**MARTIN KESSLER BOOKS**

THE FREE PRESS

NEW YORK   LONDON   TORONTO   SYDNEY   SINGAPORE

# FIXING BROKEN WINDOWS

## Restoring Order and Reducing Crime
## in Our Communities

### GEORGE L. KELLING

### CATHERINE M. COLES

THE FREE PRESS
A Division of Simon & Schuster Inc.
1230 Avenue of the Americas
New York, NY 10020

THE FREE PRESS and colophon are trademarks
of Simon & Schuster Inc.

Designed by Carla Bolte

Manufactured in the United States of America

10  9  8  7  6  5  4  3  2  1

**Library of Congress Cataloging-in-Publication Data**

Kelling, George L.
    Fixing broken windows : restoring order and reducing crime
in our communities / George L. Kelling, Catherine M. Coles.
        p.    cm.
    Includes bibliographical references and index.
    ISBN 0–684–82446–9 (alk. paper)
        1. Law enforcement—United States.    2. Crime prevention—
United States.    3. Police administration—United States.
I. Coles, Catherine M.    II. Title.
HV8141.K45      1996
364.4'0973—dc20                                    96–27232
                                                                    CIP

*This book is dedicated to our family, close and extended.*

The police at all times should maintain a relationship with the public that gives reality to the historic tradition that the police are the public and that the public are the police; the police are the only members of the public who are paid to give full-time attention to duties which are incumbent on every citizen in the interest of community welfare.

—Sir Robert Peel
Founder, London Metropolitan Police, 1829

# CONTENTS

# LIST OF FIGURES

# FOREWORD

*James Q. Wilson*

THE COMPETING DEMANDS OF LIBERTY AND COMMUNITY CONSTI-
tute a fundamental cleavage that divides contemporary political
philosophers and has produced among the public at large the American
culture war. The defenders of liberty envisage a world of autonomous
individuals who freely choose their destinies and whose liberties are essential to personal development and social democracy. The advocates
of community rejoin that no one is truly autonomous, that liberty can
only exist in an environment of reasonable order, and that personal development requires familial and neighborhood support.

This cleavage is not coterminous with that between liberal and con-
servative. The supporters of liberty include libertarians who are market-
oriented economic conservatives; the defenders of community include
liberals who think that market forces are often destructive of communal
life. John Rawls and Robert Nozick, though quite different in their attitudes toward government, are alike in basing their philosophies on
freely choosing individuals. Michael Sandel and Alasdair MacIntyre,
though perhaps in disagreement on many matters of public policy, are
alike in viewing man as a social animal whose life derives meaning from
its civic context.

On countless issues—drug legalization, school prayer, reproductive
rights, plant-closing laws, parental leave policy, crime-control strate-

gies—the competing claims of liberty and community are often heard. In this book, George Kelling and Catherine Coles explore this issue in perhaps its most common and vivid incarnation—how and to what extent should public spaces be protected?

Every day, in most big cities and many small ones, we experience the problem. Homeless people asleep on a grate; beggars soliciting funds by the bus stop; graffiti on the bridge abutment; teenagers hanging out in front of the deli; loud music coming from an open window. How should conduct in public spaces be regulated, and by whom?

For the past three decades or so, the drift in public policy has been toward maximizing individual liberty and away from enforcing communal control. Public drunkenness has been decriminalized, the mentally ill have been deinstitutionalized, public solicitations have acquired broader constitutional protection. Many of these changes were the result, not of public debate or legislative effort, but of court decisions that have endowed individuals with more, or more readily enforced, rights.

Courts are institutions whose special competence lies in the discernment and application of rights. This means that to the extent courts decide matters, the drift of policy will tend to be toward liberty and away from community. The court will, typically, hear a case brought by (or on behalf of) an *individual* beggar, sleeper, or solicitor. Such an individual rarely constitutes much of a threat to anyone, and so the claims of communal order often seem, in the particular case, to be suspect or overdrawn.

But the effects on a community of *many* individuals taking advantage of the rights granted to *an* individual (or often, as the court sees it, an abstract, depersonalized individual) are often qualitatively different from the effects of a single person. A public space—a bus stop, a market square, a subway entrance—is more than the sum of its human parts; it is a complex pattern of interactions that can become dramatically more threatening as the scale and frequency of those interactions increase. As the number of unconventional individuals increases arithmetically, the number of worrisome behaviors increases geometrically.

And so the public complains—of aggressive panhandlers, disheveled vagrants, and rude teenagers. The police have no easy response. To many of them, dealing with these minor disorders is not why they became law-enforcement officers; telling panhandlers to move on is a far cry from fighting crime. To all of them, any intervention brings the risk of adverse publicity, hostile law suits, and political debates in which, their experience tells them, rights are trumps. For nearly every kind of unconventional person there seems to be an advocacy group. Better, the police tell themselves, to pull back, do nothing. As a result, the police often fail to do even the minimal things that the courts have allowed. The public gets more upset, and the issue affects the outcome of a council or mayoral race.

For many years, George Kelling has studied this problem, advised public officials on how to cope with it, and evaluated their efforts to do so. In the process, he has become this country's preeminent authority on the problem of controlling disorderly conduct in public places. Until now, there has been no comprehensive treatment of what he has learned; now, here it is.

The title—*Fixing Broken Windows*—is an allusion to an essay Kelling and I published in *The Atlantic Monthly* in March 1982. We used the image of broken windows to explain how neighborhoods might decay into disorder and even crime if no one attends faithfully to their maintenance. If a factory or office window is broken, passersby observing it will conclude that no one cares or no one is in charge. In time, a few will begin throwing rocks to break more windows. Soon all the windows will be broken, and now passersby will think that, not only is no one in charge of the building, no one is in charge of the street on which it faces. Only the young, the criminal, or the foolhardy have any business on an unprotected avenue, and so more and more citizens will abandon the street to those they assume prowl it. Small disorders lead to larger and larger ones, and perhaps even to crime.

A rights-oriented legal tradition does not easily deal with this problem. The judge finds it hard to believe that *one* broken window is all that important or that the police should be empowered to exert their authority on people who *might* break more windows. The judge sees a snapshot of the street at one moment; the public, by contrast, sees a motion picture of the street slowly, inexorably decaying.

Kelling has seen this process unfold and understands the competing values at stake. Through his research on the history of policing in America and his work advising public agencies, notably the New York City Transit Authority, he has learned how one can deal with the problem of order in public spaces at minimal cost in individual liberty. Coles has studied the law on this matter, and sets forth with admirable clarity its hopelessly unclear condition.

The result is a book that ought to be read by every police chief, mayor, community activist, and concerned citizen. It provides practical guidance on how to cope with a problem that many of us simply debate, in increasingly strident tones, as we express our outrage over the excesses of either radical individualism or conformist communalism.

We can reclaim our public spaces without sacrificing our essential liberties, but to do so many groups—the courts, the police, and many public and private agencies—must change how they think about these matters. Kelling and Coles tell them how.

# INTRODUCTION

WITH FEAR OF CRIME AT ALL-TIME HIGH LEVELS, OUR NATIONAL political leaders propose dramatic solutions to the "crime problem." They focus on capital punishment, "three strikes you're out" incarceration policies, construction of more prisons, tighter gun control, and increasing the number of police on the streets.

Yet the current crime problem is being debated in far richer and more complex terms locally. Certainly, local politicians and media voice great concern about some of the same issues: violence, serious crime, and the prevalence of weapons on the streets. Citizens, however, are demanding that order be restored to streets, parks, and other public spaces. Their voices and demands are starting to change how local political leaders especially, but many police and criminal justice professionals as well, are redefining and addressing our cities' crime problem.

Recently, Kelling spent an evening in a tough inner-city minority neighborhood in a large Eastern city, walking with neighborhood residents, a community organizer/neighborhood lawyer, and a foot patrol officer. The residents pointed with pride to abandoned rowhouses boarded up as a result of legal action they had taken, cleaned up vacant lots, one of which had been converted to a neighborhood garden, and streets that were now empty of drug dealers. Yet at one major intersection they encountered what could only be described as an open-air

1

drug market. At first, the group watched from a distance: perhaps fifty people were on the street, some hailing cars and negotiating deals, others watching for police. A few just watched what was going on. As we approached, the watchers spotted the officer and the alert went out: "Joanna, Joanna"—the local argot for police. Dealing fell off and then stopped as dealers slowly moved in various directions—just far enough to observe the group but close enough to return later for business as usual. Many youths, especially the youngest, just stood and observed. What was most dismaying about that corner that evening was the presence of children no older than eleven and twelve. What they saw was not brutal or abusive cops, but governmental authority as a bad joke. It was clear who controlled that section of public space—not citizens or government, but drug dealers. Similar scenarios are played out on city corners throughout the United States.

We have no doubt that many of the dealers operating that night had previous records and probably were either on probation or parole or awaiting hearings on other charges. Yet where were the probation officers, parole officers, prosecutors? Why were they not out there as part of the neighborhood team to regain and keep control of the streets, sending a strong message that residents and government criminal justice agents would not tolerate dealers taking over streets and terrorizing neighborhoods? Why was the police officer, a well-intended and concerned young person who expressed indignation at conditions there, assigned only irregularly and on an overtime basis to this neighborhood rather than on a permanent fixed assignment? Of course, we know the official answers. Probation and parole agents are overwhelmed by their caseloads. Prosecutors must concentrate on serious cases and their caseload. Police are overwhelmed by 911 calls. And it is more efficient for all of these professionals to operate out of centralized facilities. But lurking behind these rationales are professional and bureaucratic models of performance and personal motivations that have little to do with neighborhood safety.

Happily, many police departments and a few probation, parole, and prosecutorial agencies are starting to seriously question their assumptions and operating strategies and shift to community, problem-solving approaches. At the same time, while citizens are demanding order and some police and criminal justice agencies are responding to them, civil

libertarians, civil liberty unions, and advocates for the homeless are
pushing in exactly the opposite direction. The vociferousness of this
controversy cannot be exaggerated. Local papers run daily news stories,
editorials, op-ed pieces, and letters detailing both public concern and
intense controversy about neighborhood disorder.

In San Francisco, one of America's most socially and politically liberal cities, for example, the last two mayoral elections have turned on
issues having to do with homelessness and disorder. During the late
1980s, Mayor Arthur Agnos refused to move encampments of the
homeless out of public parks, especially the Civic Center. Consequently, the Civic Center was dubbed "Camp Agnos" and became a
major issue in the 1991 mayoral election. Frank Jordan, a retired police
officer, was elected mayor on the basis of his pledges to restore order.
Four years later, during the next campaign, Mayor Jordan's program to
restore order, Operation Matrix, dominated the political debate. His
successor, Willie Brown, ended Operation Matrix but reassured citizens
that he would still enforce the laws against persons who camped,
drank, or committed minor crimes in parks and public places. San
Francisco's preoccupation with disorder was not unusual: during the
1993 mayoral race in New York City both candidates, David Dinkins
and Rudolph Giuliani, ran against "squeegeemen"—youths who extort
money from car drivers by washing car windows.

Such stories voice both strong indignation on the part of many local
citizens, merchants, and urban dwellers about the insults, threats, and
incivilities they face daily, and an increasingly articulate and politically
powerful demand that something be done about rampant disorder. But
they also reflect the equally forceful belief of civil libertarians and
homeless advocates that intolerance and injustice are cloaked within
the demand for order.

Why, with violence rampant in many areas of cities, are neighborhood residents preoccupied with issues such as encampments,
squeegeeing, panhandling, prostitution, and other forms of disorder?
Are they creating scapegoats of the poor, minorities, lower classes, and
youths? Helen Hershkoff of the American Civil Liberties Union argues:
"In an effort to deal with the enormous increase in poverty and homelessness in cities across the country during the past decade, numerous municipalities are enforcing with renewed vigor, long-dormant

ordinances prohibiting the destitute from asking members of the public for money."[1] Are we regressing to the idea of "dangerous classes"?

· No. Such charges merely obfuscate what are essentially legitimate claims—caricaturing them as racism and economic injustices.

Despite assertions by many libertarians, attempts to restore order do not pit rich against poor or black against white. The demand for order permeates all social classes and ethnic groups. When patrons of New York's subways demanded order, it was not bankers and stockbrokers who voiced the greatest concern—they, after all, had other options. Rather, it was working persons of all races who relied upon public transportation and craved decent and civil means of travel.

Second, those demanding order are not, for the most part, moral imperialists. Most persons opposed to prostitution in San Francisco's Tenderloin area, for example, are not prudish vigilantes concerned about commercial sex as a matter of principle. They simply object to the promiscuous behavior of prostitutes and johns, who publicly commit sex acts in parked cars, discard prophylactics and needles on sidewalks, doorstoops, and in public parks, unmindful of the play of children, and who disregard public requests for some circumspection in their behavior.

Finally, advocates for the restoration of order are not proposing some form of tyranny of the majority. Most are well aware of the excesses of the past and the dangers inherent in balancing individual rights against broader community claims. We speak here of behavior that violates widely accepted standards and norms of behavior, and about which a broad consensus exists, in spite of racial, ethnic, and class differences.

This dispute is not just political—it is legal and is being fought in the courts. As Kent Scheidegger of the Criminal Justice Legal Foundation correctly prophesied: "When a city decides to do something about public order, the first question is 'will we get sued?' The answer, inevitably, is yes."[2] And given the special role of the courts in the United States as the final arbiter of much of public policy, citizens, the media, and public professionals—especially police and criminal justice professionals—must understand the shape and logic of the legal thinking that will determine the important public policy issues about crime and its management.

Yet, as a rule, the general public knows little about these suits or the legal and social logic that resolves them. Take a recent New York City example. Two young persons, Jennifer Loper and William Kaye, moved from their parents' suburban homes onto New York City's streets in 1990. They partially supported themselves by begging in the East Village. Occasionally, police ordered them to move on under the city's anti-panhandling ordinance. Neither Loper nor Kaye suggested that police had said or done anything more threatening than ordering them to move on. Yet, in 1992, represented by lawyers who had earlier unsuccessfully challenged the New York City subway's ban on panhandling, Loper and Kaye sued the city, alleging that their free speech rights had been violated and that the city's anti-panhandling ordinance was unconstitutional. At the time, most police, even police administrators, were unaware of the existence of the anti-panhandling law, let alone the suit. Federal Judge Robert W. Sweet agreed with Loper and Kaye, elevating their begging to a political statement about poverty, inequitable distribution of wealth, and lack of adequate housing and, as such, deserving of First Amendment protection. Citizens certainly are aware of panhandling; few realize, however, that the court has essentially provided it with First Amendment protection.

Yet, as citizens experience the crime problem it includes panhandling as surely as more violent crimes. Those of us who live, work, and play in cities face an amalgam of *disorder, fear, serious crime, and urban decay*: the crime problem does not begin with serious, or "index" crime. Conceiving of it and addressing it as such, as has occurred for thirty years in national debates about crime, leads to bad public policy, poor legal thinking and practice, and distorted criminal justice practices and priorities. The distinctions among disorder, fear, and serious crime are not trivial. Citizens understand the experiences of disorder and fear, quite apart from serious crime, and want something done about them.

It is not too late to restore order and regain control of streets—if certain policy shifts are made, gains in public safety and perception of safety follow relatively rapidly. We already have examples of such successes, impressive successes in very difficult circumstances. In this book we identify realistic and attainable policy objectives that respect the legitimate rights of individuals while protecting the interest of neighborhoods and communities. This does not mean that policy shifts will be easily achieved. Powerful factors sustain the policy bias toward serious crime. After all, citizens *do* fear its dangers. Obstreperous youths may be bothersome, but unless obstreperousness turns into real danger to life and property, it is only that. All other things being equal, which they are not, it would make sense to concentrate on serious crime, especially in a world of limited resources. Two additional factors, each powerful in its own right, perpetuate the single-minded fixation on felonies: first, a broad societal ideology holds certain individual rights as absolute and virtually divorced from responsibility and obligation. This ideology gave rise to the idea that all forms of nonviolent deviance should be tolerated in the interest of liberty—a belief that order maintenance confronts directly. Second, the reigning criminal justice strategy is consistent with this libertarian ideology, internally congruent and intuitively reasonable. Its keystone is the idea of a professional "criminal justice system" as the primary means by which society controls crime. The police are the "front end" of this system—law-enforcement officers who make their primary contribution to community and neighborhood life by arresting and processing offenders into this system. Keeping the peace, solving citizen problems, resolving conflicts, and maintaining order are at best seen as distracting peripheral functions and, at worst, as despised "social work."

Alas this model has failed dismally in its own terms: serious crime has been at unacceptable levels for three decades. The model has failed because it does not recognize the links between disorder, fear, serious crime, and urban decay. And, the criminal justice system model has also failed because it ignores the role of citizens in crime prevention.

Yet, we are optimistic. Citizens are demanding policies and practices that will improve the quality of neighborhood life. They are impatient for change and have put police, prosecutors, corrections officials, and courts on notice. During the 1960s and 1970s, when prosperity was with us, when the next job would be better than the last, and paychecks would constantly expand, many citizens believed they could leave a deteriorating neighborhood for a better one. For many this is no longer possible. Residents and merchants alike are staying in Boston's Dorchester, Milwaukee's West Side, Seattle's University District, San Francisco's Tenderloin area, and New York's Columbia Heights, and demanding that deterioration be arrested and order restored. Most importantly, citizens are taking to the streets to reclaim them.

If society does criminalize certain behaviors, how do we ensure that police are kept from using these laws to harass outcasts, the poor, and minorities? This question is especially important when one understands that police and criminal justice agencies have a sorry record when it comes to respecting, let alone protecting, the rights of minorities and the poor. The racist comments of retired Los Angles detective Mark Fuhrman are but one example of unofficial police policies aimed at repressing minorities and the poor. As worrisome, many police, prosecutors, and corrections agents have been sequestered in cars or offices for so long that they have lost their street wisdom and problem-solving skills. Many, frankly, have been out of touch with the good citizens of neighborhoods for so long that they are afraid to leave their cars or offices.

In spite of these obstacles, *order can be restored in American cities.* The police are uniquely positioned to assist in order restoration and maintenance through their historical role as problem solvers in the community: in fact, citizen demands for order have been met in many cities with new police strategies emphasizing order maintenance and crime prevention, as well as citizen involvement in crime control efforts in concert with police. A new paradigm of community-based policing, and even community-based prosecution and probation, is taking hold in various forms around the country, offering citizens the opportunity to redefine and become directly involved in crime control and quality-of-life programs in their communities. The viability of life in urban America may depend upon whether order can be restored before urban decline has progressed to irreversible proportions, whether the police are permitted to play an effective role in the process, and whether the courts will uphold order-maintenance efforts on behalf of communities struggling against the very real threats posed by disorder.

In Chapter 1, we explore the consequences of misunderstanding the crime problem today, the nature of what we call disorderly behavior in cities, and the grave threat it poses to our society. Chapter 2 turns to an examination of how we got to where we are today: that is, how disorder proliferated with the growth of an ethos of individualism and increasing legislative and judicial support for protecting the fundamental rights of individuals at the expense of community interests. Chapter 3 looks more directly at policing, in particular at the failure of the old reform model that has dominated police practices and strategies for most of this century. This model is at its height with 911 policing—a serious impediment to reforms in policing that we believe are necessary. In Chapter 4, we examine in detail the New York City Police Department, which is moving strongly in the direction of community policing and focusing on order maintenance and attention to disorderly behavior, or quality-of-life crimes, as well as index crimes. Police efforts have been met with equal energy and commitment by private initiatives undertaken by citizens, merchants, and more recently experiments in the courts and community-based prosecution. With Chapter 5 we attempt to define the basic elements of the new model of policing that we believe holds great hope for rejuvenating our cities: community policing. We also meet head-on the most significant problems of implementing this new form of policing: the need for a significant amount of police discretion to be used by line officers in their daily work, and at the same time the means that might be used to control and shape officers' discretion. In Chapter 6 we turn again to an account of actual events in three cities as they have moved toward restoring order in public places. In Baltimore, San Francisco, and Seattle initiatives have arisen from different sources—merchants joining together in business improvement districts to improve downtown areas; a city administration working on all fronts with police, private citizens, and social agencies to implement a city-wide program to restore order to parks and public places; and a city attorney working closely with citizen groups and local government to implement legislation. All faced resistance to their efforts, yet all provide impressive examples of what can be achieved when resources are mustered and applied to the goal of order restoration. Finally, in Chapter 7 we put forward a community crime control model that we believe is taking form in communities throughout the country. This model restores responsibility to communities and establishes new mechanisms of police and criminal justice accountability to neighborhoods and communities.

Reducing crime through order maintenance, in the final analysis, requires the exercise of good citizenship. Citizens must accept responsibility both for their own behavior and for helping to ensure the safety and security of fellow citizens. Order arises out of what Jane Jacobs has called the "small change" of urban life: the day-to-day respect with which we deal with others and the concern that we exercise for their privacy, welfare, and safety. Such respect and concern does not divide rich from poor, black from white, or one ethic group from another. Instead, it unites divers neighborhoods against those who behave in outrageous ways, and who prey on the weak and vulnerable. Police and criminal justice agencies in a democratic society should be part and parcel of such communities—the citizens as police and police as citizens, as Sir Robert Peel the founder of modern Anglo-Saxon policing put it—both encouraging tolerance for differences and supporting citizen efforts to control the unruly and predators.

## CHAPTER 1

# DISORDER, "BROKEN WINDOWS," AND SERIOUS CRIME

IN A REPORT PREPARED FOR THE PRESIDENT'S COMMISSION ON LAW Enforcement and Crime in 1967, Albert Biderman and his social science colleagues presented an important finding from surveys of citizens: fear of crime was strongly related to the existence of disorderly conditions in neighborhoods and communities.[1] The implications of this finding should have been crucial to the formulation of public policy and shaping of police practices, for fear influences the behavior of citizens. Yet the relationship between fear and disorder was largely ignored until well into the 1980s, and even now it has had little impact in criminal justice or criminology. In certain respects, this is not surprising. During the 1960s, at the time the link between fear and disorder was first identified, serious crime was emerging as a problem of considerable political concern. Barry Goldwater and Lyndon Johnson clambered over each other to be tougher on crime during their 1964 campaign for the presidency. In office, President Johnson initiated the Commission on Law Enforcement and the Administration of Justice to study crime and society's response to it—only the second national commission on crime in the history of the United States (the first being the Wickersham Commission of the 1930s). Scholars and practitioners, too, focused almost exclusively on "serious" crimes—those that appear most

11

severe and consequential for the victim—murder, rape, robbery, assault, and burglary.

While police and criminal justice practitioners ignored disorder, however, citizens and local officials did not. For example, in San Francisco, where an ethos of tolerance for diversity, a history of political activism in public places, and a hospitable climate for much of the year all contributed to greater numbers of persons living on the streets than in most other cities, residents began to withdraw from use of the streets and neighborhoods in fear of aggressive begging. In 1991, a survey commissioned by the city of public attitudes and experiences concerning aggressive begging in San Francisco revealed that 90 percent of residents had been approached by a beggar in a public place at least once over the previous year, and that of those approached, 39 percent had been concerned for their physical safety during at least some of the encounters, while 33 percent had given money to beggars, sometimes out of perceived pressure. Survey results also indicated that over a third of all San Franciscans had avoided certain locations, stores, restaurants, or places generally because of the presence of beggars, and responses were similar from residents of the larger Bay area, who reported that they refrained from visiting the city altogether.[2] Citizens eventually moved beyond their fear and withdrawal to demand that police, prosecutors, and other government officials take action to restore order to city streets. Police and prosecutors responded, giving aggressive begging and street encampments (along with street prostitution, which was also a major concern of residents in specific neighborhoods) high priority. At the same time, however, the city's efforts to react positively to citizen demands were attacked in a legal suit challenging its reliance on a California statute that banned "accosting for the purpose of begging."

San Francisco is not unique. Right now in the most troubled neighborhoods of New Haven (Connecticut), Chicago, New York City, Indianapolis, and Milwaukee, if we ask residents, merchants, and "regulars" about the major problems in their neighborhoods, almost invariably they describe abandoned cars, graffiti, public drunkenness, street prostitution, youth gangs taking over parks, and other such disorderly behaviors. People act on these fears—many choose to leave the city. Commenting in 1994 on the responses of New York City's residents to such "minor crimes," former deputy police commissioner Jeremy Travis (who later that year was appointed to head the National Institute of Justice under the Clinton administration) remarked in an interview for *Newsday*:

> There is some fascinating survey data, done by the Commonwealth Fund. About 17 percent [of the people] who left the city said that if the Police Department had taken minor crimes more seriously, it would have had a major impact on their decision; 59 percent who left did so to improve the quality of their life. Three of five people who still live in New York City say dirt, graffiti, noise, panhandlers, homeless people, and beggars have reduced the quality of life for them and their families. This is the central issue for the future of New York City.[3]

Rather than leaving cities, other residents purchase weapons and dogs, some abandon public facilities such as public transportation, and yet others lock themselves in their residences and leave only when in the most dire need. Many have joined with neighbors to demand that police, prosecutors, and courts respond to their needs. In Seattle, elderly residents of a nonprofit housing association, along with the Seattle Indian Center, recently filed a friend of the court brief on behalf of the city to support restrictive "street civility laws," including an ordinance making it illegal to sit or lie down on public sidewalks in the downtown and neighborhood commercial areas from 7 A.M. to 9 P.M.[4] These low-income residents, many of whom had previously been homeless, worried about being able to walk safely to a corner store and felt increasingly vulnerable to criminal activity as their neighborhood was avoided by other residents who were fearful of entering the area. Joining representatives of the Indian Center, a treatment center for homeless chronic public inebriates, they argued that setting standards for behavior in the immediate area was not an assault on the dignity of the homeless, especially when the standards were necessary to helping substance abusers move beyond patterns of self-destructive behavior.

These are not isolated instances. In cities across the country, mayors like Jane Byrne of Chicago, George Latimer of St. Paul (Minnesota), and Kevin White and Raymond Flynn of Boston responded early to citizen calls for improving neighborhoods and communities through "quality-of-life" programs. More recently, mayors Stephen Goldsmith of

Indianapolis, Bret Schundler of Elizabeth (New Jersey), Frank Jordan of San Francisco, and Rudolph Giuliani in New York have emerged as outspoken advocates for restoring order, as well as for attacking serious crime. Quality of life and disorder continue to be among the most urgent issues local politicians address, regardless of party affiliation. Yet the national debate on crime focuses exclusively on serious, index crimes and related issues: capital punishment, "three strikes you're out," the need for more prisons, gun control, and the number of police on the street. The resulting discontinuity between the "crime problem" as conceived by national politicians and policy makers, and the intuition of citizens who experience and view it more broadly as a continuum encompassing disorder as well as serious crime, is troubling in two regards. First, it is unlikely that policies emanating from the national level, and funded by federal dollars, will produce programs that satisfy citizens. Second, such policies will probably not have a substantial impact on crime, however it is defined.

It is time for a sea change in our thinking about crime. Specifically, if we are to understand the crime problem as neighborhood residents, merchants, and other citizens experience it, we must go beyond narrow definitions of the problem that have characterized political, professional, and policy thinking. More importantly, if we are to address the crime problem in ways that affect the lives of citizens in their communities, we must do so with a strategy and set of tactics that respond to citizen priorities. Both of these require that we address the problem of growing disorder in our cities.

DISORDER DEFINED

What is disorder? In its broadest social sense, disorder is incivility, boorish and threatening behavior that disturbs life, especially urban life. Urban life is characterized by the presence of many strangers, and in such circumstances citizens need minimum levels of order. Whether using urban areas to reside, shop, deliver services, work, enjoy cultural opportunities, or have space for their children to play, citizens require what urbanologist Jane Jacobs has called the "small change" of urban life: "[the] built-in equipment allowing strangers to dwell in peace together on civilized but essentially dignified and reserved terms."[5]

What is this "built-in equipment"? It is the myriad of mundane street observances and rituals through which people communicate their reliability and predictability: limiting eye contact, respecting personal space, modulating voices, walking to one side of the street—the list is virtually endless. Few of these practices are codified; most are imprinted in citizens as they mature.

In small and homogenous neighborhoods and communities, where people's lives are intertwined in many ways, the "small change" of street life is least necessary. Instead, meshed obligations and familiarity are the primary guarantors of civility. Even the most seriously disturbed or deranged individuals are known personally to those in the community: everyone knows how far they will go, so their behavior is predictable, even if deviant. In pluralistic cosmopolitan areas where interaction with strangers is frequent and commonplace, we cannot be advised about those we meet by personal knowledge, history, or perhaps even reputation. Instead, we take our cues from activities observed on the street and shape our public behavior accordingly if *we* are the strangers.

Most citizens have little difficulty balancing civility, which implies self-imposed restraint and obligation, with freedom. Yet, a few are either unable or unwilling to accept any limitations upon their own behavior. At the extreme are predatory criminals who murder, assault, rape, rob, and steal. Society almost uniformly condemns such behavior: in addition to social norms and values that operate, we have also developed elaborate institutions to prevent and/or punish it—police, prosecutors, courts, and even prisons. Less extreme is disorderly behavior that, while not as serious as the crimes noted above, nonetheless can threaten social order by creating fear and criminogenic conditions. By disorder we refer specifically to aggressive panhandling, street prostitution, drunkenness and public drinking, menacing behavior, harassment, obstruction of streets and public spaces, vandalism and graffiti, public urination and defecation, unlicensed vending and peddling, unsolicited window washing of cars ("squeegeeing"), and other such acts. While many of these behaviors are designated as criminal, they are usually classified as misdemeanors or petty offenses under state laws and city ordinances, most often punishable only by fines or community service.

Virtually everyone agrees that committing a felony is wrong and deserving of apprehension and punishment, even though we do not view all felonies as equally serious, consequential, or worthy of police action. For example, spousal abuse and rape in marriage were long considered private matters, and police and prosecutorial interventions were limited and cautious at best. Now, of course, values have changed and spousal abuse and rape are considered on a par with other forms of aggravated assault and rape—perhaps even more serious given their repetitive and escalating nature. Nonetheless, for the most part, in virtually all societies murder, rape, assault, and theft of one kind or another are outlawed and deemed worthy of strong condemnation.

Disorderly behaviors are more ambiguous and less straightforward. Many more of us than would perhaps like to admit doing so have urinated in public, been drunk, asked someone for money when in a jam (for money to make a call to get help or for bus fare), bought goods or services from illegal vendors, used prostitutes, obstructed auto traffic or pedestrians on a sidewalk, committed minor acts of vandalism, or carried out other such minor offenses constituting "disorderly behavior." Why should citizens be so offended by and afraid of acts that many of us have committed at one time or another? Why should some persons guilty of such behaviors be warned and/or arrested and not others? Why is it that these behaviors, seemingly far less serious than felonies in their potential to injure or harm others, should be restricted or regulated at all?

The answer lies in the immediate fear that such disorderly behavior engenders in the local community when it reaches a critical mass, and in the potential for more serious crime, urban decline, and decay that may ultimately follow on the heels of unconstrained disorder. Neither the questions, nor the answer, are academic: disorder, fear, crime, and urban decay seriously threaten urban life and commerce in American cities today.

## DISORDER AND FEAR: THE "BROKEN WINDOWS" THEORY

During the mid-1970s, under the auspices of the Police Foundation, a think tank and research group, Kelling conducted the Newark (New Jersey) Foot Patrol Experiment.[6] While popular with many citizens and politicians at the time, foot patrol was viewed by most police executives as a waste of valuable resources that could be better used for "real" policing, that is, keeping officers on patrol in cars. During the 1960s, for example, a study of the Boston Police Department carried out by the International Association of Chiefs of Police had ridiculed the department by asserting that the "criminal element . . . is grateful to police agencies that persist in the antiquated procedure of assigning a large portion of their members to foot patrol."[7] Because of foot patrol's popularity with citizens, however, the State of New Jersey funded foot patrol as part of its Safe and Clean Neighborhoods Program. Begrudgingly, city police accepted the money, largely for the additional jobs and funding it provided. Nevertheless, foot patrol was conducted as an add-on program, an appendage to other police services, and only minimally integrated into overall police strategy.

As part of his research, Kelling spent considerable time walking with Newark police officers on foot patrol. Relatively little training or guidance was given to foot patrol officers, who were pretty much left to their own devices on beats. Yet in the myriad variety of neighborhoods officers patrolled, Kelling found that they acted in a surprisingly uniform fashion. Immersing themselves in the lives of their neighborhoods, officers were well-known, often by name, to area regulars—residents, merchants, and street people alike—and knew many of these individuals by name as well. Foot patrol officers kept abreast of local problems, assumed special responsibility for particular locations or persons, developed regular sources of information (apartment managers, merchants, street persons), became regulars at local restaurants, checked "hazards" such as bars and in one case an inner-city drug store that conspicuously displayed and sold a wide assortment of knives and straight-edge razors, and in other ways came to know and be known on their beats. Finally, in collaboration with and on behalf of citizens, officers established "rules of the street" that were commonly known and widely accepted by "respectable people," as well as "street people." These informal rules covered such behaviors as panhandling, lying down or congregating on sidewalks and in parks, drinking in public areas, and drug use. They did not merely prohibit specific acts, such as soliciting for prostitution, but often defined the conditions and manner under which activities could be carried out: for example, panhandling was permissible, but not from people standing still or waiting at a bus stop; sitting on the stoops of stores was accepted, but not lying down; drinking alcohol in public could be done only if the bottle was in a brown paper bag, and only off main thoroughfares. Not surprisingly, such rules varied by neighborhood.

Most New Jersey police chiefs were dismayed when they learned from program evaluators what (anonymous) officers, who were supposed to be "fighting crime," were actually doing while on foot patrol. For example, after being called a second time during the same evening to end brawls in the same bar, one foot patrol officer had had enough: although "bar time" was some hours away, he ordered the bar closed for the night. The bartender grumbled, closed up, and opened the next day for business as usual. When this incident was recounted to the chief of the department in which it occurred—disguised, to protect the confidentiality of the officer, so that the chief believed that it happened in another department—he responded, "That wouldn't happen in my department, the officer would be fired."

If police officials were unimpressed with foot patrol, however, citizen responses were uniformly positive, even in predominately black neighborhoods patrolled by white officers. Overwhelmingly, fear declined and citizen appreciation for police soared. Although foot patrol did not reduce the incidence of serious crime, residents of foot-patrolled neighborhoods felt more secure than did those in other areas, believed crime to have been reduced, and appeared to take fewer measures to protect themselves from crime (such as staying home behind locked doors).[8] Foot officers, in turn, were more favorably disposed toward citizens in their neighborhoods and experienced higher morale than did their colleagues who patrolled in cars. Similar research in Flint, Michigan, by Michigan State University Professor Robert Trojanowicz, produced virtually identical findings, showing additionally that patrol officers themselves were less fearful while patrolling solo, on foot, than were officers riding two in a car, in the same areas.[9]

At the time it was not entirely clear why citizen fear in Newark should have been so dramatically affected by foot patrol. One answer is that foot patrol caused citizens to be more conscious of a police presence (since residents were extremely sensitive to adding or withdrawing foot patrol), and therefore more secure. Yet no neighborhood received more than a total of thirty hours of foot patrol per week on average—so a pretty small dosage of foot patrol delivered a hefty amount of fear reduction. More likely, the reduction in citizen fear of crime resulted from what the police were doing while on foot patrol. In essence, the experiment documented foot patrol officers engaged in managing and controlling disorderly behavior. How was this played out? Officers obtained their order-maintenance authority not only from criminal law, or their police organizations, but as a broad mandate from those they policed, that is, from citizens who used the streets, lived in or conducted their businesses in the local neighborhood, and even those who "hung out." Over time, through daily transactions, citizens and police came to know each other and to recognize their shared interest in the peace and order of the streets. Eventually police and citizens negotiated a "disorder threshold" for the neighborhood, and rules of conduct that would be applied when that threshold was breached. While the officers' immediate involvement in this process was key, their activities may also have helped to develop a consensus regarding appropriate neighborhood conduct strong enough to persist even during times of police absence, thus heightening the effect of actual police presence.

The results of the *Newark Foot Patrol Experiment* were published in 1981. Building upon the findings from Newark and their own respective research, in 1982 Kelling and James Q. Wilson, then a Harvard professor with an ongoing interest in policing and public order, published an article in the *Atlantic* that directly addressed the significance of order-maintenance activities by the police and attempted to bring it before the public.[10] "Broken Windows," as the article would become known popularly, used the analogy of a broken window to describe the relationship between disorder and crime: "if a window in a building is broken *and is left unrepaired*, all the rest of the windows will soon be broken. . . . [O]ne unrepaired broken window is a signal that no one cares, and so breaking more windows costs nothing."[11] Kelling and Wilson described the process in concrete terms:

A stable neighborhood of families who care for their homes, mind each other's children, and confidently frown on unwanted intruders can change, in a few years or even a few months, to an inhospitable and frightening jungle. A piece of property is abandoned, weeds grow up, a window is smashed. Adults stop scolding rowdy children; the children, emboldened, become more rowdy. Families move out, unattached adults move in. Teenagers gather in front of the corner store. The merchant asks them to move; they refuse. Fights occur. Litter accumulates. People start drinking in front of the grocers; in time, an inebriate slumps to the sidewalk and is allowed to sleep it off. Pedestrians are approached by panhandlers.[12]

Therefore, the analogy goes, disorderly behavior unregulated and unchecked signals to citizens that the area is unsafe. Responding prudently, and fearful, citizens will stay off the streets, avoid certain areas, and curtail their normal activities and associations. As citizens withdraw physically, they also withdraw from roles of mutual support with fellow citizens on the streets, thereby relinquishing the social controls they formerly helped to maintain within the community, as social atomization sets in. Ultimately the result for such a neighborhood, whose fabric of urban life and social intercourse has been undermined, is increasing vulnerability to an influx of more disorderly behavior and serious crime. Again, in the words of Wilson and Kelling:

> serious street crime flourishes in areas in which disorderly behavior goes unchecked. The unchecked panhandler is, in effect, the first broken window. Muggers and robbers, whether opportunistic or professional, believe they reduce their chances of being caught or even identified if they operate on streets where potential victims are already intimidated by prevailing conditions. If the neighborhood cannot keep a bothersome panhandler from annoying passersby, the thief may reason, it is even less likely to call the police to identify a potential mugger or to interfere if the mugging actually takes place.[13]

In reporting the causal link between disorderly behavior and citizen fear Wilson and Kelling relied upon the findings of the Newark Foot Patrol Experiment, surveys conducted in a variety of other places—Portland, Baltimore, and Boston—and on specific surveys of the elderly. While they presented the causal relationship between disorder and fear as an empirical fact, the links between disorder and serious crime, and disorder and urban decay, were set forth as hypotheses that required further empirical testing.

Unfortunately, such testing would not occur and produce concrete results for nearly a decade. In the meantime, responses to "Broken Windows" were clearly ambivalent. For many citizens, the argument formulated and legitimized deeply held convictions about neighborhood and community problems, setting forth the relationship between neighborhood disorder and fear in terms that citizens themselves used with each other and in talking to police. Surely it articulated a latent but increasingly strong citizen demand for the restoration of order in public spaces. For some police, "Broken Windows" put the relationship between disorder and fear in terms that helped them to understand the high priority citizens placed on disorder, and perhaps verified their own beliefs about the linkages between disorder and crime. As Dennis Nowicki, former Chicago Police Department executive and now chief of police in Charlotte, North Carolina, remarked shortly after "Broken Windows" appeared, "I knew it. When we stop kids from panhandling on the El [Chicago's subway system], we are preventing robberies. Kids start out asking for money; they then find out that people are scared in the subway and begin to try to intimidate them into giving them money. It's a short step from intimidation to simply taking the money."

Nevertheless, "Broken Windows" also reopened a Pandora's box that police and other criminal justice agencies had kept closed, anticipating that dealing with disorder would be both inconsequential and risky. It raised questions within the realms of public policy, criminal justice, policing, and constitutional law (specifically, legal protections for individual rights), challenging developments that had taken place during the 1960s and 1970s. For example, the dominant criminal justice paradigm held that police were law-enforcement agents whose purpose was to intercept serious crimes in progress or investigate serious completed crimes and, through arrest, to initiate the processing of criminals through the "criminal justice system." Recognizing order maintenance by police as significant in reducing fear levels among citizens, and ultimately in preventing serious crime, lay outside this prevailing conception of legitimate police work. Most police considered themselves too busy responding to calls for service and dealing with serious crime to give attention to disorder. Similarly, for many civil libertarians efforts to reduce disorder would impermissibly violate constitutional protections for the fundamental liberties of individuals who had committed no "criminal" act. In particular, advocates for the mentally ill, the homeless, and minority groups expressed outrage over what they perceived to be an attack on the poor and disadvantaged.

## THE DANGERS OF IGNORING DISORDER: FEAR, CRIME, AND URBAN DECLINE

During the 1980s, a few social scientists began to follow up on the link between fear and disorder, confirming the linkages between disorder—the "signs of crime"—and fear, first discovered by Biderman.[14] The growing impact of this research and the ideas presented in "Broken Windows" led the National Institute of Justice (NIJ) to solicit experimental research in the area of "The Order Maintenance Functions of Police Departments" in late 1982.[15] Since an experiment is the most powerful form of research methodology to determine causality, it would put "Broken Windows" to a rigorous test: if disorder and serious crime are linked, the policy implications, especially for police, would be crucial, since maintaining order could prevent crime. Funds for research were awarded to the Police Foundation, a Washington, D.C.–based think tank that focused on police policy.[16]

The researchers were not unaware of political concerns about research into order maintenance. In an independent assessment of the legal and constitutional issues raised in "Broken Windows" commissioned by the Police Foundation, attorney Robert C. Black reiterated the reservations of opponents to order maintenance generally:

> There is still another constraint on the execution of the fear-reduction strategy which almost "goes without saying" and perhaps for that very reason needs to be said. Though the strategy envisages some police work not necessarily intended to eventuate in arrest for and conviction of crime, ultimately the criminal sanction underpins any authoritative police action, even a simple order to move on. . . . Wilson and Kelling evidently look to renewed use of traditional streetsweeping laws—against public drunkenness, vagrancy, disorderly conduct, loitering, etc.—to control undesirables. These laws and the manner in which the police enforce them, are subject to constitutional constraints.[17]

In fact, the ideas presented in "Broken Windows" were antithetical to the use of "streetsweeping" tactics targeted on "undesirables"; rather,

they advocated close collaboration between police and citizens, including street people, in the development of neighborhood standards.
Moreover, neighborhood rules were to be enforced for the most part
through non-arrest approaches—education, persuasion, counseling,
and ordering—so that arrest would only be resorted to when other
approaches failed.

Yet Black was not alone in his interpretation of "Broken Windows":
the distinction between order maintenance and "streetsweeping" was
not always apparent to police either, at least during the early 1980s.
One attempt at implementing an order-maintenance approach conducted in Chicago in 1982 used police officers brought in on overtime
assignments to sweep through troubled areas and arrest youths congregating on streets. While these sweeps may have been directed against
disorder, they did not constitute order maintenance of the ilk Wilson
and Kelling had in mind in "Broken Windows," or in Kelling's *Newark
Foot Patrol Experiment*. Clearly, all police actions involved in order
maintenance would have to be grounded in law and subject to clear
constitutional constraints against infringement of individual liberties.

Despite the enthusiasm of NIJ and the Police Foundation team for
conducting a major experiment into the relationship of order-maintenance activities to fear reduction, political concerns in the United
States Attorney General's Office largely thwarted this intent. Originally, Attorney General William French Smith was to announce a
major experiment in order maintenance to be conducted in Newark
and in Houston. Reviewing plans for the experiment that the Police
Foundation had submitted to NIJ prior to a press conference in
Newark, however, Smith's representatives insisted that the entire effort
be renamed and its focus shifted from "Order Maintenance Experimentation" to "Fear Reduction Experimentation."[18] This shift was more
than nominal: it entailed a fundamental change in emphasis to fear
reduction in general, rather than the specific relationships among disorder, fear, and crime as had been envisioned in the original NIJ solicitation. During implementation the actual focus was further altered by
local police officials in pursuit of their own interests in fear reduction.
As a consequence, in Houston the experimental efforts included developing community police stations, community organizing, and citizen
contact patrol, none of which was concerned directly with disorder. In

Newark, one effort concentrated on order-maintenance "crackdowns," with the remaining efforts paralleling those in Houston. "Crackdowns," like "streetsweeps" of course, were far different from the ideas proposed in "Broken Windows."

The shift in focus in the NIJ experiment from fear reduction through control of disorder to fear reduction by any means did not preclude it from making significant contributions to developing police theory, especially community policing theory.[19] Nonetheless, many of the basic policy issues were ignored or set aside. Were disorder and fear causally linked with serious crime and urban decay? If so, could police actions to control disorderly behavior and citizen fear also reduce crime? A crucial opportunity to test linkages among disorder, fear, crime, and police order-maintenance efforts experimentally was lost. The issues raised in "Broken Windows" were just too controversial and out of the mainstream of conventional thinking to be endorsed by national politicians, even so far as justifying their exploration in an experiment.

Fortunately, even after the Police Foundation study, Northwestern University Political Science Professor Wesley Skogan continued to pursue his long-standing interest in the linkages among disorder, fear, and crime. Merging the data collected for the evaluation of the Houston and Newark experiments with two other data sets—from three cities he and Michael Maxfield, then a graduate student, had studied earlier, and from surveys in Chicago and Atlanta—Skogan not only replicated the finding of a relationship between disorder and fear, but established the causal links between disorder and serious crime—empirically verifying the "Broken Windows" hypotheses. The results were published in 1990 as *Disorder and Decline: Crime and the Spiral of Decay in American Neighborhoods*.[20]

Taken as a whole, Skogan's research made use of two types of data: first, in surveys of 13,000 individuals in forty urban residential neighborhoods in Atlanta, Chicago, Houston, Philadelphia, Newark, and San Francisco, citizens were asked about their experiences with crime, their fears, actions they took to defend themselves, and their perceptions of neighborhood disorder. Second, independent and objective observations of neighborhoods made by field researchers in ten of the forty neighborhoods documented conditions there, recording instances of graffiti, gang-related congregations, street prostitution, public drunkenness, drug dealing, and other such behaviors. Three important findings emerged when Skogan analyzed the data.

First, regardless of ethnicity, class, or other characteristics, residents within a community or neighborhood generally concurred about what constituted disorder and how much disorder was present locally. Although types of disorderly behavior and conditions varied by community and neighborhood, in terms of total responses across all communities residents reported the following forms of "social disorder" (that is, behaviors as opposed to physical conditions) most frequently: public drinking and lounging drunks; loitering youths and corner gangs; drug use; noisy neighbors; panhandling and harassment on the streets, especially when carried out by those apparently mentally ill; and street prostitution. Several forms of physical disorder were closely related to these disorderly behaviors: commercial sex shops; vandalism consisting of graffiti and damage to public spaces such as schools, bus shelters, street signs, and vending machines; accumulations of rubbish and refuse; and dilapidated and abandoned buildings.[21]

A second key finding in Skogan's analysis was a direct link between disorder and crime: in other words, "disorder and crime problems go together in a substantial way." In neighborhoods with higher crime levels, disorder was linked more strongly with crime than were other characteristics of the areas—poverty, instability in the housing market, and predominantly minority racial composition among residents.[22] Finally, Skogan found that disorder, both directly and as a precursor to crime, played an important role in neighborhood decline. By lowering community morale and giving the neighborhood a bad reputation throughout the city, disorder both in itself, and through increased crime, undermined the stability of the local housing market: fearful residents moved out, and real estate values plunged. At the same time local businesses could not attract customers, and investment in the community plummeted.[23] All of these factors contributed directly to decline and decay. Professor Skogan concluded that meaningful research on neighborhood crime had to include an investigation of problems of disorder, which "both directly and through crime . . . plays an important role in neighborhood decline. 'Broken windows' do need to be repaired quickly."[24]

Beyond providing empirical proof to confirm Wilson and Kelling's hypothesis, however, Skogan's results offer both rebuttal and assurance to opponents of order-maintenance programs. First, critics of order maintenance as the ideas were discussed in "Broken Windows" raised legitimate concerns that varying definitions of order might result in a "tyranny of the majority," by one group in a neighborhood over others, with police order-maintenance activities becoming the means by which that control was established and maintained. Professor Skogan's findings suggest that since wide agreement exists among citizens in specific neighborhoods about what disorderly and threatening behaviors are present and how serious a problem disorder poses, order-maintenance activities need not be divisive in communities. This conclusion was borne out in the Newark Foot Patrol Experiment, where officers enjoyed broad support for their activities from all citizens, including street people. The issue is similar on city streets: people recognize disorder when they see it, and uniformly want something done about it.

Skogan's research also confirms that citizens' fear of disorder is neither an unreasonable nor extreme reaction, since disorder does indeed precede or accompany serious crime and urban decay.[25] In a fundamental sense this finding affirms the long-standing intuition and experiences of citizens. For example, in Ridgewood, a Queens neighborhood in New York City adjacent to a seriously troubled and decayed Brooklyn neighborhood, residents have fought hard to maintain a stable, working-class community. Paul Kerzner, chairman of the Greater Ridgewood Restoration Corporation, describes what it takes to maintain the neighborhood: "It's always an uphill battle. When you see graffiti, you have to clean it up right away. When you hear of a drug location, you have to scream bloody murder to the police captain until you get results. Little by little, you create a climate of civility that people respect, and you make sure that standard never gets lowered."[26]

If citizens' perceptions are correct, they must hold the line against disorder in order to stave off more serious crime and urban decay. To ignore disorder would be to court potential disaster for their communities. The logical correlate of this position is that on a different level, when local or federal officials involved in crime control ignore disorder and fear, they act contrary to the best information that both citizens and social science have to offer. They risk, ultimately, irreversible urban decline and decay for large portions of our cities.

Skogan's research established clearly that citizen demand for government to deal with the "crime problem" is substantially different from official representations of both the problem and demand. The fact that citizens want attention paid to disorder as well as serious crime may explain what appears to be a contemporary anomaly in crime-fighting efforts today: even though the incidence of serious crime may level off or decline, fear of crime will not abate and may even continue to rise where disorder is not addressed. Yet asking political leaders, criminologists, and police officials to incorporate fear and disorder into their thinking about crime, into crime-fighting programs and strategies, is not as easy as it may sound. Fundamentally, such a change requires reconceptualizing our notion of what constitutes "crime" and rethinking how we determine the relative seriousness of particular types of crime.

## CRIME AND THE OFFICIAL CRIME PROBLEM

Official data about America's urban "crime problem" generally are derived from the Uniform Crime Reports (UCR). The UCR are published annually, with data for each preceding year preliminarily released the following spring and the final report, *Crime in the United States*, published in late summer.[27] The UCR were originally developed during the 1920s by the International Association of Chiefs of Police (IACP), under the leadership of Bruce Smith,[28] and later were adopted by the IACP as the first standardized crime-related record keeping system.[29] In 1930, the Federal Bureau of Investigation (FBI) took over the collection, compilation, and publication of crime information based on data provided by local and state police departments. The original "index" for assessing local crime rates was comprised of seven crimes: murder, rape, robbery, aggravated assault, burglary, larceny, and motor vehicle theft. Arson was added in 1979.

Since the 1960s, criminologists and police alike have acknowledged serious limitations in using the UCR as a statistical measure of crime rates and police performance. First, the UCR, by definition, chronicle *recorded* (reported crimes that police accept) as against *reported* crimes. The difference between reported and recorded crimes can be trivial, but examples abound in policing of "cooking the books" to keep crime statistics low.[30] Second, aside from the vulnerability of UCR to manipulation, especially at the local level, the primary substantive problem with the UCR is that they fail to record *unreported* crimes.[31] As a consequence, recorded crime data substantially underrepresent actual crime levels. Third, the UCR are extraordinarily selective. Ignored in the UCR index crimes are financial and white-collar crimes, serious problems in their own right. Finally, UCR classifications mask the complexity of the crime problem. Buried in the legal nomenclature of robbery, rape, and assault, just to use three examples from the index crimes, is a multiplicity of issues that cross-cut the index crime categories. One of these is stranger versus nonstranger perpetration of crimes. In 1993, for example, of the estimated 9,898,980 violent crimes committed in the United States (rape, robbery, and assault), more than half, 5,045,040 (51 percent), were committed by nonstrangers.[32] Classification methods of the UCR draw attention toward one facet of the crime problem and away from others, often with unintended although serious consequences.[33]

Despite the weaknesses of the UCR, they continue to be relied upon for a number of important purposes related to policy-making. During the years between World War II and the 1950s, comparatively quiet as far as UCR crime statistics were concerned, police were quick to use the UCR in order to claim credit for the relatively low crime rates. This honeymoon ended during the 1960s, when the "crime problem" exploded into a national issue. Since then the UCR have been used as a measure for the incidence of crime, thereby framing the terms of the "crime problem" for both the media and the general public. Yet UCR statistics have come to serve purposes other than indicating the supposed incidence of crime or police effectiveness. Linked with calls for service (that is, calls for assistance from citizens to the police), UCR crime categories serve to establish, virtually alone, what police view as the citizen demand for services. This understanding of demand, in turn, underlies beat (the primary geographical unit to which officers are assigned) construction, the allocation of patrol officers to particular neighborhoods by time of day or night, and a setting of priorities for responding to specific calls for service.

Inherent in the UCR organization of index crimes is the view that the crime problem consists solely of committed acts of index crime: disorder, fear, and community decline are unrecognized as integral to the crime problem. Implicit in this model also are judgments about the relative severity of particular crimes—judgments that were made originally by police during the development of the UCR and continue to be widely accepted today. Few would disagree with the values imbedded in the police ordering of priorities: the most serious crime is murder; other crimes like rape and robbery with violence or the threat of violence follow; crimes against property that do not involve violence or threat of it are at the third level of this hierarchy. For a number of reasons, however, criminologists have attempted to develop more sophisticated measures of crime severity. One such rationale is that even within categories—say robbery—relative degrees of harm can be experienced by victims that are not reflected in official statistics. Another is that in the determination of overall crime rates, each discrete incident involving the same crime is not equally important, and some incidents should count more than others.

Criminologists Thorsten Sellin and Marvin E. Wolfgang first addressed these issues in their 1964 book, *The Measurement of Delinquency*.[34] After considerable research into the problems of determining the relative severity of crimes and the methods used to solve those problems, the Bureau of Justice Statistics published *The National Survey of Crime Severity* in 1985.[35] The methods used were an elaboration of the original Sellin-Wolfgang approach: present citizens, in the latter case a broadly representative sample of 60,000 individuals, with a series of crime scenarios, and then ask them to score the relative seriousness of each scenario.

Basically, the empirical approach of Wolfgang and his colleagues, as reported in the 1985 national survey, broadly supported the intuitions of those who created the UCR. The 1985 survey concluded: "The overall pattern of severity scores indicates that people clearly regard violent crimes as more serious than property offenses."[36] In these rankings, the most serious offense identified, with a score of 72.1, was the planting of a bomb in a public building that resulted in the death of twenty persons. The second most serious crime, 52.8, was the forcible rape and murder of a woman. The third, 47.8, was a parent killing a child with his fists. Far, far down on the list were some of the problems about which this book is concerned: a noisy person disturbing the neighborhood, 1.1; a group hanging around a neighborhood after being told by the police to disband, 1.1; a person drunk in public, 0.8; a sixteen year old breaking curfew, 0.7; and, at the bottom of the list, a person under sixteen playing hooky, 0.2.

How can these data be reconciled with the central thesis of this book, that for many citizens and communities the most serious problems are those rated least serious in the national survey? The reflection of criminal events in relatively brief surveys, as sophisticated as they may be methodologically, takes criminal acts out of their context. This is crucial, for criminal behavior is meaningful to all of us not merely because it involves an act of violence against a person or property. Any act becomes more serious if the setting in which it is carried out heightens the act's intensity, the resulting fear, and propensity for damaging the community as a whole. This does not mean that murder or assault in virtually any set of circumstances is not a serious crime. It does mean that because of the context in which it occurs, such a crime may have a grave impact not only on the victim and his or her family and friends, but upon the larger community as well. The raping and killing of a young child is not only unspeakably tragic for the child, her family, and relatives, but it shatters the social bonds among neighbors by making them fearful of each other and any strangers they encounter. Disorderly behavior as well may take on added significance because of its impact on the life of a community.

## MEASURING WHAT MATTERS: DISORDER AS SERIOUS CRIME

When are disorderly acts really *serious*? At what point does their seriousness merit intervention? Why should some persons engaging in disorderly behaviors be warned and/or arrested, and not others? The answers to these questions require a determination based upon two measures: first, the seriousness of virtually any crime—major as well as minor—is determined not solely by the heinousness of the act itself, but also by the context in which the behavior takes place. Second, the seriousness of any crime is similarly dependent not upon the harm done to the immediate victim alone, but also upon the injury to and impact on the entire community. Because of the context in which it occurs, disorderly behavior may be serious, if not to the specific individual who is the target or victim, then to the community whose social life may be gravely and even tragically affected.

Some disorderly behavior can be even more consequential for neighborhoods than are serious index crimes. For example, during the early 1990s businesspersons from the Upper West Side of Manhattan, in New York City, requested a meeting with both their police precinct commander and a representative of the district attorney's office to voice their objection to police placing high priority on robberies, yet practically ignoring illegal vending in their community. But it was even more complicated: illegal vending actually was less the problem than were drug users, who were selling "hot" merchandise to the illegal vendors, "hanging out," using drugs, panhandling, and harassing shoppers and pedestrians. Business owners made it clear that while they feared robbery, robberies could be "managed" through security, control of merchandise, and control of cash flow. They could not survive, however, if shoppers were unwilling to cross the phalanx of importuning street people, for businesses would languish and ultimately fail—a personal financial loss to the merchants, but a loss to the neighborhood as well. Here the context of disorderly behavior, in this case illegal behaviors associated with vending, made it more consequential for a particular neighborhood than the more "serious" crime of robbery.

The recognition of context as an element adding meaning to crime, and even as a factor in determining an appropriate response by authorities, is not new. In fact, it happens regularly and frequently. For example, police may evaluate the context of an act in deciding whether to intervene, even where a crime has technically occurred. This was long true for spousal abuse. Traditionally, police expected disputants to solve their problems on their own, regardless of the fact that an assault had taken place and likely could recur. The context within which the assault took place—by a family member, within the home—shaped police practices. The values being protected by such policies may or may not have been legitimate. Certainly, they included a deference to the authority of husbands and fathers over their wives and children, a value that has since been largely rejected, and a reluctance for government to interfere in family life, a value that society still holds in esteem but must be balanced against the costs of uncontrolled violence within family life. Similarly, police determinations of whether to intervene in specific disorderly incidents, while ultimately grounded in law, must arise out of an assessment of the seriousness of behavior within its context. Despite the existence of a city ordinance closing neighborhood parks at 10 P.M., on a sweltering summer night police officers might choose not to enforce it, instead permitting local residents and their families to remain in the park so long as they are quiet and generally respectful of the circumstances. Police officers evaluating the situation perceive the context created by a neighborhood park, that could provide a welcome refuge from the heat and humidity in a dense urban area, to a peaceful group of neighbors, and tailor their responses accordingly. For now we merely make this point explicit—that context adds meaning to an act, and is a key element in police officers deciding whether to intervene or to enforce the law strictly. We leave a more detailed discussion of the process involved, and a response to the legal challenges raised against the use of such police discretion, to Chapter 5.

What are the elements of context that give added meaning to disorderly behavior, and that cause disorderly behavior to have as serious implications for a community as does more serious crime? These elements number at least five: time; place; previous behavior by a disorderly person; the condition of the "victim" or observer of the disorderly behavior relative to the perpetrator; and the aggregation or clustering of incidents of the specific act involved, particularly as it may affect the entire neighborhood or community. Apart from their individual significance these five elements frequently interact, compounding their total effect.

## Time

At a macro level, we all understand that behaviors appropriate at one time are inappropriate at another. To a degree, appropriateness depends upon our expectation of certain predictable behavior; it may also depend upon the specific audience expected to be present. Holidays and festivals are good examples. New Year's Eve is a time for revelry, and many communities work hard to ensure a safe time for celebrants (for example, by augmenting public transportation). Halloween is a time for costumes, begging, pranks, and scaring people. The Fourth of

July is a time for fireworks and noisemaking. Most of us are more tolerant of carousing and merrymaking at these times than we might otherwise be. Similarly, excessive noise on Friday and Saturday nights is more broadly acceptable than on weeknights when most people have to work the next day. A panhandler standing peacefully in front of a brownstone during the middle of the day is probably not threatening to most persons; yet the same panhandler, behaving the same way at dusk or after dark, can be quite threatening. Two panhandlers standing at the top of a stairway leading from the subway up to the street during rush hour is a different matter than the same two, behaving identically, standing there at midnight when few other people are around. A prostitute standing on the corner in a mixed residential/commercial neighborhood at 2 A.M. is different than at mid-afternoon when children are returning home from school. People lying across a sidewalk in a commercial district during shopping hours are more disruptive to pedestrian traffic than would be true during off-hours. In each case, everything else in a person's demeanor and behavior can be the same, yet the time at which behavior occurs endows it with special meaning and produces a differing impact on individuals and the surrounding neighborhood.

## Place

In like manner, even when everything else is the same, location can affect the meaning and impact of particular acts. Panhandling, again, is a good example, for the same form may have quite different meanings in residential as against commercial areas. The bustling crowds of Harvard Square in Cambridge (Massachusetts) make a solitary panhandler sitting on the stoop of a fast-food store relatively innocuous. The same panhandler sitting on the stoop of an apartment building for the elderly in a residential neighborhood of Cambridge could be quite threatening to the residents. Someone offering to "watch your car" at midday on a public street might be easy to turn down; however, the same act might be far more intimidating in an underground public garage when no one else is around. Likewise, selling merchandise alongside a park may be a manageable problem—passersby can avoid congestion by walking into the park or crossing the street. In a commercial area that depends upon window-shopping and easy access to stores, vending can spell disaster not only for commerce, but for citizens who live in the neighborhood and depend on local dealers.

## Previous Behavior of the Disorderly Person

The behavior of persons, either chronically or immediately preceding the commission of a disorderly act, also gives added meaning to the immediate act. Thus, for example, a person who has chronically terrorized a neighborhood by threatening persons, striking out at them, throwing feces at them, or attempting to block their passage, yet who begs passively in any particular incident, nonetheless is threatening and engenders fear because of his or her reputation for previous aggressive behavior. A person staggering from drug use or inebriation and who is seen behaving erratically, but who suddenly stands rigidly upright and puts out a cup without otherwise moving, may seem a threat because of her/his previously observed drug or alcohol-induced erratic behavior.

## Condition of the Victim or Observer Relative to the Perpetrator

The age, physical condition, gender, and other characteristics of the victim/observer that make him or her vulnerable in relation to the perpetrator also intensify the significance and threat posed by any single act of disorderly behavior. Thus, a drunk gesturing wildly and yelling at a pregnant woman holding a young child and waiting for a bus is different than the same drunk behaving the same way to two college students. We worry about the vulnerability of the woman, the impact on the child, and the difficulty they would have removing themselves from the presence of the drunk. We worry much less about the ability of sturdy youths in similar circumstances who, if the situation became especially threatening, could flee or defend themselves more easily. Other persons are similarly vulnerable—children, the elderly, the physically or visually impaired, persons in wheelchairs, to give some examples—so that particular acts of disorder or incivility directed at them could be more serious when carried out by an individual who is physically stronger or more powerful, and may be menacing or threatening.

*Numbers or Aggregation*

The number, or aggregation, factor of a specific act has a significant impact both on an individual's perceptions of and responses to that act, and on the health and vitality of the neighborhood itself. As Wilson and Kelling showed, disorderly conditions indicate that no one cares. The greater the disorder, in aggregate terms, the stronger the message to observers and "victims"—those toward whom the behavior is directed. One panhandler might say little about neighborhood conditions; ten might say a lot. One person lying down across a sidewalk in a commercial area is probably a minor inconvenience; thirty interfere with commercial functioning and pedestrian traffic. One or two persons sleeping in a park may make a stroller uneasy; an encampment of 200 may destroy the park for public use entirely. A single youth playing hooky may pose little threat to a small town, yet thousands of youths skipping school represent a major threat to neighborhoods in Philadelphia or New York. In each case, those who might seek to oppose or curtail an individual act become increasingly fearful and less likely to do so as the number of perpetrators and acts grows. At some point disorderly behavior reaches a critical mass so that fear on the part of citizens turns to avoidance and retreat, and serious crime begins to make inroads into the neighborhood. It is not just the individual observers or "victims" who are harmed, for as Skogan's work reports, neighborhood decline and decay may well follow.

Because of the social contexts in which they occur, the acts that we have labeled "disorderly behavior" may take on much more threatening, menacing, and destructive meanings than simple behaviors alone would carry—making them serious indeed to witnesses or "targets." More than one judge has asked in recent cases involving just such acts by the homeless, or street people, "do we really want to criminalize behavior that all of us might be forced into or need to do at some time or another in public?" We would answer this question by referring to the context in which such acts are performed: it is one thing if a person, including a homeless person, has to urinate and behaves discreetly: that is, finds an isolated location (say an alley), positions her/his body as modestly as possible, makes sure that children are not present, and in other ways communicates both literally and symbolically that he or she respects the rights of others and is doing her/his best to do so in an emergency. It is something else when, as we have observed, a person stands on Fifth Avenue in New York City and openly urinates into the gutter without concern for others.

Many times citizens themselves will act to stem such behavior, without substantial police intervention. However, when the context and or number of such acts produces a setting in which fear or actual physical conditions prevent citizens from acting and from using a public space in its intended fashion, then disorderly behaviors should be subject to more formal legal restrictions and controls that ultimately become the basis for police intervention. Recently residents of several San Francisco neighborhoods asked the city to close their local parks, remove play equipment and benches, and fence the grounds off or even bulldoze the land. The reason for these requests was that the parks had been taken over by encampments, drug dealers, and prostitutes, making them too dangerous for social and recreational use by residents and their children. Instead, the parks had become magnets that attracted additional crime into the area.[37] In such cases, when the normal constraints of mutual obligation and decency break down so grossly, police, prosecutors, and judges will have to intervene to ensure that the "small change" of urban life persists.[38] A community's life may depend upon such intervention.

## CAN WE RESTORE ORDER?

The discontinuity between citizen demands for order and police and criminal justice priorities persists. Police and criminal justice agencies use formal measures of demand based on judgments of crime seriousness that are intuitively reasonable and supported by sophisticated research. Citizen demands are based on their experiences in public spaces (the context) with what they correctly believe are the precipitating signs of crime—disorder and media coverage of crime. Small shifts in levels of reported crime simply have no practical impact on the vast majority of citizens. Their daily "in your face" street experiences do. Yet virtually no police department or criminal justice agency has established formal mechanisms for collecting data about the problems that bother citizens most, or for acting upon these concerns.

At first thought Skogan's admonition that broken windows need to be repaired quickly seems a reasonable idea. Yet the practical implications of restoring order are actually radical: asking political leaders, criminologists, and police officials to incorporate fear and disorder into their crime-fighting programs and strategies implies a fundamental reordering of political and professional priorities, and challenges a criminal justice system paradigm that remains vigorously entrenched to reform criminal justice education and develop a new conception of the criminal justice "system." Asking the courts to recognize a community's interest in maintaining order as compelling, and empowering the police to intervene when disorderly acts are carried out, is perceived by many as a direct challenge to the legal and constitutional protections for fundamental liberties that have grown up since the 1960s.

Nevertheless, the efforts of some cities to restore order and prevent or reverse the decline of urban neighborhoods are beginning to pay off. We can learn from their successes—in legislatures and city councils, in the courts, and on the streets—and from the failure of others. Restoring order and preventing or reversing urban decline are feasible goals. The strategy proposed here involves, as a first step, exploring more fully what disorder is and is not, and attempting to understand just how America's cities became arenas in which disorderly acts could flourish under constitutional protection while community standards were increasingly threatened. Many of those opposed to restricting disorderly acts claim to be acting on behalf of the poor or disadvantaged, under the guise of legal principles that purport to protect fundamental liberties. Since their arguments frequently prevail in the courts, thereby forestalling progress toward restoring order, answering them is an important task with which to begin.

## CHAPTER 2

# THE GROWTH OF DISORDER

OPPOSITION TO RESTRICTIONS ON DISORDERLY BEHAVIOR HAS been strong, organized, and in many cases effective. Most often it takes the form of a local chapter of the American Civil Liberties Union or some other advocacy group, acting on behalf of the "homeless" or a group of persons who have camped or engage in disruptive behavior on streets or in other public places, bringing a legal suit against a city for passing, or a police department for enforcing, legislation restricting disorderly acts. A number of arguments are raised to attack such legislation: it represents, in essence, a war waged by the rich upon the poor; it is merely an attempt to push society's most marginal and disadvantaged out of sight and out of mind; it assaults the fundamental liberties of individuals to speak out and remind us—even by their very presence on the streets—of their condition in society and our collective responsibility to them; and at the least, it is an effort by an intolerant and tyrannical majority to impose its standards upon those who are "different." Illustrative of such arguments are the words of Candace McCoy, in the *Criminal Law Bulletin*,

> "Broken Windows" contains an argument that seems to be based on the middle-class yearning for order and decorum. "A place for everything and everything in its place" is the housekeeper's physical manifestation of a

deeper psychological preference for predictability and control. This tidiness becomes a moral command: It is bad to be "out of place," that is different. People who are dirty and different are bad.

Wilson and Kelling are not so out of touch with the still vigorous liberal tolerance for nonviolent deviance that they would argue baldly that the homeless should be institutionalized because they are bad people. . . . Rather, the Broken Windows thesis as presented is behavioral, supposedly based on an empirical description of the effects of the homeless on community life, not on a judgment of their moral character.[1]

Others are more ambivalent about the problem of disorder and attempts to restrict disorderly acts. In an article in *The New Yorker*, James S. Kunen initially accepts the apparent need to maintain order, and even acknowledges the practical benefits of doing so:

The notion that disorder on the street may help generate crime makes sense. Rowdy or unpredictable behavior scares people, so they stay indoors, and when they do go out they keep to themselves. Citizen surveillance thus decreases, making the streets more attractive to criminals. . . .

In theory, then, reducing disorder ought to reduce crime—and that appears to be happening in New York City. Misdemeanor arrests are up 32 percent this year, and the bulk of them have come in poor, high-crime precincts—a rebuke to the assumption that the Mayor's purposes were merely cosmetic. Felony arrests are up, too. And, as of late October, there were 1,352 homicides, down from 1,641 during the same period last year. Reported robberies declined from around seventy thousand to around sixty thousand.

Yet in conclusion he falls back on the adage that reducing disorder means attacking the homeless:

. . . We can define certain people out of the community—even read them out of the human race. . . . But we can't make them cease to exist. Homeless people who are terrified of city shelters can be chased out of Central Park or Grand Central, but they still need to sleep somewhere.[2]

How we get from enforcing laws against disorderly behavior to reading people out of the human race, or casting them aside, is a rather tortuous bit of logic. Yet it is one that even some judges apply, as did Federal

District Court Judge Robert Sweet in ruling against a panhandling statute in New York:

> A peaceful beggar poses no threat to society. The beggar has arguably only committed the offense of being needy. The message one or one hundred beggars sends society can be disturbing. If some portion of society is offended, the answer is not in criminalizing these people, debtor's prisons being long gone, but addressing the root cause of their existence.[3]

We believe the approach expressed in these three examples to be essentially flawed, as well as ultimately counterproductive. Apart from granting absolution to those who abuse alcohol and drugs, coerce or intimidate others, or act unlawfully, this line of reasoning errs by relying upon several faulty assumptions concerning the "homeless," who they really are, and the "harmlessness" of aggregate acts of antisocial behavior on neighborhoods and communities. As often as not, those portrayed as "homeless" in court cases brought by advocates seeking to ensure their continued right to a presence on streets, in parks, and in other public places, are mentally ill, multiple substance abusers, or even criminally motivated. When used to justify keeping substance abusers or mentally ill individuals on the streets rather than moving them into shelters or treatment programs, arguments on their behalf are more destructive than constructive in outcome, merely ensuring their continued deprivation and vulnerability to crime and serious physical harm.

Even more important, however, and contrary to what critics of order maintenance contend, criminalizing the poor or homeless is *not* the central issue or the foundation of legislation against disorderly behavior. The problem is not the *condition* of being homeless or poor; it is the *behavior* of many persons, some homeless but others not, who violate the laws of the city and state. The disorder that we describe consists of physical acts, such as panhandling, and the residual physical conditions that result from disorderly behavior, such as graffiti and abandoned cars. The *act* of panhandling, the *act* of public drinking, are disorderly behaviors of concern here—not being poor, or even being recognized widely as a prostitute or public inebriate. The issue is behavior.

Yet, how did we permit disorderly behavior to grow to its current proportions in our cities? And how it is that the debate over restricting disorderly behavior has come to center on questions of "victims' rights" or the "homeless"? The intense public, professional, and legal debate taking place today over such issues as homelessness, economic injustice, and whether society's "victims" should be punished, is framed in large part by an ethos of individualism that grew and flourished through the middle years of this century.

## THE GROWTH OF INDIVIDUALISM
## AND INDIVIDUAL RIGHTS

A revolution in social thinking was afoot in the United States during the 1960s, in particular, that ultimately shifted the balance among individual rights and freedoms, personal responsibility and accountability, and community interests.[4] Lawrence Friedman, in *The Republic of Choice*, describes the developing culture that emerged:

> In our individualistic age the state, the legal system, and organized society in general . . . seem more and more dedicated to one fundamental goal: to permit, foster, and protect the self, the person, the individual. A basic social creed justifies this aim: each person is unique, each person is or ought to be free, each one of us has or ought to have the right to create or build up a way of life for ourselves, and to do it through free, open, and untrammeled choice. These are the unspoken premises of popular culture.[5]

A number of ideas relevant to our discussion of increasing disorder evolved as part of the social and conceptual revolution that produced this popular culture: the primacy of the "self" and the right to be "different"; a corresponding emphasis on individual needs and rights, and the belief that such rights were absolute;[6] a rejection, or at least serious questioning, of middle-class morality; the notion that stigmatizing individuals as criminals or deviants turned them into criminals or deviants; and the positing of solutions such as mental hospitals, therapies, and other interventions as more invidious than the problems they were designed to address. In the judicial arena, the courts developed a corresponding body of legal precedent in which constitutional protections for the fundamental rights and liberties of individuals were expanded and elevated to a position of far greater significance than either the responsibilities of individuals, or community interests.

The increase in urban disorder that has occurred in the past thirty years, in many senses, is rooted in these very changes: the emphasis on individual rights tied to the culture of individualism helped spur an increase in deviant behavior on city streets, while changes in legal doctrine, especially in constitutional and criminal law, not only permitted such behavior to continue but safeguarded the rights of those behaving in a deviant fashion. Said in another way, disorder grew and was tolerated, if not ignored, because the expression of virtually all forms of nonviolent deviance came to be considered synonymous with the expression of individual, particularly First Amendment or speech-related, rights.

It is important to note at the outset that not all increases in protection for individual rights had a negative impact—or indeed any impact—on the growth of disorder or society's tolerance for it. Recall that during the 1960s, serious crime was a major issue of national concern. Initially it seemed that the most serious and consequential changes in legal protections for fundamental rights would be those restricting police practices as they investigated criminal activity and dealt with those accused of criminal acts. The 1930s Wickersham Commission first put a national spotlight on the serious abuses that existed in police investigatory and evidence-gathering practices. Although most police leaders decried tactics such as the "third degree"—relentless interviewing that, at minimum, bordered on torture—similar practices nonetheless continued and were tolerated by the courts through the 1950s. During the early 1960s, however, a series of Supreme Court rulings handed down in rapid succession fundamentally reshaped police investigatory practices. Among the most significant of these decisions by the Court were: that evidence illegally seized by police could not be used against defendants in state courts—thus extending the exclusionary rule that had previously applied in federal courts to the states as well (*Mapp v. Ohio*, 1961); that those accused had the right to consult with counsel, and to have counsel present during interrogation, prior to indictment (*Escobedo v. Illinois*, 1964); and that suspects held for interrogation had to be informed of their rights to remain silent, and to have counsel present during an interrogation— today referred to as Miranda rights (*Miranda v. Arizona*, 1966).[7]

When these decisions were handed down, many in the police community bitterly attacked the Supreme Court, predicting ominous consequences.[8] The fear was that the Court's decisions would interfere with the ability of police to obtain evidence needed for convictions. Despite early protests, however, few in policing believe today that the decisions had a serious deleterious effect on the ability of police to carry out criminal investigations or prepare cases for court; rather, police were prodded into developing improved investigatory skills and capacities, and in doing so came to understand that formerly they had relied too greatly on interrogation. An even more positive outcome of the Supreme Court decisions was to put police on notice that, in the United States, their functions properly included not only law enforcement and the protection of the community, but the protection of individual rights as well. For the most part police incorporated both these legal requirements into their values and their activities. Crime fighting and the concern with serious crime went on.

While the Court's expansion of these protections for the fundamental rights of the accused was surely not insignificant, and received the greater attention, the growth of constitutional protections in other areas that more directly increased and even shielded disorderly behavior on the streets was less heralded, yet equally crucial. Two developments in particular produced a significant increase in the incidence of disorderly acts in public places, and concomitantly legal protections for these acts that reduced the ability of police to deal with them: the deinstitutionalization of the mentally ill and the decriminalization of public drunkenness.

## DISORDER INCREASING—THE DECRIMINALIZATION OF DRUNKENNESS AND DEINSTITUTIONALIZATION OF THE MENTALLY ILL

Traditionally, both handling the mentally ill and dealing with drunkenness were important functions for police. For example, in Seattle in 1945, arrests for drunkenness comprised 70 percent of total arrests for that year.[9] In Milwaukee in 1936, the 8,112 arrests for drunkenness made up 52 percent of all arrests.[10] Similar arrest ratios obtained in San Francisco during the 1940s and 1950s, when arrests for drunkenness comprised 61 and 71 percent, respectively, of the total number of arrests.[11] Even these figures substantially underestimate the number of arrests for drunkenness, since many drunks were arrested under disorderly behavior or vagrancy statutes.

Similarly, handling mentally ill persons has always been a de facto responsibility of police, although no laws existed, such as drunkenness statutes, that specifically criminalized emotional illness. Nonetheless, the demand that police "do something" about the emotionally or mentally disturbed—either for their own protection or because they were disruptive—led to police using disorder and vagrancy statutes to take such persons into custody. Most of the actions taken by police in dealing with disturbed persons were informal and "unofficial," with no involvement by any social service or medical agency; therefore, data are not readily available to establish the dimensions of these efforts.[12] Yet they were likely substantial. Philip Taft wrote in 1980 that "Police . . . had long been overtaxed dealing with 'mentals.' . . . Chicago's 12th district had been scooping 50 to 100 people off the streets daily and holding them overnight in jail 'for their own safekeeping' said one veteran of the force."[13]

Although police had long dealt with the disruptive behavior of those not institutionalized, by the 1950s "warehousing" of the mentally ill had become a common abuse. What began as a legitimate move to correct this abuse eventually led, under the tutelage of R. D. Laing, Thomas Szasz, Erving Goffman, and others, to a rejection of the concept of mental illness completely: individuals were not ill; society's response to them was.[14] And what began in the deinstitutionalization movement as the right to treatment eventually became the right to *refuse* treatment, based upon one's liberty interest. In 1975, in *O'Connor v. Donaldson*, the Supreme Court held: "A finding of 'mental illness' alone cannot justify a State's locking a person up against his will and keeping him indefinitely in simple custodial confinement. . . . [A] State cannot constitutionally confine without more [than this] a nondangerous individual who is capable of surviving safely in freedom by himself or with the help of willing and responsible family members or friends." The Court also held that a state could not confine the mentally ill simply to provide them a standard of living greater than what they would have in a private community, or to keep those harmless mentally ill apart from other citizens solely to save those not mentally ill from "exposure to those whose ways are different."[15] The issue of commitment had moved from being a medical question to a legal one, and the mentally ill could legally choose "freedom" on the streets over hospitalization or institutionalization.

The movement to deinstitutionalize the mentally ill became the model for diffusing the culture of individualism throughout public policy generally. Indeed, the same logic would shape the movement to decriminalize drunkenness, which followed and largely paralleled the deinstitutionalization experience. In 1967, the President's Commission on Law Enforcement described the routine treatment of individuals arrested for drunkenness: an offender was frequently placed in a barren holding cell that might contain as many as forty or fifty drunks, with little room to sit or lie down and inadequate sanitary facilities. Virtually no medical care was provided. Offenders able to afford bail usually were released when they sobered up and could often avoid prosecution, whereas those too poor to afford bail had to appear in court. The majority of defendants who ended up serving a jail sentence did so in county jails with appalling conditions that had "a destructive rather than a beneficial effect not only on alcoholics . . . committed to them but also on those others who are convicted of the most petty offenses."[16] Appropriately concerned about police and criminal justice handling of drunkenness, reformers during the 1950s and 1960s first redefined the problem by moving it from the criminal arena into the medical world, where drunkenness became an illness in need of treatment. Yet most of these reformers—social workers, criminal justice practitioners, medical personnel, and "alcohologists"—agreed that up to two-thirds of those chronically inebriated would not pursue treatment. Thus long-term *involuntary* treatment was proposed as an alternative to punishment, jails, and prisons.

At this point, however, civil libertarians again entered the fray and, as Robin Room of the University of California School of Public Health noted in 1976, just as they had converted the issue of commitment of the mentally ill from a medical into a legal question, so they succeeded in transforming institutional commitment for alcoholism from a medical question into a legal one:

The lawyers broke into the developing cycle of alcoholism-thought by bringing with them firmly held and concretely based perspectives forged in the battles over involuntary commitment for mental illness. . . .

At an annual meeting of the National Council on Alcoholism, Peter Hutt, the ACLU Counsel . . . stated the lawyers' position unequivocally: "We have not fought for two years to extract DeWitt Easter, Joe Driver, and their colleagues [persons arrested for drunkenness] from jail, only to have them involuntarily committed for even a longer period of time, with no assurance of appropriate rehabilitative help and treatment. The euphemistic name 'civil commitment' can easily hide nothing more than permanent incarceration.[17]

President Johnson's Crime Commission solidly endorsed the decriminalization of drunkenness, pronouncing: "Drunkenness should not in itself be a criminal offense. Disorderly and other criminal conduct accompanied by drunkenness should remain punishable as separate crimes."[18] And while the commission recognized that implementing decriminalization would require the development of adequate civil detoxification procedures, it adopted the civil libertarians' position regarding involuntary commitment. To wit, drunkenness would result neither in arrest, nor in commitment.

Decriminalization of drunkenness and the deinstitutionalization of the mentally ill had an enormous impact on urban life. Adequate numbers of community mental health and detoxification centers had not been built to provide care for those now out of institutions.[19] Without comprehensive psychiatric care, many mentally ill refused to take their medications. Many mentally ill as well as alcohol abusers asserted their "right" to deviance and refused all forms of assistance. And, as the sheer numbers of the mentally ill and/or drunk increased on city streets, so police ability to "manage" the disorder such individuals posed decreased.

Although most police handling of mentally disturbed persons remains informal and, as a consequence, "unofficial," problems associated with the mentally ill on city streets have worsened since the deinstitutionalization movement. Rael Jean Isaac and Virginia C. Armat provide statistical evidence of the sheer increase in numbers in *Madness in the Streets: How Psychiatry and the Law Abandoned the Mentally Ill*:

In Buffalo, in the course of 1982, seventy-two discharged psychiatric patients were arrested as they wandered on the grounds of Buffalo State Psychiatric Center and three general hospitals with psychiatric units—

most of them charged with trespassing. There are twice as many mentally ill persons on the streets and in shelters as there are in our public mental hospitals. There are as many individuals suffering from serious mental disorder in our jails and prisons as there are in our public mental hospitals. A study followed a sample of 132 patients released from Central Ohio Psychiatric Hospital in the first three months of 1985. Within six months of their release, *over a third* had become homeless.[20]

Similarly, Christopher Jencks reports that nationwide, by 1987, approximately 100,000 working-age persons with mental problems severe enough to preclude their holding a job were homeless.[21]

Considerable anecdotal evidence also exists about the consequences of turning the emotionally disturbed out onto the streets without adequate care. The Larry Hogue fiasco in New York City provides a recent example. Larry Hogue was a "homeless" individual with a history of drug use who literally terrorized a New York neighborhood. In a classic catch-22, when Hogue was in the hospital and not under the influence of crack, he posed no imminent danger to himself or to others: ergo, he was released. When back on the streets, Hogue used crack—and then proceeded to vandalize and defecate in cars, set fires, and threaten, physically abuse, and assault citizens. On one occasion he punched a young girl and pushed her in front of a bus. When police intervened, Hogue was so obviously and seriously disturbed that he was hospitalized. Once back in the hospital and withdrawn from crack, Hogue was no longer an imminent danger to himself or others, refused further treatment, and left the hospital. Similar tragedies are enacted daily on city streets throughout the United States.[22]

The impact on cities following the decriminalization of drunkenness is reflected in police data regarding arrests, which illustrate the lessening control over street life by police. In San Francisco, where during the 1940s and 1950s arrests for drunkenness constituted between 60 and 70 percent of the total number of arrests, this percentage dropped sharply to 44 percent in 1967, and down precipitously to 17 percent in 1992.[23] This trend is reflected as well in the limited national data that are available. In 1967, President Johnson's Crime Commission estimated that one-third (2,000,000) of all arrests nationwide were for drunkenness.[24] By 1992, government estimates of arrests for drunkenness had dropped to 6 percent of the total (approximately 880,000 of 14,200,000 arrests).[25]

Nevertheless, while arrests for drunkenness declined, citizen demand for police to "manage" drunks continued, for high-level policy-making notwithstanding, alcohol abusers continued to create problems in urban neighborhoods and public spaces, if not by their behavior at any given moment, then by the threat of their alcohol-induced unpredictability. Police therefore continued their informal handling of drunks—taking them home, reprimanding them and threatening arrest if they did not behave properly, calling family, walking them away from some location or situation to end a conflict, locking their car keys in the car's trunk so they could not continue to drive, and other such "unofficial" acts. Yet the legal changes accompanying decriminalization stripped police of much of their legal authority to control alcohol-related behavior, for police could no longer rely on the ultimate sanction—to arrest for drunkenness. When citizens complained that a drunk had committed some minor crime—a misdemeanor—police often could take no action, since arrest for a misdemeanor was permissible only when police themselves viewed the act. In the meantime, law-abiding citizens and the neighborhoods frequented by alcohol abusers suffered. For many citizens, especially in inner cities, the inability of police to take actions when drunks were merely threatening, or when police had not viewed the offense themselves, added to the view of police as "not caring" or being unwilling to take action.

Added to these serious repercussions of decriminalizing drunkenness, however, is another of equal weight: drunkenness and alcohol abuse may not merely be serious problems in their own right, they may also contribute to the overall crime problem in a major fashion. Recent surveys of jail inmates show that 49.5 percent of those arrested for homicide and 44.3 percent of those arrested for assault had drunk alcohol before committing the crime that led to their incarceration.[26] Based on prison surveys conducted by Christopher Innes, Harvard University professor Mark Klieman estimates that approximately 40 percent of those now in state prisons were drinking at the time of their offense, and concludes "if alcohol contributes even 20 percent to the problem of street crime, the control of alcohol-related crime ought to be a major consideration in framing alcohol policy."[27]

It is clear now that the decriminalization of drunkenness and the deinstitutionalization of the mentally ill had momentous consequences for our cities. Apart from increasing the level of disorder on streets, these movements undercut the basic authority of police to intervene and manage two important types of disorder. Yet greater tolerance for disorder, and the erosion of legal bases for restricting acts of disorder, have come from other sources as well.

## THE EROSION OF LEGAL AUTHORITY FOR CONTROLLING DISORDER: LEGISLATIVE DEVELOPMENTS AND CHANGING LEGAL DOCTRINE

Authority to regulate behaviors such as panhandling, prostitution, public drinking, soliciting for charitable contributions, picketing and parading, and appropriate use of parks and city streets, resides in the states' constitutionally derived power to provide for the police protection, health, safety, and quality of life of their citizens.[28] Each state may delegate to municipalities the power to regulate completely or partially in these areas; conversely, a state may choose to preempt regulation of an entire field. Yet attempts to restrict and regulate many disorderly acts today take place in an area of the law uncertain enough, as defined by the courts, that a pamphlet published by the Criminal Justice Legal Foundation to aid cities in constructing anti-panhandling or begging statutes advises a city to anticipate legal challenges:

> Any effort to restrict panhandling will be met with vigorous opposition from well-organized, well-funded, and extremely litigious organizations. Their point of view is shared by a significant minority of judges, particularly in the federal courts. It is therefore impossible to write a panhandling ordinance that will not be challenged. It is also impossible to guarantee that an ordinance will withstand challenge, even though it may, in reality, be perfectly valid.[29]

The tension between "rights" proponents, who argue that curbing disorderly conduct, often described by them as "speech" or expressive behavior, violates their fundamental liberties, and "communitarians" or "universalists," who contend that the rights of individuals must at times give way to communal values and structures so that basic order can be maintained in a larger community, is readily apparent in these suits and in the debate over legislation that they reflect.[30]

As we noted above, opponents of legislation directed at controlling disorder often cast their arguments in terms of the need to protect the rights of the "poor" or "homeless." Traditional bases for controlling disorder in society did rely upon restrictions placed explicitly upon the poor and vagrants. Yet our courts have appropriately taken us far beyond the old vagrancy laws that permitted the poor or minorities to receive discriminatory treatment. Today, both legislation and legal doctrine concerned with restricting disorderly behavior in public reflect this evolution. The question is, however, whether the courts have gone too far.

From the time of Union, the states sought to regulate both vagrancy and begging, and even movement by the poor into their regions. The Articles of Confederation prevented paupers from exercising the right to enter and leave, freely, any state, and excluded them from enjoying those privileges and immunities reserved to all other citizens.[31] Local authorities could oust newly arrived poor, removing them to their last place of residence. In 1791, when the Bill of Rights was ratified, eight of the fourteen states then in the Union specifically prohibited begging by statute; four other states and the District of Columbia followed by 1812.[32] In many locations, only those who had resided for lengthy periods in a particular location were eligible to receive public assistance.[33] All such laws were heirs to the British tradition of regulating the "dangerous classes,"[34] and the United States Supreme Court fully supported them: in *Mayor of New York v. Miln* (1837), Justice Barbour wrote that the State of New York had acted wisely in excluding paupers arriving by ship for it was "necessary for a state to provide precautionary measures against the moral pestilence of paupers, vagabonds, and possibly convicts; as it is to guard against the physical pestilence . . . from unsound and infectious articles."[35]

With the Tramp Acts of the 1870s, the states made it a crime for workers lacking visible means of support to travel about the country: these laws were directed toward preventing marginal elements of the working class from moving into criminality or becoming involved in community labor disputes. Implementation and enforcement of such statutes continued through the Great Depression and into the middle of this century. By 1960, under the guise of legitimate exercise of their police powers, all states except West Virginia had passed, and enforced, vagrancy laws against the unemployed poor.[36] State statutes were supplemented in many locations by municipal ordinances. While legislation varied from state to state, in the tradition of the "dangerous classes" approach such laws clearly punished status—the poor and the idle, able-bodied individuals who could work, but did not. No illegal act was required: vagrancy alone was sufficient cause for arrest.

Following the Depression and World War II, criticism of vagrancy and loitering laws in the United States by legal scholars and welfare practitioners escalated,[37] and the courts began to move toward eliminating status as a constitutionally permissible basis for criminal punishment. Tracing this process briefly up to the present, we find that legislation and corresponding legal doctrine applicable to the control of much disorderly behavior have passed through several phases in the United States: in the first, early *vagrancy laws* and other legislation making a status a criminal offense were passed; these were soon supplemented, or replaced through intended reform, by *anti-loitering laws* directed more specifically at certain acts or behavior; when the courts began to hold vagrancy as well as loitering laws unconstitutional, these laws were supplanted by more specific prohibitions against *loitering "for the purpose of"* some criminal activity (such as prostitution or drug dealing). The trend through these first three periods was toward a rejection of status-based legislation, and a requirement that criminal offenses be based upon specific behavior. Today, in the face of legal challenges to "loitering for the purpose of" laws, legislation restricting or prohibiting specific behaviors, such as lying down on a sidewalk, asking for money aggressively or more than once, or intentionally blocking pedestrian movement on sidewalks, is being developed and tested in the courts.

## Vagrancy Laws and Status-Based Legislation

The first successful legal challenges to vagrancy and loitering laws were directed at the exclusion by states of the itinerant poor. In *Edwards v. California* (1941), the Supreme Court struck down a California law prohibiting the importation of paupers into the state.[38] And although the Court's holding was based upon California's violation of the Commerce

Clause—in attempting to isolate itself from the effects of the Depression—concurring opinions by Justices Douglas and Jackson foreshadowed later Supreme Court decisions, attacking vagrancy as a status more directly. Relying on the Privileges and Immunities Clause of the Fourteenth Amendment, the two justices wrote that property status alone was not acceptable as a basis for limiting the rights of citizens. Justice Douglas also insisted that the California law had violated the fundamental right to interstate mobility, a right incident to national, as well as to state, citizenship.

The Court continued along this path with *Shapiro v. Thompson* (1969), finding that requirements in Pennsylvania, Connecticut, and the District of Columbia for a year's residence prior to applying for and receiving welfare benefits violated the fundamental right to travel among the states, and to equal protection.[39] Even though the states' avowed purpose was to inhibit an influx of needy persons in order to preserve the fiscal integrity of their public assistance programs, the Court held that this goal was constitutionally impermissible: while the states could legitimately attempt to limit expenditures, even for public assistance, they could not do so by creating an "invidious distinction" between new and old residents who were needy or destitute.

In addition to these pronouncements with respect to the status of poverty, the Supreme Court further developed its approach to status-based legislation generally during the 1960s. Two decisions are noteworthy for the present purposes: in the first, *Robinson v. California* (1962), police had examined the accused, Robinson, one evening on a Los Angeles street and found needle marks and scabs on his left arm. Robinson also admitted to the occasional use of narcotics. He was arrested and charged under a California statute making it a misdemeanor punishable by imprisonment for one to use or be addicted to the use of narcotics. California courts had construed the statute as making the "status" of narcotic addiction (that is being "addicted to the use" of narcotics) a criminal offense for which an offender could be prosecuted at any time before he reformed: thus a person could be guilty of the offense if addicted, regardless of whether he or she had ever possessed or used any narcotics within the state. The United States Supreme Court struck down California's law, finding that imprisonment of an individual where he or she might never have touched a narcotic within the state, nor carried out any irregular behavior there, inflicted cruel and unusual punishment, in violation of the Eighth and Fourteenth Amendments.[40]

A few years later, in *Powell v. Texas* (1968), the Court considered whether a section of the Texas Penal Code prohibiting intoxication in public fell within the ambit of *Robinson* as impermissible, status-based legislation. Powell, a chronic alcoholic with a long history of arrests for drunkenness, was arrested and charged with being found intoxicated in a public place. In defense, he asserted that because of his chronic alcoholism, his actions were involuntary and therefore could not constitutionally subject him to criminal punishment. At trial, Powell was found guilty. Upon appeal, a divided Supreme Court upheld his conviction and the constitutionality of the law, finding that unlike the California statute, the Texas provision did not seek to punish status, but rather to impose "a criminal sanction for public behavior which may create substantial health and safety hazards . . . and which offends the moral and esthetic sensibilities of a large segment of the community."[41]

Although handed down in the 1960s, *Robinson* and *Powell* figure significantly in recent cases brought by advocates for needy persons (the "homeless," the mentally ill, and substance abusers) against cities that attempt to restrict their behavior. Specifically these cases are raised because they deal with the issues of status, and related "involuntary acts" by individuals of a particular status in public. The question posed in current suits is whether *Robinson* and *Powell* should be interpreted to say that life-sustaining acts of homeless individuals—lying down, sleeping, eating, storing property, even begging—are involuntary as carried out in public and cannot legitimately be restricted since they are tied to the "status" of "homelessness." *Powell* in particular is troublesome as a guide because it represents a plurality opinion by four justices of the Supreme Court rather than a clear majority. The plurality opinion did address the issue of involuntary acts by way of a return to the *Robinson* decision. Yet it did not adopt the position advanced by advocates for the needy:

It is suggested in dissent that *Robinson* stands for the . . . principle that "[c]riminal penalties may not be inflicted upon a person for being in a condition he is powerless to change. . . ." Whatever may be the merits of such a doctrine of criminal responsibility, it surely cannot be said to follow from *Robinson*. The entire thrust of *Robinson's* interpretation of the Cruel and Unusual Punishment Clause [of the Eighth Amendment] is that criminal penalties may be inflicted only if the accused has committed some act, has engaged in some behavior, which society has an interest in preventing, or perhaps in historical common law terms, has committed some *actus reus* [a guilty, physical act]. It thus does not deal with the question of whether certain conduct cannot constitutionally be punished because it is, in some sense, "involuntary" or "occasioned by a compulsion."[42]

The debate over how *Powell* is to be applied arises from the concurring opinion of Justice White, who voted with the plurality to determine the outcome of the case, but explained his rationale in a separate opinion: while Powell might have proven that he had no choice as to whether he could drink at all, he did not prove that he had been compelled to drink in public.[43] Advocates for the homeless have seized upon Justice White's words to assert that if Powell had been homeless, he would have been powerless *not* to drink in public, and therefore his conviction would not have been upheld by the Court—an argument that raises homelessness itself to a status. Advancing the argument further, "status-based" restrictions on "life-sustaining acts" when carried out by the "homeless" in public parks, on city streets, and in municipal buildings such as parking garages, should be found impermissible, since homeless individuals presumably have no access to private space and therefore no choice but to perform such acts in public.[44]

Most courts to date have not adopted the view that homelessness is a status, or the applicability of Justice White's opinion in *Powell* to the activities conducted by the homeless in public.[45] Instead, they have adhered to the plurality opinion in *Powell* and to a recognition that the Supreme Court itself has not held the Eighth Amendment prohibition of cruel and unusual punishment to preclude punishing acts derivative of a person's status. For example, the California Supreme Court recently upheld a Santa Ana ordinance that proscribed camping on public property, finding it permitted punishment only for proscribed conduct, and that it was not clear that the petitioners actually had no alternatives "to either the condition of being homeless or the conduct that led to homelessness and to the citations [for camping on public property]."[46] Similarly, when advocates for the homeless brought a challenge to San Francisco's Matrix Program, which was aimed at ending street crimes in parks and neighborhoods by prohibiting public drinking and inebriation, obstruction of sidewalks, camping in parks, public urination and defecation, graffiti, street prostitution, street sales of narcotics, aggressive panhandling, and dumping of refuse, the federal district court found in *Joyce v. City and County of San Francisco*:

> homelessness is not readily classified as a "status." Rather, as expressed for the plurality in *Powell* by Justice Marshall, there is a "substantial definitional distinction between a 'status' . . . and a 'condition.' . . . While the concept of status might elude perfect definition, certain factors assist in its determination, such as the involuntariness of the acquisition of that quality (including the presence or not of that characteristic at birth) . . . and the degree to which an individual has control over that characteristic."[47]

Although such holdings are not uniform, the position taken by most courts is that homelessness is not a status, nor are acts deriving from the condition constitutionally protected from legitimate regulation.[48]

### Attempts to Regulate Behavior: Loitering Laws

Even before vagrancy and status-based legislation was widely invalidated by the courts, laws directed at the *act of loitering* also were passed and enforced. Many courts perceived loitering laws as one and the same with status-based legislation, even though some loitering laws had been passed to replace vagrancy statutes, presumed to be unlawful, with a constitutionally permissible form of regulation. Nevertheless, during the 1960s and 1970s federal and state courts began to strike down legislation regulating or prohibiting loitering as well as vagrancy.[49] Two landmark cases by which the Supreme Court dealt a fatal blow to vagrancy and loitering statutes based upon the status of poverty, or vagrancy, were *Papachristou v. City of Jacksonville* (1972) and *Kolender v. Lawson* (1983).

In *Papachristou*, eight individuals, some of whom were black and others white, had been charged with various acts of vagrancy for "prowling by auto" and loitering. They were convicted of violating a Jacksonville, Florida, vagrancy ordinance: "Rogues and vagabonds, or dissolute persons who go about begging . . . , persons wandering or strolling around from place to place without any lawful purpose or object . . . shall be deemed vagrants." Justice Douglas's majority opinion invalidated the ordinance as "void for vagueness," because it failed "to give a person of ordinary intelligence fair notice that his contemplated conduct is forbidden by the statute" and encouraged "arbitrary and erratic arrests and convictions." Elaborating on these points the Court emphasized that the Jacksonville ordinance was impermissible because it made criminal, innocent acts such as "wandering or strolling" from place to place that had long been part of the American tradition. The result of casting a net so widely, according to the Court, was to place "unfettered discretion" in the hands of police. The Court also rejected the rationale that vagrancy laws would prevent criminal behavior, since the Fourth Amendment guaranteed arrest only upon probable cause.[50]

While in *Papachristou* the Court focused primarily upon the requirement of providing adequate notice as to what specific conduct constituted criminal activity, in *Kolender v. Lawson*, the Court placed greater emphasis on the danger of potentially discriminatory enforcement by police. Lawson had been stopped by police, asked for identification, and detained or arrested fifteen times between March 1975 and January 1977, each time while walking late at night on an isolated street near a high-crime area or in a business area where burglaries had been committed. He was charged under a section of the California Penal Code that stated:

> Every person who commits any of the following acts is guilty of disorderly conduct, a misdemeanor: . . . (e) who loiters or wanders upon the streets or from place to place without apparent reason or business and who refuses to identify himself and to account for his presence when requested by any peace officer so to do, if the surrounding circumstances are such as to indicate to a reasonable man that the public safety demands such identification.

Writing for the Court, Justice O'Connor found the statute facially vague under the Due Process Clause of the Fourteenth Amendment for failing to "define the criminal offense with sufficient definiteness that ordinary people can understand what conduct is prohibited and in a manner that does not encourage arbitrary and discriminatory enforcement." Specifically, the statute lacked an explicit standard for determining how a suspect could satisfy the requirement of providing credible and reliable identification, and thereby encouraged arbitrary enforcement by police, who would have to determine whether the requirement had been met in each case.[51]

Following the Supreme Court's decision in *Papachristou* and to a greater degree after *Kolender*, other courts overturned many vagrancy and loitering laws under the Due Process Clause of the Fourteenth Amendment. Ordinances and statutes that failed constitutional tests were generally criticized on vagueness grounds for failing to provide guidelines so that reasonable persons could avoid specifically unlawful behavior, and for leaving police officers with unwarranted discretion in determining when behavior was unlawful and whether to arrest an individual. On overbreadth grounds, legislation was found fatally flawed for impermissibly restricting First Amendment constitutional freedoms. These court decisions sent a message to states and municipalities that even though their laws had not been tested, they probably would not pass constitutional muster. As a result, police ceased to enforce, and district and city attorneys to prosecute under, many laws that remained on the books. Other states and cities relied upon, or moved to pass new, statutes and ordinances directed at specific *behaviors* rather than the poor or itinerant.

## Loitering "For the Purpose Of" Laws

The permissible constitutional alternative to vague and overbroad status-based legislation was greater specificity and behavior-directed statutes and ordinances. Even before the *Papachristou* decision the courts began to define what would be required for legislation to withstand constitutional challenges. In *Shuttlesworth v. City of Birmingham* (1965), the Supreme Court considered an ordinance providing that "it shall be unlawful for any person . . . to so stand, loiter or walk upon any street or sidewalk in the city as to obstruct free passage over, on or along said streets or sidewalk," and that "it shall also be unlawful for any person to stand or loiter . . . after having been requested by any police officer to move on." The Court held that even though the ordinance, *as written*, would violate the First Amendment, when construed more narrowly, it would pass constitutional muster, since it "applies only when a person who stands, loiters, or walks on a street or sidewalk so as to obstruct free passage *refuses to obey a request by an officer to move on*."[52] Then a series of New York cases beginning in the late 1960s set forth the rule that legislation prohibiting loitering alone was unconstitutional, but where "loiter" was used along with or to describe another specifically proscribed act that legislation would be valid.[53] Drafters of such legislation believed the specific intent element contained in a statute incorporating the words "loitering for the purpose of" in conjunction with another unlawful activity, or specifying the manner of loitering so as to link it to that unlawful act, should ward off challenges based upon overbreadth or vagueness. In effect, the specific intent element would serve as notice that certain conduct was proscribed, as well as provide police with guidance for limiting their discretion and the equivalent of probable cause to stop and arrest. California's Penal Code section 647(d), which provides that any person "who loiters in or about any toilet open to the public for the purpose of engaging in or soliciting any lewd or lascivious or any unlawful act" is guilty of a misdemeanor, is typical of such legislation. The Supreme Court of California upheld the statute in *People v. Superior Court (Caswell)* (1988), finding that the requirement of knowledge that certain conduct was unlawful, and language specifying the place of enforcement, readily mitigated any potential vagueness by serving fair notice of the acts proscribed and providing adequate guidance to police to reduce their use of "unfettered" discretion in enforcement.[54]

"Loitering for the purpose of" legislation has produced a mixed bag of results, however, when tested in the courts. Some courts have followed the same rationale as the California Supreme Court, upholding statutes or ordinances modeled on this format.[55] A Milwaukee, Wisconsin, ordinance prohibiting loitering or prowling in a place, at a time, or in a manner not usual for law-abiding citizens under circumstances that warrant alarm for the safety of persons or property in the vicinity, and which provided for explanation and required probable cause for detention by the officer, was upheld in the face of a vagueness attack. The Wisconsin Supreme Court found the time, place, and manner language, and a listing of factors that police officers should consider in determining whether "alarm" was warranted, to provide sufficient specificity to avoid vagueness, and quoted the U.S. Supreme Court's words regarding the degree of definitiveness required: "There are areas of human conduct where, by the nature of the problems presented, legislatures simply cannot establish standards with great precision."[56] The city continues to enforce this ordinance as well as two new ordinances aimed at loitering for the purpose of prostitution and loitering for the purpose of drug dealing.[57]

Not all courts have accepted the constitutionality of "loitering for the purpose of" laws, however. In *Wyche v. State of Florida* (1993), the Supreme Court of Florida addressed the facial constitutionality of a Tampa ordinance making it unlawful for any person to loiter "while a pedestrian or in a motor vehicle, in or near any thoroughfare or place open to the public in a manner and under circumstances manifesting the purpose of inducing, enticing, soliciting, or procuring another to commit an act of prostitution . . . or other lewd or indecent act." As does much "loitering for the purpose of" legislation, the ordinance specified several acts and circumstances that could satisfy the "manifestation" element:

> . . that such person is a known prostitute, pimp, sodomist . . . and repeatedly beckons to, stops or attempts to stop, or engages passers-by in conversation, or repeatedly stops or attempts to stop motor vehicle operators by hailing, waving of arms . . . for the purpose of inducing, enticing, soliciting, or procuring another to commit an act of prostitution. . . . No arrest shall be made for a violation of this subsection unless the arresting officer first affords such person the opportunity to explain this conduct, and no one shall be convicted of violating this subsection if it appears at trial that the explanation given was true and disclosed a lawful purpose.[58]

Renetha Wyche was arrested under the ordinance after police observed her standing on a streetcorner in a "skimpy outfit," waving to passersby, and then getting into a car that stopped near the curb.

The Florida court struck down the ordinance, reasoning that it inhibited and infringed upon constitutionally protected activity that an innocent person might undertake—such as window shopping, sauntering down a sidewalk, waving to friends or passersby—by allowing arrest and conviction for loitering under circumstances that merely *indicated the possibility of intent* to engage in prostitution, rather than requiring *proof* of unlawful intent as an element of the offense. Furthermore, the court declined to "write in" requirements of specific intent to engage in prohibited activity, or sufficient overt activity to clearly manifest that intent, and it refused to find that police themselves could constitutionally exercise discretion to differentiate between "constitutionally protected street encounters and acts reflecting the state of mind needed to make an arrest."

Other "loitering for the purpose of" legislation has also floundered in the courts where the act to which loitering is tied is a constitutionally protected act. Legislation aimed at restricting "loitering for the purpose of begging" is a prime target in this regard, under attack as increasing numbers of courts have found begging and panhandling to constitute speech or communicative activity protected by the First Amendment. A key case in this area was decided in July 1993, when the Second Circuit Court of Appeals upheld a federal district court's finding that New York State's "loitering for the purpose of begging" law was unconstitutional.[59] The grounds for the decision were not vagueness or due process; rather the court held that begging was communicative activity protected by the First Amendment. In other recent decisions, both state and federal courts have accorded First Amendment protection to an increasing number of acts carried out on city streets that we label here as disorderly behavior—camping in parks, begging and panhandling, obstructing sidewalks in commercial areas, among them.

With the uncertain response from the courts to "loitering for the purpose of " legislation, many cities and states today are turning to legislation that departs entirely from the legacy of loitering or vagrancy statutes and instead targets specific acts that contribute to disorder and fear on the streets.

### The Next Phase of Legislation: Targeting Specific Behaviors

Across the country, "loitering for the purpose of" laws are still on the books and still enforced in many communities. Increasingly, however, cities and states are adopting legal provisions for addressing directly a range of behaviors that contribute to high levels of disorder on city streets, from aggressive begging and panhandling, accosting for the purpose of begging or soliciting for alms, lying down, sleeping, or camping in public parks or on sidewalks (sometimes limited to designated areas or particular hours), to obstructing pedestrian traffic on sidewalks, threatening or harassing or intimidating individuals, drinking alcohol in public, and defacing public property. The particular legislation relied upon by any city reflects to a degree the types of problems faced by that community. We provide specific examples of this type of legislation, and the experiences of cities and towns attempting to implement and enforce it, in the form of case studies in Chapters 4 and 6.

Challenges to these forms of order-maintenance legislation are a matter of course for cities. Legal advocates for those prosecuted continue to attack statutes and ordinances as impermissibly status based, aimed at the poor and homeless. Increasingly, however, they frame their analyses in terms of the affirmative First Amendment rights of speech and expressive conduct, and other fundamental rights of those poor and homeless on the streets, such as the right to travel and of association, almost invariably raising due process and equal protection claims.[60] The Equal Protection Clause of the Fourteenth Amendment prohibits a state from "deny[ing] to any person within its jurisdiction the equal protection of the laws," thereby requiring that all persons similarly situated be treated alike.[61] Equal protection challenges are brought frequently as class action suits on behalf of the "homeless" within a particular community, and charge that a particular statute unfairly targets the poor or homeless.

Under equal protection analysis, legislation is presumed valid so long as the classification drawn is rationally related to a legitimate state interest, a relatively easy standard for a city or state to meet. The problem arises when the burden is placed upon the city or state to meet a much higher standard—that of strict scrutiny. Where state action represents intentional discrimination (as found in the statutory language, or where "invidious discrimination" is at work) on the basis of a "suspect classification," such as race or national origin, that is, discrimination against members of a group historically the subject of invidious discrimination, it is subjected to strict scrutiny. Similarly, strict scrutiny is applied where a classification infringes upon a fundamental, constitutionally protected right, such as speech, voting, or interstate travel.[62]

"Strict scrutiny" often spells doom for a city's order-maintenance legislation: to prevail in such cases, the government must show that the legislation constitutes a finely tailored means for effectuating a *compelling government interest*. This standard is considerably higher and more difficult for a city or state to reach than the rational relationship level.

Whether the poor or homeless bringing suit constitute a suspect class is key, therefore, to a city's effort to succeed with legislation that targets specific acts. The answer to the question as established by the Supreme Court in a series of decisions appears to be no. For example, in addressing government funding for abortions, the Court found that indigence did not create a suspect class for equal protection purposes, and upheld a Connecticut welfare regulation providing poor pregnant women with funds for childbirth but not for nontherapeutic abortions.[63] The Court reached the same conclusion for poor pregnant women in New York City who challenged funding restrictions on payments for medically necessary abortions.[64] And in the realm of education, poor Mexican-American parents of children residing in districts with less taxable wealth and lower per-pupil expenditures failed in their equal protection challenge to the Texas system of financing public education based upon local property tax bases.[65] Lower courts have followed suit: just as most courts have refused to acknowledge homelessness as a status, so they have declined to recognize the poor or homeless as a suspect class and thereby invoke the application of strict scrutiny in their analyses.

Even though strict scrutiny may not apply on the basis of the homeless as a suspect class, it may be invoked where a fundamental right is violated through a classification. And when confronted with charges of due process and equal protection violations implicating speech and other constitutional rights, courts around the country have not responded uniformly in their evaluation of legislation directed at specific behaviors apart from loitering.[66] For example, two federal district court judges within the Ninth Circuit recently came down on different sides of the same issue—whether a city may regulate sitting on a sidewalk in a commercial area. In March 1994, Federal District Court Judge Barbara Rothstein (W.D. Wash.) upheld, on First Amendment, due process, equal protection, and right to travel grounds, Seattle, Washington's, sitting ordinance that prohibited, in part, sitting upon a

public sidewalk between 7:00 A.M. and 9:00 P.M. in designated downtown and neighborhood commercial zones. With regard to the First
Amendment challenge in particular, Judge Rothstein commented,
"Plaintiffs' argument [that the mere presence of an unkempt and
disheveled person sitting or lying on a sidewalk communicates the need
for assistance and society's failure to address that need] would require
the conclusion that every public act by homeless people is expressive
conduct protected under the First Amendment because they are by
their very presence making a continuing social statement. The court
rejects this argument as not supported by First Amendment precedent."[67] Yet in May 1995, Berkeley, California, was enjoined from
enforcing its ordinance that banned, in part, sitting down upon a public
sidewalk within six feet of a building in a commercial zone between
7:00 A.M. and 10:00 P.M.: according to Federal District Court Judge
Claudia Wilken (N.D. Cal.), sitting down on a sidewalk constituted
protected, expressive conduct under the First Amendment, communicating messages of both neediness and passivity.[68]

Judge Wilken's according of First Amendment protection to the
nonspeech behavior of individuals may be unique in its application to
sitting on a sidewalk, but is not atypical of the trend toward the courts'
extending such protection to many acts, beyond speech, carried out by
persons in public places. No longer confronted with legislation that
clearly targets the status of individuals—such as the old vagrancy and
loitering statutes—and having decided for the most part that homeless
and indigents do not constitute a suspect class, the courts now are
grappling with advocates' contentions that a message is being communicated by the actions, even mere presence on the streets, of the persons whom they represent—whether begging, lying on sidewalks, or
camping in parks. We examine some courts' specific holdings in the
face of such First Amendment challenges to order-maintenance legislation targeting specific behaviors in later chapters, and suggest the legal
arguments that cities will need to anticipate and meet if they are to
succeed in developing and defending their legislation.

Yet, as is clear from the Berkeley and Seattle cases, if one digs deeper
than the judges' ultimate rulings, the success of a city's legislation and
enforcement program in the courts often will depend not merely upon
the content of the legislation; rather, it turns as well upon the ability of

advocates for those prosecuted under it to portray the offenders as disadvantaged, poor, and victims of discrimination. In answer, the city will need to present a record of its overall efforts to deal fairly with the problems of the poor and homeless, as part of a carefully crafted legislative and policy strategy to provide and maintain quality of life for *all* citizens. The cities of Seattle and San Francisco are exemplary in this regard, as we show in greater detail in Chapter 6. Equally important is the need to dissuade the court from identifying poverty and homelessness with the problems of antisocial and criminal behavior that threaten order, safety, and the long-term viability of urban neighborhoods.

## WHAT DISORDER IS AND IS NOT: THE DANGERS OF CONFUSING DISORDERLY ACTS WITH POVERTY AND HOMELESSNESS

We support fully the movement by the courts away from allowing persons to be penalized for their status. We have no wish to return to vagrancy laws, which are unjust and inappropriate in a democratic society. And we have the same concerns about homelessness, poverty, and social injustice as do the vast majority of the population: we wish opportunity to be equitably distributed, and we want to ensure that persons seeking adequate jobs and homes are able to have them.

Homelessness and poverty are serious conditions in their own right. Nonetheless, we believe that some courts, mistakenly seeing status-based legislation whenever homelessness and poverty are mentioned, are going too far in striking down loitering "for the purpose of" laws. For the most part, these courts are failing to discern the very real distinctions between legislation directed at a *status* (as are vagrancy and loitering laws) as opposed to specific *acts* (as is loitering "for the purpose of" legislation). Furthermore the courts have an unrealistic and perhaps uninformed view of the effects of implementing and enforcing legislation that will only pass constitutional muster with greater and greater specificity built in, a problem that we address in Chapter 5. Above all, the courts, as do many in society today, fail to recognize that confusing poverty and homelessness with disorderly behavior has serious consequences.

First, using "homeless" as a euphemism for a panorama of antisocial and/or unlawful activities, and for "the poor," gives all who are poor a bad name, and ignores the reality that most poor are law abiding, embody a sense of decency and respect for others, and take responsibility for their own obligations. As Alice S. Baum and Donald W. Burnes, who have worked extensively in social service roles with homeless persons, point out:

> By perpetuating the myth that the homeless are merely poor people in need of housing, . . . advocates reinforce and promote the most pernicious stereotypes about poverty in America. The vast majority of poor people in America are not homeless. Poor people do not live on the streets, under bridges, or in parks; do not carry all of their belongs in shopping carts or plastic bags; do not wear layers of tattered clothing and pass out or sleep in doorways; do not urinate or defecate in public places; do not sleep in their cars or in encampments; do not harass or intimidate others; do not ask for money on the streets; do not physically attack city workers and residents; and do not wander the streets shouting at visions and voices. . . .
>
> We fear that the political strategy of portraying the homeless as simply "the poor" in order to gain sympathy has resulted in convincing many Americans that all poor people behave in ways that are inconsistent with common standards of decency. Not only has this resulted in a backlash against the homeless, but, we believe, it has also fueled the growing hostility toward the poor, immigrants, and minorities.[69]

The characteristics of many plaintiffs in suits against order-maintenance activities frequently reflect this discrepancy between those who are poor and the "homeless." In Santa Ana, where the city was sued over an ordinance banning camping on public property, the California Supreme Court found the nine declarants claiming to be "homeless" for purposes of the suit to have a variety of reasons for camping in public, ranging from missing a bus to the shelter, not being able to sleep in a noisy and congested shelter, to feeling safer in a civic center area than in a shelter. One was not homeless at all, and another had not even been cited under the ordinance.[70] Similarly, in *Joyce v. City and County of San Francisco*, the four plaintiffs were homeless for the following reasons: one had been invited by a daughter to live with her, but refused; then found housing provided by a housing clinic unsatisfactory; could not find a roommate who was "suitable;" and refused to sleep at a shelter because of the homeless people who stayed there. The second had housing and at most had been on the streets only a few nights. The third had housing and received assistance and food stamps from the city. And the fourth had received assistance from the city, but was suspended for missing appointments.[71] Among recipients of general assistance in the city, those who were homeless received the same amount in benefits as those who had obtained housing from the city; yet many homeless refused to stay in either transitional or permanent housing.[72] Clearly, not all those designated as "homeless" in these suits are in this condition involuntarily. Yet their choice to live on the streets is disruptive to others.

Second, lumping all the homeless together into one population ignores the very real emotional, psychological, and physical needs of subsets of the homeless who are extraordinarily disturbed and/or criminal. For example, research conducted in New York City in 1989 on those who used the subway for shelter found them to be a particularly troubled and troublesome population, with many having lengthy histories of arrest for both minor and serious crimes.[73] Metropolitan Transportation Authority estimates indicated that at least 40 percent of subway homeless were mentally ill, and substantial portions were chronic alcohol and drug abusers. More recent research indicates that 80 percent of the males in New York's armory shelters abuse drugs or alcohol.[74] Moreover, Baum and Burnes have found the popular portrayal of the "homeless problem" to be way off the mark:

> Newspapers, magazines, books, and television programs reported stories of homeless two-parent rust-belt families temporarily down on their luck or of homeless individuals who had recently been laid off from permanent employment. These stories led policymakers, politicians, and advocates to frame the issue as one of people not having homes and therefore being "homeless." None of these descriptions bore any resemblance to the people we knew. Nor were they consistent with the emerging research, which documented that up to 85 percent of all homeless adults suffer from chronic alcoholism, drug additions, mental illness, or some combination of the three, often complicated by serious mental problems.[75]

Information from other such sources suggests that the origins of many problems of those labeled homeless are not solely economic, as advocates would have us believe, but instead are rooted in mental illness, chronic alcoholism, drug addiction, and often the interaction of the three.[76] To advocate for the rights of individuals with these characteristics to live on the streets, or in subway tunnels, often means that nothing is done to address the cause for their being where they are and that they are left vulnerable to the very real dangers inherent in their surroundings. Yet, as one of us, Kelling, observed, advocates for the homeless in the New York City subway tried to talk persons who accepted police offers of food and a bus ride to a shelter out of the bus and back into the subway—when up to twelve persons a month without known addresses were dying there from causes ranging from hypothermia, to electrocution from the "hot" third rail in the subway, to being burned to death while huddling near a hot plate for warmth, to murder.

A third problem of the homelessness/disorder dilemma is confusing homelessness with criminal activity. A significant subgroup of those identifying themselves as homeless are actually using an identity of homelessness as a camouflage for carrying out criminal acts. For example, in San Francisco, city workers attempting to carry out cleaning and maintenance activities in public parks, plazas, and streets were physically threatened by people living in encampments there, and faced significant health risks from having to pick up debris consisting of needles, human waste, and garbage. In addition, these encampments became centers for drug use, crack cocaine dealing, and theft that spilled over into surrounding neighborhoods. Individuals intoxicated by alcohol or drugs lounged and slept in doorways of businesses or even homes, and intimidated residents, customers, and pedestrians.[77]

That advocates should preserve the myth that every person who begs aggressively, who lives in an encampment in a city park, or who urinates, defecates, or engages in sexual acts in public, is homeless is not surprising. After all, making the problem of homelessness seem as vast as possible lends a compelling urgency to their argument. And virtually every antisocial behavior can be framed as one of "homelessness." For example, Brad Lichtenstein, a member of the New York volunteer group Streetwatch, which monitors police handling of the homeless, criticized Mayor Giuliani's support for a measure put before the New York City Council during the fall of 1994, to make it illegal to solicit money near automatic teller machines, arguing "if the measure passes, there will be one more in a long list of reasons to arrest homeless

New Yorkers."[78] Granted that some who panhandle at automated teller machines may be homeless and unthreatening, many others are robbers, muggers, and scam artists, some of whom are homeless and others not. *Disorderly behavior is not the sole province of the homeless.*

Finally, confusing the acts of disorder taking place on streets with homelessness as a status draws attention away from the enormous social consequences of the acts themselves. As Skogan's research has clearly shown, apart from driving citizens from parks and streets, disorder may eventually lead to the elimination of entire neighborhood shopping centers and threatens the social fabric and commercial viability of our cities. While the rich and well-to-do can avoid and flee from this behavior, the poor and working classes in cities cannot.

Is there a more useful way of approaching the street population that advocates call the homeless when thinking about the problems of disorder? Perhaps one of the keenest observations about the relationship between different populations on streets and disorder has been made by Kent Scheidegger of the Criminal Justice Legal Foundation. Drawing from the work of Baum and Burnes and others, Scheidegger breaks the homeless into three subgroups: the *have-nots*, the *can-nots*, and the *will-nots*.[79] The have-nots are the genuinely poor, who are on the streets due to some emergency, need temporary shelter, and who will move back into the mainstream—a relatively small percentage of those commonly thought to be the homeless. The can-nots are the seriously mentally ill and addicted, perhaps the largest of the three groups. The will-nots are those for whom living on the streets and hustling, including criminality, has become a life style. In the debate over disorder, the have-nots are not generally the problem; repeated and continuous antisocial behavior by the can-nots and will-nots is.

Whether truly homeless or not, the can-nots and will-nots are indeed the responsibility of our society. We are far from having exhausted attempts to develop more satisfactory and productive means of providing for and treating their specific needs. Yet neither the mentally ill and substance abusers, nor those who live on the streets by hustling and unlawful activity, should be permitted to threaten the viability of social and commercial life in our cities by repeatedly crossing the boundaries of civil and lawful behavior. Our responsibility to them is not met by allowing our cities to deteriorate in furtherance of the mistaken notion that we are protecting their—and our own—liberties. Neither is our responsibility met by a movement that seeks to protect their "rights" to remain on the streets or in subway tunnels and to engage in disorderly behavior.

Understanding how we arrived at our current state and levels of disorder is an important first step in addressing the problems of neighborhood crime and decay. Yet the social changes and evolution of legal doctrine and legislation recounted here have been accompanied by an equally significant trend toward reducing the traditional order-maintenance role of the police. If changes in legal doctrine, legislation, and social thinking have all contributed to an increase in urban disorder, so too has the ineffectiveness of policing strategies. We have not used the police effectively to help maintain order or, as it turns out, to reduce and control crime generally. Instead, during much of this century we have defined a narrow role for police as professional crime fighters, removed from involvement in local neighborhood life, responding to more "serious" crimes, and apprehending criminals. And as police have moved out of many order-maintenance activities in neighborhoods, disorder has moved in.

## CHAPTER 3

# THE FAILURE OF
# PAST POLICING STRATEGIES

FROM THEIR EARLIEST DAYS, AMERICAN POLICE PROVIDED ASSIS-
tance to communities that extended far beyond crime control and law-
enforcement activities. Indeed, they have always been an essential
component in maintaining order in communities and on neighborhood
streets. During this century, however, a new paradigm has taken over
policing. In this model, order maintenance has been eclipsed by a focus
on "fighting crime." As professional crime fighters, police came to constitute the "front end of the criminal justice system," aloof from the citizens and communities they policed, and accountable not to citizens
but to the principles of their profession. This model gave rise to 911 systems, around which much of policing is now organized. Police themselves helped to shape and to promulgate this new ideology that
defined them as crime-fighting professionals. At the same time, the
courts saw ample justification for reducing the discretion of police to
deal with low-level street encounters as a means of minimizing the possible abuse of power by police.

The problem today is that the professional crime-fighting model of
policing has failed, and to such an extent that some police have all but
given up on the idea that they can significantly affect crime. In particular, 911 systems drain police resources from where they could be used
more effectively to prevent crime; isolate police from neighborhoods;

and in many areas are not consistent with citizen priorities or responsive to citizen demands. Maintaining order, an integral function of policing since the early to mid-nineteenth century, has come to be perceived by many of us, even police themselves, as a degrading non-police function.

How did we reach this dilemma? To look for the answers, in this chapter we examine the development of American policing, especially those basic shifts in strategies and tactics that have proved so consequential for police efforts to deal with crime today. The history of police involvement in order maintenance, and the consequences of recent changes in policing systems, provide insight into why disorder has increased in our cities, and how police have become less able to help maintain or restore order. Above all, they suggest a logically inescapable, yet startling, conclusion: if order is to be restored to public spaces, it will not be without cost, and in the current context of limited funds for urban problems, the likely cost will be in terms of different police priorities and a substantially different role for citizens in maintaining public safety. To begin at the beginning, we must understand the nature of the tradeoffs made by an earlier generation of police leaders to deal with early twentieth-century problems; only then can we ascertain the tradeoffs that must be made now.

## THE FAILURE OF POLICING PARADIGMS: THE OLD REFORM MODEL AND THE WARRIOR STRATEGY

No police system in the world is as radically decentralized and localized as is the American system. As a local institution serving local needs, policing in the United States was multifaceted and broad in function from its earliest beginnings. Originally, the business of police was to keep the peace and to prevent crime—as Sir Robert Peel, the architect of modern policing in England, put it, "Keeping peace by peaceful means." Crime *prevention* was the primary police function. Police would prevent crime by their conspicuous presence—that is, they would be dispersed throughout the population—and by dealing with the conditions that created crime (disorder, drunkenness, gambling, and prostitution, for example). Arresting people was only one of their responsibilities, and there were many others.

Not atypically, New York City's charter laid out the broad functions of its police at the beginning of the twentieth century in the following terms:

Sec. 315. It is hereby made the duty of the police department and force, at all times of day and night, . . . to especially preserve the public peace, prevent crime, detect and arrest offenders, suppress riots, mobs, and insurrections, disperse unlawful or dangerous assemblages, and assemblages which obstruct the free passage of public streets, sidewalks, parks, and places; protect the rights of persons and property, guard the public health, preserve order at elections and all public meetings and assemblages, regulate, direct control, restrict, and direct the movement of all teams horses, carts, wagons, automobiles, and all other vehicles in streets, bridges, squares, parks, and public places, for the facilitation of traffic and the convenience of the public as well as the proper protection of human life and health, . . . remove all nuisances in the public streets, parks, and highways; arrest all street mendicants and beggars; assist, advise, and protect emigrants, strangers, and travelers in public streets, at steamboat and ship landings, and at railroad stations; carefully observe and inspect all places of public amusement, all places of business having excise or other licenses to carry on any business; all houses of ill-fame or prostitution, and houses where common prostitutes resort or reside; all lottery offices, policy shops, and places where lottery tickets or lottery policies are sold or offered for sale; all gambling-houses, cock-pits, rat-pits, and public common dance-houses, and to repress and restrain all unlawful and disorderly conduct or practices therein; enforce and prevent the violation of all laws and ordinances in force in said city; and for these purposes, to arrest all persons guilty of violating any law or ordinance for the suppression or punishment of crimes or offenses.[1]

Note the operative words: *preserve, prevent, detect, arrest, suppress, disperse, protect, direct, remove, assist, advise, repress,* and *restrain.* Submerged in each of these terms are complex sets of responsibilities. As part of their protection function, police provided urban residents and newcomers with an array of social services that are not now broadly acknowledged. Police stations were built with space for migrants moving into the cities to sleep for several nights until they found work and shelter.[2] The original food and soup lines were also developed by police. Provision of social services was not limited to adults and homeless immigrants: one of the major nineteenth-century responsibilities of urban police was finding lost children and returning them to their parents or referring them for services.

Even with these good works, police gained a reputation for brutality, inefficiency, and corruption during the late nineteenth and early twentieth centuries. This reputation grew out of the integration of police with local political machines governing cities from "smoke filled rooms." As adjuncts of ward-based political machines, police were not only indispensable in providing ward services, the source of their jobs— ward-based patronage—ensured their loyalty to local politicians.[3] Consequently, one form of police corruption involved using their power to keep politicians in office. Police also accepted payoffs for under-enforcing unpopular laws, especially vice laws that targeted alcohol consumption. Moreover, abuse of minorities, especially but not limited to African Americans, also characterized early policing. Reflecting on the vehemence with which police were attacked by late nineteenth-century reformers, Egon Bittner dryly notes: "Of all the institutions of city government in late-nineteenth-century America, none was as unanimously denounced as the urban police. According to every available account, they were, in every aspect of their existence, an unmixed, unmitigated, and unpardonable scandal."[4] This is an exaggeration: reformers had their own agendas and political axes to grind. The earliest residents of cities, English and Dutch settlers who were displaced by immigrants claiming political control, resented that police were not aggressive enough in policing vice. Late nineteenth-century industrialists feared the working-class sympathies of police would make them unreliable in policing the strikes that plagued the era. Political "outs" resented police involvement in elections (since, not surprisingly, police worked on behalf of the "ins"—from whom they often got their jobs in pre–civil service days). Journalistic muckrakers berated police for their corruption and inefficiency. Ministers denounced police venality from their pulpits.[5] Milwaukee provides one example of how troubled early police were in many cities. During the 1880s alone, Chief Daniel Kennedy was fired for mistreating prisoners; Chief Robert Wasson for corruption (his officers were noted for drunkenness and abuse); Chief Lemuel Ellsworth—the first Republican reformer—for a kickback scheme and his inability to control the department; and his successor, Chief Florian Ries, was fired after a scandal involving robbers paying off detectives and police.[6]

Despite calls for reform from outside policing, and piecemeal reforms such as the creation of a civil service that ended the awarding of police jobs as political patronage, police continued to be viewed as a sorry lot until well into the twentieth century. Then, a succession of internal reformers allied themselves with the Progressive movement and developed a police reform strategy that would dominate policing during most of the twentieth century—at least until the 1980s. In this vision, police were to become highly disciplined and closely controlled crime fighters, focusing on murder, rape, robbery, and assault. As professional crime fighters, police would be relieved of their service and order-maintenance functions: social workers could take care of those problems, "real" police fought crime. In respects the strategy they developed was brilliant. It largely removed police from politics; substantially reduced corruption; created a vision of policing that was widely accepted by the general public, political and media elites, and line police personnel; and, when supported by the Supreme Court decisions regarding criminal investigation noted earlier, it significantly reduced police abuses. Unfortunately, the strategy failed on its own terms.

In the United States, as we have seen, local politicians and ward bosses created police departments. Leaders in Boston and New York learned how officials in London were dealing with the problems of urbanization—disorder, crime, and riots—and implemented American variations on London's innovation. Then early in the twentieth century, August Vollmer emerged as America's first visionary police leader. During his tenure as chief in Berkeley, California, from 1909 to 1932, Vollmer attempted to create a genuinely professional model of police, governed by its own knowledge and skill and independent from political manipulation. At a time when few departments even required a high school education, he emphasized the need for police officers to have higher education, professional autonomy, and to use their discretion broadly. Gene and Elaine Carte describe Vollmer's approach in Berkeley and his philosophy of policing generally:

> The Berkeley success came from Vollmer's ability to find good men to be police officers and to use their talents well. Professional policing began when Vollmer decided, rightly or wrongly, that the police officer required significantly special skills to do his job, skills that could not be learned on the beat by a recruit who was indifferent to the "higher purposes" of policing. That is why it was inconceivable to him that a policeman should become identified with workingmen whose sense of occupational purpose extended only so far as a decent wage and adequate conditions on the job. . . .[7]
>
> He expected each man to be the "chief" of his beat, to bear responsibility for dealing with problems of any nature that came up within the area he patrolled. . . . He was to work closely with merchants to establish preventive measures and to know the families on his beat well enough to detect delinquency problems or unusual needs. . . .
>
> In other words, in Vollmer's philosophy, the patrolman did not merely work within a professional organization; he was a complete professional in himself, selected through rigorous testing, trained in a progressive police school, and imbued with the ideals of service and efficiency.[8]

Many of Vollmer's early ideas were to reemerge in the movements known as community and problem-solving policing that developed much later in the century, and to which we turn our attention in coming chapters. However, they did not prevail in mainstream policing, which at this time moved in a different direction. Instead, Vollmer's protégés—especially O. W. Wilson, the dominant police theorist of the twentieth century—became the primary advocates of a new view of policing substantially at odds with that of the early, practicing Vollmer. Where Vollmer had wanted to broaden police functions, Wilson and others wanted to narrow them. Where Vollmer recognized police discretion and recruited highly educated persons to manage it, reformers sought to drastically limit, or eliminate, discretion and saw little need for more than a high school education for officers. Where Vollmer experimented with collegial control, reformers imposed military-like command and control.

Why Wilson's view superseded Vollmer's is hard to say. Genuine professionalism was in its infant stages at the turn of the century, even in medicine. Given the level of police practice, it might well have been hard for most police to comprehend just what was entailed in Vollmer's model. Moreover, Frederick Taylor's scientific model of organization and management—with its the preoccupation with control, job routinization, and simplification—was coming into vogue then.[9] And, given the mystique of science during the early twentieth century, "scientific" might have seemed to be a far more palatable and communicable vision of what most reformers had in mind for policing. Indeed, many reformers dubbed their model of policing "scientific." By the 1930s, even Vollmer was writing of "scientific" policing, "scientific" investigation and patrol methods, as well as "scientific" recruitment of officers (through psychological testing), construction of beats, and allocation of patrol officers.[10] Regardless, what had been inconceivable to Vollmer during his tenure in Berkeley—that policing should be identified with a narrow bureaucratic vision—would become the standard operating assumption for most policing during the 1930s.

To eliminate political influences in police departments, gain control of officers, and establish crime fighting priorities, the prevailing reformers advocated a series of changes in policing:

- Police would abandon many of their service-related activities and narrow their function to law enforcement;
- Within police departments, authority would be centralized and the power and influence of precinct captains and commanders checked;
- The intimate links between patrol officers and neighborhoods would be severed, primarily through the implementation of motorized patrol and newly developed patrol allocation systems. Idle conversation with citizens was to be forbidden, in many cities;[11]
- To reduce claims by neighborhoods and local politicians on police, patrol beats would no longer be congruent with neighborhoods but would be constructed "scientifically," using crime rates, calls for service, and desired travel times as the principal determining variables. Moreover, demands for police services would be centrally channeled, at first through simple telephone and radio systems, later through elaborate "enhanced 911" computer aided dispatch systems;

- To further extend the influence of chiefs into precincts and neighborhoods, many specialized units would be created—these units would be prestigious groups formed by "creaming" the most talented officers from routine police work in the precincts, and would be based in a central police headquarters, but operate city-wide;
- Officers would be recruited on the basis of psychological screening mechanisms and civil service standards; and,
- "Scientific" organizational structures and management systems would be established and maintained.

In other words, the *function* of police would shift from crime prevention and the provision of services to criminal apprehension through law enforcement. In terms of *tactics* for carrying out these functions, intimate collaboration with citizens would be replaced by more remote and reactive procedures, such as rapid response to calls for service and patrol by automobile, that would hold police back from interacting with citizens. Finally, police reformers would create *organizational structures* and *managerial processes* to support these new functions and tactics. All of these changes represented a substantial departure from Vollmer's early vision of policing, and ironically they were antithetical to the development of policing as a profession. Together, they represented an entirely new strategy of policing—the reform model.

## The Reform Model: Police Functions, Tactics, Organization, and Management

Police in the United States had high hopes about their ability to control crime during the first half of the twentieth century. At first, cars emerged as the new technology that would permit significant advances: they would allow supervisors to get to beats to oversee officers; and they increased the range of patrol officers, who could patrol a beat, be picked up, then taken to patrol another beat, and so on. As time went on and more cars were available, more and more police were assigned to cars. Not only could police cover more territory, police in cars were easier to supervise—it was harder for them to get "lost" in a car, especially one with a two-way radio. During the 1930s, when cars proliferated and police were shifting to motorized patrol, some believed that they could wipe out urban crime altogether.[12] The anticrime strategy developed tactics centered around the use of cars and technology:

> By means of police radio, headquarters can broadcast information instantly to every precinct station and every police auto. Orders can be given to descend upon the scene of the crime from various directions by police cars. The net is quickly formed and tightened. Often the criminal is caught at the scene of the crime: usually not far away. If he should get outside of the net, the chase may be taken up and directed by radio.[13]

By the 1940s O. W. Wilson, who had started as a police officer under August Vollmer in Berkeley, California, and become an academic and superintendent of the Chicago Police Department, had developed his theories about police tactics as well. Wilson's thinking went beyond the simple explanation that cars would increase the range within which police could work effectively and make them easier to supervise, to propose a new theory of how automotive patrol could impact upon crime control. The focus was *preventive patrol,* and *rapid response to calls for service*: police cruising randomly and unpredictably through city streets in cars could create a feeling, among both good citizens and criminals, of police omnipresence. Moreover, police in cars with radios could respond instantly to calls for service, and the authority of officers would be enhanced by placing them in conspicuous, powerful automobiles.[14] Wilson's theories were widely accepted, and by mid-century, police "business," that is, fighting crime, was carried out through riding in cars. Preventive patrol, conducted by police rapidly cruising through city streets, ostensibly intimidated criminals and reassured citizens by creating the illusion that police were everywhere. Motorized patrol increased the surveillance capabilities of police, increasing the likelihood of intercepting crimes in progress. Finally, in cars police were constantly available to respond to calls for service: to be "in-service" meant officers were riding in cars; to be "out-of-service" meant police officers were dealing with citizens. Organizational pressure was placed on officers to be in-service—waiting for the next call.

The organizational structures and managerial processes advocated and implemented by early twentieth-century police reformers were heavily influenced by and patterned after the "scientific" theories of

Frederick Taylor. Taylor's factory model advocated centralization of authority, creation of middle management to standardize and routinize tasks, increasing layers of control, finding the appropriate ratio of over-seers to workers (known as span of control), and unity of command. Workers, stripped of their craft skills, were seen as easily replaceable commodities who could be shifted from job to job and shift to shift with impunity. Labor was assumed to have little or no investment in work itself, or the products of work: left to their own devices, laborers would malinger and/or get into trouble. Supervisors *oversaw*, mid-manage-ment *thought* and *ordered*, and line personnel simply *did*. Thus, officially at least, the police job was routinized. Police were viewed as law enforcers who used little or no discretion. "Complex" work was carried out by health, social service, traffic, and federal and state law-enforce-ment agencies, while city police handled simple, residual work.

Although this organizational structure and associated managerial forms were touted by the reform model's champions as the "professional model of policing" by the 1940s and 1950s, calling the model a profes-sional one was, and is, a gross misnomer: patrol officers in the reform model were the equivalent of line factory workers, a tradition main-tained even today in police uniforms in many cities, with command per-sonnel, captains and above, wearing white shirts, and lower ranks wearing blue shirts. In fact, police reformers viewed line personnel with condescension, if not disdain.[15] As sociologist Egon Bittner understood, police were to have "the 'manly virtues' of honesty, loyalty, aggressive-ness, and visceral courage."[16] They need not be very bright. Indeed, the essential preoccupation of police reformers was *control*, neither a surpris-ing nor inappropriate result of the legacy of corruption and abuse that had grown up in policing by the early years of the twentieth century. Control of officers pervaded every aspect of the reform strategy. To keep police from being unduly influenced, they would be sequestered in cars and isolated, not just from politicians, but from all citizens. To ensure that individual police officers carried out the priorities of police depart-ments, demand was channeled centrally via 911. To prevent the corrup-tion of police through interaction with citizens, especially in vice control, neighborhood officers were discouraged if not forbidden from dealing with problems on their beats like prostitution and drugs, and conversing with citizens. And in spite of variation in implementation of the reform model, measures of performance reflected the narrow focus of reform policing: arrests, crime rates, and response time.

## The Spread of the Reform Model

"Modern" police departments rushed headlong into this new policing strategy, adopting the function, tactics, structures, and managerial processes we have described, for they combined the best of all possible worlds: enhancing control over police officers, introducing "scientific" practices, augmenting the power of officers, and gaining their support, for riding around in cars was far more comfortable than plodding through city streets, especially in inclement weather. Those cities that continued foot patrol, like Boston, were ridiculed by the International Association of Chiefs of Police (IACP) for sticking to antiquated tactics. With the advent of computers during the 1960s, many cities put 911 systems in place to further improve the capacity of departments to take calls and respond quickly. If citizens did not like the changes, and some did not, they were expected simply to defer to the professional wisdom of police officers. In the late 1960s, when Boston finally installed a computerized 911 system, citizens continued to call district stations. The police promptly cut off the district lines.[17] Police actions in the context of the reform model were premised upon a defined role of citizens, who were to support police, act as their eyes and ears, stay out of the way when police arrived, testify in court, and essentially act as passive recipients of crime fighting services. Citizen influence over, or involvement in, policing activities was seen as political encroachment into the professional domain.

The decentralization that we have described among police in the United States led to change proceeding department by department, and to considerable variation in departments as the reform model was implemented in different cities. While it was agreed among reformers, for example, that removing political influence from police departments was essential, how this was to be achieved was unresolved and varied by city. The purpose of rejecting such influence was, at best, not to make police unaccountable to city government, but to maintain the professional integrity and independence of the police by insulating important organizational processes—such as hiring, reward and promotion systems; police assignments; and the allocation of police to neighborhoods—from partisan political manipulation. Cities achieved this goal in different ways, and sometimes accountability suffered. In Los Angeles, an extremely tight civil service system was established to control all promotions within the police department, right up through the chief of police. Alternatively in New York City, appointments and promotions were, and continue to be, controlled by civil service through the position of captain; while positions above captain are appointed by the commissioner of police; and the commissioner is appointed by the mayor. The strengths and weaknesses of each system are apparent: in New York City, the appointment and promotional system establishes clear accountability to political leadership, so that elected officials can determine the overall policies of the police department through their power to appoint top police management. The danger is that an unscrupulous mayor can reach into the department by appointing a political hack as commissioner and distribute appointments above captain on the basis of party loyalty. In Los Angeles, given the lock civil service has over appointments and promotions, there is virtually no way a mayor can demand loyalty from the police department, since the system insulates the police from political accountability. The consequences of this lack of accountability were evident in the aftermath of the Rodney King affair, when Chief Daryl Gates was able to dictate his own terms for departure. Moreover, even if a chief is recruited to Los Angeles with a strong mandate for change, as was Willie Williams, he or she will have an extremely difficult time implementing this agenda given his/her limited ability to appoint key staff at senior levels. While the goal of ensuring a police department's freedom from political corruption thus shapes both systems, the outcome is significantly different in New York and Los Angeles. Each case presents a tradeoff. In the New York City model, accountability to city government is assured by the power of the mayor to appoint the commissioner and the power of the commissioner, in turn, to appoint all positions above captain. The risk is political meddling. In the Los Angeles model, political meddling into the police department is averted by having all positions covered by civil service. Here, the risk is unaccountability.

Despite these and other variations that have arisen, the assumptions underlying local implementation across the country essentially conformed to the reform model. The reform strategy itself energized police and captured the public imagination. Starting with the television series "Dragnet," generations of programs portrayed police whizzing about in powerful cars and responding to calls, fighting crime and the bad guys. Powerful metaphors were developed to portray this strategy of police: "the thin blue line;" "wars" on crime, drugs, and violence; and "crime fighting." Robocop was born of a fallen street "warrior."

*The Emergence of Police as Warriors, "Law Enforcement,"*
*and the "Front End of the Criminal Justice System"*

By the 1950s and 1960s, reformers had been so successful in insulating police from external influences that the police were virtually unaccountable to anyone. Attempts to influence police policy, regardless of motive or intent, were seen by police as political meddling. Isolation and unfamiliarity bred contempt and antagonism. Policing was *police business* and, as such, best left in the hands of professionals. Most chiefs took the position that civilians had no business in police departments.[18] During the 1960s, the Supreme Court rulings on criminal investigations, the civil rights demonstrations, the Vietnam War disturbances, and the urban unrest that characterized the era exacerbated what was becoming a siege mentality in policing. In the midst of this national turmoil, President Johnson established his commission to examine policing.

Needless to say, most police were not terribly enthusiastic about having a national commission, especially one created by a liberal president and staffed by liberals from academia, intrude into police business. Ironically, however, the most powerful endorsement of the reform model of policing came from President Johnson's Crime Commission. Certainly, the commission saw weaknesses in the *implementation* of the reform model: better personnel should be recruited; training improved; technology enhanced; small police departments and some functions, like crime laboratories, consolidated; and public relations efforts targeted on minority communities. And the commission did call for research into the effectiveness of patrol and innovations like team policing. One of the commission's task forces even published a comprehensive and valuable report, *The Police*, that fully recognized the complexity of police business.[19] Nevertheless, the reform view of the police function as "crime fighting" was strongly validated, first, by the commission's endorsement of police as *law-enforcement* agencies and, second, by its adoption of the idea that the conglomeration of police, prosecutorial, court, probation, parole, and prison agencies comprised a *criminal justice system*, with police as the front end of that system.

Introducing the use of "law enforcement" as synonymous with policing represented an attempt by the commission to resolve a turf conflict. Sheriffs were concerned that if the commission wrote about "police" and used police as a generic term, it would demean or downplay the role of sheriffs in the public eye. Consequently, in a move to mollify sheriffs, and seeking a more broadly inclusive term by which to designate all policing agencies in the United States, whether local police, county sheriffs, state patrol officers, or federal agents, the commission settled on "law enforcement."[20] That such labeling would lend support to a narrow, ideological view of policing was unforeseen.

The conceptualization of the police as the front end of a criminal justice system further strengthened the narrow view of police as *law-enforcement officers*. The idea of a criminal justice system originated during the 1960s with staff of the American Bar Foundation (ABF), who noted that arrestees moved from police, to prosecutors, to the courts, and so on, and surmised that, to offenders at least, this process must appear to be a system. ABF researchers also noted that changes in one agency affected other agencies: if police made more arrests, then prosecutors were impacted, as were courts and corrections.[21] At this time, the notion of a system, which was derived from the biological sciences where it constituted a coherent natural order with high levels of interdependency, built-in feedback, and self-regulation, was being imported into social science analysis.

Yet in the case of police and the other criminal justice agencies, imposing a systems analysis was faulty in a number of senses. Obviously, the different institutions are not part of a natural order. More importantly, they are not designed or governed by a single or even collective intelligence. Agencies operate and are governed independently, often with disparate goals. Police want "bad guys" off the street and "know" that they are guilty—otherwise they would not arrest them. Prosecutors want "good" cases and reject others. Judges want good criminal process and "justice." Police and prosecutors want "bad guys" in jail and prison; jail and prison administrators, confronted with overcrowding, want them out. To be sure, while these agencies may have congruent goals in particular cases, this does not make a system. Moreover, mere impact upon one institution by the acts of another does not create an overarching system. Because criminal justice agencies do not have the characteristics of a system they cannot achieve what a system can: self-regulation and integration of component parts that work together toward a coherent goal.[22]

Whether the system metaphor as applied to the criminal justice "system" was grounded in reality or not, the impact of its application was crucial. Historically, police had been conceived of as an administrative branch of local government, accountable to it for the provision of a variety of services. As part of a criminal justice system, they became accountable to that system, to the law, and to their profession. Moreover, the larger social role police once had is further discounted in the system model. In the minds of reform chiefs, the president's Crime Commission stressed what police were really about: arresting criminals and processing them through the criminal justice system. Police executives now had it both ways: a strategy that freed police from political manipulation now had a crime-fighting imprimatur stamped upon it by a national commission. The job of police was to arrest criminals and present them to the criminal justice "system" for processing. If they carried out this task and crime still escalated, then someone else was failing—soft judges, plea-bargaining prosecutors, or bleeding hearts that freed known criminals. The academic criminal justice industry spawned by the Law Enforcement Assistance Administration would become the primary vehicle for disseminating this view of police to generations of students. And the ideology itself became part of the common wisdom: police were part of the criminal justice system, its front end.

Lost in all of this was the idea of prevention, except in a narrow, technical sense: crime prevention would be achieved through the police role as the front end of the criminal justice system, that is, by making arrests. Police officers were expected to make arrests *automatically*—not using judgment or discretion to manage situations (and maybe keep them from getting out of hand), but responding to crises already in progress. Arrests, then, would result in incarceration (offenders who are in jail or prison cannot commit crimes), primary deterrence (potential offenders are deterred by the certainty of their arrest), secondary deterrence (potential offenders are deterred through their awareness that others are arrested for criminal behavior), and/or rehabilitation (those who are apprehended are rehabilitated through some form of social or psychological intervention and do not commit further crimes). True, *preventive patrol* was believed by some to be a means of crime prevention, but the idea of omnipresence implicit in preventive patrol was a tentative and unproven assumption at best. More than anything else, the idea of omnipresence did little but turn police work into riding around in cars, rather than dealing with citizens. As token recognition of other forms of crime prevention, some departments created special crime-prevention units consisting of small numbers of officers who advised citizens about locks and other such issues. In the police culture, however, crime prevention had moved so far out of the mainstream of police thinking that in one department officers in such units were dubbed "the empty holster crowd"—the same label given to officers deemed by police administration as too unstable to carry their weapons and who were on some form of special non–law-enforcement assignment. Other police departments had equally demeaning tags for crime-prevention officers. "Real" police work was riding in cars, responding to calls, and arresting criminals.

## The Collapse of the Law-Enforcement Strategy

Still optimistic during the 1960s, and facing that generation's crime wave, chiefs throughout the United States pledged to their city councils that if only they could have x number more police officers, they could significantly reduce crime. Yet, one can hardly overstate the extent to which the warrior strategy was failing, even during these tumultuous times. Today, there is barely a dimension—whether it be keeping the peace, or controlling crime, fear, or officers themselves—in which this strategy has succeeded. Perhaps nothing in recent history symbolizes the failure of the reform strategy as did the Rodney King event in Los Angeles and the subsequent collapse of the Los Angeles Police Department in the riot that followed the first trial of the police officers. During the 1950s, William H. Parker molded the LAPD into *the* national model of reform policing: small, relative to city size; mobilized in cars; militarized; isolated from political influences by civil service right through the position of chief; and "tough." As such, it was lionized in radio, television, and films. The LAPD presented itself through a succession of chiefs— Parker, "Ed" Davis, and Daryl Gates (who had been Parker's driver as a rookie)—as a lean, tough, no-nonsense police department—a deserving model for the rest of the United States. Yet, when all was said and done, officers had remained out of control and the command structure had collapsed in a crisis. For many in policing, it was the collapse of a strategy, not just the LAPD.

Confidence in the reform strategy began to erode during the 1970s. First, more and more citizens, especially minorities, voiced complaints about the remote, officious, and brusque behaviors of officers. "Just the facts ma'am"—Sergeant Joe Friday's motto in "Dragnet"—just was not satisfactory. More citizens also started to demand that police return to the use of foot patrol. Mayors began to get wind of this: it was no accident that during every mayoral election in Boston from 1972 to 1984 Mayor Kevin White announced the assignment of foot officers to neighborhoods. Despite the animosity of the police to foot patrol, cities such as Newark, Flint (Michigan), Boston, Baltimore, Arlington County (Virginia), Fort Worth, Nashville, and Washington, D.C., all restored the use of foot patrol during the mid-1970s.[23] Although few were really aware of it at the time, a demand was developing in cities throughout the country for a qualitatively different form of policing that would deal with problems other than serious crime alone.

Second, interception patrol—patrol designed to nab offenders in the act of committing crimes—was not paying off. Research conducted by Albert Reiss in Chicago suggested that 93 percent of arrests were the result of citizen-initiated actions—citizens contacting the police to complain about crime.[24] Contrary to "common sense," police on random interception patrol come upon so few crimes that any contributions to an overall crime control strategy are minimal.

Third, the idea that motorized patrol either created a feeling of police omnipresence or intimidated criminals was largely invalidated by the 1974 *Kansas City Preventive Patrol Experiment*.[25] Results of the study showed that substantial changes in levels of preventive patrol had no impact on levels of crime or citizen perceptions about the safety of neighborhoods. Regarding the latter, police cars going through neighborhoods was not a memorable event for citizens: therefore, police could substantially increase or decrease levels of patrol with little awareness of such changes by residents.[26] This finding contrasted sharply with results obtained in foot patrol experiments, which showed that citizens *were* sensitive to increases or decreases in foot patrol levels. In Newark, for example, research staff conducting the foot patrol experiment and then Police Director Hubert Williams had to answer to politicians in order to finish the experiment: only assurances that neighborhoods losing their foot officers during the experiment would get more than their share when the experiment was over placated elected local leaders.

Fourth, the assumptions that underlay the reform strategy's organizational structure and managerial processes—that police officers were akin to factory workers, used little discretion, and conducted routine, repetitive activities—were undermined by research accumulating during the 1960s and 1970s. Police Foundation researcher Mary Ann Wycoff summarized this research: despite all the efforts of reformers over decades, research evidence consistently demonstrated that citizen demand shaped police work, crime-related problems constitute a small portion of that work, and police respond to that demand in highly discretionary ways.[27] The incongruity between police work as actually practiced and as conceived in the reform model is stark, as Bittner has described:

> The official definition of the police mandate is that of a law-enforcement agency. . . . The internal organization and division of labor within departments reflect categories of crime control. . . . Recognition for meritorious performance is given for feats of valor and ingenuity in crime fighting. But the day-to-day work of most officers has very little to do with all of this. These officers are engaged in what is now commonly referred to as peace-keeping and order maintenance, activities in which arrests are extremely rare. Those arrests that do occur are for the most part peacekeeping expedients rather than measures of law enforcement of the sort employed against

thieves, rapists, or perpetrators of other major crimes. For the rich variety of services of every kind, involving all sorts of emergencies, abatements of nuisances, dispute settlements, and an almost infinite range of repairs on the flow of life in modern society, the police neither receives nor claims credit. Nor is there any recognition of the fact that many of these human and social problems are quite complex, serious, and important, and that dealing with them requires skill, prudence, judgment, and knowledge.[28]

It is difficult, as well, to exaggerate the impact of these incongruities on the beliefs, attitudes, and practices of street police officers and the police unions they have developed during the past thirty years. Certainly increased feelings of cynicism and isolation on the part of officers are one result.[29]

Finally, a police "culture" evolved that viewed whole segments of society—especially inner-city minority youth—as "the enemy." Most police have working- or middle-class origins and are unfamiliar with minority neighborhoods. Their training has focused on the problems and dangers of such areas, but they know little else about them.[30] Isolated in cars and having contact only with the most troubled and troublesome people of communities, police can easily become suspicious, cynical, and fearful of citizens, especially in minority communities. The "thin blue line" mentality had an impact. Police saw themselves as warriors, defending the good against the bad; the problem was, with few contacts in many local communities police had a difficult time sorting out the troublemakers from ordinary citizens.

That the reform strategy has failed is now widely acknowledged by police leaders. The notion that policing is primarily a law-enforcement profession founders on the idea that in a democratic society the responsibility of police includes protecting the constitutional rights of *all* citizens, the law abiding as well as criminal suspects. Concentrating on serious crime ignored a broadly based demand for the restoration of order, a demand growing louder in the face of increasingly outrageous street behavior by the mentally ill, chronic drug and alcohol abusers, prostitutes, and many youths. Furthermore, the reform strategy failed in terms of its own defined goals: crime control and law enforcement. Not only did the tactics of motorized, random patrol prove unsuccessful, but research about crime, criminals, and victims suggests that police are limited in their crime control functions by a variety of other factors, such as the timing and location of crime and the relationship between criminals and their victims.

Awareness of these issues has led a new generation of reformers to seek a broadening and redefinition of police functions to include order maintenance, to revamp their organizational structures and managerial processes so as to reflect actual police work, and to develop new tactics. Yet they have been severely hampered in their efforts by 911 systems that were developed and put in place as the epitome of the reform strategy. Today 911 dominates virtually all policing as well as the expectations of citizens as to what they will receive in police services. So long as 911 persists in its present form, policing cannot move forward into a new strategy.

## THE FAILURE OF 911 POLICING

Rapid response to calls for service is an intuitively appealing idea: if police can get to the scene of a crime quickly, they will more likely be able to protect or rescue victims, make arrests, capture criminals in the act of committing crimes, and therefore make strong cases against them in court. Whether opening their windows and calling for help, running to police stations, capturing the attention of patrolling officers, or telephoning for assistance, citizens have properly expected that police would rush to the scene of criminal events or emergencies.

The ancient precursor to rapid response and 911 was the hue and cry—the premedieval English system under which able-bodied men were required to have weapons nearby so that if criminals struck, citizens could grab their weapons and pursue and subdue them.[31] The tradition of citizen response to emergencies and pursuit of villains continued in colonial America with pursuit taking the form of posses. When police departments were created in cities, they assumed the responsibility of pursuit. Early twentieth-century police relied heavily on cars and radios to respond to crime and emergencies. Certainly, with this combined technology, and later with computers added, police could reach the scenes of crimes and emergencies considerably faster than when on foot patrol, except for those times when a foot officer was serendipitously close to some event. Police were so certain of the benefits of rapid

response to calls for service that until the early 1970s "full-service" policing meant that police would respond to *all* calls for service and attempt
to reach the scene within three minutes. Response time—the time it
takes once a call is received by the police department for an officer to
arrive at the caller's location—became for many, and for many still is, a
key measure of police productivity and effectiveness. Rapid response was
not only believed to be effective, it was equitable: anyone should be able
to obtain police service simply by dialing the police emergency number.
Today 911 systems are at the core of contemporary policing.

Organizing a police department to enable it to respond rapidly to
calls for service is a complicated process involving up-to-date technologies such as telephone systems, computers, and radios, not to mention cars. In more sophisticated systems such as enhanced 911,
computers in cars and computer-based automatic vehicle-locator systems that project the location of cars onto screens so that dispatchers
can visually identify the closest available car to the location of the call
and dispatch it, are also used. Rapid response has an impact on more
than a police department's technology, however. It has implications for
staffing: police must be scheduled to work during periods of high 911
demand. It has implications for beat construction: beats (defined patrol
areas) must be constructed to reflect relatively equal numbers of calls
for service to ensure that neighborhoods are treated similarly and that
officers have equitable workloads. Rapid response also determines how
police patrol an area: to keep response time low, police must be in-
service and ready to respond immediately. It has an impact on police
priorities: police may decide to concentrate on a particular crime problem, but be constantly called away from it to respond to calls. Supervi-
sory relationships in departments are also affected: police may develop
work plans for a shift with a supervisor, but have to scuttle those plans
as soon as the first call comes. Finally, 911 impacts on police contacts
with citizens: organizational pressure is placed on officers to be in-service as much as possible so that they can respond to calls for service
quickly. Therefore, interactions with citizens must be handled rapidly
and efficiently. There is virtually no aspect of police functioning, tactics, or organization today on which 911 does not have a major impact.
Well integrated into the reform strategy and tactics, rapid response
keeps officers in cars and under centralized control, focuses police

activities on city-wide priorities, is congruent with interception and preventive patrol, and is not intrusive into neighborhood life—since by definition it is reactive.

*From Full Service to Emergency Response:*
*Does Rapid Response Matter?*

"Full-service" policing created an enormous demand. During the 1970s, calls for police service began an inexorable climb: citizens were calling police for virtually everything. In nearly every city, calls for service escalated to the point that police departments were being overwhelmed. Boston is an example: over the period 1975 to 1991 the total number of 911 calls per year rose approximately 33 percent. This rise in total 911 calls appears unrelated to index crime frequency, for while index crime levels themselves declined from highs of 80,000 in 1975 and 1981, to 62,000 in 1991, during the same period calls concerned with nonindex crimes increased from 350,000 to nearly 600,000.

Why do citizen calls for service continue to increase despite a leveling off or decline in crime rates? We do not know, although we can surmise. Fear of crime could be one reason. The absence of a felt police presence on the streets could be another. Aggressive marketing efforts by police departments to sell 911 certainly have had some impact. Another interpretation is that citizens are reaching out to the police for more than emergencies and crime control: citizens persist in calling police about pervasive neighborhood problems. Attempts by police to foil citizen attempts to bring them into neighborhoods, by ignoring calls for "minor problems" like youths taking over a corner, are often thwarted when citizens deliberately "up the ante" by reporting "a man with a gun"—a report that virtually guarantees immediate response by multiple cars in most cities. Citizen refusals to view 911 as solely an emergency system, especially when coupled with demands for foot patrol, might have been early signs that the reform strategy of policing did not meet their needs for service that went beyond mere crime control.

Regardless of the reasons, increasing demands placed upon 911 during the 1970s stimulated researchers and police to study the impact of variations in response time. Although earlier studies of response time had been conducted, the first study of response time based upon data other than those routinely generated by police departments (subject to considerable error) was a spin-off of the Kansas City Preventive Patrol Experiment and was published in 1976. Using the Kansas City data, Tony Pate, a principal researcher in the Kansas City experiment, and his colleagues examined the relationship between response time and citizen satisfaction with police service in response to calls. While previously police had assumed a direct relationship between response time and citizen satisfaction, that is, the shorter the response time, the greater would be citizen satisfaction with police service, Pate found that citizen satisfaction with police response time was shaped by an intervening variable: citizen *expectation* of response time.[32] In other words, *absolute* response time was less important than the relationship between the response citizens expected from police and the actual time it took for police to arrive. For example, if police arrived at a call in five minutes, but citizens had expected them in eight minutes, citizens tended to be pleased, whereas if citizens had expected police in three minutes, they tended to be displeased.

A second response time study conducted in Kansas City during the mid-1970s was equally important, not only in its findings, but because it constituted the first major research effort independently designed and executed by a police department, with the aid of civilian researchers, to study the efficacy of police tactics. Obviously, police insularity had begun to erode under leaders like Kansas City Police Chief Clarence Kelley. The purpose of this second study was to determine the impact of variation in response time on arrests. The results were stunning: *rapid police response led to an arrest in only 3 percent of serious crimes.*[33] The primary reason for this negligible impact was citizen behavior: as a rule citizens do not call police immediately after a crime, even a violent one. Most citizens, whether victims or witnesses, delay somewhere between twenty and forty minutes. Some victims and/or witnesses go into shock. Others, especially those victimized by friends or family, are uncertain about whether to call the police at all, and frequently contact someone close first to ask for advice. Many are frightened and want to be certain that the criminal is completely clear of the vicinity. Some businesses, fearful of violence on the premises, instruct their employees not to call police until they are sure that the perpetrator of a violent crime, such as a robber, has left the scene.

Almost everyone considers his or her situation carefully after being victimized. Some individuals, after careful consideration and, perhaps, after consultation with a friend or loved one, decide to call the police; many others, also after consideration, decide not to. We know that roughly half of all serious crimes go unreported.

The second Kansas City response-time study was considered so important and counterintuitive that it was replicated during the late 1970s in four other cities—Jacksonville, Peoria, Rochester, and San Diego—with funds from the National Institute of Justice.[34] In each case, the findings were identical: *less than 3 percent of reports of serious crime led to arrests as a result of rapid response.* Yet William Spelman, the primary author of the report, went even further: using his data about citizen behavior and police responses, Spelman calculated the impact if *all* delays in calling the police were eliminated. Even under such circumstances, an unachievable goal of course, Spelman concluded that no more than seventy crimes per thousand would lead to arrests as a result of rapid response.[35] Again, police were stunned.[36]

The overwhelming number of calls for service and increasing doubt about the efficacy of rapid response to calls for service led to a fundamental shift in thinking by the late 1970s. As a result, the idea of full-service policing—immediate response to all calls for service—was scuttled, to be replaced by 911 as an *emergency* response system for critical calls. Along with it the idea of "differential response" to calls for service was born, and call diversion programs developed that would prioritize calls according to their seriousness. In these schemes, police respond immediately only to calls of the highest priority; other calls are handled via telephone, followed by a request that citizens come to police stations or, during quiet times, by sending an officer. Subsequent research has shown that if treated properly citizens do not object to such procedures, but are quite satisfied so long as telephone operators explain the range of alternative services and police actually follow up on them.[37]

Nevertheless, the findings of response-time studies create a policy quandary. In many individual cases 911 systems and police responses have had wonderful and heart-warming outcomes—e.g., a child who is even too young to know her address nonetheless dials 911 after an injury to her parents and, because enhanced 911 systems automatically

94  *Fixing Broken Windows*

record the calling number, saves her family and herself.[38] Such stories have enormous appeal, and television has made the most of them. Yet on an aggregate level, cases in which 911 technology makes a substantial difference in the outcome of criminal events are extraordinarily rare. Spelman's policy recommendation regarding 911, made in a section entitled "Programs that Probably Will Not Reduce Citizen Reporting Time," stated: "there was nothing to show that installing 911 results in significant cuts in citizen reporting time. . . . When people call operators instead of 911, delays increase by only about ten seconds: not a significant figure within the general context of typical reporting times of five minutes or more."[39]

### The Costs of 911 Policing: Police-Citizen Interactions

Given these findings it is worthwhile to attempt to balance the benefits of 911 policing against its costs. For the time being, let us put aside the issue of financial costs, substantial as they are, for conceivably society might be willing to pay them in order to obtain even a small benefit. Other costs of 911 policing also figure in the balance, however. Here we discuss two of the most significant: negative effects of 911 policing on interactions between police and citizens, and lost opportunities for crime prevention and restoring communities to full functioning after a crime.

THE IMPORTANCE OF "CONNECTING." Things happen when police officers get out of their cars and systematically interact with citizens, through foot patrol or some other tactic. Let us provide an example observed by Kelling in walking foot patrol on the streets of Newark, New Jersey, during the mid-1970s. This was a time when most of the citizens in the area were black and the officers were white, when memories of the 1960s riots in American cities were still fresh. As two officers patrolled a Newark street, they came upon a pregnant African-American woman with a young child at a bus stop being harangued by a drunk African-American man. Both the woman and child were obviously terrified. The officers knew the man and addressed him by name: "Joe, you must leave this woman alone." When Joe protested, one of the officers took him firmly by the shoulders, turned him around, and began walking him away from the woman. Joe continued to protest: "I'm not doing anything wrong." His street companions, who were standing alongside nearby buildings and watching, began to comment: "Oh, oh, Joe wants to get arrested." The officer walked Joe about ten yards away from the woman and instructed him: "I'm going to let you go, but keep walking. I don't want you to bother this woman anymore." Joe continued to protest, and when the officer let him go, he took a couple of steps forward, then tried to run around the officers and back to the woman and child. The officers immediately grabbed Joe, wrestled him to the ground, handcuffed him, and called for a car to take him to the station for booking. During the twenty-minute wait for the car, Joe continued to protest, ranting and raving in a drunken fashion. One officer held Joe down, while the other exchanged comments with citizens, including the woman and child who had been harassed. Joe's street colleagues never came to his aid, but ridiculed him for behaving as he had. Finally, a police car came, the officers put Joe in the backseat, the car pulled away, and citizens dispersed.

How different this event might have been if the officers and citizens had been unfamiliar with each other. For many white officers, making such an arrest on a Newark street, when the vast majority of passersby were African Americans, would have been a nightmare scenario. As it was, however, the scene was relatively relaxed. Indeed, throughout their foot patrols white officers in Newark moved easily along city streets, chatted with citizens, explained to miscreants why they had to behave, ordered people to "move on," and occasionally, made arrests. In effect, these officers were exercising the very authority ideally accorded to police that we described in Chapter 1, an authority negotiated as citizens and police came to know and trust each other and to recognize their mutual interest in maintaining order on the streets.

What happens when police get out of their cars? First, the needs of police and citizens are so congruent that they reach out to each other. Even during the 1970s when chiefs were doing all they could to ensure the insularity of police from citizens, police and citizens found ways to make contact. Regardless of the neighborhood, citizens enjoy seeing police on the street. Residents greet them. Merchants welcome them. Slowly police get to know more and more people—apartment managers, neighborhood "politicians" and "figures," restaurant owners and workers, young children who approach them freely and curiously. Soon police start to discern the "wannabes" from troublesome gang members. They absorb information about community standards, troublemakers, problems, neighborhood happenings. To use New Haven police chief Nick Pastore's word, police and citizens *connect*. The reactions of citizens and police to each other are quite different when "warriors" intervene in a neighborhood dispute, or conduct "sweeps" or "crackdowns," as strangers—fearful, outnumbered, not knowing anyone, not understanding the history of the territory. Professor David Bayley of the State University of New York–Albany, who has studied police behavior throughout the world, has documented this variation:

> Black and white residents in the Kenwood–Hyde Park area of south Chicago say that the behavior of police toward residents varies sharply depending on the nature of their assignment (personal communication, 1991). The best were the community police officers who were permanently assigned to patrol on foot. They knew many people by name, could often distinguish local people from the visitors drawn to the area by its movie house and fast-food restaurants and were viewed as friends. Next best were the mobile patrol officers from the precinct who came into the neighborhood on routine patrol. Although they were less discriminating in their choice of interventions, they reacted largely to radio-dispatched calls for service and left order maintenance on the street to the foot patrol officers. Lastly, the officers who exhibited the worst behavior toward community residents were those outside the precinct who came into the area mostly to eat at local restaurants or to back up emergency calls. They were the ones who accosted people on suspicion and acted as if their responsibility was to "keep things under control" by demonstrating an intrusive, hard-edged presence.[40]

Secondarily, a "connection" between police and citizens in a neighborhood is crucial in shaping positive reactions of each toward the other. Where such a connection exists, when an officer makes a mistake, his or her reputation in the neighborhood assures citizens that it *is* a mistake, and not incompetence or racism. At the same time police themselves become less fearful and more trusting in their contacts with citizens. On the other hand, police insularity characterizes the day-to-day experiences of police and citizens as they operate within 911 systems. Compare the responses of the Newark police officers arresting Joe and the citizens present at the scene, with this remark from a young officer in a midwestern city as he rode past a public housing development: "Everybody that lives in there hates us" were his words, and unfortunately they are understandable, based upon his experiences. A citizen calls 911 for service and police respond; as they try to sort out the problem, other neighborhood residents watch impassively or sullenly, offering little or no information or support, some glaring at officers with overt hostility. Yet, the officer was wrong: residents of that same development had indicated to Kelling that they were weary of not being able to protect their children or their property, and knew that police would come quickly and leave as fast, without establishing a permanent presence in their neighborhoods. The officer perceived hostility, but the residents were responding out of fear and intimidation, confronted daily with gangs, drug dealers, and other predators who *had* established a permanent presence and were prepared to intimidate, harass, and even use mayhem to keep control of the neighborhood.

For police themselves, the consequence of isolation has been the emergence of a siege mentality. Because they only interact to intervene in a serious crime, they have no other relationship with citizens. And whether it is during day-to-day confrontations, or more serious disturbances, the alienation of officers from the communities they police interferes with the effective exercise of their basic authority, forcing police to rely inordinately on the use of force. As strangers in communities, police feel compelled to draw upon "preemptively coercive means, such as intimidation and threats,"[41] if not the direct application of force, and ultimately arrest. Many police tend to meet even the most modest resistance, indeed on occasion even to meet passivity, with preemptive coercive techniques—ordering, threatening, physical posturing, presenting weapons, and other such authoritative means. Because police believe that they must *win* any confrontation (with some good reason) regardless of who is initially confrontational, citizens—most often male youths—must *lose*, deserving or not.[42] At worst, reactive 911 policing can create a chasm between citizens and police so wide that it threatens the stability of cities and neighborhoods. During the 1960s in the United States, for example, virtually every major urban riot was precipitated by a clash between citizens and police. Fortunately such riots are relatively rare. Nevertheless, the problem of confrontations between police and citizens is a chronic one, born of suspicious or unruly citizens, fearful police unfamiliar with citizens in the area, training that leaves officers unfamiliar with racial and ethnic minorities, policing tactics that are oriented around preemptive moves if the circumstances appear threatening, and an overall police strategy emphasizing control over officers rather than service to the community.

While police do have to use preemptive coercion on many occasions, as a general principle to guide policing it is worrisome. Not only is such coercion antithetical to policing a democracy, it may create the very resistance it is intended to forestall, and lead to self-fulfilling prophecies and a downward spiral in which police become more aggressive and youths increasingly embittered and resistant. For when crises occur, when police need information and support, police coercion may ensure that help will be withheld—not only by youths who have been in trouble, but by other citizens who have observed earlier rousting, or been mistakenly rousted themselves and resent it, or who feel intimidated by the hostile relationship between neighborhood youths and police. Thus our third point concerning what happens when police get out of their cars: where police do establish a presence in a neighborhood, connect with citizens there, building trust and lessening fear, the ability of police to control the public behavior of citizens without resorting to the actual use of force is greatly enhanced. And when force itself is required, the officer familiar with a community is much more likely to be able to use it with the support and trust of the citizens who live and work there.

THE LOSS OF OPPORTUNITIES FOR CRIME PREVENTION AND DAMAGE CONTROL. By definition, 911 systems are reactive rather than proactive, aimed at responding to a crime or emergency rather than preventing such an occurrence. By keeping officers at a distance from citizens, 911 systems deprive police from acquiring intimate knowledge of and contacts within a community that could be invaluable in crime-prevention efforts. The connection between police and citizens is central to crime prevention.

Broadly construed, crime prevention surely includes peacekeeping, crowd-control, and riot-control functions. The potential for riots, such as those in Los Angeles that followed the first trial of officers linked to the arrest of Rodney King, will always exist. Police possess the latent ability to act as a restraining and calming influence in communities if they "connect" with citizens and residents. David Bayley sets out the preventive capabilities of police in "The Best Defense":

> Fearful and apprehensive about the possibility of collective violence, police leaders face a cruel choice. They can do nothing, which may leave them defenseless, or they can prepare, which usually means intensifying training for riots, including the formation of specialized riot-control units. The problem with the positive strategy is that it may seem provocative. As a result police departments tend to shy away from it. The current posture generally is to worry privately but do nothing publicly. No wonder police executives are fearful.
>
> There is, however, . . . a third option, that is positive without being provocative. Police executives can adopt the programmatic initiatives contained in community- and problem-oriented policing philosophies. Together, these approaches constitute, I believe, a strong defense against outbreaks of urban rioting and disorder.[43]

This does not mean that police will be able to prevent every disturbance, but even when disturbances do break out, truly preventive police work will involve helping citizens to limit the damage and to restore the community's functioning.[44]

In the summer of 1994, in New Haven, Connecticut, two African-American women and their four children moved from a housing development to a quiet residential neighborhood in which most residents were white. Soon after, a lingering dispute from the housing development followed the women to their new home, erupting into violence when someone fired seventeen shots into the next-door neighbor's house, believing it to be the new residents' home. Neighborhood tensions rose. About a month later the two women had a birthday party for one of their brothers. The party grew loud and moved outdoors, with music resonating from speakers placed in the yard. The family next door, whose house had been shot at, called police three times starting at 10:30 P.M.: the police came to the house shortly after midnight. After the police left once, and later returned, a major conflagration ensued with ten officers injured, ten citizens arrested, and someone at the party throwing a radio through the window of the next-door neighbor. The next evening a rock was thrown through another window. Charges flew: racism, illegal search, police behaved like "animals," "officers were shoved and pushed," "the party lasted for hours," and so on. The community had been seriously frayed by these incidents, and the potential for ongoing trouble, perhaps involving many more neighbors, was great. New Haven police could simply have left it at that: they had reacted and had quelled the disturbance. After visiting both families, however, Chief Nick Pastore decided to go further. He contacted a local mediator, Charles Pillsbury, to establish a mediation process between the families. Several weeks of mediation followed, and the process was concluded with a neighborhood picnic involving the two families, other neighbors and friends, and police. Months have now elapsed, and the neighborhood remains calm.

While the New Haven police were not able to prevent the immediate neighborhood conflict, when it did erupt they moved to limit the damage and aid the community in restoring itself. They were surely a preventive force in the sense that they helped to ensure peace in the long run. Police have a deep vested interest in all three outcomes: prevention, limiting damage, and restoration of individual, family, and community functioning. The orientation of 911 emergency response systems ignores these key interests, and in doing so, fails to address crime-prevention needs in a significant sense.

When it comes to index crimes such as homicide, there is growing evidence to suggest that police attention to "quality-of-life" issues and low-level crimes, making use of tactics significantly at variance with 911 policing, may have a significant impact in lowering incidence rates of index crimes. For example in New York City, as of June 30, 1995, the rate of reported murders by handgun was down 40.7 percent from the previous year, largely attributable, according to federal and local officials, to "quality-of-life" enforcement by the police.[45] We discuss these findings in greater detail in the chapters that follow, but suffice it to say here that the reactive nature of 911 policing emergency-response systems offers little in the arena of prevention for such crimes.

## Having Police Hurry

Suppose the research is right: regardless of how sophisticated the communications systems, how fast the cars, how motivated the officers, rapid response to calls for service is simply a failed tactic. No "tinkering" at the fringes—automatic vehicle-locator systems, enhanced 911, or differential response to calls for service—is going to result in a substantial gain in reducing crime and disorder. If true, this is a tough social policy pill to swallow. Considerable financial investments have been made in such systems. Politicians, even some who advocate community policing, continue to promote the idea of rapid response to calls for service so strongly that many police chiefs find it difficult to be honest with citizens about its potential. Some chiefs have given up: one, quoted by David Kennedy, a research fellow in the Kennedy School of government, says "People expect us to come when they call; that's an absolute. Believing anything else is a pipedream."[46] Other chiefs have been more courageous. Benjamin Ward, police commissioner of New York City from 1984 to 1989, faced a community meeting sponsored by the New York City Police Foundation at which a citizen stood up and said "We've got our foot patrol officer, now we want faster response." Ward responded: "You can't have both. They just don't go together." Generally, the news about rapid-response systems is so bad and hopes for it have been so high that it is easier for politicians and police to try to accommodate tactically to 911 while chipping away at it. Call-diversion programs have been developed, split forces created with some officers on patrol and others responding to 911 calls in cars, and new allocation systems attempted in which chunks of time are acquired for officers to work directly with citizens in neighborhoods by allocating other officers to respond to calls for certain periods.

Yet, aside from the costs associated with 911 policing enumerated above, if it does not work, it does not work. And if it does not work, then citizens are lured into a false sense of security and done a disservice if city and police officials continue to foster belief in its effectiveness. By continuing to market 911, police and politicians may also unwittingly interfere with the development of alternative social or policy responses to emergencies, and to crime, that would be more efficacious.

What might these responses be? Citizens might begin to understand the limitations of policing and know that they must take some responsibility to protect themselves, their families, their neighbors, and even strangers using the streets. This responsibility would include cultivating a sense of alertness in residents and all who use the streets so as to establish control over the territory and, while welcoming strangers into the neighborhood, nonetheless send out strong messages of community solidarity under threat. Physical structures and use of space can be designed to facilitate and encourage residents and citizens to oversee and claim this space. Ultimately citizens themselves must help develop a sense of order in a neighborhood that will discourage opportunists from testing the ability of residents or neighbors to defend themselves.

In the mid-1980s a woman in Boston was attacked on a bridge. Citizens heard her screams for help and called police. Twenty minutes later the woman was still calling for help and no police had arrived. Another twenty minutes later she was still without help. When these facts were made public, media and citizens were indignant. An investigation was initiated by then Mayor Raymond Flynn. The blue-ribbon commission appointed by the mayor, among other changes, recommended the installation of enhanced 911. Yet, it was not simply a case of police failure. The community failed as well. Where did citizens get the idea that when they call police their responsibilities as citizens end? Why were not elderly or incapacitated citizens in the neighborhood creating a ruckus by blinking their outdoor lights, yelling and shouting, calling other neighbors by the telephone, doing anything? Why were not healthy young persons, men and women, coming out of their homes, making their presence felt, trying if by nothing but numbers to intimidate and scare off the assailant and, if necessary, using baseball bats and other weapons to drive him off? While many answers could be given, one fair response is that for generations police have advertised the fact that crime is their business, that citizens should meet their responsibilities by reporting crimes and being good witnesses, and that handling crime is best left to the professionals.

## THE NEW REFORM: THE REDISCOVERY OF POLICING

What then is the proper role for police? Clearly, we want police to attend to emergencies, to come to the aid of citizens. They must also help citizens develop their claim over the local territory, back them up, and assist them in dealing with neighborhood problems. At times police will make arrests, and even protect offenders if citizens become too vigilant. But the central point of the argument is this: *we should not be relegating police to their cars, keeping them away from dealing with problems in neighborhoods in the name of waiting for calls or shortening response times.* No one has calculated the financial costs of holding police officers in cars waiting for calls against the benefit derived in those rare cases where rapid response makes a positive difference in the outcome of the incident. Probably it is astronomical, so costly as to be absolutely unacceptable.[47] This does not mean that police should not hurry to emergencies. They should. It does mean that issues like allocating police, configuring beats, calculating workloads, planning police activities, and determining priorities should be determined on the basis of a crime-prevention approach rather than a reactive law-enforcement model.

American policing is now changing, and while the public is certainly aware of this fact, the scope, dimensions, and contours of the transformation are not immediately apparent. The shift in police strategy can, however, be approached through an example. In an economically depressed section of Buffalo in the early 1990s, eleven girls between the ages of nine and sixteen were raped over a period of fifteen months. Although police determined after the third attack that a serial rapist was stalking young girls on their way to school, they did not circulate a sketch of the rapist or go public with the information until five months later, only after the *Buffalo News* inquired about the attacks. By that time eight more rapes had occurred. The chief of detectives defended the department's decision by explaining how news coverage might have hindered their investigation by alerting the rapist.[48] Residents and parents were appalled, but Buffalo police believed they were doing their job: arresting criminals in the act of committing crimes and investigating, post hoc, "successful" crimes. The decision of these officers illustrates the power of the law-enforcement ideology in shaping conventional responses to problems: the business of police is capturing criminals. Police in Buffalo probably used additional methods to try to apprehend the rapists: certainly, they increased levels of patrol, and they might have used stakeouts—inconspicuous officers surveilling locations at which another attack might take place. But the purpose of these tactics was to apprehend the perpetrator *in the act.* Although unintended, the practical consequence of interception tactics was to leave neighborhood children as bait for predators.

The newer model of policing now gaining ground contrasts starkly with the strategy of police in Buffalo as they dealt with this series of rapes. While it is frequently referred to today as community policing, or problem-solving policing, we shall call the new policing model the *preventive* model, and note at the outset that its strategy would posit the business of police in far different terms than the old reform strategy: *stop the next rape!* Of course, one means of achieving this is by identifying, arresting, and incarcerating the rapist. Aside from mere law enforcement, however, a preventive police approach immediately would have involved the community and would have included notifying all residents and officials (via newsletters, community meetings, telephone calls, informing school officials and children, etc.) about the rapes and providing, at the very least, the mode of operation and whatever descriptive information was available (it was determined after the third rape that a serial rapist was involved—this means that police had a rudimentary knowledge of a pattern and description even then). Parents, children, other citizens could have been mobilized to take individual and/or group preventive action. A total approach would have included limiting the damage. Children, aware of the danger of a sexual predator, are traumatized. Additionally, many are grieving for their friends. They need reassurance, information, and understanding. Schools and parents need advice about how to handle their children's concerns and how to protect them. Events like serial rapes strain relations in neighborhoods and communities. Suspicions spoil neighborliness and trust at a time when it is most required. Part of the responsibility of police is to help repair the damage that has been inflicted, certainly to the victims and their families, but also to other children, their families, and the community as a whole.

Admittedly, the circumstances described in Buffalo are a dramatic example of a narrow law-enforcement approach, but it is far from atypical in arrest-oriented departments. Even though it may be distasteful to suggest that children become "bait," it is not too strong a term. A preventive approach would have been to stop the event from happening in the first place. Happily, police are moving in this direction. In 1994 in Boston, for example, children in an inner-city neighborhood reported several attempts by a man to lure them into cars. The pattern was similar in each case. Commissioner Paul Evans immediately contacted city and private agencies, met with citizens, issued statements through the media, and made other attempts to mobilize parents, the neighborhood, and community resources. To be sure, some children, made hypersensitive by their fears and the publicity, reported events that either never happened or were exaggerated. Better that, however, than having more children victimized, kidnapped, or killed.

In 1961, when police were still confident about the efficacy of their law-enforcement tactics and well before research began to undermine them, Jane Jacobs wrote of another view of street safety. In this view police were not central; indeed, they were incidental to street safety:

> The first thing to understand is that the public peace—the sidewalk and street peace—of cities is not kept primarily by the police, necessary as police are. It is kept primarily by an intricate, almost unconscious, network of voluntary control and standards among the people themselves, and enforced by the people themselves. In some city areas—older public housing projects and streets with very high population turnover are often conspicuous examples—the keeping of public sidewalk law and order is left almost entirely to the police and special guards. Such places are jungles. No amount of police can enforce civilization where the normal, casual enforcement of it has broken down.[49]

Police in such a model are the "or else" of society. They assist citizens in casual order maintenance, help to restore order when it breaks down, and use their capacity for forceful action when conditions warrant it.

This view of the relationship between the public and police is not new. The Principles of Law Enforcement developed by Sir Robert Peel in 1829, as part of a mission statement for the newly created London Metropolitan Police Force, memorialized an identical set of values. The principles included:

1. The basic mission for which the police exist is to prevent crime and disorder. . . .
2. The ability of the police to perform their duties is dependent upon public approval of police existence, actions, behavior, and the ability of the police to secure and maintain public respect.

3. The police must secure the willing cooperation of the public in volun-
tary observance of the law to be able to secure and maintain public
respect.

4. The degree of cooperation of the public that can be secured dimin-
ishes, proportionately, the necessity for the use of physical force. . . .

5. The police seek and preserve public favor, not by catering to public
opinion, but by constantly demonstrating absolute impartial service to
the law, in complete independence of policy, and without regard to the
justice or injustice of the substance of individual laws; by ready offering
of individual service and friendship to all members of society without
regard to their race or social standing. . . .

6. The police should use physical force to the extent necessary to secure
observance of the law or to restore order only when the exercise of persuasion, advice, and warning is found to be insufficient. . . .

7. The police at all times should maintain a relationship with the public
that gives reality to the historic tradition that the police are the public
and that the public are the police; the police are the only members of
the public who are paid to give full-time attention to duties which are
incumbent on every citizen in the interest of the community welfare.

8. The police should always direct their actions toward their functions
and never appear to usurp the powers of the judiciary by avenging individuals or the state. . . .

9. The test of police efficiency is the absence of crime and disorder, not
the visible evidence of police action dealing with them.[50]

Peel's principles stand in equally good stead today as a guide for policing, as well as for the development of an effective and productive relationship between police and citizens.

If we adopt the approach implicit in Peel's principles, what are the
tradeoffs that today's citizens and police must make to restore order to
our cities? We must move away from the use of reactive, 911 policing
and return to a model of policing in which basic strategies are aimed at
crime prevention and order maintenance. A critical first step is that 911
and rapid response must be demarketed. Politicians and police must provide leadership and be explicit with citizens about the cost of 911 to
communities. In partnership with the police, citizens themselves must
once again accept mutual responsibility for their own prudent, effective,

and legally permissible involvement in crime prevention and order maintenance. It is unimportant whether citizens, their elected leaders, or the police lead the way in moving toward these goals, so long as the process begins. In the next chapter, we provide an early example of a police organization taking the initiative in reestablishing order in New York City, and explore the dramatic effects of order maintenance.

# TAKING BACK THE SUBWAY

### New York City's Quality-of-Life Program

HOW DO WE ACTUALLY BEGIN THE PROCESS OF RESTORING ORDER in our cities? In many urban centers problems of disorder become so great that order maintenance must start with a campaign to "take back the streets," reestablishing a modicum of civility and safety for ordinary citizens who travel daily along streets and by public transportation to work, to school, to shop, in pursuit of all the ordinary activities of everyday life. Given the work that police engage in on a day-to-day basis, they may be uniquely positioned to take the lead in this effort. Ultimately, to succeed, police must work in tandem with political leaders, citizens must support their efforts, and courts must validate policing activities. Yet the potential exists for police to make substantial contributions to neighborhood order and crime reduction within a relatively short period of time.

In New York City, the impetus for change in police priorities had its origins in a pervasive sense among citizens that community life in their own neighborhoods was not what it ought to be, and in a relatively inchoate demand from the public that police and political leadership move toward restoring order. Soon citizens began to organize and take action themselves, at the same time putting direct pressure on police and other officials to adopt priorities consistent with their order-related concerns. The result was a range of order-restoration initiatives. We discuss several examples of these efforts in New York City here: the first, carried out in Times Square and Bryant Park during the late 1970s, was an early experiment and cooperative endeavor by the mayoral administration and police to regain control of Bryant Park.[1] The strategy embodied many elements of what would later be known as the broken windows approach—yet the effort was eventually aborted due to lack of police interest. After police abandoned their activities, a privately funded and organized attempt to restore order in Bryant Park moved in a different direction, and ultimately produced what today is described as an "urban jewel." Bryant Park has become one of many success stories growing out of strategic planning for and investment in the local community undertaken by private corporations and commercial enterprises, frequently through the creation of business improvement districts (BIDs).

Another impressive order-restoration undertaking occurred in "taking back" the New York City subway, initially targeting graffiti on subway trains, and later increasing levels of disorder identified as "homelessness." Restoring order in the subway was not only important in its own right, but gave rise as well to the New York City Police Department's (NYPD) current anticrime strategy. For the person charged with implementing order-maintenance policies in the subway—Chief of the Transit Authority Police Department, William Bratton—would later become Commissioner of Police for New York City under Mayor Rudolph Giuliani. Bratton himself is largely responsible for moving the NYPD, as he did previously with the Transit Authority Police, into community policing and with focusing the attention of each organization on maintaining order.

Other actors and forces were equally important in the struggle to regain control of public spaces in New York City. Most notably, neighborhood associations and citizen groups were influential, both in pressuring police to be responsive to their needs and in taking to the streets themselves to restore control over their neighborhoods. Similarly, prosecutors began to take tentative steps to reach out to the community, experimenting with various "community prosecution" programs. And we would be remiss in failing to note that Bratton's second appointment and fundamental changes in the NYPD came about only after a political contest for mayor in which quality-of-life issues, symbolized in particular by "squeegeeing" (unsolicited washing of car windows), dominated the campaign. Indeed, by the early 1990s, the once inchoate citizen demand for order had crystallized into an urgent call to action, and thus became a political priority. In this milieu, characterized by the emergence of a new urban consensus, police and private-citizen initiated responses moved closer together, working increasingly in a synchronous, integrated fashion.

Nevertheless, it is primarily the process of change in strategies of policing that we seek to capture, and to illuminate, in this chapter: a view of the Transit Authority Police Department (TPD) and the NYPD over this period of rapid change and redirection provides an example of the new preventive model for policing in action, and the benefits it may confer. In each case, as the organization moved to develop a capacity for engaging in order maintenance and different forms of crime prevention, progress occurred through fits and starts. Resistance to the transformation arose from within the police department as well as from other sources in the community. Civil libertarians and advocates for the homeless attacked the programs as favoring the interests of the economically advantaged over and against those of the poor, minorities, and otherwise disadvantaged groups. Both the Transit Authority and the NYPD were sued. Moreover, the successful attempt by the New York State judiciary to have all quality-of-life offenses virtually decriminalized, as occurred when legislation was attached to the state budget in June 1995, removing jurisdiction for these violations from the state criminal courts, provides evidence of the continuing lag on their part in understanding the importance of disorder as a destructive force and its links to crime and urban decay.[2]

Nevertheless, police efforts to date have resulted in effects that are in some respects truly astonishing. Not only have the police garnered wide citizen support for their programs; order has been restored to the subway and certain petty crimes have been significantly reduced or even eliminated on city streets. Preliminary indications also suggest a linkage between the quality-of-life program and a decrease in violent crime: robbery has been dramatically reduced in the subway, and murder is declining in the city. While we do not yet understand the precise nature of this linkage, and current police efforts extend beyond order-maintenance activities alone, many police posit a direct correlation between restoring order and reducing violent crime in New York City.

## A BURGEONING DEMAND FOR IMPROVING THE QUALITY OF LIFE: PUBLIC AND PRIVATE INITIATIVES

### Operation Crossroads

During the late 1970s, at the initiation of Herb Sturz in the Mayor's Office, the New York City Police Department engaged in an experiment called Operation Crossroads, to clean up Times Square, and in particular to address problems of prostitution, hustling, gambling, scams, and drug dealing that were prevalent and troublesome to merchants and citizens alike.[3] Up to this time, police had used aggressive sweeps as their primary tactic for reducing these activities. After identifying a problem area, NYPD would mobilize a squad of officers and arrest all those found loitering there. The tactic had little effect, for soon after they were arrested perpetrators were back on the streets. The courts eventually declared sweeps unconstitutional.

Then Operation Crossroads took a new approach. Trained observers would identify areas in which disorderly behavior appeared high, whereupon police would implement a high-visibility, low-arrest strategy to interrupt and deter such activity. Police would educate, advise, cajole, and use generally noncoercive methods to discourage disorderly behavior; arrest would be a last resort. A crisis in Bryant Park, adjacent to the main branch of the New York Public Library, provided the opportunity to test the approach in Operation Crossroads. Parks Commissioner Gordon Davis threatened to close the park when drug dealing reached epidemic levels and police failed to control it. Police managers responded to Davis's threat by implementing the low-arrest tactics of Operation Crossroads. The results were dramatic: the number of persons engaging in selling, buying, and using drugs decreased by 85 percent, and the number of people involved in "positive" activities increased by 79 percent. Furthermore, the presence of some officers, either stationed in one spot or on directed patrol, appeared more critical to affecting conditions than the absolute number of officers.

The order-maintenance activities of police in Operation Crossroads clearly translated into improved conditions on streets that citizens could appreciate. Nevertheless, as soon as the "crisis" in Bryant Park passed, police aborted the project, transferring key personnel elsewhere. They were not about to abandon their traditional ways of evaluating officer performance and assigning officers to specific beats. And in the park, conditions again worsened after the demise of Operation Crossroads. By the early 1980s they reached crisis proportions, with muggings and robberies regular events, and drug sellers approaching library patrons as they entered and left the public library. Pressure mounted from the chairman of the Library Board of Directors Richard Salomon, the next Director Andrew Heiskell, and the Rockefeller family (which was prepared to invest $3 million) for a renewal of order restoration efforts in the park. Then in 1980 the Bryant Park Restoration Corporation was created, with Daniel Biederman at its head. Yet opposition to these efforts effectively precluded implementation of a concrete plan for ten years, in spite of the fact that, during the mid-1980s, two citizens were killed in the park.

Finally, in 1990, Biederman was able to move ahead with concrete plans for the restoration. His strategy would be to identify those elements fundamental to maintaining orderly, safe, and amiable environments in other public places that were models of success, and then to re-create them in some fashion in Bryant Park. With Rockefeller Center as an exemplar, he compiled a list of ten essential characteristics, including: minimal sanitation levels maintained—parks had to be clean and litter-free; a sense of security—with full-time policing of facilities; adequate lighting—the park could not be turned over to predators at night; physical facilities maintained—vandalism and graffiti had to be attended to immediately; excellent concessions—with high-quality food and service provisions; beautiful flowers and trees; clean, well-run rest rooms—with no need for public urination or defecation; interesting entertainment programs—which would bring visitors to the park; key elements of design—the park would be visually transparent, with wide, unobstructed entrances, at least one fountain, so as to be pleasant while facilitating the operation of normal social control; and clearly posted rules—notifying everyone of expected behavior in the park.[4] Restoration efforts commenced with the hiring and training of private security personnel; food vendors were carefully selected; signs delineating park rules were designed and posted in conspicuous locations; entertainment was planned. The park was reopened in 1992. It is a model for other restoration efforts.

## The Grand Central Partnership and BID

The private model of order restoration implemented in Bryant Park took another form in commercial areas, with the creation of private improvement districts, BIDs, in which property owners voluntarily tax themselves and use the money to improve conditions and thereby the quality of life within the boundaries of the district. The original raison d'être of BIDs was to restore order primarily by maintaining the physical environment and security of commercial areas to ensure their viability. Later, BIDs broadened their focus from physical conditions alone to include disorderly behavior. Today thirty-three business improvement districts operate in New York City. One of the most active and successful is the Grand Central BID, whose management is headed by Daniel Biederman.

In operation since 1988, the Grand Central BID covers seventy-five blocks in midtown Manhattan's central business district, with Grand Central Terminal at the core. It is a high-rent commercial area in which numerous historical and architectural landmarks (such as the Chrysler Building, the Daily News Building, and St. Bartholomew's Church), well-known hotels and businesses, and noted institutions and clubs are located. The Grand Central Partnership carries out the functions for which the district is organized. Uniformed street sweepers clean seven days a week, collecting litter, removing graffiti, and emptying refuse bins. A Multi-Service Center offers hot meals, counseling, job training, and housing placements for the homeless, and former employment trainees help to run the center. Additionally, the partnership provides multilingual visitor services, sponsors a full public-events program of live and video performances (including a First Night arts festival that attracts thousands of people), and carries out a number of projects focused on improving the physical appearance of streets, intersections, crosswalks, street-signs and lamps, and building facades. To deter crime, approximately fifty uniformed security officers, on foot patrol between 7 A.M. and 11 P.M., are linked by radio communication with the three NYPD precincts that cover the district. All of these services are supplemental to those provided by the city itself.

From December 1989 to December 1992, reported crime in the area dropped 42 percent.[5] So the program seems to be working. Yet there are challenges to it: recently the Grand Central Partnership has been accused of tolerating, if not encouraging, abuse of some "homeless" by former street people it has hired as outreach workers. This attack on BIDs has come primarily from the Coalition for the Homeless—a group that has opposed virtually all public and private attempts either to restrain the excesses of street people, or to offer them services other than those prescribed by the Coalition itself.[6] While the facts have been obscured by contradictory testimony, even the liberal *New Yorker* weighed in on behalf of the Partnership: "On balance, the Partnership's programs have done a great deal more for the homeless than the Coalition's sandwiches, and possibly its advocacy. . . . In retrospect, the Partnership can be seen to have performed an indispensable function: It has tested the limits of a powerful new idea."[7]

For the most part these private and governmental efforts to address disorder in the City of New York were initiated before the police themselves were prepared to contemplate or undertake internal change in their own strategies for crime control—perhaps reflecting the degree to which police had insulated themselves from citizen input. While citizens could exert pressure on elected officials, and could form groups such as BIDs to spend private funds, they had not as yet been able to find a channel for prodding police into a meaningful response to public demands for order. True, under Police Commissioner Benjamin Ward the NYPD began a shift toward community policing, but it was implemented as an add-on, well outside the mainstream of policing in New York City. It was the transit police who first got serious about restoring order.

## THE SUBWAY EXPERIENCE: A PILOT FOR CHANGE

The New York City subway provides a system of transportation that is crucial to the viability of social life and commerce in the city. Built largely during the first quarter of this century, the subway's twenty-six transit lines cover 230 route miles with 465 stations; more than 5,000 train cars are in use during peak periods. More than 3.5 million riders use the subway on an average working day. Aside from dwarfing most other major systems, the New York subway differs from virtually all others in two important respects: it operates twenty-four hours a day, and it is an *urban* system that transports citizens exclusively *within* the city, as opposed to systems such as Washington, D.C.'s Metro or San Francisco's BART (Bay Area Rapid Transit), which function primarily to transport persons into and out of cities. The New York City subway provides stations and stops in nearly every New York City neighborhood, even the most troubled. As such, it is a mass transit system that truly serves the basic requirements of those most in need of public transportation.

Although subway trains and tracks were refurbished and brought up to high standards during the mid-1980s, many stations were deteriorating, sending a strong message of lack of care. Two highly visible problems in particular created a quality-of-life crisis in the subway during this time, accelerating its deterioration and undermining public confidence in the safety of the system for riders. The first was graffiti; the second was disorderly behavior and petty crime that became known popularly as "the homeless problem." When ridership began to decline and popular dissatisfaction with subway conditions became evident, Robert Kiley, chairman of the Board of the Metropolitan Transportation Authority (MTA), and David Gunn, president of the New York City Transit Authority (NYCTA), understood that if the subway was to be fully restored, order had to be reestablished.

## Graffiti and Disorderly Behavior in the Subway

With graffiti now largely gone from the subway, it is hard to describe just how intractable the problem seemed during the early 1980s, when graffitists' logos, slogans, and portraits—"tags"—covered nearly every car. For apologists such as Norman Mailer, graffiti was a vibrant art form, hardly deserving of police action. Many, even those who did not share Mailer's taste in art, believed that police had more important matters to deal with than minor crimes like vandalism. Yet for others, such as Harvard education professor Nathan Glazer, graffiti signified that graffitists, other disorderly persons, and criminals "who rob, rape, assault, and murder passengers . . . are part of one world of uncontrollable predators,"[8] and gave evidence to citizens that public officials were unable to secure the subway environment even from relatively minor lawbreakers, let alone serious predators. Glazer's 1979 article in *Public Interest*, "On Subway Graffiti in New York," galvanized thought about graffiti's potential for disruption in urban settings.

At the time Glazer wrote, six years of effort had gone into eradicating graffiti, to no avail. Glazer despaired that it might be an insoluble problem. The youth subculture emblazoning subway cars appeared to be a permanent part of New York's culture. Both mayors Lindsay and Koch had launched major anti-graffiti efforts. Detaining youths and forcing them to clean cars failed because of the expense, and also because it provided graffitists with inside knowledge about painting and cleaning technology. Putting trains in "target hardened" locations didn't work because the areas were so vast that they could not be secured—youths simply cut through fences, and media pressure prevented the use of attack dogs to protect trains. Arrests of graffiti vandals increased yearly, without impact.

Despite these failures and the widespread belief that nothing could be done about graffiti, New York City subway trains are now among the cleanest in the world, thanks to the Clean Car Program initiated in May 1984 by Transit Authority President David Gunn. The idea was straightforward: *once a train was entered into the program and cleaned, it would never again be used while graffiti was on it.* Graffitists would never see their tags on clean trains again: they might be able to paint over other graffiti on cars that weren't entered into the program, but not on clean cars. Initially, trains were pulled out of service, cleaned, and entered into the Clean Car Program; any further graffiti would be removed from cars within two hours or they would be taken out of service until cleaned. Transit police were assigned to ride full time on the first clean trains and to protect clean trains in special yards. Special arrest and prosecution programs targeted graffitists who hit clean trains.

This effort succeeded while others failed for several reasons. First, David Gunn was absolutely committed to the program: he found graffiti intolerable and made graffiti removal his administration's earliest and highest priority. Moreover, the program succeeded because it attacked the basic motives of graffitists who, above all else, wanted their work seen. The strategy of never permitting tagged trains to be used meant that graffiti would be defeated. Officials knew they were winning when graffitists who managed to penetrate yards repainted graffiti-covered cars rather than tag clean ones.

Finally, the NYCTA succeeded because the Gunn administration abandoned the use of a law-enforcement strategy in dealing with graffiti. Early efforts to deal with graffiti had approached it as a law-enforcement problem for police to deal with. They did—arresting graffitists again and again, and over and over. More trains were tagged, but arrests increased. Police believed they were "doing their job"; meanwhile, other NYCTA departments, such as maintenance, conducted their own "business as usual," viewing graffiti as a law-enforcement problem. Gunn took a new approach. He understood that the graffiti problem was a complex mix of vandalistic behavior, poor maintenance, inadequate leadership, and lack of resolve. Under his close supervision an interdepartmental task force was charged with increasing the number of clean cars in the program each year—a goal the NYCTA exceeded every year. In five years, graffiti on trains was wiped out.[9] On May 12, 1989, the last graffiti-covered train was removed from service and cleaned.

Despite the victory over graffiti, lawlessness still reigned in the subway during the late 1980s. Panhandling, one of its most highly visible and intrusive signs, was endemic. In addition to peaceful and passive beggars, stupefied addicts slumped over cups, hustlers or representatives of service organizations (it was often impossible to tell the difference) lectured train passengers about their obligations to help the needy and solicited for "donations," panhandlers aggressively thrust their hands or cups into the faces of subway users and glowered at them demanding money. Service organizations and churches were attempting to turn some stations into feeding and clothing distribution centers, attracting even more indigents.[10] Often the recipients of donated clothing would strip and change clothes in the middle of stations or platforms, and with the lack of toilet facilities, many persons urinated or defecated in public places, including train cars. At times, entire cars were taken over by indigents who sprawled over seats and on the floor. Approximately 1,200 to 2,000 persons a night were sleeping in the subway, and the number was rapidly increasing.

Farebeating created an additional sense of lawlessness. Popular scams included jumping over or backcocking turnstiles (placing backward pressure on turnstiles and then slipping through them without paying); coin sucking (blocking the token receptacle with some foreign object and sucking out a deposited token); and most outrageously, disabling all the token receptacles, holding open gates, and collecting fares from persons entering the system. During rush hours, this latter maneuver resulted in bedlam, with confused passengers being channeled to one gate and confronted by intimidating youths who extorted fares from them. Chairman Kiley himself was caught in one of these fiascos and watched with dismay as police seemed to do little about it. Youths emboldened by the apparent anarchy attacked token receptacles, having developed a technology for quickly springing the door of the receptacle. Hundreds or thousands of tokens were stolen in a matter of seconds, with thieves fleeing into the subway or street. When receptacles were hardened with vaults, predators turned on tolltakers collecting tokens from the vaults, assaulting and robbing them. Estimated losses from the various fare scams and thefts ranged from $60 to $120 million a year, not to mention the indignation, demoralization, and fear that paying passengers and on-site transit staff felt. Following on the heels of disorder and petty crimes, robbery and felonies started a steep increase in 1987.

For the most part, the media portrayed conditions in the subway as one more manifestation of society's larger problem of homelessness. Officials of the MTA and NYCTA, sharing this concern, also labeled the problem as "the homeless." Consequently, early efforts to deal with subway disorder reflected the same assumptions that the general public held: the homeless were victims of public neglect, inadequate housing, changing economic conditions, and inequitable distribution of wealth, in need of jobs, treatment, and a temporary shelter until they got on their feet. Initial efforts attempted to link those homeless who frequented or inhabited the subway with outreach workers. The MTA established close ties with New York City's Human Resources Administration (HRA) and the Volunteers of America (VOA)—the latter, funded by the MTA. To facilitate outreach efforts, the transit police department created a special unit, the fifteen-person Homeless Task Force. Officers in this unit met nightly with outreach personnel and accompanied them to locations where vagrants congregated, attempting to encourage them to accept offers of help.

Yet the impact of these efforts was negligible: the vast majority of those "hanging out" in the subway—more than 90 percent—rejected shelters. The reason they gave most often was that the subway was safer than shelters. And the issue of safety was used by advocates as a justification for allowing homeless persons to use the subway as a shelter. Yet statistics compiled on behalf of the Transit Authority at this time documented that an average of six homeless persons a month died of preventable (that is, not natural) causes in the subway during 1989, with the worst month being December, when fourteen died.[11] On one December weekend alone, four street persons died in the subway: one hit by a train; a second killed by another homeless individual; and two from hypothermia. Furthermore, the most disturbed and deranged homeless sought refuge deep in the tunnels where conditions were not only appalling but genuinely life-threatening: hot third rails posed a danger of electrocution; damp, cold, and dark tunnels were infested with rats, vermin, and filth and filled with discarded syringes and needles; side rooms contained worn electrical wiring that was exposed. Only specially trained transit police were permitted back in these areas of the tunnels—yet advocates argued that the homeless should be permitted to stay, rather than be taken by bus to shelters. Clearly those who chose to stay in the subway, and their advocates, either were seriously mistaken about its safety, or were using the safety argument as a cover for a political statement about their view of shelters.

Nevertheless, with increasing numbers of street people using the subway and rejecting shelters, the problems on the subways worsened. In light of these conditions, ridership on the subway was seriously declining, threatening a multibillion dollar rejuvenation project which had already substantially improved the infrastructure and enhanced the timeliness and quality of subway service. Although New York City's faltering economy was one factor contributing to a reduction in subway use, marketing surveys and focus groups conducted by the MTA indicated that the major determinant was fear of crime. Surveys of riders reflected this fear: 97 percent reported taking some form of defensive action before entering the subway; 75 percent refrained from wearing expensive clothing or jewelry; 69 percent avoided "certain people"; 68 percent avoided particular platform locations; and 61 percent avoided specific train cars.[12] Responses revealed that the core of the problem was public unease with the "homeless" who were turning the subway, as well as Grand Central Terminal and Penn Station, into gigantic surrogate shelters. Furthermore, attitudes toward the homeless in the subway were changing: public sympathy was turning into public antipathy. Although concerned about conditions for the needy and homeless, the public found incivilities to have become so pervasive in the subway—drunkenness, vomiting, urinating and defecating in public, conspicuous drug use, threatening and insulting behavior toward passengers, open sexual behavior, intimidating panhandling—that it sought the restoration of public order.

In April 1989, Kiley called together the chiefs of the three transit police departments under his direction, the New York Transit Authority Police Department, the Long Island Rail Road Police Department, and the Metro North Police Department, to demand that they do something about the problem of homelessness in the subway, Grand Central Terminal, and Penn Station. Kiley and Gunn were particularly vexed by the inability of police to draft a realistic plan to deal with disorder because of the previous victory over graffiti. Yet the response of police leaders to Kiley's demand was mostly equivocating: police did not have the authority to do anything about the homeless; nothing they had tried had worked thus far; the homeless were the responsibility of social workers, not police; and typically, police were preoccupied with the increase in robberies. Nonetheless, a week later subway police came up with a proposal: cleaning crews would move into an area in which homeless persons had congregated, hose it down, and aggressively clean it. An enhanced Police Homeless Task Force would eject the homeless in support of these activities, and maintenance crews would haul away whatever debris was left. Dean Esserman, legal counsel to the TPD and now chief of the Metro North Police Department, who was highly critical of the plan, dubbed it "Commando Cleaning." Fortunately, Kiley and Gunn rejected the proposal.

What Kiley and Gunn did do was to establish a multilayer, multibureau study group to develop police plans for restoring order in the subway. Kelling, who at the time was acting as a policing consultant to the MTA generally, became the study group's advisor in June 1989. Transit police officers assigned to the study group were dubious of the entire business, never having been involved in such a process and having no faith in top command's willingness to place any value on their views. For these officers, the issue of explicit and public authority was the acid test of management's commitment to solving the disorder problem: they wanted explicit authority to deal with disorder, and they wanted that authority made public. As one officer said to the group, "When somebody is whacking me with an umbrella because I am 'denying the rights of the homeless,' I want to be able to point to a sign that makes it clear that I am just doing my job." The game, they feared, was going to be "covering your ass." They were familiar with the old saw in policing told by Hubert Williams, president of the Police Foundation and former director of the Newark Police Department. The mayor calls the chief of police and says: "Bums are bothering secretaries in the park at lunch. Don't do anything illegal, but get them out of there." The chief calls in the deputy chief and starts the order down the line: "Bums are bothering secretaries in the park at lunch. Don't do anything illegal, but get them out of there." The message gets to the patrol officers responsible for the park. They understand the real message: "Do what you have to do and cover your ass." The TPD's command staff's "commando cleaning" proposal to deal with subway disorder was of this ilk: the line officer is the dirty worker, doing what has to be done to solve the problem, regardless of its morality or legality. Transit officers wanted the NYCTA firmly behind them, even if they went to court. Kelling's first job, therefore, was to convince line officers that no "dirty work" would take place: the MTA's actions would be made public, be legally defensible, and would take the high moral ground away from homeless advocates and civil liberties lawyers. From the first meeting of the task force, participants were continuously asked "Why are we doing this?" "Whose interests are being served?" "How do we ensure that the genuinely needy are not hurt by what is done?" "Will this be defensible in court?"

The first task for the study group was to gain a precise understanding of the problems existing in the subway.[13] They reviewed the literature concerning transit problems and homelessness. The group held meetings with other police and transit agencies to find out what other departments were planning or had learned. They met with social agencies to alert them to the possibility of increased demands for services. The group also spent time in the subway detailing actual conditions, taking pictures and videos of problematic activities and locations, and talking with homeless persons, transportation employees, and police.

The problem identified in this process was multifaceted, and different from what most participants on the task force had believed it to be. While homelessness was a factor that aggravated the situation in the subway, few genuinely homeless individuals sought refuge there. The most significant problem was outrageous and illegal behavior by a relatively large population of subway users, some of whom *appeared* to be homeless but many of whom were not, a high proportion of whom were severe alcohol and drug abusers and/or seriously mentally ill, and many of whom were using the subway as a shelter.

Fortuitously, one member of the Police Study Group, Captain Richard Gollinge, was already dealing with the problem of disorder in his district. Gollinge was an unabashed "Broken Windows" advocate and a tough cop who had earlier managed special anticrime units. For Gollinge, dealing with the homeless problem was just good policing, although he worked at this endeavor at his own risk and without sanction from top management. He realized that transit police in the subway had an advantage over city police in the streets in dealing with obstreperous and disorderly behavior: public behavior could be regulated in the subway to a greater degree than in the streets because of the dangers inherent in an electrified, high-speed train system used by a high number of paying riders. Gollinge was prepared to use the authority afforded him in the subway system. His officers were under strict orders to respect riders, regardless of their status, but to enforce regulations aggressively.

On his own initiative, Gollinge had sent his officers a clear statement in the form of a memo of their responsibility to maintain order. The document defined the disorder problem as behavior, not economic condition; described specifically the behaviors of concern; cautioned police that homelessness was not a target of enforcement; and specified police activities that should be taken in response.[14] Not only was Gollinge explicit about what he expected his officers to do, he actually led them into the subway to enforce applicable rules. While not documented empirically at the time, conditions in Gollinge's district were noticeably different than in others: far fewer people were sprawled out on the floors and behaving in an unseemly fashion. Predictably, Gollinge's efforts had been publicly noted and, having received little internal support, they were under attack by advocates and civil libertarians who enjoyed broad media attention. Nevertheless, his limited efforts provided the basis for developing a general transit police policy.

Even with Gollinge's model in hand, the study group faced a number of other tasks in developing plans for restoring order in the subway as a whole. The Transit Police Department also reviewed its own values, to ensure that they would guide both rules and methods to be applied. The study group considered all existing subway rules and regulations in light of constitutional law and changing legal, social, and moral traditions. The assumption from the beginning was that the rules, and the subway plan generally, would be tested in court. Rules that could not stand up to legal scrutiny would not be adopted or implemented in the first place. One rule, against "obstructing," was especially troublesome. It was sufficiently vague both to invite legal challenges, and to trouble line officers charged with enforcing it. Was a person lying halfway across a walkway that was otherwise unimpeded obstructing? How about a person who stopped at the bottom of stairs, just to get oriented? What about someone who set his luggage on the platform, inadvertently blocking free movement? Was this person obstructing and therefore deserving of police attention? Police were nervous that too much discretion was involved in answering these and a myriad of other questions about obstructing. As the group took photographs and videos of actual subway conditions and played out enforcement scenarios, members realized that the problem was not really obstructing, but *lying down*. They decided, therefore, to request that the MTA Board of Directors change the rules to target lying down and scrap the rule against "obstructing"—which the board did.

The rules that were finally adopted for enforcement prohibited acts such as applying graffiti, farebeating or tampering with fare collection boxes and turnstiles, solicitation, begging and panhandling, drinking alcoholic beverages or entering a transit facility or conveyance while unable to function safely due to the influence of alcohol or drugs, littering, urinating outside provided facilities, and lying down on a floor, platform, or stairway, or blocking free movement in such locations. Soliciting for licensed charities, public speaking, leafleting, and other speech-related activities were permissible in certain locations where they would pose no threat to the safety of transit system users.[15] TPD and transit legal staff developed enforcement policies in cooperation with prosecutors' offices.

A debate surfaced early about how much the public should be informed of the planning effort. Opposition to going public came primarily from the top command of the TPD, and on the surface seemed reasonable: given the attention span of the media, the general public, and politicians, publicity could lead to expectations of success that might prove difficult to meet. The expectation was that, like graffiti, dealing with disorder would be a long-haul effort requiring at least five years. Yet, the study group pushed for high visibility: in the trade-off between high expectations and nonexistent expectations, the group believed the only way to get and keep the attention of top management was to create a public perception that the Transit Police Department was on the move. Kelling, also, pushed for high visibility, believing that the policy issues involved should be aired fully before the public, in order to educate it. The definition of the subway's problem as "homelessness" was a tragic misnomer that ill-served the suffering population attempting to use the subway for shelter. It excused outrageous and illegal behavior by a large number of petty and serious criminals, exempted police from meeting their responsibilities, and invited "solutions" that were irrelevant to the problems. Ultimately the decision was Kiley's, and he chose to be "out front" about the philosophy and tactics of the order-maintenance strategy. The messages to be communicated to the public would include:

- the sense of disorder and fear that resulted from rule violations;
- the link between disorder and crime;
- the toll, in terms of safety and health, that the homeless paid for their attempts to use the subway space for shelter;
- the good-faith efforts that the MTA and the NYCTA had made and were continuing to make to find appropriate services for the genuinely homeless; and
- that regaining control of the subway would take a long time.

The final thorn in the planning process involved the date of program initiation. Kelling pushed for an October 1 beginning. Driving this date were the need for police to gain experience and skill in handling disorderly behavior and the needy, and getting the program started well before cold weather set in so that those using the subway as a surrogate shelter would have an opportunity to find alternate accommodation. A later, December 15, beginning as proposed by those in the NYCTA responsible for signs, pamphlets, coordination with other agencies, and other such matters, would be a strategic disaster. Kelling anticipated advocates for the homeless using the media to fight the program, with the message: "Merry Christmas, homeless and needy of New York. Our gift to you is ejection from the subway." Finally, after hearing both sides, Kiley determined that the starting date would be October 25, 1989. Officers were trained, the public was notified of the impending program through the distribution of millions of leaflets to subway users, rules were posted conspicuously throughout the system, rule violators were handed ticket-like brochures alerting them that after the initiation of the program they would be cited for their rule-violating behavior, other police departments, service agencies, and transportation agencies were briefed on the plans, and each transit police officer was provided with copies of a brochure setting out the legal base and rationale for order-maintenance efforts. On October 25, 1989, Operation Enforcement was initiated.

SURVIVING A LEGAL CHALLENGE. Aware of the MTA's plans, advocates for the homeless had demanded two things from Kiley: "nooks and crannies" in which homeless could establish shelters and the right to panhandle. Kiley was firm as to both: no nooks and crannies; no panhandling. When program implementation began, advocates for homeless persons and the New York Civil Liberties Union confronted police in the subway almost nightly, appearing in stations in which many street people congregated as officers attempted to enforce the new rules. Many events were staged: a man would walk into a subway station followed by TV cameras, lawyers, and advocates. With cameras running, the man would lie in front of a turnstile, blocking access. An officer would ask him to move. When the offender refused, the officer would order him to move. Lawyers on the scene would challenge the authority of the officer to take action and attempt to involve him or her in a legal debate in front of the cameras. Such oft-repeated scenarios would end with the person being ejected or arrested, or with the officer simply moving away without taking action, not wishing to create another media event.

On November 28, 1990, two homeless men and their advocates challenged the NYCTA in federal district court with a class action suit, alleging that the free speech rights of homeless persons in the subway were being violated by Transit Authority regulations. Three weeks later, Federal District Court Judge Leonard Sand issued an oral order temporarily halting enforcement of the rule against panhandling. Since virtually all the materials that had been distributed in preparation for the program included the rule against panhandling, every poster and sign had to be removed from the subway and all other published material withdrawn from circulation. The ban on enforcement was made permanent in February 1990.[16]

The court's opinion in the case, *Young v. New York City Transit Authority*, gave full credence to the First Amendment speech rights that were claimed to be involved in begging and panhandling. According to First Amendment jurisprudence, legislation that restricts pure speech is presumptively unconstitutional, particularly where the government attempts to regulate on the basis of *content or viewpoint*. Content regulations are rarely permissible and generally held to a standard of strict scrutiny, requiring a compelling government interest and means that are narrowly tailored and necessary to achieving it.[17] The government has greater leeway when it attempts to impose *content-neutral* restrictions on speech, which are generally adjudged according to a lower "reasonableness" standard requiring only that restrictions be narrowly tailored to serve a significant government interest and leave open alternative channels for communication. A statute or ordinance subjected to this more lenient test has a greater chance of being upheld than one warranting strict scrutiny, which represents a considerable hurdle not only for legislation under equal protection analysis, but for a First Amendment challenge as well.

The First Amendment affords protection not merely for speech, but for expressive conduct as well, where the act and expression are "inex-

tricably joined," the action is undertaken with the intention of convey-
ing a specific message, and there is a reasonable likelihood that the
message will be understood by those viewing or receiving it.[18] First
Amendment protection applies to expressive conduct such as students
wearing black armbands to protest American involvement in the Vietnam War; burning an American flag during a protest rally; and picketing and parading in various settings.[19] Yet expressive conduct does not
receive the same degree of protection as pure speech, for the United
States Supreme Court has held that an important governmental interest in regulating the nonspeech element of expressive acts may sometimes justify incidental limitations on First Amendment freedoms.[20] In
these cases, a more lenient level of scrutiny is applied, requiring that a
regulation be within the constitutional power of government, further a
substantial government interest, be content-neutral, and be no greater
than is necessary to further the government's interest. As we noted
above, the level of scrutiny applied by a court is not merely academic,
but is an important predictor of whether the court will uphold legislation or strike it down as unconstitutional. Arriving at the appropriate
standard to be applied to particular legislation facing a First Amendment challenge depends, then, upon a determination of whether the
law restricts pure speech or expressive conduct, and whether the
restriction is content-neutral. It also depends upon two other factors:
the *forum* in which the speech occurs, and whether the legislation constitutes a valid *time, place, or manner restriction*.

Under forum analysis, the court must balance the government's
interest in restricting speech or acts on its property against the interests
of those seeking to use the property for expression, and the standard
used for judging whether a regulation of speech is permissible varies
with the character of the property.[21] In traditional *public fora*, primarily
streets and public parks, and in *designated fora*, those areas set aside for
use by the public for expressive purposes, the content of speech may be
regulated only where it is necessary to serve a compelling interest and
the restriction is narrowly tailored to that end—in other words, the
strict scrutiny standard must be met. But in a *nonpublic forum*, which is
an arena not set aside for public communication—a military base, a
sidewalk leading from a parking lot to the entrance of a U.S. Post

Office, an airport terminal operated by a public authority[22]—the government may regulate speech and expressive activity where necessary, in accord with the property's intended use, so long as the restriction is not directed at a particular viewpoint. And the court will judge such restrictions by a lower reasonableness standard. Finally, regardless of the forum in which they occur, various forms of expression protected under the First Amendment (whether oral, written, or symbolic action) may also be subject to *time, place, and manner* restrictions. So long as they are content-neutral, such restrictions are judged according to a reasonableness standard.[23]

These four elements of First Amendment jurisprudence—whether a regulation is content-neutral, whether it affects speech or expressive conduct, the type of forum in which the restriction applies, and whether it can be justified as a time, place, and manner restriction—developed as key elements in the *Young* case. And they remain at the core of virtually all judicial challenges to order-maintenance legislation today.

In the case of the Transit Authority regulations, Judge Sand found begging to be protected speech because it was indistinguishable from charitable solicitation. The Supreme Court has found that solicitation by organized charities implicates free speech interests because it is frequently intertwined with speech that informs about, or seeks support for, a particular cause or viewpoint: without the solicitation, "the flow of such information and advocacy would likely cease."[24] Although he found that the Transit Authority restrictions on begging were not content based, he contended that in effect the Authority had shown that the system could accommodate appropriate free expression, and explicitly permitted it by charitable organizations in some locations. Therefore, he treated the subway as a designated public forum. Considering then whether the regulation was a permissible time, place or manner restriction, he held that a *total* ban on begging and panhandling in the subway was not permissible, for it was not narrowly tailored; and the interests advanced by the Transit Authority—protecting the public from harassment, intimidation, and fraud—were not significant enough to justify restricting the rights of beggars. He cited other regulations not challenged in the case as permissible time, place, and manner restrictions—such as the prohibition of solicitation conducted in a manner reasonably intended to annoy, alarm, or inconvenience others, or that would constitute a breach of the peace.[25]

On the one hand, Judge Sand's ruling was a disaster. The police doubters and fencesitters had their day. Taking the posters down was an especially dispiriting exercise: the multitude of blank spaces where signs had been displayed gave tangible evidence of what appeared to be a major defeat. On the other hand, the editorial outcry that followed the decision was a surprise to almost everyone. Previous news and editorial comments had been extraordinarily cautious about the MTA's enforcement policies, and solicitous of the homeless. Yet Judge Sand's decision about panhandling apparently hit a raw nerve in New York City, for virtually every editorial opposed and/or ridiculed the decision. Editorial criticism ranged from careful analysis of the legal issues to "who is this suburban judge who has never ridden a subway to tell New Yorkers what we have to endure?" Enough was enough, order had to be restored to the subway.

The speed with which the MTA legal staff appealed the district court decision vindicated officers who had placed their trust in Gunn's and Kiley's pledges that they were determined to restore order, regardless of setbacks. Temporary relief from the court's decision was obtained in a few weeks. Moreover, the MTA appeal would ultimately be successful. The Second Circuit Court of Appeals disagreed with much of the district court's reasoning and overturned its decision, upholding the Transit Authority regulation prohibiting all begging and panhandling in the subway system, while permitting charitable solicitation by organizations in limited areas. Writing for the appeals court, Judge Altimari determined that begging was not speech: he disagreed with the district court's finding that begging should be entitled to protection as charitable solicitation, concluding instead that the dissemination of information, discussion, and advocacy of public issues furthered by charitable solicitation were not intertwined with the act of begging.[26] He noted in particular that Transit Authority regulations distinguished between the harmful effects caused by begging and First Amendment rights implicated in charitable solicitation as carried out by organizations by permitting solicitation in limited areas of the system. Even so, such action by the Transit Authority did not create a public forum. Judge Altimari accepted the Transit Authority's judgment that problems associated with begging and panhandling could not similarly be contained in limited areas, but could be addressed only through a complete ban.

Judge Altimari also addressed the issue of whether begging was deserving of First Amendment protection as *expressive conduct*, "inseparably intertwined" with a specific message.[27] His answer was no, based upon the reasoning that most individuals beg in order to collect money. If some beggars do intend to send a more specific message, such as about homelessness or the inadequacy of government benefits, he concluded it unlikely that subway passengers witnessing the conduct would discern the message, because circumstances in the subway would cause them to feel threatened and harassed instead.

Not stopping with his conclusion that begging was not expressive conduct, however, Judge Altimari proceeded to assess the permissibility of legislation regulating expressive conduct. His threshold inquiry clearly showed that the regulations at issue were not directed at suppressing the content of the expression; furthermore, he found substantial governmental interests in providing a safe environment and preventing intimidation and harassment, and held that "the only effective way to stop begging . . . was through . . . a total ban."[28] In reaching these conclusions, Judge Altimari relied heavily upon evidence presented by the Transit Authority from its own studies conducted in the transit system to evaluate "quality of life problems" experienced by riders. Passengers reported feeling continually harassed and intimidated by panhandlers, and objected to "unwanted touching, detaining, impeding, and intimidating" by beggars and panhandlers. Results of a second study, conducted by George Kelling, were also presented to the court: they suggested that lack of free mobility in the subway system due to physical space constraints on crowded platforms, ramps and stairways, and in trains, created a feeling of intimidation in passengers unable to move away when approached by panhandlers. The study found that real dangers for injury or accident were posed by an exhibition of threatening behavior in this setting.

Judge Altimari was able to conclude, then, that even if begging and panhandling did constitute protected expressive conduct, the Transit Authority regulation was not in violation of the First Amendment. On balance, he found the district court's analysis to reflect "an exacerbated deference to the alleged individual rights of beggars and panhandlers to the great detriment of the common good."[29]

THE LEADERSHIP CRISIS. While the battles in the courts over subway policies proceeded, the effort to deal with subway disorder on the ground was languishing by the end of 1989—numerous officers and mid-managers were simply ignoring their responsibilities. A January 1990 *New York Times* article described the effort as a failure. While this was premature—many police were trying to maintain order—things were not going well. From the outset, Kiley and Kelling were aware that while a study group with Kiley's support could devise a plan, formulate and implement a training program, and develop necessary supportive services, ultimately the leadership of the TPD police would have to drive policy. Despite the study group's requests for more "white shirts"—captains and above—to provide leadership in the subway akin to Gollinge's, especially at night when most of the confrontations with libertarians took place, they were rarely to be seen. Worsening the situation, the police union chimed in with explicit opposition to the plan. For management and the unions the business of the police was *law enforcement*. As one patrol officer angrily yelled at Kelling, "Where in the hell did you ever get the crazy idea that disorder was police business? Our job is fighting crime." His anger was fueled by a sense that he was being forced to do work beneath his, and policing's, dignity. It was quite clear that unless something radical happened in the TPD, efforts to restore order would wither within a matter of months.

In April 1990, William Bratton was recruited to lead the Transit Police Department (TPD). His mandate was to revitalize efforts to restore order to the subway. Moving quickly to energize the TPD, Bratton met with officers, created a tightly knit management team, reorganized the department, published a plan of action, fashioned a marketing plan for communicating with the public, and devised new subway tactics, while simultaneously seeming to be everywhere throughout the subway. In a telling move, Bratton promoted Richard Gollinge *three* ranks from captain to a one-star chief—an act unprecedented in New York City.

Central to all his actions was Bratton's clear sense of the new "business" of the TPD. Whether meeting with officers, speaking on a radio talk show, meeting with his command staff, or planning tactics, the theme of the new TPD mission permeated everything Bratton did and said. The theme had two elements. First, the mission of the TPD was "Taking Back the Subway for the People of New York."[30] Implicit in this motif were both an admission of serious problems—the subway had to be taken *back*—and a promise of action—the subway had to be *taken* back. Bratton conceded that the policies and practices of the Metropolitan Transportation Authority and its police departments had "lost" the subway and train stations to their then-current level of chaos. The problem was not just more youths, more homeless, more drugs and alcohol; the overall strategy of the MTA and the TPD had also failed to maintain order. Moreover, Bratton emphasized that the subway could be taken back by a substantial change in transportation and police strategy. Transit and police activity could restore order and prevent crime. The second element of Bratton's new theme was that the three problems plaguing the subway—farebeating, disorder, and robbery—were in reality one problem, linked conceptually and sequentially. To deal with one was to deal with all three.

Under Bratton, police activities to restore order increased immediately. Primarily, police were encouraged to inform citizens of their misbehavior, warn them if necessary, and eject them from the subway or arrest them if they persisted in violating subway rules or the law. Ejections for misbehavior *tripled* within a matter of months after Bratton took office and continued to escalate even after Michael O'Conner became chief of the TPD in 1992, as Figure 4.1 illustrates.

As Figure 4.2 demonstrates, arrests for minor crimes, misdemeanors, followed virtually the same pattern, jumping immediately after Bratton became chief in April 1990, and then continuing to escalate. At the same time, as Figure 4.3 indicates, fears that complaints about police aggressiveness would increase were unwarranted.

While restoration of order was a primary goal, great effort was also made to reduce farebeating. To ensure that these efforts were equitable, special anti-farebeating teams operated throughout the city: the well-to-do who refused to pay their fair were to be targeted as well as the poor. To ensure that tactics were not overly punitive, booking procedures were brought to arrest sites in the form of a "booking bus," to facilitate booking and release on the spot. After all, despite farebeating

**FIGURE 4.1**

*Ejections from the New York City Subway, Jan. 1987–July 1994*

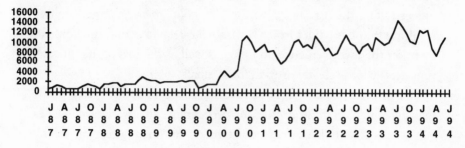

**FIGURE 4.2**

*Arrests, New York City Subway, Jan. 1987–July 1994*

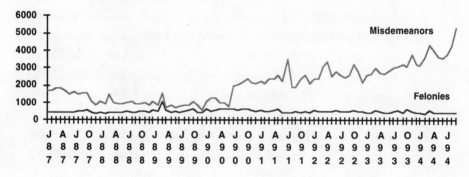

**FIGURE 4.3**

*Citizen Complaints about Police, New York City Subway, Jan. 1987–July 1994*

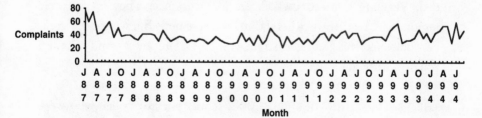

costing tens of millions of dollars in lost revenue, on a case-by-case basis farebeating amounted to a theft of $1.25. Routine booking procedures upon arrest as practiced in New York City at the time involved an officer taking the arrestee downtown to police headquarters, thereby resulting in the offender losing a whole day's income and time, not to mention the inconvenience and fine, as well as the loss of the officer's time on the job—clearly overkill for a "small" offense.

During the early days of the farebeating effort police discovered that a high percentage of those arrested for farebeating either were carrying illegal weapons or had warrants outstanding for their arrest on felony charges, many for crimes committed in the subway. In certain neighborhoods, as many as one arrestee in ten was either wanted on a felony charge or carrying an illegal weapon. This was an unexpected development. For while it had been anticipated that crime would decrease in tandem with declining levels of disorder, it came as a surprise that so many farebeaters would be carrying weapons or have outstanding warrants. Perhaps nothing so convinced police about the linkages among disorder, farebeating, and robberies as the finding, time and time again, that many farebeaters were robbers as well and offenders guilty of "disorderly acts." Consequently, when action was taken against farebeaters, serious crime dropped. And consequently also, police morale soared—they really could make a difference. Soon the farebeating-disorder-robbery trilogy was adopted by line police officers as part of a single effort. When Richard Vigilante, then editor of the Manhattan Institute's *City Journal*, was mugged outside a subway station, his assailant immediately fled into the station. A plainclothes anti-farebeating team was just inside the turnstiles and when the mugger, pursued by Vigilante calling for help, leapt over the turnstiles, he was immediately apprehended. When the dust settled, Vigilante thanked the officers for assistance. They immediately responded: "Yeah, it was a good thing we were here. But we got this great new chief and this great new strategy: robbery, farebeating, and disorder; you deal with one, you deal with all."

THE STATION MANAGER PROGRAM. It was not just police who were responsible for the changing conditions in the subways: civilians played an important role as well. Although the first steps targeting disorder in the subway were taken under Kiley and David Gunn, it was Alan Kiepper, then president of the NYCTA, who hired Bratton as chief of the Transit Police Department in April 1990. Gunn had left in early 1990 to take, in effect, a sabbatical. Kiepper shared with Kiley and Gunn a concern for restoring order, but believed that along with it an overall improvement should be made in the "quality of life" of the subway. Seeking ways to increase the user friendliness of the subway and improve conditions in subway stations, Kiepper created the post of station manager—relatively high-level and highly paid staff whose responsibility would be to coordinate all services provided to each station by the subway bureaucracy. Like most other governmental bureaucracies at this time, the NYCTA operated through departments organized functionally: thus, at each station, cleaning issues would be dealt with by one department, safety by another, repairs by yet another, and so on. No single individual was in charge of any particular station—until the position of station manager was created.

From the outset, station managers took seriously their responsibility to improve the quality of subway life. They were highly visible to passengers, especially during rush hours, providing information and reassurance that someone was "in charge." They were particularly aggressive in their insistence that subway users follow subway rules. Unstintingly, station managers chastised smokers, rebuked obstreperous youths, rousted persons who seemed to be "casing" toll booths (favorite robbery targets), warned persons who lay down that they were violating subway rules, and in other ways policed "their" stations. Moreover, they oversaw public toilets to ensure proper maintenance and prevent people from "hanging out" in them, and got burned-out lightbulbs replaced and cleaners quickly to the location of "spills."[31]

Although major stations such as Times Square, 34th Street, and 42nd Street (Grand Central Station), had their own assigned station managers, most subway stations had, at best, part-time oversight by station managers. And no station had a station manager for more than forty hours per week. Yet, station managers were extraordinarily effective in asserting authority over their stations. In effect, they provided three means of reasserting order and controlling crime in the subway. First, they were the equivalent of "shopkeepers" described by Jane Jacobs in *The Death and Life of Great American Cities*. With a deep vested interest in the viability of neighborhood streets, "storekeepers and other small businessmen are typically strong proponents of peace and order . . . ; they hate broken windows and holdups; they hate having customers made nervous about safety. They are great street watchers and sidewalk guardians."[32] "Owning" subway stations gave an urgency to the work of the station managers that was atypical in a bureaucratic organization. When lights were out in the 42nd Street station, this was not one lighting problem on the list of a centralized bureau head; for a station manager, it was *my* light is out in *my* station and *I* must get it taken care of. This ownership scenario was played out regarding signs, care and use of toilets, "hangers out," sprawled out drunks or addicts, and an infinite list of details affecting conditions in a station.

Additionally, station managers initiated and oversaw improvements in the environment that facilitated its control by police, other transit employees, and subway users themselves. A prime example was closing rarely used passageways and blocking access to remote sections of platforms—unused "nooks and crannies" that become locations for drinking, drug use, sexual and other such activities. Although station managers could not close such areas themselves, they were able to identify problems, and by their persistence focus the NYCTA's attention on the need for action to solve them.[33]

Finally, station managers' activities contributed to *situational crime prevention*, by reducing opportunities for crime.[34] Situational crime prevention concentrates not on the criminal or the origins of criminality, but on increasing the efforts that criminals must expend to commit successful crimes, increasing the risks criminals must take when they commit crimes, and reducing the rewards of criminal activities. In the subway, vandal-proofing the turnstile coin receptacles was an example of forcing increased efforts by criminals; greater surveillance by station managers increased criminals' risks; and elimination of graffiti reduced the rewards of criminals (they could not see their work).

The introduction of subway station managers, then, was a powerful adjunct to a series of moves to improve services and restore order in the subway. Although transit police played the key role, a total problem-solving approach, integrating the activities of various governmental agencies and departments, made the overall effort infinitely more effective.

For those concerned about the problem of disorder, fear, and crime in neighborhoods, it is fair to ask whether or not the subway experience with its crime problem can be generalized to community or neighborhood life. After all, a subway is substantially different from a community: the system is spatially bounded, with formal entrances and exits; as a system it is "simple" when compared to the complexity of a community; the system is set up to provide a single service; riders pay to use it; and they ride it for relatively short periods of time. Moreover, transit police are not constantly confronted with 911 calls for service, and consequently, they are free to deal with problems without constant interruption. It may be that in such a limited setting the impact of policing policies and practices will be more immediate and powerful, and therefore easier to measure.

But as it turned out, the subway experience would provide the blueprint for restoring order on the streets of New York City in two ways. First, the policies adopted for the Transit Authority provided the prototype for city-wide practices that would be developed and utilized by NYPD. Second, the person responsible for implementing the changes in the subway, William Bratton, would become the city's police commissioner under Mayor Rudolph Giuliani. And Bratton had learned two important tactical maxims in the subway that would hold him in good stead on city streets. Restoring order reduces crime. Moreover, crime is reduced at least in part because restoring order puts police in contact with persons who carry weapons and who commit serious crimes. These principles would be expanded in the New York City Police Department.

## TRANSFORMATION IN THE NYPD

Within the New York City Police Department, a reorientation toward crime control with a strong order-maintenance component was several years behind the Transit Authority experience. In fact, police treatment of panhandlers and an anti-begging section of the state penal code were challenged in court before the NYPD had even turned its attention to order maintenance. It was only when Police Commissioner Raymond Kelly launched an effort to combat squeegeeing in 1993 that the breakthrough in the NYPD's approach to disorder and quality-of-life issues occurred. When appointed commissioner, Bratton then went on to implement plans developed originally under Commissioner Kelly; but he would take even stronger steps to restore order in New York City.

Disorder was not an explicit and central concern for the NYPD during earlier administrations, even though previous commissioners did lay the groundwork for an order maintenance program. Commissioner Benjamin Ward (1984–89) started the Community Police Officer Program (CPOP); however, it was limited to a relatively small proportion of officers, and met considerable resistance throughout the department. Later, Mayor David Dinkins and Commissioner Lee Brown (1990–92) created a strategic plan to implement community policing city-wide that included the addition of 5,000 more police. In spite of the efforts of many individual officers, especially those in CPOP, to deal with problems of disorder, however, the NYPD culture viewed problems like squeegeeing, panhandling, and other petty crimes as beneath the dignity of self-respecting police.

## An Early Loss: Panhandling on the Streets

The NYPD's relative lack of concern about disorderly behavior during the late 1980s and early 1990s would create problems for it in the future, when the same advocates and attorneys who sued the New York City Transit Authority (NYCTA) pursued their anti–order-maintenance agenda further by filing suit against the City of New York for enforcing a section of the state penal code that prohibited "loitering for the purpose of begging." This statute was so rarely invoked that most police and city officials were largely unaware of its existence: a few officers had made a small number of arrests under the law, but panhandling was at the periphery of the NYPD's concern. Police officials were largely ignorant of the statute; training for enforcing it was nonexistent; and NYPD policy statements were silent concerning its enforcement—all factors that would weaken the city's case. When Kelling was asked by a representative of the city's Corporation Counsel to help prepare the defense, he found that the NYPD was standing largely aloof from the suit, providing minimal information. Only when Kelling called then First Deputy Commissioner Raymond Kelly, a friend and former student, and Kelly intervened, did the NYPD became fully involved.

The matter also appeared to be of little concern to Corporation Counsel interests, although those attorneys who handled the city's case were deeply committed to pursuing the issues raised in the lawsuit and developed significant expertise in the area.

The begging statute itself provided that a person was guilty of loitering when he "loiters, remains or wanders about in a public place for the purpose of begging."[35] As in the subway case, the suit against New York City was brought as a class action, by representatives of "needy persons" living in New York who begged on public streets or in public parks.[36] The individuals bringing the suit had themselves never been arrested under the statute for begging; they had merely been asked by police officers to "move along." The NYPD, as defendants, responded that the challenged statute was an essential tool in addressing disorderly conditions on the streets, for beggars tended to congregate in certain areas, becoming increasingly more aggressive and intimidating to residents and local businesses. Police described panhandlers stationing themselves in front of banks, bus stops, automated teller machines, and parking lots, frequently blocking sidewalks and following pedestrians with threats. Police further contended that panhandlers often moved on to committing more serious crimes, and that eventually neighborhoods could be ruined from the progression of criminal activity. In a striking departure from the reasoning of the appeals court in the NYCTA suit, Federal District Court Judge Robert Sweet struck down the statute, declaring it unconstitutional.

In contrast to the appeals court decision, Judge Sweet recognized begging as deserving of the same First Amendment protections as charitable solicitation, finding that both conveyed the same message to listeners. Further, he concluded that begging was expressive conduct, with an act and expression inextricably intertwined. Applying a time, place, and manner test for regulations that restricted protected speech in a public forum (on city streets), and the test for regulating expressive conduct, he found at the outset that the statute failed the content-neutrality standard since it discriminated between solicitation by an organized charity and a beggar. Judge Sweet concluded that this differential treatment was based upon the content of the message communicated by beggars, that social and economic conditions and opportunities forced some people to rely on begging to support themselves. Judge Sweet also found that the statute's total ban on begging left no alternative means of presenting this message.[37]

Judge Sweet spent considerable time in his opinion in balancing the various interests involved, including not only the interests of beggars and the government, but also those of the specific audience and the general public. The audience's interest, according to Judge Sweet, lay in receiving available information, especially about social conditions, in not being defrauded, and only to a lesser degree in being left alone. This last interest paled, according to Judge Sweet, alongside the overriding interest of the audience in receiving information and the ability of individuals to turn away, avert their eyes, refuse to respond, or in some other way to evade "captivity." Between audience and beggar, as between government or the public and "speaker," Judge Sweet found that the scales tipped in favor of the beggar communicating a message. Even the government's interest in maintaining public order, or preventing fraud, could not save the statute. Contesting data from studies that showed the link between disorderly behavior, such as begging and panhandling, and more serious crime, Judge Sweet wrote: "A peaceful beggar poses no threat to society. The beggar has arguably only committed the offense of being needy. The message one or one hundred beggars sends society can be disturbing . . . the answer is not in criminalizing these people . . . but addressing the root cause of their existence."[38]

The Second Circuit Court of Appeals affirmed the lower court's decision, finding that begging implicated First Amendment protection as expressive conduct or a communicative act.[39] Writing for the court, Judge Miner applied a strict scrutiny analysis, justified for a regulation that restricted speech on the basis of its content and in a public forum. He also reviewed the statute under the time, place, and manner test. It failed under all these measures. In particular, he found the state's interest insufficient to justify a complete ban on peaceful begging on public streets while leaving no alternative channels open for communication by beggars. He specifically contrasted the court's prior holding in *Young*, permitting restriction of begging in the subway, as justified by virtue of the special conditions in the subway system.[40] Similarly, Judge Miner referred approvingly to a Seattle ordinance that prohibited the obstruction of pedestrian or vehicular traffic and aggressive begging because it restricted specific conduct only, whereas the New York statute impermissibly prohibited verbal speech and communicative conduct.[41] It appeared that the NYPD was stopped before it could even begin to restrain panhandling.

## The First NYPD Success: Squeegeeing

Nonetheless, Commissioner Kelly (appointed by Mayor David Dinkins in 1992) wanted to do something about squeegeeing. Squeegeeing, or unsolicited washing of car windows, was widespread in New York City during the early 1990s. Squeegeemen operated in groups of three to six, with a few locations having as many as fourteen to sixteen, usually youths in their late teens or early twenties. The most popular locations for such activities were at entrances and exits to tunnels, bridges, and highways where cars were backed up, or at intersections. Some window-washers worked sites regularly, others only occasionally. Hard-working window washers claimed to earn $40 to $60 a day; some made over $100 a day if they persisted. At many sites, window-washing continued day and night, year around, although activity was heaviest during warmer months.

The behavior of squeegeers toward occupants of cars varied. Many squeegeers worked hard, running back and forth between cars, even climbing on the bumpers of trucks to wash windows. Some appeared good natured, clowning around and verbally sparring with each other and with drivers, generally behaving in ways that they believed citizens would not find threatening. If drivers waved them off or turned windshield wipers on to dissuade them, many squeegeers would retreat. Nevertheless, others behaved in a manner clearly calculated to menace: if drivers said no to them, these squeegeers would drape themselves over the hoods of cars to prevent them from moving, even after traffic lights changed. Some squeegeers would spread soapy water or spit on car windows, leaving them dirty and streaked. Often two, three, or even four window washers would swarm around a car, washing all the windows in spite of the driver's protests. A few squeegeers appeared to be mere pathetic hangers-on, burnt out and seriously under the influence of alcohol, drugs, or both, staggering bewilderedly between cars, gesticulating at drivers and passengers. Carrying only rags or newspapers, they rarely washed windows or received "tips."

Commissioner Kelly contacted Kelling during the summer of 1993 to aid the NYPD in getting control of squeegeeing. Kelly himself had recently been "serviced" by squeegeemen, one of whom had spit on his windshield, while driving into the city with his wife. Acknowledging his own rage and frustration, Kelly appreciated how threatened and power-less citizens felt after such assaults. Using a problem-solving approach akin to that followed the subway's study group, Kelling and NYPD staff, then Assistant Chief Michael Julian, and Sergeant Steve Miller began their work by unobtrusively observing and videotaping squeegeemen. They had plain-clothes officers drive an unmarked car through inter-sections to make it available for window washing, interviewed "squeegee-men" and neighborhood police officers, and examined police department criminal records. Background information on the squeegeemen arrested during the study period provided a picture simi-lar to that gained in the Transit Authority. The popular conception of squeegeemen was a group of homeless individuals simply "down on their luck." Norman Siegel, head of the New York Civil Liberties Union, urged that political leaders "could better solve the problem by providing apartments and jobs to those who squeegee."[42] Yet the data collected on squeegeers portrayed a different scenario: of those arrested during a sixty-day experimental period, approximately three-quarters had legitimate addresses at which they resided; half had previous arrests for serious felonies such as robbery, assault, burglary, larceny, or carrying a gun; and almost half had previous arrests for drug-related offenses. Squeegeers were not merely a troubled population, they were capable of considerable mayhem. Citizens had good reason to be fearful.

Dealing with squeegeemen had proven to be an extraordinarily frus-trating job for the few police officers who took it seriously. Because offi-cers in cars and special units ignored squeegeeing, neighborhood officers were left to deal with the problem. Yet when they did so, the officers received only scorn from other officers who viewed squeegeeing as unworthy of police efforts or attention. Even more chafing for conscien-tious officers was the response of squeegeers. Since squeegeeing was a minor infraction, it was punishable only by a fine or community service. Consequently, officers were limited to giving squeegeers Desk Appear-ance Tickets (DATs), known derisively by New York police as "Disap-pearance Tickets" because offenders generally failed to appear to pay their fines, and warrants for arrest that were issued subsequent to non-appearance were never served. As in most departments, warrants issued for nonappearance were sent to a central warrant-service unit, where they were relegated low priority as against a flood of warrants outstanding on more "serious" matters. Squeegeers learned this quickly, and would all but tell officers to "Keep your DAT, I've got plenty of them."

A simple comment by a patrol lieutenant proved to be the key to solving the problem. His suggestion—"If only we [neighborhood officers] could get the warrants for nonappearance for the DATs"—made sense, for while squeegeeing was not a jailable offense, nonappearance was. While a DAT for a minor offense might not mean much to a central warrant bureau, it meant a great deal to officers trying to restore order to neighborhoods, who were being responded to with scorn and derision. Arrangements were made with Paul Schectman, then counsel to Manhattan District Attorney Robert Morganthau and now New York State's Commissioner of Criminal Justice, to have warrants for nonappearance for squeegeeing flagged and sent directly to the officer who had issued the DAT in the first place. Thus, when an officer served a DAT for squeegeeing and the offender did not appear, that officer could make an immediate arrest, and jail time would follow. With punishment swift and certain, squeegeeing died out in a matter of weeks.

## A New Mission for the NYPD

The anti-squeegee campaign took place during the 1993 Dinkins-Giuliani mayoral campaign, when squeegeeing became a metaphor for all that was wrong with New York City. Rudolph Giuliani ran for office as a strong anticrime candidate. A former federal prosecutor, he laid claim to a special competence for dealing with New York City's crime problem; like many other local political leaders he was also "streetwise," and understood the consequences of disorder and fear in New York City. And he appointed Bratton as Police Commissioner of New York.

Several factors made Giuliani's choice of Bratton to head the NYPD a key to dealing with disorder in New York City. First, the new commissioner would have to make major changes inside the NYPD itself. As an outsider, Bratton was fully prepared to do this. Most of the NYPD command staff had been in place since the mid-1980s. Moreover, in 1993 the department was being racked by a series of corruption scandals that, while not implicating command staff, nonetheless suggested that a "hunkering-down" mentality had developed in the upper levels of the department, discouraging sergeants and mid-managers from bringing forward charges of corruption or abuse. Many in policing believed that a "stay out of trouble," do-nothing mentality had developed in the ranks of the department as well. The department was described by many as a bloated, inefficient bureaucracy that was controlling neither crime nor its officers very well. And although the department had made a commitment to community policing on paper, it was still deeply mired in a narrow law-enforcement strategy. Aside from being an outsider, Bratton's success in implementing a preventive order-maintenance strategy in the Transit Police Department (TPD), as well as reorganizing and energizing the department itself, made him a logical candidate for the commissioner's job in a Giuliani administration.

On taking over the NYPD, Bratton adapted and then implemented many of the techniques conceived by aggressive chief executive officers (CEOs) in both the public and private sectors to strategically reposition their organizations. He also repeated many of the tactics he had used as TPD head. He devolved authority from the fifty-five top-level chiefs downward to precinct commanders, primarily captains. At the same time he made it clear that precinct commands would be given only to the best and brightest captains, and that future promotions would come from this pool of precinct captains. As this message was disseminated in the NYPD, many precinct commanders retired, giving Bratton the flexibility to assign young and aggressive captains to command precincts: the average age of precinct commanders dropped from the sixties to the forties.

Bratton initiated a number of other moves, including gaining control of a runaway budget, especially for its spending on overtime; improving training for officers; using task forces to study departmental problems; involving precinct commanders in corruption control; and surveying officers to determine their views about improving the department and the quality of their working conditions. He reduced the number of special units, and developed a variety of internal communication channels (such as videos and internal newsletters) for sending information from himself and other key personnel directly to line officers. And finally, the new commissioner established clear, measurable goals for the department, which he communicated to the public by publishing seven strategic plans that covered everything from improving the quality of life in the city to managing domestic violence and controlling corruption.

While all of these changes were important, and many comprise the standard approaches of leaders trying to reinvigorate moribund organizations, Bratton was also implementing nothing less than a new strategy of policing—community policing. Embodied in the new strategy was a strong, simple, and straightforward message about the business of the organization and the function of policing. And fundamental to the new strategy was the development of greater accountability to the community and involvement in solving local problems.

Bratton's message about the business of the NYPD in a community policing strategy focuses on crime. The logic is this: first, even though policing involves broad and numerous functions, the *core function* of police is crime control, aimed at disorder, fear, and index crime. Second, police have the capability for preventing crime. Third, officers must be both aggressive and respectful in their activities: being aggressive in crime control does not require being combative, nor does being respectful of citizens embody weakness. Finally, although comprehensive organizational change is likely to take years, gains in crime control will accrue rapidly if police are energized and carefully directed. For Bratton, community policing can be "hard on crime," and he is convincing police officers as well as the public that he may be right.

Community policing as Bratton conceives it is a far cry from community policing as seen by many other police leaders, who couch their descriptions in "soft," social science terms. In their view, community policing is antithetical to the "crime-fighting" function that defined the role of police for decades. Faced with this notion of community policing, many police officers find unpalatable what they believe is in store for them if they adopt it: a strategy that is soft on crime, has little impact on it, emphasizes social work, cares more about the rights of offenders than the interests of the community, and is in the "grin and wave" tradition of community relations. Bratton had to convince officers otherwise, and so he did, in both the TPD and the NYPD.

Bratton's approach starts where officers stand in their own thinking, that is with *crime*, and then attempts to move them beyond their traditional, narrow law-enforcement view. By communicating to police what we know about the links between disorder, fear, and crime, and helping them to interpret it in relation to their own street experiences, Bratton has steered the NYPD into some initial successes similar to those achieved by the transit police. Squeegeeing was a quick win and immediately attracted the attention of the public as well as that of the officers themselves. And, just as searching farebeaters in the subway yielded weapons and sent a message through the TPD that fighting disorder was effective as a means of addressing crime generally, so similar accounts are making their way throughout the NYPD: a person arrested for urinating in a park, when questioned about other problems, gave police information that resulted in the confiscation of a small cache of weapons; a motorcyclist cited for not wearing a helmet, on closer inspection, was carrying a nine-millimeter handgun, had another in his sidebag, and had several high-powered weapons in his apartment; a vendor selling hot merchandise, after being questioned, led police to a fence specializing in stolen weapons. These stories made concrete the importance of dealing with minor problems in order to forestall major problems. Just as every farebeater was not a felon, not every petty criminal is a serious criminal; yet enough are, or have information about others who are, that contact with petty offenders alerts all criminals to the vigilance of the police and gives police legitimate access to information about more serious problems.

To implement his community policing strategy successfully, Bratton needed simultaneously to empower his new precinct heads and to create a means for holding them fully accountable. The process developed to serve these two ends—Crime Control Strategy Meetings—rivets the attention of managers on what is happening in the neighborhoods for which they are responsible, thereby creating another sense of accountability to the local community. Each Wednesday and Friday, from 8:00 to 11:00 A.M., NYPD precinct commanders from one of the five boroughs convene in the command center at One Police Plaza, the NYPD's central headquarters, for these meetings. Also present are Deputy Commissioner for Crime Control Jack Maple, the NYPD's chiefs of patrol (Louis Anemone) and detectives (Charles Reuther), all five borough commanders, and representatives from schools, district attorneys' offices, and the parole department.

The format for each meeting is the same: in turn, each precinct commander, accompanied by a detective lieutenant and other representatives of the precinct, takes the floor to report formally on current conditions in the precinct, including problems related to disorder, crime prevention and control, efforts being undertaken by the district police to address them, and results. Portrayed overhead on a large screen for all to see are precinct data on index crimes, numbers and geographical distribution of arrests, shooting victims and incidents, precinct residents on parole who have outstanding felony or parole warrants, and whatever other data are available that reflect on the quality of life in the district. Data are organized by week, month, and year to date and are compared with the previous year's statistics. The precinct commander is questioned by Deputy Commissioner Maple and others present about specific problems: rapes may be up; robberies staying at high levels; grand larcenies down—and precinct commanders have learned that they must not only be intimately familiar with the data looming over their heads, but must be able to "unpack" them when queried. Officers from other precincts may offer suggestions to the solution of particularly troublesome problems arising from their own experiences or may share information about a common problem. The themes that continually shape the discussion are Bratton's four guiding methods of crime control: accurate and timely intelligence; rapid deployment; effective tactics, and relentless follow up and assessment. Finally, each presentation generally closes with the introduction of a patrol officer or officers who have been particularly resourceful in dealing with some neighborhood problem—as likely a quality-of-life issue as any other crime problem.

The Crime Control Strategy Meetings have sparked the New York City Police Department. In an elegant and simple way they constitute a process that embodies the decentralization of authority to precinct commanders, establishes the terms of accountability, dramatizes the department's new procedures for providing services to communities, and reinforces Bratton's vision of policing. Most importantly, the seriousness of the meetings, the status of those required to attend, the presence of their peers, the incessant grilling and challenges, and the

high visibility of the process force precinct commanders to focus attention constantly on their neighborhoods.

With these changes, the NYPD has undergone a major reorientation
and reorganization, embracing fully a quality-of-life approach to crime
prevention and control. While all the elements of organizational
change are not yet in place, the NYPD has gone through a substantial
shift in its strategy, a shift that is no longer merely nominal, supported
only by the highest levels of command and in a few isolated outposts in
the department. Capitalizing on early wins and considerable reductions
in serious crime, the new leadership is changing not only the structure
of the NYPD, but its entire culture.

Recently these gains faced a new threat, this time not by court challenges, but by bureaucratic court representatives who, in the name of
"clearing the docket" of a backlog of court cases, managed to slip into
the state budget a provision that would virtually decriminalize all
minor offenses by removing them from the jurisdiction of the state
criminal courts.[43] In effect, this provision strips the city of the authority
to arrest persons who refuse to respond to citations for minor misdeeds,
say, for example, squeegeeing. Recall that the only measure finally
bringing squeegeeing under control was the reality that squeegeers
would be arrested and go to jail if they did not pay their fines. Decriminalizing such offenses robs police of their "or else"—the authority to
arrest persons who persist in illegal disorderly conduct. It is impossible
to exaggerate the extent to which this move undermines the ability of
police to restore and maintain order. By slipping this provision into
state law, court officials, intentionally or not, played directly into the
hands of radical libertarians who would perpetuate urban chaos in the
name of "liberty interests" and exaggerated fear of police abuses.

## THE NEW URBAN CONSENSUS AND BROAD-BASED
## QUALITY-OF-LIFE INITIATIVES

The legal anomaly noted immediately above aside, increasingly, police
initiatives in order maintenance and crime prevention are merging and
being coordinated with efforts taken in the private and public sector.
Working cooperatively with representatives of the New York Civil Liberties Union, the New York City Council and NYPD have drafted an

aggressive panhandling ordinance to replace the begging law that was invalidated in the *Loper* decision.[44] Introduced before the City Council on October 12, 1994, the proposed ordinance is modeled on Washington, D.C.'s 1993 aggressive panhandling ordinance.[45] It prohibits in public places such acts as: approaching, speaking to, or following a person in connection with soliciting (including asking or begging) for donations, or the sale of goods or services, where the conduct is intended or likely to cause a reasonable person to fear bodily harm, damage, or loss of property, or to be intimidated into giving; continuing to solicit after a negative response has been given; intentionally touching a person without consent while soliciting, or intentionally blocking or interfering with that person's passage as a pedestrian or in a vehicle; and using violent or threatening gestures toward a person being solicited. In addition, soliciting within twenty feet of an automated teller machine or check-cashing business, or on private property, without permission from the owner, is also proscribed. And finally, operators and occupants of motor vehicles on streets may not be approached for soliciting or the sale of a good or service.[46]

This new legislation reflects a distinct evolution in the approach of New York City government to quality-of-life issues, which have shifted to center stage in the Giuliani administration. Similar movement, if more tentative, is occurring in other arenas. For example, quality-of-life crimes are the focus of a unique new community court established in 1993 as a three-year, public-private, experimental effort to bring justice back into the community.[47] The Midtown Community Court, located next to the Midtown North Police Precinct Station, operates in the Times Square neighborhood of Manhattan. It is an arraignment court for quality-of-life crimes committed in the community—misdemeanors such as shoplifting, prostitution, graffiti, low-level drug possession, petty larceny, and unlicensed vending. Those who plead not guilty go to trial at a downtown criminal court; however, approximately 70 percent of those arraigned plead guilty, and are sentenced at the community court. Roughly 80 percent of all sentences contain orders for performing community service in the neighborhood in which the crimes were committed (usually beginning immediately or within twenty-four hours), for enrolling in social service programs, or both; other sentences may include jail time, counseling sessions, or drug treatment.[48] Using a computer-generated database, the court has immediate access to records on each defendant (covering arrest information, criminal record, and prior record of compliance, history of substance abuse, mental illness, employment, and housing information) for use in sentencing, so that sanctions can be "matched" to a defendant.[49] The court also monitors the progress of each defendant sentenced and requires periodic appearances by offenders when sentences include ongoing treatment or service. Compliance rates for community treatment and short-term social services are high—77 and 72 percent respectively—and those who fail to appear for community service are rearrested quickly and sentenced to jail.

The court's successful operation rests upon close collaboration with police in the three precincts covered by the court's jurisdiction and with the community. A community advisory committee made up of residents, attorneys working in the area, administrators of social service providers, and officials of quasi-governmental agencies keeps the court informed of neighborhood problems and concerns, and aids in marshaling local resources required to provide social service support and community service projects. More than fifteen local groups supervise community service projects to which offenders are sentenced, including various cleaning and beautification activities in public spaces (streets, parks, the Port Authority Bus Terminal, and subway stations), feeding the homeless at soup kitchens, painting housing units managed by a housing development corporation, painting over or removing graffiti on buildings, stuffing envelopes for nonprofit organization mailings, and cleaning the courthouse itself. Instead of being arraigned and rapidly returning to the streets to commit further crimes, the majority of offenders moving through the Midtown Community Court perform immediate and visible service to the local community as restitution for their offenses. Punishment is swift and certain, and meaningful to both the defendant and the community. Following their performance of community service and involvement in counseling, a number of former offenders actually have become volunteers at the courthouse or in court-affiliated work projects.

The Midtown Community Court has strong support from New York's criminal court administrative judge Robert Keating, who facilitated its organization, the Mayor's Office, as well as local community residents and businesses. Both command and line officers from the

NYPD are also enthusiastic proponents. The Manhattan District Attorney, however, remains critical of the substantial resources devoted to the Midtown Court's operation compared with other criminal courts.[50] Indeed, funding is an ongoing concern for this type of project, for the Midtown Court must marshal significant appropriations from public and private (including corporate) sources to keep itself in operation beyond the initial three years. And although the court has been successful enough that a second community court is planned for the Red Hook section of Brooklyn, a community containing nearly 8,000 public housing residents, this second court will materialize only if sufficient funds can be raised. Clearly, the results of programs targeted at quality-of-life issues will need to justify continued, or greater, expenditures in support of order restoration and maintenance. Fortunately, the results to date are not only positive and affirming of current efforts, they are in some respects truly astonishing.

## ASSESSING THE RESULTS OF RESTORING ORDER

For those who live and work in New York City today, the changes in the subway and on many streets and public places are palpable as order is restored to the city. Graffiti is gone from subway trains. The facilities of Grand Central Terminal, Penn Station, and the Port Authority Bus Terminal have changed dramatically: one has only to walk through one of these stations to feel the difference, see the cleanliness, and notice that a sense of mutual respect now characterizes citizen interaction. Bryant Park has been restored and is a joyous place. Central Park has been largely reclaimed. Squeegeemen are off the streets. People who left the city during the late 1980s and now return to visit are stunned by the differences in the subways, parks, and on the streets. News articles about New York regularly highlight the improvements. In sum, independent of statistics, the experiences of citizens in New York are changing. Where many used to find life in New York City an unrelenting hassle, they now feel a renewed sense of urban pleasure.

And while change is clearly evident in terms of quality of life and a reduction in low-level crimes and incidents of disorder, a new development is the dramatic reduction as well in index crime, as reflected not only by what citizens experience but also in the crime statistics. Declines

FIGURE 4.4

*New York City Subway Felonies and Robberies, 1988–1994*

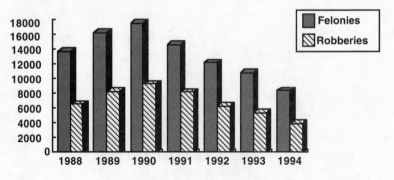

in crime in the subway began immediately after the institution of an order-maintenance strategy by Bratton in 1990 and have continued to the present time. Figure 4.4 illustrates the increases both in all felonies (including robberies) and in robberies, perhaps the felony of greatest concern in the subway, prior to 1990; it also indicates the decreases that began the next year and have continued since. These are startling statistics, unparalleled in the crime control literature: since the institution of an aggressive order-maintenance strategy, *felonies have declined 75 percent and robberies 64 percent.* In effect serious crime has ceased to be a major problem in New York's subways.

Although the order-maintenance program in the subway was not introduced or studied experimentally, at least two factors suggest that order-maintenance activities caused a reduction in crime. First, the onset of declines in crime occurred almost immediately after Bratton introduced the police order-maintenance activities. Second, although administrative and organizational alterations were plentiful in the Transit Police Department, *tactical* changes were limited to targeting on farebeating and restoring order: no major anti-robbery or felony tactics were introduced. Are the changes in crime rates solely the result of police efforts? No, not likely. We believe that, most likely, they have come about as a result of the Metropolitan Transportation Authority's total commitment to order restoration, which included eliminating graffiti, "target hardening" (that is, making targets less accessible), assertion of civilian control over territory through the station managers program, as well as police efforts.

FIGURE 4.5

*New York City Murder Rates, 1988–1994*

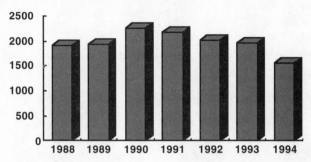

This same pattern is now visible in New York City as a whole, where in 1995 citizens were less likely to be victimized than at any time since 1970. Figures 4.5 and 4.6 illustrate the significant declines that have occurred in violent crime, noticeable especially in 1994, during Bratton's first year as commissioner. Some of these declines are unprecedented. For example, the drop in the murder rate is without historic parallel in cities throughout the United States. During 1994, homicide declined nationally by 5 percent, while the decline in New York City was 17 percent. Moreover, robberies declined in 1994 to their lowest rate since 1973. Assault declined as well. Preliminary statistics for 1995 suggest that the rate of decline in all categories of violent crime is even steeper than in 1994.[51]

As with declines in crimes against persons, property crimes have also

FIGURE 4.6

*New York City Robberies and Assaults, 1988–1994*

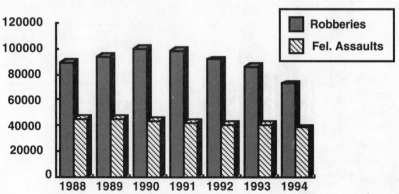

decreased in New York, shown in Figure 4.7. In 1994 the burglary rate was down from 1993 levels by 10.9 percent; larceny 10.8 percent; and motor vehicle theft 15.2 percent. Preliminary reports from 1995 again indicate that the rates of decline are accelerating.

Aside from looking at the data themselves, we can also test our conclusion that order-maintenance efforts have led to reductions in crime generally by returning to the perceptions of citizens in New York. Most believe that something quite profound is happening in their town. While the citizens with whom we have spoken may not represent a random sample, there is little doubt that for them the quality of life in New York City is improving appreciably. One survey has a particularly suggestive finding. The widely reported Quinnipiac College poll regularly reports the most important concerns of New Yorkers. Its most recent findings were presented in a November 6, 1995, press release: "For the first time in a Quinnipiac College poll, New Yorkers list unemployment as the 'most important problem facing New York State today.' In April, New Yorkers listed taxes. In prior polls, New Yorkers always had listed crime as the biggest problem."[52] Adding up the changes in the subways and parks, as well as in the streets in many areas, over the last five years New York has become a much different place. We suggest that order-restoration efforts are a significant reason.

Because New York is a media center, and because the order-maintenance activities there are the cornerstone of police crime-control activities, considerable controversy has developed over whether or not Bratton's policies are responsible for New York City's widely reported

FIGURE 4.7

*New York City Property Crimes, 1988–1994*

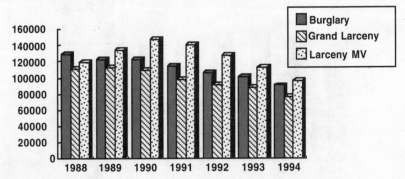

reductions in crime. Within criminology circles, this debate has been rigorous indeed. The issue of whether crime is declining as a result of police actions raises some of the thorniest problems of causality in social science. How do we know that crime has actually dropped? Are the "books being cooked"? Are citizens changing their reporting habits, say out of concern for corruption? Are the changes a temporary blip that over time will return to previous "normal" levels? If crime has dropped, how can the effect be parsed out? What role does sentencing play? The increase in prisons? Are there structural changes in society—say changes in poverty levels—that could be responsible for the shifts? These and other legitimate questions abound.[53]

This debate has also been rancorous, because deep-seated ideologies are involved. One side argues that poverty, racism, and social injustice cause crime, and since police can do little about these structural features of society they will never be able to do much about crime either.[54] An alternative and more optimistic view, to which we subscribe, asserts that addressing the "root causes" of crime, whatever they may be, need not be the only way of reducing crime itself: in fact, regardless of the causes of crime, police can, through the use of the proper strategy and a variety of tactics, affect crime rates. The key question for those who espouse this latter view is whether and how police can help to create the conditions in neighborhoods and communities that will allow other institutions—the family, neighborhood, church, community agencies and government, and commerce—to deal with these basic problems of society.

We believe the statistics reflecting current drops in index crime in New York City illustrate just these processes and effects. Specifically, our confidence that the crime reductions in New York City are real and have to do with police and community actions rests on a line of reasoning that goes something like this: prepare a city for twenty years; develop strong community movements; organize BIDs and private security; clean up the mess in the subway; restore parks (often privately, and keep them under private oversight); develop a community court and close linkages with prosecutors; and then have a new mayor and police commissioner walk in and say to the city, "Oh by the way, I have 38,000 police that I am going to assign to work with you and hold them closely accountable both for results and their behavior." In such circumstances, we would be surprised if crime did not drop.

Many of the initiatives for restoring order in New York City exist in cities throughout the country. For a movement is gaining ground. This movement represents a basic shift away from the 1960s "criminal justice system" model, with its intolerance of citizen and private input into maintaining order and controlling crime, and its insistence that such matters are best left to professionals. To be sure, the move toward community collaboration and accountability is at this stage far from efficient and lacks refinement. But citizen initiatives are visible everywhere, as grass-roots involvement, through neighborhood organizations, citizen advisory councils, and crimewatch groups. Private and corporate security organizations are reaching out to establish new relationships with citizens and with public sector agencies. Community- and problem-oriented prosecution, courts, and corrections efforts, widely dispersed and in their infancy, are affecting community efforts unevenly. Yet, there is hardly a city in which the outlines of a community-based crime prevention paradigm are not apparent.

The shift to a community-based, problem-oriented approach to maintaining order and reducing crime, as promising as it is for cities, contains real dangers. The "system" model was reactive: as such, it used authority narrowly and frugally. The community model is active and interventionist, involving police intimately in neighborhoods as they attempt to solve problems before they worsen, and to some degree justifying intervention by citizens, directed at crime prevention, as well. Such actions by police and citizens must arise out of a broader base of authority and wider network of collaboration. How such use of authority is to be controlled so as to protect the fundamental rights of all citizens is a major issue in a democratic society.

C H A P T E R  5

# COMMUNITY-BASED CRIME PREVENTION

THE STARTLING CHANGES IN THE NEW YORK CITY SUBWAY AND other public spaces such as Bryant Park, and what appears to be a replication of the subway success above ground, all have drawn considerable attention worldwide to New York City's order-restoration efforts and current experiment in policing. Political and police leaders from Singapore to California and from Saudi Arabia to England have visited the NYPD, many specifically to attend crime-control strategy meetings. Yet criminologists and academics are still debating how much, if any, of New York's recent crime reduction can be attributed to aggressive order maintenance and police rejuvenation. Responding to Mayor Giuliani's and Commissioner Bratton's tough talk on disorder and crime, some have suggested that New York City is returning to the old-fashioned "police are in-charge, citizens sit back while crime fighters define and solve problems" mentality. Others, convinced that Bratton is making significant advances in implementing community policing, nonetheless worry that the media and a number of political and police leaders and academics are putting the wrong spin on what is happening in the city, thereby jeopardizing important and valuable strategic shifts in policing.

All of this begs the question "What constitutes community policing?" When departments tack overtime foot or bicycle patrol onto an otherwise unchanged 911 strategy—even with a specific mandate to restore order in certain neighborhoods—does this constitute community policing? Does having eight or so community officers out of a total of 400 police officers mean that a department has implemented community policing? Is aggressive order maintenance coupled with a strong anticrime orientation, as undertaken by the NYPD, antithetical to community policing? For many these are serious questions, since community policing has come to mean all things to all people. Others believe that community policing is no more than an undefinable set of concepts and a public relations con intended to restore unwarranted public confidence in a seriously tarnished and disgraced occupation. While these critics are wrong in their basic premise—that community policing is undefinable—they do make one valid point. Overtime foot patrol or a small number of community officers by themselves simply do not constitute community policing. In reality, community policing is nothing less than a completely new paradigm, in which a focus on crime prevention replaces the old reactive policing model.

Community policing must necessarily take a variety of forms, since individual communities or even districts within cities will emphasize different elements to reflect discrete local needs, traditions, and values. Regardless of how it is implemented, however, community policing requires the restoration of public order and the involvement of police in order maintenance.

## COMMUNITY POLICING, AGGRESSIVE ORDER MAINTENANCE, AND QUALITY-OF-LIFE ISSUES

Essentially, the changes currently underway in the NYPD are congruent with the basic elements of community policing. What are these fundamental tenets?

The first is belief in a broad policing function, embracing more than law enforcement in response to felonies. Police work includes keeping the peace and public order, protecting constitutional liberties, ensuring security, resolving conflicts, assisting persons who are in danger or cannot help themselves, managing problems that endanger citizens and/or communities, and responding to emergencies. When street people take over parks and make them unusable by families and children—as happened in

San Francisco—this is a police problem, even if street people are not committing major crimes. Historically, police have always had many of these responsibilities, which are essential to the prevention of crime and protection of citizens and communities.

Community policing also acknowledges the reliance of police on citizens, in multiple senses: for authority to police neighborhoods, for information about the nature of neighborhood problems, and for collaboration in solving problems. In the Boyd Booth neighborhood of Baltimore, for example, citizens had to be intensely involved with police to regain control of streets from drug dealers. This does not mean that police do not initiate actions on their own. Where citizens are unaware of the existence of certain problems, or a neighborhood is so far out of control that citizens cannot organize on their own behalf, police will need to take the lead, acting on behalf of citizens.

Community policing recognizes that organizational structures and administrative processes that treat officers like factory workers have failed. Police work, unlike factory work, is not simple and routine, but complex; it is usually conducted by one or two officers in the field, without direct oversight, who must use considerable discretion in handling problems. When officers confront complex life and death decisions, success depends not on direct supervision or rote application of specific rules, but on the application of general knowledge and skill, obtained through prolonged education and mentoring, to specific situations. Community policing aims to develop administrative techniques that recognize this complexity in the work of police officers. Sergeants, for example, become mentors and coaches, not overseers. Their focus is on assisting officers in solving neighborhood problems, not adherence to organizational rules.

Along the same lines, community policing eschews *general tactics*, like preventive patrol and rapid response to calls for service, in favor of *specific tactics*, targeted on particular problems and developed in collaboration with citizens and city, governmental, and private sector agencies. Squeegeeing in New York City was not eliminated by "sending a police car," but through the collaboration of prosecutors and police, and the judicious use of warrant service. Solving a larger problem, disorder in the subway, demanded an integrated effort by a plethora of units and agencies—from public relations departments to station managers to social service agencies. Eradicating graffiti in the subway succeeded through mutual commitments from maintenance units and prosecutors, as well as subway officers.

Because problems are most often local—requiring identification and crafting of responses at this level—authority must be devolved to lower levels of the police organization if a department is to be responsive to neighborhood needs. Beats, areas, and/or districts should therefore be congruent with neighborhood and community boundaries and police personnel should be assigned to such geographical units on a relatively stable basis. Attempting to deal with neighborhood problems by using special units as opposed to local patrol units is not always effective, for all other things being equal, patrol units with their closer linkages to citizens and neighborhoods are best equipped to manage problems in accord with neighborhood standards. Neighborhood officers in New York City resolved the squeegeeing problem, not special units. Special police units and efforts were required in Baltimore's Boyd Booth neighborhood to *establish* control, but regular neighborhood and foot patrol officers were required to maintain it.

Community policing recognizes that police serve multiple aims, as reflected in their broad functions. Crime reduction is certainly one priority; others include policing in accordance with the law as well as properly in civil and moral terms, reducing fear, protecting neighborhoods, and helping citizens manage problems. The broadest goal is to help communities maintain a safe environment, in which basic institutions (the family, churches, schools, commerce) can operate effectively and thrive. Establishing the priority of goals, and selecting the means to obtain them, whether by individual police officers in a neighborhood or by precinct commanders in a community, requires the exercise of considerable discretion—the logic of which should be developed under public scrutiny.

In virtually every dimension, the shifts in the NYPD's strategy are consistent with these basic tenets of community policing. Functions have been broadened, and explicitly include order maintenance; police officials are collaborating with citizen groups and private security to prevent crime; substantial amounts of new authority have been devolved to precinct commanders to achieve neighborhood goals. Is the NYPD now fully implementing community policing? No, but like many other departments it is moving in this direction—probably more rapidly than most.

Nevertheless, in its emphasis on *aggressive order maintenance*, the NYPD appears to some to have moved outside the pale of community policing and to be involved in a revival of reform-model policing. Several elements of the NYPD's current program might appear at first glance to support such a conclusion. First, the department has relied explicitly on aggressive order-maintenance activities as a cornerstone of its overall strategy. Commissioner Bratton has attempted to energize officers at least in part by using language that resonates with them—for example, community policing can be "tough on crime." Bratton's tough talk in this regard, especially in the context of Mayor Giuliani's hard line on crime, is worrisome to many both within and outside of policing who fear that aggressiveness is or will become combativeness, especially in minority communities. With some exceptions, advocates of community policing generally have been reluctant to emphasize the crime control capabilities of community policing or order-maintenance activities, emphasizing instead broader concepts like quality of life, fear reduction, or problem solving.

Although the current NYPD strategy strongly emphasizes responding to citizen demands, and collaboration with citizens and both public and private agencies in response to problems, the department is also developing extensive proactive, problem-scanning capacities that enable it at times to take the lead in neighborhood problem solving. New York is not alone in this regard. Various police technologies—problem-oriented policing such as practiced by Chief Daryl Stephens in Norfolk, Virginia, and more recently in St. Petersburg, Florida, and crime pattern and mapping efforts, "hot spot" analyses, such as those in Kansas City, Missouri, and Indianapolis—are akin to New York's analytic approach. Properly used, these scanning capacities permit police to catch some problems early and nip them in the bud, before they are widely recognized or a community can mobilize to confront them. This does not mean that citizens are excluded from problem solving; rather it emphasizes the full capabilities of police in the areas of crime prevention and order maintenance.

Finally, although Bratton is sensitive to existing social, racial, and economic inequities, he does not believe that police are helpless to deal with crime until these problems are solved. Instead, the NYPD is now acting under the assumption that dealing with crime can assist society in achieving if not social justice, at least the preconditions under which it can be developed. For example, a community cannot thrive economically when delivery trucks stay out of it to avoid being looted by bands of marauding youths. Again, the NYPD's approach is not unique: a problem-solving approach rests on the assumption that dealing with a wide array of neighborhood problems—from abandoned cars to the dumping of hazardous waste—will address these problems in their own right while at the same time increasing the capacity of the neighborhood to protect itself and enhancing its quality of life, preconditions for other economic and social institutions to thrive.

These elements present in current NYPD efforts might contrast with the "softer" approach to crime control adopted by some community policing advocates, but they hardly warrant characterizing NYPD accomplishments as a return to the reform model. In reality, the current debate over whether the NYPD is engaged in community policing illustrates how this new policing paradigm is easily misunderstood. To many, community policing, with the emphasis on the word "community," connotes a "soft," unaggressive, or "friendly" style of policing. Programs cited frequently as examples of community policing—"officer friendly" programs in schools, for example—contribute to this point of view.

Yet in fundamental respects, the old reform model of policing was far less aggressive than is community policing. Although it *looks* aggressive—powerful cars roaring about, sirens screeching, cops brandishing guns—at the core it is passive. War metaphors to the contrary, reform-model policing holds police in cars, prevents their integration into neighborhoods, discourages contacts between police and citizens, and emphasizes *counter*action rather than *pro*action. Libertarians supported this strategy because it was congruent with their views about how society should be policed: police were not to intervene with youths, the mentally ill, drunks, and street people unless a serious crime or breach of peace was committed. For the most radical libertarians, this even included banning attempts by police to assist the homeless through referring them to agencies—which the ACLU was successful in achieving in Baltimore, as we shall see in the next chapter. Libertarians who argue today that police shouldn't waste their time with disorder when serious crime is such a problem, are harkening back to this understanding. Police leaders supported such a strategy because it enhanced the control capability of police departments by restricting political and other forms of citizen input into police priorities and tactics. Both points of view have some legitimacy: police have systematically violated the liberty interests of subgroups of the population; identifying rogue cops and ousting them from police departments is an important organizational responsibility. During the last decade, however, civil libertarians have recognized that when police departments officially reinstate order maintenance as an important police priority, the tacit alliance between libertarians and the police is over. A flurry of litigation over police practices has resulted.

Whether explicitly or not, libertarians understand that the shift toward community policing, with the accompanying commitment to order maintenance and problem solving, represents a movement toward a far more aggressive and interventionist police strategy than characterized the old reform model of policing. And they are correct. The old model of policing dealt with incidents. A chronic neighborhood quarrel erupts: police respond. It erupts again: police again respond. And so on. In practical terms for police, incidents have neither a history nor a future. Consistent with their reactive, unintrusive model, police are to refrain from taking action until an incident erupts.

Order maintenance and problem solving eschew such a "hands-off" approach. Order maintenance brings police into greater contact with citizens on a routine basis, and specifically with offenders for a greater variety of behaviors than criminal offenses. Problem solving defines not merely an incident but the *problem* that gives rise to the incident, with its history and potential future, as the fundamental unit of police interest and work. Thus, if a police department has fifteen repeat calls to an apartment building over a period of several weeks, the obvious question in a problem-oriented department is "why wait for the next call and the possibility that someone is going to be seriously hurt?" Like order maintenance, problem solving shifts police from a reactive to a preventive posture: stop the next incident/disorder/crime/injury. Contrary to many popular views, community policing, with its focus on order maintenance and problem solving, is *by its very nature* more aggressive and interventionist than traditional 911 policing. Herein lies the source of many potential problems.

## Problems in Carrying Out Aggressive Order Maintenance

In New York as elsewhere, the order-maintenance function that is basic to community policing rightfully raises concerns from many corners. At minimum, in a world with high levels of "serious crime" it seems counter-intuitive to concentrate on minor offenses, especially since most police now in leadership positions were reared within the old reform model of policing that tailored itself to deal with "serious crime." Yet this concern can be met with a reasonable answer. Targeting minor offenses would seem to be justified since surely we cannot afford the neighborhood disintegration and decline that will follow in the wake of uncontrolled levels of disorder. Furthermore, early reports from New York suggest that decreasing levels of index crimes may indeed be tied to the implementation of a quality-of-life program aimed at order maintenance.

Much more significant than this concern, however, are the worries of civil libertarians, advocates for the homeless or minorities, police leaders, scholars, and even proponents of aggressive order maintenance themselves, over whether police can be trusted to maintain order equitably, justly, and in ways that preserve public peace. For while it does not have to, order-maintenance policing can enforce a tyranny of the majority, a repression of minority or marginal elements within the community. Critics to the contrary, most police leaders are themselves worried about police abuse of citizens, especially minorities. Many of the current generation recall vividly the role of police in the 1960s riots, as well as the more recent riots in Miami and Los Angeles, and are deeply committed to avoiding the abuses and mistakes by police that cast them as aggressors rather than peacemakers in many communities. Moreover, minority police executives and many others are often loathe to authorize police order-maintenance activities out of fear that it will signal an "unleashing" of the police in minority neighborhoods. And frankly, as early proposals to deal with the "homeless" in the New York City subway demonstrate, those concerned about the perpetuation of abusive police tactics have good reason to be fearful.

These concerns intensify in the face of a significant corollary: police order maintenance inevitably raises the issue of *police discretion*, which even the most thoughtful and successful police executives have largely ducked during the last thirty years. The earlier law-enforcement reform model of policing was premised upon police responsibility for a relatively narrow set of problems, felonies, and a response to felonies that was essentially straightforward—if someone committed a felony he or she would be arrested. It was just that simple, yet fundamentally wrong: for virtually every problem with which police deal originates in complex interactions or phenomena and requires for its management that police select from a repertoire of potential reactions and responses, only a few of which have to do with law enforcement. Said in another way, police—whether line officers, supervisors, or managers—use discretion in their day-to-day work. It is not merely an oddity, required in the occasional solution of selected problems: police must educate, cajole, comfort, inform, warn, threaten, and even coerce, all subject to their own reasoned and professionally formed judgment. Such is the stuff of order maintenance, and of police discretion.

To understand just how and why such discretion is a necessary part of order maintenance, we might look at policing activities as they were carried out in 1982, in a massive and troubled public housing project in Chicago—the Robert Taylor Homes.

> . . . problems persist [in the Robert Taylor Homes], chief among them the presence of youth gangs that terrorize residents and recruit members in the project. The people expect the police to "do something" about this, and the police are determined to do just that.
>
> But do what? Though the police can obviously make arrests whenever a gang member breaks the law, a gang can form, recruit, and congregate without breaking the law. And only a tiny fraction of gang-related crimes can be solved by arrest; thus, if an arrest is the only recourse for the police, the residents' fears will go unassuaged. The police will soon feel helpless, and the residents will again believe that the police "do nothing." What the police in fact do is to chase known gang members out of the project. In the words of one officer, "We kick ass." Project residents both know and approve of this. The tacit police-citizen alliance in the project is reinforced by the police view that the cops and the gangs are the two rival sources of power in the area, and that the gangs are not going to win.[1]

Anyone familiar with police practices understands that under the police rubric of "kicking ass" various methods, most of them verbal, are involved. Another officer in Chicago described in similar terms how he dealt with gang members who would not follow his orders: "I say please once, I say please twice, and then I knock them on their ass." The officer meant it: although a courteous and generally congenial man, he had grown up in Chicago's public housing developments and was not prepared to stand by and watch gangs terrorize his family, friends, and neighbors.

Clearly order-maintenance activities were needed in this community. Yet the officers faced a dilemma: official police policies about what to do in such circumstances were largely ambiguous or nonexistent. No concerted effort had been made to analyze citizens' problems, assess the authority that police had, develop additional authority if need be, and formulate the guidelines and tactics required to deal with the problems created by gangs in Chicago. Watching innocent citizens being preyed upon and needing protection, individual police officers were left to their own devices. The surprising result was not that police officers occasionally *exceeded* their authority or were abusive, but that they were as *restrained* as they were. Such gangs are an extraordinary irritation for police. They defy police publicly, virtually challenging them to turf wars. Yet given police reliance on generic tactics, sending a car when citizens call, police departments leave officers bereft of tactics other than their own improvisation or occasional special unit sweeps. Sweeps, inherently a short term and legally marginal placebo, often worsen the situation for residents and local police: they alienate innocent youths caught up in them (as well as their parents), and are meaningless to real troublemakers for whom an arrest is a minor irritant.

To many citizens, lawyers, and judges, order-maintenance activities in the name of regaining control of neighborhoods is nevertheless a hard sell. Granted, in such a situation the potential for police abuse is rife. Yet proposing, as civil libertarians do, that police can and should do nothing about serious neighborhood problems unless faced with criminally illegal behavior is no answer, for it represents both an unrealistic view of the ability of legal categories to capture complex social problems, and an unrealistically narrow view of the police function. To frame all police-citizen interactions according to the standards of *criminal* law and procedures, with their elaborate protections, ignores the broad police authority to protect public health and safety under civil as well as criminal authority. The risk of such unrealistic and narrow views and policies is potential anarchy and chaos, caused not merely by predators, but possibly by citizens in the form of vigilantism, and by police in the form of zealotry. At the same time, when police are not provided with explicit authority to deal effectively with the problems they encounter and/or that citizens call to their attention, they often unwittingly become dirty workers, furtively "doing what has to be done" through the exercise of their discretion. This is often the case when it comes to controlling or restricting disorderly behaviors. It is easy then for the boundary to be crossed: where police have no explicit and realistic "rules" to follow, zealous police action on behalf of citizens may either become, or be interpreted by some segments of the community as, abuse. And in spite of the apparent need for discretionary action on the part of police, when unsupported by legislation or other sanctioning guidelines, such actions are unlikely to be unsuccessful in long-range terms.

Indeed, the problems in the Robert Taylor Homes, if anything, have worsened since 1982. Gangs, now much more heavily armed and vicious, continue to terrorize residents. Chicago's former dedicated overseer of public housing, Vincent Lane, struggled to help citizens gain some form of control over their turf after persistent random gunfire threatened residents, their children, and employees attempting to maintain the building. Lane implemented emergency household searches after particularly serious barrages of gunfire. Yet "liberty interests" prevailed as the American Civil Liberties Union, representing four tenants, opposed security measures that would have included metal detectors to prevent gang members from bringing firearms into buildings, a photo ID system for visitors, and a policy permitting guards and police to conduct emergency searches without warrants "in response to barrages of gunfire."[2] Ironically, the ACLU objected to tenants' groups entering the case in opposition to it, and attempted to reassure tenants that the ACLU and its four clients would adequately represent the interests of all 144,000 public housing residents.[3] Most galling, this arrogation of representation was accepted by Judge Wayne Anderson, who refused to certify the democratically elected tenants' association leaders who supported Lane's policies.[4] We do not believe the interests of poor minority residents of the Robert Taylor Homes were genuinely served by the "protection" they received against supposed police abuse of their rights. Yet what then is the answer?

## Bases for Order Maintenance

The very real potential for police abuse reminds us that even though citizens of all backgrounds may agree on the need to control disorder (as Skogan's work tells us), and even though order-maintenance activities may reduce fear and serious crime and improve the quality of life in neighborhoods (as experience confirms), these findings may be *necessary but not sufficient* bases for police to engage in order maintenance. Three additional elements are integral to all order-restoration efforts by police.

First, police and local communities must form an ongoing partnership that provides a mandate for police to act genuinely on behalf of the community, and that leads to the development of a consensus about appropriate neighborhood standards of order and civility. The precise nature of this partnership and the processes by which it is formed and a consensus evolved within the community need a great deal of study, for we know little about them now. Yet the participation of community members in this partnership is essential, because the ultimate goal of order-maintenance programs and community policing is the reintroduction of social control that will be exercised primarily by citizens, and facilitated or backed up by police. In order for order-maintenance activities to be undertaken equitably in a community, the partnership must be inclusive: no social, economic, racial, ethnic, religious, or other group can be excluded. Police must use their authority to restore and maintain order equitably among all, regardless of the distinguishing characteristics of any particular individuals or groups. And finally, the partnership must be dynamic, subject to continuous renewal and reaffirmation, so that police order-maintenance activities reflect and are truly responsive to the mandate given them from the community.

Second, the problem of potential abuse of minorities and the poor by the police is really part of the fundamental problem of protecting the individual rights of all citizens. And individual rights are on the line when police engage in order maintenance—civil libertarians properly remind us of this. Therefore, utilitarian justifications for order must be reconciled with the protection of constitutional liberties and political freedoms of all citizens, and order itself must grow within this context. In other words, police must act in full accordance with the law, no matter what acts they perform under the guise of order maintenance. The authority accorded police by law and the mandate from the community under which they operate do not constitute a license for them to violate individual rights; at the same time, however, police must be able to intervene in the interest of the community (and the state) when the behavior of individuals threatens public order.

Finally, we must recognize and accept the legitimate use of police discretion, while finding ways to shape and limit its exercise. In this regard, police officers in American cities, whether in public housing projects, minority neighborhoods, residential or commercial areas, need several things. Most important is the legal authority to respond to citizen demands for assistance in maintaining minimal levels of order. This authority must be specific enough to ensure that individual freedoms are protected but general enough to allow police to respond to the ambiguities and complexities of real life—that is, they must be given authority to exercise discretion where it is required. Finally, this discretion must be carefully shaped and controlled by law and policy to ensure that police authority is used equitably, and that police order-maintenance activities strengthen lawful citizen control over neighborhoods while ensuring tolerance for diversity.

Unfortunately, community policing may fail to achieve its full potential with respect to order maintenance if problems associated with police discretion are not fully attended to. This is our primary focus in the remainder of this chapter, as we explore more fully, and attempt to answer, the following questions: Why is discretion so important? What problems are associated with it? What is the danger of failing to acknowledge discretion? And finally, how can discretion be most usefully shaped and controlled?

## COMING TO GRIPS WITH POLICE DISCRETION

That police use discretion in their work is, on one hand, obvious. Most people have experienced police use of discretion or wish they had.

Traffic enforcement is the best example: anyone stopped for speeding hopes that an officer will use discretion and give a warning rather than a ticket. In other criminal justice agencies discretion is used as well: prosecutors decide whether to formally charge an offender with a crime, and through plea bargaining use their discretion in charging to exchange a lesser charge for information about an accomplice or a guilty plea. Prison officials and judges, struggling with overcrowding in jails, turn one person out the back door when someone else comes in the front.

Nevertheless, the scope, magnitude, and pervasiveness of such discretion is not well understood either by the public or many policymakers. For discretion, although it operates in criminal justice agencies at virtually all levels, is frequently invisible, performed out of public view and with little public oversight. For example, in state prosecutors' offices, district attorneys may set policies for plea bargaining that go largely unrecognized by the public. In policing, sergeants can determine policing priorities in neighborhoods simply by requiring their line officers to make many arrests; captains and lieutenants assign and reassign police to different neighborhoods, discretionary acts that influence public safety in these areas; and police chiefs may determine policies regarding the enforcement of local ordinances against various forms of disorder. And, while the use of discretion by sergeants, lieutenants, and captains (mid-level managers and supervisors) may not have as much impact day to day on city streets as the discretion used by line officers, mid- and high-level discretion shapes the overall strategy of the police department over extended periods of time and has long-term consequences. Thus in New York City's subways the decision of high-level police managers not to enforce the rules of the subway but instead to concentrate their efforts narrowly on robbery had enormous implications over extended periods of time, seriously jeopardizing the viability of the subway. In similar fashion, policy decisions by district attorneys not to prosecute quality-of-life crimes such as prostitution and panhandling have a substantial impact on neighborhood and community life.

Police departments, like other professional agencies, shield their use of discretion for a variety of reasons. They do not believe that the public will understand or approve of some of the practices. They question the negative effects of making certain policies public, such as one tolerating speeds up to five miles over the official speed limit. They fear the antagonism of legislative bodies to agencies that interpret or ignore legislative intent. They believe in the legitimacy of secrecy in particular areas, such as the use of decoy operations and informants. They wish to "mystify" their practices so as to enhance the prestige of their occupation. Or they just do not believe in the propriety of sharing knowledge of internal operations and practices with the public.[5] And when police agencies do attempt to communicate with the public about their exercise of or need to use discretion, their message competes with the dominant images and metaphors of reform-model policing: "no nonsense about crime," "crime fighting," "warriors," and being "tough on crime." Unfortunately, few metaphors have developed that convey simply and powerfully the truly complex realities of policing in the realm of disorder, fear, and crime.

Up to the 1950s, little enough was known about police use of discretion that we can say it was officially "discovered" only at this time. Criminal justice agencies were primarily "black boxes": police, lawyers, probation officers, and others worked in them and citizens were "processed" by them, but what and how things happened was largely unknown to the lay public. Surveys of police and other criminal justice agencies prior to the 1950s concentrated on the extent to which they adhered to reform strategy standards of criminal justice administration as reflected in official reports and statistics. Police effectiveness in particular was measured by arrest statistics; prosecutorial effectiveness was adjudged by numbers of cases disposed of successfully through trials or pleas and sentencing. Much of what police and prosecutors actually *did* remained out of public view.

All this changed when, early in the 1950s, the Ford Foundation funded a major investigation of criminal justice agencies to be conducted intially by the American Bar Association (ABA) and later by its research unit, the American Bar Foundation (ABF). Under the leadership of the late Frank Remington (formerly professor of law at the University of Wisconsin Law School) and Lloyd Ohlin (formerly Touroff-Glueck Professor of Criminal Justice Emeritus at Harvard Law School), the survey studied the law *as it operated* and as such was "different from earlier studies, much less concerned with official summary statistics and more concerned with the analysis of the criminal justice system in daily operation."[6] The study was conducted in three states, Kansas, Michigan, and Wisconsin, and relied heavily on observational data of low-level decision making. Researchers systematically studied all the major players in criminal justice agencies—police, prosecutors, judges, and corrections officers—as they went about their daily routines. The decision to study law as it operated was crucial in light of our purposes here: it signaled the beginning of the end of the reform model in policing, for the research findings turned conventional "common sense" about police and criminal justice agencies on its head.

The study found that discretion operated at all levels of criminal justice organizations. Its use was linked to the complex application of criminal law—whether by police officers, prosecutors, or other criminal justice officials. Low-level decision making by line personnel in light of practical and real-life considerations thus contributed to the crime-control and problem-solving capacity of criminal justice agencies. The idea that police officers made arrest decisions simply on the basis of whether or not a criminal law had been violated was determined to be inaccurate. Instead, the survey found that "persons were routinely taken into custody to conduct further investigations; for harassment, as a means of controlling a problem; to preserve testimony; and for safekeeping."[7] Moreover, police were found to use a lion's share of criminal justice discretion: Professor Kenneth Culp Davis, who wrote the 1969 classic *Discretionary Justice: A Preliminary Inquiry*—a work that has framed contemporary policy discussions about discretion in criminal justice—estimated that of all the discretion used in criminal justice agencies, about half was used by police.[8] He described police as "among the most important policy makers of our entire society. . . . [who] make far more discretionary determinations in individual cases than any other class of administrators; I know of no close second."[9]

The study also illuminated the use of criminal law to solve many social problems, not just serious crime. Behaviors designated as unlawful in criminal codes—such as assault—were found to be extraordinarily diverse, including everything from private debt settlement, to spouse abuse, to attacking strangers. And finally, the policies of each criminal justice agency were found to have an impact on other criminal justice agencies, which led other researchers to conclude that together, the agencies comprised a criminal justice "system."[10]

These findings stunned the legal, academic, and criminal justice communities. They challenged virtually every aspect of conventional criminal justice thinking, suggesting that: performance should be judged by how problems were solved, not rote application of arrest; training should focus on proper thinking rather than obedience to overseers; police supervision should concentrate on examining alternate means of solving problems, instead of numbers of arrests or citations; police practices and tactics/methods should be tailored to individual circumstances, not broad legal categories such as assault.[11] In policing, as in other criminal justice organizations, the implications of the findings were not immediately apparent; yet over the next two decades the irreconcilability of the realities of police work with the reform model of policing became overwhelmingly clear.

Although publication of the major findings of the ABF report took fifteen years, the results were widely disseminated and immediately influential. Public concern over crime during the 1960s was high. Television showed low-level actions of police handling civil rights and anti-war demonstrators, raising public concern about police abuse. Of equal importance, however, was the fact that staff of the ABF survey moved into prominent positions around the country, both in government and in education. When President Johnson created the Commission on Law Enforcement and the Administration of Justice in 1965, Lloyd Ohlin became an associate director of the commission's staff. Other former ABF staff served as consultants for the president's commission. Later they, and staff from the president's commission who were heavily influenced by the ABF report, went on to prominent careers in prestigious think tanks, foundations, and universities—Wisconsin, Yale, Harvard, and Carnegie-Mellon, to name just a few. Remington and Ohlin were also instrumental in the formation and shaping of criminal justice programs in other universities, consulting, as they did, with the State University of New York-Albany, which became the flagship of university criminal justice education centers.

Similarly, the "discovery" of discretion in the ABF survey stimulated and channeled subsequent research. The finding of considerable low-level, low-visibility discretion exercised by line police officers caused a generation of researchers during the 1960s and 1970s to examine police functioning, particularly low-level decision making by patrol officers.

Not surprisingly, study after study confirmed the ABF survey findings: police work is complicated; a small proportion of police time is spent on criminal matters; and police use discretion throughout their work.[12] At the same time, a few scholars and policy makers also began to study and address the idea of controlling or shaping discretion, with some advocating the elimination of police discretion altogether, at least in the decision to arrest. Joseph Goldstein stated this point of view most strongly:

> The ultimate answer is that the police should not be delegated discretion not to invoke the criminal law. . . . [T]he police should operate in an atmosphere which exhorts and commands them to invoke impartially all criminal laws within the bounds of *full enforcement*. . . . Responsibility for the enactment, amendment, and repeal of the criminal laws will not, then, be abandoned to the whim of each police officer or department, but retained where it belongs in a democracy—with elected representatives.[13]

Goldstein's approach has been most intensely debated as it pertains to domestic violence—a problem largely invisible to the public prior to the ABF report.[14] This issue is complicated because of the values at stake—the traditional reluctance of government to become involved in family matters versus the ongoing suffering of family members in abusive relationships—and because the research into the effectiveness of police and prosecutorial intervention tactics has been contradictory and inconclusive. The findings of the first experiment in police handling of domestic abuse, in Minneapolis in 1983, suggested that women whose husbands were arrested suffered less in the future than women whose husbands had not been arrested.[15] Consequently, many states and municipalities mandated arrest in all cases of spousal assault—the strongest position yet against police discretion. Subsequent replications of the Minneapolis experiment in three other sites, however, failed to replicate its findings. This suggests that domestic abuse is a more complicated problem, perhaps one in which police and prosecutorial discretion is required to balance the goals of limiting suffering and solving problems with the desire to bring abusive spouses to justice.[16]

Despite the experiences after the Minneapolis experiment, eliminating police discretion completely, even in the decision to arrest, has always been a minority view. Mainstream thinking, from the "discovery" of discretion during the 1950s and 1960s onward, focused on developing measures for shaping rather than eliminating its use entirely.

*Limiting Police Discretion Through External Controls*

Limitations on police discretion arising from outside police organizations themselves have developed from a number of sources. University of Wisconsin Law School professor Herman Goldstein has listed some of the forms that such attempts to influence or control police have taken:

> Legislatures have enacted statutes that curtail, clarify, guide, or mandate police actions (e.g., regarding stopping and questioning, strip searches, use of force). City councils have used their budgetary and legislative powers to set police priorities (e.g., marijuana enforcement, the decision to prosecute drug cases under federal law) and to control investigations (e.g., surveillance of political groups). The citizenry, through initiatives and referenda, have sought to provide more specific guidance to their police on the issues of local concern (e.g., marijuana enforcement, use of force). Prosecutors have been more assertive in making policy decisions affecting police practices regarding matters that are substantially of concern to them.[17]

In addition, the courts themselves have developed a number of constraints on police activity, particularly in the areas of search and seizure, and in the handling of suspects in custody. Organized interest groups, such as community crime-control organizations and the American Civil Liberties Union, attempt to shape criminal justice discretion through these different institutions. For example, advocates for causes such as the homeless sue police—as they did in New York's subways; community crime prevention and business groups organize and apply pressure on police to modify their priorities or tactics—as Herb Sturz did in New York City; prosecutors within one agency or at different levels, such as city and county, agree to handle or not to handle cases referred to them by police in particular ways—forcing, for example, police to refer all cases of prostitution to the city attorney, thereby frustrating police attempts to get more serious state charges against some prostitutes; mayors and city managers put direct pressure on police—as

Mayor Frank Jordan did in San Francisco to ensure that police gave serious attention to disorderly behavior (an effort discussed in detail in Chapter 6); and so on. Most recently, as in the 1995 O. J. Simpson trial (but there are many other examples), we have seen juries attempt to shape police use of discretion in their judgments—by refusing to convict offenders when they suspect or have evidence of police abuses.[18]

Yet external control over low-level decision-making by police is necessarily limited. *Judicial* oversight of police is constrained because courts can only examine those issues brought before them in specific cases; and because courts have heavy caseloads and can hear only so many cases.[19] *Legislative* influence is limited by legislatures' tendencies to balk at high-visibility problems by passing overly vague and punitive laws and to provide insufficient resources for their full enforcement, and by legislators' lack of technical knowledge about the issues. *Prosecutorial* oversight of police use of discretion is limited by the differing functions and constituencies of police and prosecutors; the reality that prosecutors can overrule police decisions to arrest simply by their choice of which cases to prosecute, yet basically cannot influence the decision not to arrest; and the additional reality that few prosecutors are interested in calling much attention to police discretion out of fear that prosecutorial discretion might become the next issue. Finally, the capacity of *local government* to shape police discretion is limited by the success of police reformers during the first half of the twentieth century to define virtually any political influence over police as *corrupt* influence. And, in spite of their financial control over police departments, many local politicians have been reluctant to get too close to police or policing issues for fear that they will get "burned" by what appears to be a never-ending crime problem.[20]

A major element in the current crisis over control of police discretion is the result of high levels of citizen demand for order, police attempts to respond to this demand, and successful legal challenges by civil libertarians and advocates to legislation that criminalizes disorderly behavior as well as to police who act on the authority of such legislation. Panhandling is a good example. Recall that laws against begging have gone through certain stages: from vagrancy, to loitering, to loitering "for the purpose of" panhandling. Currently, laws against loitering for the purpose of panhandling (and/or other offenses like prostitution) are now under legal assault. Eventually this issue may move to the Supreme Court for ultimate resolution, but it has not reached that stage yet. The legislative response, invited in the *Loper* decision (striking down a New York statute making loitering for the purpose of begging illegal in public places), has been to try to be increasingly specific. Accordingly, new laws target *aggressive* panhandling as the appropriate behavior to be regulated. New York City, as noted in Chapter 4, is now attempting to draft an ordinance aimed at this behavior to replace the state law.

Superficially, it would seem that if aggressiveness is defined in the ordinance, as indicated by acts such as obstructing, blocking, touching, using profane or abusive language, or following a person in connection with requesting money or goods, such an ordinance would be easy for police to enforce. Unfortunately, this is not the case. The nuances of behavior—panhandling is the behavior, aggressiveness is the nuance—are not inherent solely in those acts of touching, blocking, obstructing, or pursuing, but in the context as well: the time, location, the number of such acts, the condition of the person who panhandles relative to the person who is the target of the act. In terms of the perceptions of the person from whom money is sought, what is not aggressive in one context may seem extremely aggressive in another. As we wrote in *Public Interest*:

> What appears passive in one setting may seem aggressive in another: one person standing on a sidewalk at mid-day in a business area with a cup in his hand, quietly asking for quarters, is not particularly threatening; the same person, with exactly the same demeanor, standing at 9 P.M. in front of a brownstone when an elderly person returns and must unlock the door, is ominous. Similarly, four panhandlers standing in front of a restaurant, even if they are not behaving aggressively, may be more threatening than one panhandler in the same place. And just two passive panhandlers, framing each side of a subway entrance after the rush hour, can be menacing.[21]

Those drafting statutes and ordinances have attempted to counter the difficulty of legal overspecificity by inserting language making it unlawful to beg with the intent to intimidate another person into giving money or goods. Intimidation is usually defined with reference to particular acts (touching, following) such as would make a reasonable person feel compelled, or fearful of imminent harm or the commission of a criminal act upon his or her person or property.[22] We discuss this approach as it was used in Seattle in the next chapter. Such language appears to open the door to overbreadth challenges, however, as it did in *Roulette v. Seattle*: there, the federal district court held that the aggressive panhandling ordinance could be saved only by a limiting construction, making it applicable where there was an intent to threaten the person solicited.[23] Other courts have not been so charitable.[24] Furthermore, the threat of imminent bodily harm, as described by the courts, ignores real-world complexity in which context, and not merely words or actions, creates a threat.

What is clear is that the problems and incidents with which police deal are incredibly complex, and are influenced by many social, demographic, and situational factors. As police respond to these highly variable situations they select from a range of potential actions, beginning with education and instruction of the offender, and extending across the spectrum, ultimately to the use of force. Given such circumstances, although tightly drawn laws and ordinances are highly desirable and may be effective in particular areas (such as search and seizure), it is impossible for legislators to pass laws that cover every nuance and eventuality that police will encounter in their varied duties. Anyone familiar with urban street life understands the lengths to which street hustlers, scam artists, and criminals will go to intimidate and threaten citizens, especially those who are vulnerable: hold open doors at automatic teller machines; get cabs for "fees"; "watch" or park cars in public garages; "assist" people buying subway tokens or, in San Francisco, cable car tickets; carry luggage at airports. The list is endless. Developing overly specific laws in the name of limiting discretion will only involve police in endless street quibbles with "curbstone lawyers." Moreover, the sheer volume of the laws, rules, and regulations with which police have to cope makes it virtually impossible for officers to remember all the specific detail: creating ever more specific laws is an exercise in futility. Finally, ongoing external review of police practices by prosecutors, judges, or other outside or civilian groups is literally impossible, since much order-maintenance activity is invisible.

Nevertheless, the task remains: how to determine when external controls on police actions are inappropriate and largely ineffective or counterproductive; how to find effective means of eliminating *unnecessary* use of discretion by police; and how to develop measures for shaping and controlling the use of *necessary* discretion.[25] To return to one of our earliest questions, if we criminalize activities like panhandling and public urination, how do we ensure that police will use their discretion equitably and justly and not, as libertarians fear, to oppress minorities, the poor, and youth? In the same vein, when prosecutors or police use discretion in handling a case, how can we ensure that the discretion applied is not merely a personal inclination, but represents well-reasoned, professional judgment?

### Limiting Discretion Through Internal Controls on Police

In 1965, Frank Remington, based on his work on the ABF survey, began a new line of thought about policing. He believed that police, in light of their complex responsibilities and necessary use of discretion, should play an important and explicit role in developing crime-control policies in communities and proposed the development of standards, or guidelines, through some form of public process akin to the rule-making processes of administrative agencies.[26] President Johnson's Crime Commission also endorsed the development of guidelines for controlling police discretion in its report, *The Challenge of Crime in a Free Society*:

> Police departments should develop and enunciate policies that give police personnel specific guidance for the common situations requiring exercise of police discretion. Policies should cover such matters, among others, as the issuance of orders to citizens regarding their movements or activities, the handling of minor disputes, the safeguarding of the rights of free speech and free assembly, the selection and use of investigative methods, and the decision whether or not to arrest in specific situations involving specific crimes.[27]

When might such guidelines be useful or necessary? Consider the decision by a police officer not to arrest when a crime has been committed. As many authors have noted, not arresting someone for committing a crime is the *most invisible* decision, and one not subject to judicial oversight or supervision.[28] There may be very good reasons for police to exercise discretion and refrain from making an arrest even though a crime has been committed: a primary reason is that complainants may not want police to press charges beyond a certain point, which is often so in cases of domestic abuse or violence. Since significant numbers of crimes are committed by friends, lovers, business associates, and family members, victims frequently want help from police in managing a crisis, but once it is over prefer to see the matter closed. Consequently, police often decide not to arrest. The decision is an important one, yet the ability of external agencies to influence control over the discretion exercised by an officer is limited. Official guidelines, on the other hand, could be extremely useful for the officer in such situations.

For clarity in this discussion some general definitions are required here. By *guidelines* we are referring to broad policy statements that deal with substantive problems (for example, how police should use their discretion in dealing with panhandling): they incorporate democratic and organizational values with policing knowledge, values, and skills; and they prescribe specific procedures and rules and regulations. *Procedures* refer to distinct methods police use in specific situations, such as handcuffing any prisoner during transportation. *Rules and regulations* are specific prohibitions against deviant behavior—drinking on the job, for example—or proscriptive instructions such as against transporting accident victims in police vehicles.

Prior to the ABF study and the president's commission, police had already developed extensive administrative rules and regulations in their organizations, particularly with regard to the care of equipment, off-duty behavior, scheduling of court appearances, handling of prisoners and their property, and the use of weapons. Some rules and procedures clearly affected police street practices, such as those governing the use of weapons and preliminary criminal investigations.[29] Yet, as a long line of scholars (including Frank Remmington, Wayne R. LaFave, Herman Goldstein, and Kenneth Culp Davis), courts, and the president's commission have noted, most departments were silent about the routine day-to-day activities of police: "What such manuals [rules and regulations] almost never discuss are the hard choices policemen must make every day: whether or not to break up a sidewalk gathering, whether or not to intervene in a domestic dispute, whether or not to silence a street-corner speaker, whether or not to stop and frisk, whether or not to arrest."[30]

The advice to develop guidelines and training that acknowledge both the complexity of the situations with which police deal and the range of possible police responses in many critical areas of police practice, including order maintenance, has been largely ignored by police. LaFave has pointed out the detrimental effects of the lack of guidelines in several senses: in regard to search and seizure doctrine, the Supreme Court and appellate courts have not benefited fully from police guidelines because they have not sufficiently encouraged such guidelines, they have inadequately evaluated such guidelines, and litigants have not focused on such guidelines and their rationale.[31] LaFave also sets forth several positive effects of developing rigorous guidelines: they allow for the meaningful input of police into policy making and legal deliberations. Furthermore, Fourth Amendment (search and seizure) theory suggests that police guidelines which grapple with the complexities of real work experiences can have enormous influence in shaping court doctrine. Although cautious in his comments, LaFave notes that under administrative law doctrine "courts give some deference to professional judgment."[32] But it is clear that to be accorded such deference, guidelines must survive a court's "hard look" review: that is, they must reflect rigorous thinking and appropriate use of data.[33] To date, most police guidelines by and large do not meet this standard.

Generally speaking, academicians, foundations, and others lost interest in guidelines after the 1970s, although a few articles about controlling police discretion continued to appear into the 1980s, mostly in law journals. The idea of model policies and rules and regulations was somewhat resuscitated by the development of the accreditation movement in policing during the 1980s; however, the process had relatively little impact on how line officers used their discretion. Instead, largely as a result of the early work of the Police Foundation in Kansas City and Cincinnati, research shifted to experiments in police tactics. A crucial movement in policing—developing guidelines to shape police discretion—lost its impetus, perhaps as much as any other reason, because the field simply was not yet ready for it during the 1970s. Police business was still police business.

Recently, when Kelling was asked to testify in a hearing about disorder and its impact on the quality of life in neighborhoods in a major city, he contacted the local police department for background material. He asked a representative of the department for any policy statements, guidelines, rules and regulations, or training materials the department had concerning problems such as panhandling, public urination and defecation, sleeping in public spaces, and other such issues. Kelling was certain that a pivotal issue in the outcome of the case would be police discretion, and he wanted to be able to testify knowledgeably about local policies. The only response that the department could give was that training of police for handling problems of disorder was accomplished through "oral traditions" in the field training program. (Field training programs are apprenticeships conducted after a recruit finishes police academy. Before recruits go into patrol either alone or with a partner, they are assigned to work with specially designated field training officers for mentoring and supervision for a designated time.)

The phrase, "oral tradition," was obviously intended tongue-in-cheek: although the police representative knew what issues were important, the department simply had not developed policy guidelines or a systematic curriculum. This is not surprising given the current state of policy development in policing. Three problems characterize current police rules and regulations. First, they are long on the internal operations of a police department—rules that cover the internal "manners and mores" of departmental operation. Second, to the extent that departments have strong policy guidelines, they focus on the "sexy" issues: use of deadly force, "hot pursuit," and arrest procedures—often because police have been forced to develop guidelines by the courts. Finally, existent guidelines do not systematically deal with discretion: acknowledging that discretion exists in some decision making, as many policy statements do, is in the right direction but woefully inadequate as a guide to officers.

Clearly, "oral tradition" does not typify many departmental rules and regulations. Rules and regulations that control the internal relations among ranks, personnel procedures and obligations, filling out forms, and other organizational issues are often clearly and carefully stated, frequently with a painful degree of detail. Moreover, police rules andregulations over time also evidence considerable lag, trivia, and inconsistency. For example, the 1932 edition of the rules and regulations of a large midwestern department admonishes officers: "A patrolman shall familiarize himself with the locations of fire and police signal boxes and all telephones on his beat available for use." The 1950 edition uses identical wording. The 1992 draft edition updates the admonishment only by changing officer gender: "The Officer shall familiarize himself/herself with the location of fire and police signal boxes and all telephones on his/her beat available for his/her use." The trouble is, signal boxes no longer exist and officers carry personal radios. The preoccupation of police departments with relatively trivial issues is further demonstrated in a mid-sized eastern city, where a training bulletin on issuing motor vehicle citations lists as points one and two: "Summons and misdemeanor forms should be neatly printed;" "Enough pressure should be applied during printing so as to make clear copies." Other points are of a similar nature. Discretion in the application of traffic citations is completely ignored. Most importantly, however, 80 percent of police work—especially preventive aspects of policing—goes largely unguided, unrecognized, and unrewarded in police departments.

A few leaders have been genuinely courageous in developing internal police controls about substantive police issues: police use of deadly force has been substantially curtailed, "hot pursuit" brought under departmental guidance, inventory search of vehicles subsequent to arrests carefully controlled, and investigatory and arrest practices brought into line with Supreme Court standards. Many departments developed internal rules under considerable duress. As Samuel Walker notes in *Taming the System: The Control of Discretion in Criminal Justice, 1950–1990*: "In important respects, the dynamics of the changes in domestic violence policy were similar to the changes in deadly force policy. In both cases there was a well-organized political constituency pressing for change. Police shootings was an African-American civil rights issue; domestic violence was a feminist issue." This does not do justice, however, to police leaders like Patrick V. Murphy who seized upon the use of deadly force during the early 1970s as Commissioner of the New York City Police Department. At that time most chiefs vigorously opposed delimiting police use of force. His restriction of use of deadly force to life threatening encounters, rather than permitting police to shoot at fleeing felons, not only reduced the number of deaths of citizens, it reduced the number of officer deaths as well.[34] Yet almost all of these internal rules deal either with highly dramatic aspects of policing, such as use of deadly force and hot pursuit, or with the formal aspects of law enforcement, such as investigatory and arrest practices, that will be reviewed by prosecutors and courts as cases are processed. We must remember that most officers rarely, if ever, use their weapons, that hot pursuit remains a relatively rare event despite media portrayals to the contrary, and that law-enforcement activities comprise less than 20 percent of officers' workload.

As for guidelines and training in the area of order-maintenance activities, they were sparse and often inconsistent or even contained double messages about discretion. Early 1990s New York City Police Department training materials set out training for disorder control as a one and one-half hour lesson under "Additional Police Science"—the same amount of instructional time given to "Safeguarding Property of Deceased Persons." It is not surprising that many officers did not know the elements of any law, let alone policies or guidelines, dealing with panhandling when the *Loper* case was being prepared for.[35] The San Francisco Police Department has issued a carefully crafted general order about panhandling that is augmented by a film offering guidance for applying police discretion with aggressive panhandlers. These materials provide the rationale for Operation Matrix, a highly controversial order-maintenance and homeless effort in San Francisco discussed in Chapter 6. After introductory comments, the first statement under "Policy," however, is: "Enforcement of [law designated] is a responsibility for the Department; however, officers are reminded that their primary enforcement objective is preventing and suppressing serious crime." The message is clear: we have to do this but our basic business is something else. No wonder one officer in this department indicated that "Nine out of ten officers never even read HQ [headquarters] directives about Operation Matrix."[36]

There are a few promising exceptions. The New Haven Police Department, for example, has developed a policy statement that begins with a careful pronouncement of values, followed by the goals to be achieved, and the legal authority under which police are to act; another carefully defines the rights of the homeless, and admonishes police to respect them scrupulously. Often such statements go on to acknowledge discretion, but do so in an extraordinarily narrow fashion. For example, the following paragraph is found in a memorandum from a deputy chief to area commanders:

C. *Offer Alternatives.* Officers shall maintain the element of discretion when dealing with first-offense violations. If, upon request, the violator complies with the law, then verbal admonishment, referral, and facilitation to service providers may be appropriate where feasible. Officers shall, in a humane attempt, identify location of homeless and dysfunctional persons and notify the appropriate agency when feasible with a request that the agency respond, intervene, and offer services. A list of service providers is attached. However, if the violator refuses to comply or is found to be in violation of a second or subsequent offense, the enforcement action may be taken.[37]

To be sure, this memorandum in its totality puts forward positive values about how police should treat the homeless—a considerable improvement on the materials that most police departments have available. Yet, the mere acknowledgment of discretion is insufficient. No one intimately familiar with police practices really believes that police will use discretion only with first-time offenders. Some officers will repeatedly warn offenders, keeping behavior like public drinking under control by insisting that street people, as long as they behave in other ways, drink in inconspicuous locations. Note, as well, the last phrase, "then enforcement action *may* be taken." What factors determine whether or not enforcement, or any other action for that matter, is taken? Such limited guidelines look like "unfettered discretion" to judges and the general public.

The answer to the question, "Why did you handle that problem as you did?" so often given by police, "Well, its a matter of common sense," is not satisfactory. Certainly, the vast majority of police *do* use good common sense, but it is not merely some personal inclination or attribute that is unavailable for analysis. The "common sense" police use is framed by the context in which the behavior in question takes place. One factor police will certainly pay attention to will be the condition of the offender (a first-time offender), as instructed in the memorandum, but officers should and will consider many others as well (time, location, number, and condition of victims and witnesses). Again, the memorandum is a substantial improvement over those of most departments, but it remains incomplete. It neither communicates internally to officers the criteria they should use when applying discretion, nor reassures citizens, political and community leaders, and judges that they can be comfortable with police use of discretion.

The central point to be made here is that despite significant development in police practice, theory, and research during the past three decades, efforts to shape routine work have largely stalled. Frank Vandall, professor of law at Emory University, noted the state of the art in 1976: "An examination of contemporary police training materials reveals that they fail to deal with the concept of discretion in law enforcement. They use such vague phrases as 'proper action,' 'necessary action,' and 'cool thinking' to gloss over the common discretionary problems involved in dealing with common situations."[38] Twenty years later, such phrases are still the state of the art.

These circumstances have not gone unnoticed in recent court decisions assessing police handling of disorder. In Baltimore, for example, one of the issues raised in a suit against the city and its anti-panhandling law, was the adequacy of police training for dealing with special populations. It consisted of one hour preservice training for recruits on gay and lesbian issues, Alzheimer's, and homelessness (fifteen minutes—a ten-minute video and a five-minute discussion) and fifteen minute in-service training (the same video and discussion) for experienced police. Federal District Court Judge Frederic N. Smalkin denied the Baltimore police commissioner's motion to dismiss the suit, in part because he found that training of officers may have been sufficiently inadequate to constitute "deliberate indifference" to the population being policed, and thereby to provide grounds for a civil rights suit against the city and police department. Furthermore, he quoted specifically the deposition testimony of several Baltimore police officers who stated that they had not been kept abreast of changes in laws pertaining to vagrancy and panhandling.[39] The result was a settlement agreement, entered into by the city, in which written policies on police interactions with the homeless and panhandlers and future training and education of officers in this area were in effect dictated to the Police Department by advocates (attorneys) for those suing the city, and which involved payment by the city and police commissioner of attorneys' fees and costs.[40]

As a consequence of the lack of carefully thought-out guidelines and policies, most police departments will have a very difficult time withstanding the legal scrutiny resulting from litigation over their order-maintenance practices and policies. Without adequate guidelines, police use of discretion will always seem to be based on the arbitrary inclination of individual officers. This is not, or at least ought not to be, its true meaning. Police discretion means that in any given situation police officers, as any professionals who use discretion, apply the profession's knowledge, skill, and values to that specific situation. The problem is that when police knowledge, values, and skills are uncodified, as they are in too many departments, officers cannot counter effectively either the claims of litigators or the naiveté of judges about police street practices. One can hardly blame judges or libertarians for the shortcomings of city and police policy makers. But most importantly, the lack of guidelines and the activities associated with their development retards the development of true police professionalism. One is struck when observing police how skillful they can be; one is also struck by their almost complete inability to explain their actions beyond saying: "It was just good common sense." Too many values and skills, and too much wisdom, are lost in this formulation.

Beyond the development of police professionalism, why should citizens worry about police discretion and why do we devote so much space to it here? One way to answer this question is to review the activities of foot patrol officers in Newark and the officers in the Robert Taylor Homes in Chicago. In each case, police officers responded to citizen demands for order with, for the most part, impressive and restrained actions. With some exceptions that we have noted above, they operated within the law to negotiate neighborhood rules and enforce them. Although the officers in Newark maintained order more successfully than did those in the Robert Taylor Homes, a variety of factors—including the assignment of officers (in Chicago they were on regular preventive patrol by automobile, not on foot patrol) and the physical and demographic makeup of the neighborhoods—could explain the differences. Yet, these attempts to restore and maintain order were unofficial: no records were kept of police activities; no rules and regulations, procedures, guidelines, or training prepared officers for this work; and, because the work was unofficial it offered no opportunity for departmental recognition, promotion, or, unless citizens complained about police behavior, sanctions for inappropriate behavior. In other words, a substantial proportion of police behavior, as we noted above up to 80 percent, falls out of the official purview of police administration.

Our concern for guidelines and admonitions that citizens and political leaders should insist on their development are based only in part on the demands that courts are placing on police. In a larger sense, we seek to ensure, first, that police respond to citizen demands; second, that police and citizens negotiate a consensus about the nature of neighborhood problems and what is to be done about them; third, that police policies and practices in neighborhoods are official, legitimate, and have continuity over time; and finally, that both citizens and police develop yardsticks to measure their mutual performance. What principles should shape police guidelines? What should guidelines contain and what should they look like? We would argue that nine principles must shape police guidelines, or alternatively, that nine substantive needs must be met by them.

First, the guidelines must recognize the inherent complexity of police work. Not only are the problems police confront inherently complex in their own right, but the task of assessing a single incident within the context in which it has occurred is also complicated. Most police work involves conflicts and disputes, neither the origin nor solution of which is readily apparent to a police officer who comes onto the scene of a problem, whether it be handling a domestic disagreement, a landlord-tenant dispute, troubles associated with neighborhood parking in congested cities like Boston, or a myriad of other problems. Few problems are what they initially seem, yet citizens expect police to respond to them wisely, compassionately, even-handedly, instantly, and forcefully, if need be.

Second, the guidelines must acknowledge that police will use discretion in handling discrete problems, both in assessing their meaning within a context as perceived by the observers, participants, and victims, and in deciding upon an appropriate response. Depending upon his or her assessment of the situation, an officer will have to decide to educate the offender, refer him or her to an agency for help, give a warning, order the offender to move on, cite him or her, make an arrest, or take some other action. Guidelines can and should specify the situational factors officers should consider, the range of possible responses, and provide guidance as to which responses are appropriate in specific contexts. For example, policies regarding the treatment of panhandlers can be tailored to time of day, activities of panhandlers, and location in the city.

Third, guidelines must be developed in collaboration with practicing police officers and citizens. Line police and citizens, who have firsthand knowledge of problems and their consequences, are best positioned to define problems, consider solutions, and assist in solving problems. In effect, policy guidelines for solving problems establish a contract between police and citizens, informing each of their responsibilities and the outcomes they can expect. Moreover, all citizens should be involved. In Somerville, Massachusetts, for example, a police officer negotiated with both residents and youths about how a park in a residential neighborhood should be used during evening hours. The park closed at 10 P.M.; yet, on warm summer nights, older youths had no other place to go. Negotiating with residents and youths, the officer established a policy under which youths could stay in the park until 11 P.M., so long as they refrained from playing loud music and drinking alcohol, and left quietly at 11 P.M. without having to be reminded by police. The policy reflected the development of a consensus among youths and residents, and became self-enforcing.

Fourth, guidelines must be publicly promulgated, so that they are clear to officers, the general public, community stakeholders, and the courts. In the Somerville case, all police who worked the area, all nearby residents, and local political leaders were informed of the new policy—otherwise it could have been inadvertently violated by police or citizens. As a general principle, it should be remembered that guidelines are written for both officers and citizens. Consequently, they should not be set out in either "legalese" or bureaucratic jargon.

Fifth, guidelines should include rules about what officers *may not do*. In the case of panhandling, for example, police may not make decisions based on the race or social class of the beggar. Likewise, officers in Somerville, while free to exercise considerable discretion, could not authorize drinking by under-age youths. Further, officers need to be protected from inappropriate or unrealistic demands of citizens—not all citizen demands for service are moral, legal, or justifiable. Clear statements about what officers may not do will allow officers to educate citizens about their responsibility to be tolerant of noncriminal deviance.

Sixth, because outcomes of police interventions are often wildly unpredictable, regardless of officers' skill, intent, values, or whatever, guidelines must emphasize police adherence to a *process* (application of knowledge, skills, and values), rather than any specific outcome. A successful police handling of a problem is one that it is *done well*. For example, warrants must be obtained for search. The right to counsel must be observed. These principles must be followed even if they result in cases being lost. The same holds for other police work.

The seventh principle follows on this: guidelines must protect officers from mistakes. The organization, not the officer, must be liable for good faith but mistaken use of discretion. This is partially accomplished by acknowledging points one and six. Good officers, as do incumbents of every occupation, make mistakes. They may be tired, use poor judgment, misread a situation, rush too fast to action, overrespond. Yet, making a mistake is different than being incompetent. Incompetence can be inferred from repeated mistakes, poor judgments, or inappropriate use of force—in other words, from *patterns* of performance.

The eighth principle also follows on these points: guidelines must establish standards of accountability that permit identification of competent and/or excellent performance (even when such performance violates organizational rules), and standards that identify incompetent or uncaring work (including performance that is within organizational rules). Caring violations of rules should be considered better policing than uncaring adherence to trivial rules. An example is required to fully understand the implications of this principle. A police department and department of public welfare in a midwestern city have an agreement: abandoned children become the responsibility of the department of public welfare once a police officer contacts a social worker. At about 11 P.M. one evening, a single male resident in an apartment calls police about two young girls who have been left alone for several days in the downstairs apartment. An officer goes to the scene and finds the two girls, ages seven and nine, alone and without food. In accord with the policy, he contacts an on-call social worker. The social worker refuses: instead he instructs the officers to ask the man who called to report their situation if he will keep the girls for the rest of the night—"He obviously has the girls' interests in mind"—and the social worker will come first thing in the morning. Despite policy, the officer refuses, buys some food out of his own money, and transports the two girls to the police station where they spend the night. The officer's concern for the welfare of the children would not allow him to follow policy. Who knows? The social worker's plan might have worked out fine. But the officer put his values—and hopefully his department's values—of protecting young and vulnerable children above departmental policies. An uncaring officer could have followed the policy, with potentially grave consequences.

Finally, developing guidelines must be recognized as an ongoing, continuing process. Changing circumstances and problems in neighborhoods require constant review, updating, amending, and even elimination of guidelines, procedures, and rules and regulations. Ever new players, circumstances, and problems ensure that this is a never-ending process—an integral part of police work.

Virtually all of these principles could be found in the work of one of the most innovative chiefs of the 1970s, Robert M. Igleburger of Dayton, Ohio—whose work, unhappily, is largely forgotten. Most efforts at that time to shape discretion focused on *model* rules and regulations that were to be available for adoption by individual police departments.[41] Igleburger and his then administrative assistant Frank A. Schubert, a protégé of Herman Goldstein at the University of Wisconsin Law School, changed both the substance and methods of guideline development. Not only did they develop guidelines around *specific neighborhood problems*, often with respect to *particular locations*, they also integrated patrol officers and citizens into the process.[42] Guidelines were to grow out of police-citizen actions to solve problems, not out of some abstract general notion or model.

An example of neighborhood guideline development in Dayton at this time portrays the process and its outcomes. At this time conflicts had arisen between students and residents in a working-class neighborhood adjacent to the university. Not atypically, students who wanted to live off campus sought inexpensive rooms and apartments nearby.

Problems arose in the evenings, when students finished studying and wanted to "party," while workers with children, especially on weeknights, wanted peace and quiet. The result, of course, was conflict between students and other residents, and repeated calls to the Dayton Police. Disturbance violations of one form or another, especially noise violations, were the most common complaints. Because of the repeated calls, the police department experimented with guidelines specific to the problem for officers who were assigned to this area.

As part of the policy-making project Schubert, along with neighborhood officers, polled residents and students, met repeatedly with both, and learned more about the neighborhood and its problems. Once police understood neighborhood standards about noise and other neighborhood issues that could be sources of conflict between students and other residents, they developed guidelines that police would use to enforce those standards. The standards and guidelines were then printed and widely disseminated among all the concerned parties.[43] This was not a once and for all determination: each year the process was repeated to update policies and to ensure that new students, residents, and police themselves understood and endorsed police policies regarding the enforcement of noise and other disturbances.[44] When Igleburger retired as chief of the Dayton Police Department in 1973 the effort faded away, not unlike other model rule-making efforts. Reports on the policy-making project were never published or disseminated, except in one brief article in the *American Bar Association Journal* (1972) by Igleburger and Schubert on shaping discretion through public-police partnerships.[45] Like several other efforts during this era, the work of Igleburger represents a promising start to a line of thought that unfortunately was aborted during the 1970s, but desperately needs to be revived now if the quality of policing is to be substantially improved.

Two final notes about public policy making by police. Unfortunately, public participation in policy making has been a lost thread in police innovation over the last decades. Police leaders during the 1960s and 1970s were not ready for public participation. Most were still too imbued with the idea that crime fighting was a police responsibility and that citizens should limit their activities to "supporting your local police department" and being good observers and witnesses. Yet most are ready for public involvement now, as is the public itself. Nevertheless, as police researcher Mary Ann Wycoff points out, considerable experimentation will be required to determine both the forms that public participation should take and the issues that are proper subjects for citizen participation.[46] This process can and should be a valuable contribution to developing the partnership between police and the community that we believe is essential for effective order maintenance. In effect, it allows for the creation of a "contract" between police and citizens, strengthening police accountability to the community they police and incorporating the legal bases for their actions.

Second, we are not so naive as to believe that merely developing written guidelines, even if they are carefully and properly developed, will solve the problems of managing discretion. We have alluded to the need for strong leadership, training, and education at all levels of police organizations; additionally, departments must strengthen supervision and mentoring and develop appropriate measures of police performance and reward systems. But developing strong guidelines that codify appropriate measures of police discretion is an essential ingredient of any attempt to restore order.

# TAKING BACK THE STREETS

*Restoring Order in Baltimore, San Francisco, and Seattle*

BECAUSE OF THE NATURE OF THEIR ROLE AND THE SPECIFIC ACTIV-
ities they carry out, police will be important to any attempt to restore
order in our communities. Yet the impetus for restoring order can origi-
nate with other actors as well, as indeed it does in many cases. Private
citizens may join together in associations to address safety in their
immediate neighborhoods, prodding politicians and the police to take
action on their behalf. Businesses and commercial enterprises may form
BIDs (business improvement districts) with public safety and service
provision components of an overall program to restore order in the
downtown. A mayor may embark upon a comprehensive program that
draws together citizens in neighborhood organizations, police activities
in enforcing criminal laws, and provision of appropriate social services.
A city attorney can attack sources of disorder through civil enforcement remedies, targeting crack houses, abandoned properties, or even
gang behavior as public nuisances, and developing city ordinances to
prohibit particular behaviors that are troublesome locally. A local prosecutor or district attorney may decide that trying cases for crimes
already committed is only one part of the job, and go on to mobilize
resources throughout the community to address crime and disorder on
a neighborhood by neighborhood basis, working closely with citizen
advisory councils, schools, and the courts.

Whatever the origin of order-restoration efforts, the task itself is not an easy one. Success on the ground and viability of programs in the face of legal challenges depend in large part upon careful planning and attention to a number of elements. A city's intent to help the poor and disadvantaged, not simply to abandon, displace, or make scapegoats of them, must be clearly documented. This record must show, above all else, that the city has acted morally, and with integrity. Citizens must actively and visibly support the city's actions. Those responsible for the task must craft legislation narrowly and carefully, so that it is legally defensible. Police and other officials must be trained and then proceed to careful implementation of programs and legislation. All initiatives, including the drafting of legislation, and its enforcement, must respect and protect the individual rights of all citizens.

When some or many of these elements are not present or attended to, the results of attempting to restore order may be "two steps forward, one step back." For example, in the accounts that follow, private business concerns in Baltimore were largely successful in their order-restoration program while the city and police were forced to compromise based upon problems with legislation and its enforcement when both were faced with a legal challenge from advocates for the "homeless." In San Francisco, citizens voted Mayor Jordan out of office late in 1995, despite his aggressive Operation Matrix which addressed disorder in various neighborhoods. And even where city officials and private citizens work together to formulate and implement a careful order-restoration program, the courts are the final arbiter and the last hurdle. In Seattle, city officials still await, with cautious optimism after nearly two years, a final decision from the Ninth Circuit Court of Appeals as to the legality of their carefully crafted ordinances targeting disorderly behavior on sidewalks.

## BALTIMORE: PRIVATE CITIZENS AND BUSINESSES TAKE THE INITIATIVE

Baltimore is one of America's historic East Coast commercial and transportation centers. Situated on the Chesapeake Bay at the mouth of the navigable Patapco River and linked during the mid-1800s with the Midwest by the Baltimore and Ohio Railroad, Baltimore remains one of the busiest ports in the United States. Its economy today is driven by its industrial, research, and educational institutions. Natural boundaries of bays, waterways, railroad tracks, and main radial traffic arteries, coupled with unique brick rowhouses that comprise half of the city's housing stock, have made Baltimore a city of neighborhoods. The city's planning department in 1994 identified 266 distinct neighborhoods, represented by 400 community associations.[1] Baltimore's neighborhood groups, citizens, and private business concerns have spearheaded attempts to restore order in the city—although with strong support from the mayor and his administration.

As in many other Eastern cities, demographic, social, technological, and economic changes during the last three decades have created problems of poverty, urban blight, and crime in Baltimore's older neighborhoods. During the decades prior to the 1990s, considerable attention was given to restoring commercial and downtown areas: development of the Charles Center (1960s, downtown buildings), the Inner Harbor (office buildings, parks, the National Aquarium), Harborplace (1980, restaurants and shops), and Camden Yard (1992, the location of Baltimore's new and popular baseball stadium)—all led to a reinvigorated downtown area. Yet in inner-city neighborhoods dramatic increases in crime since 1988, much of it associated with the crack cocaine epidemic, created a crisis. Violent crimes increased by 53 percent between 1987 and 1994. Murders jumped from 213 in 1985, to 352 in 1993. Moreover, the population decline from 776, 885 in 1980, to 724,000 in 1992, created many abandoned houses, especially in older rowhouse neighborhoods, where deserted furniture was strewn around yards and public walkways, crack houses flourished, and drug dealers and users congregated. Rowhouses presented serious fire hazards since fires could easily spread, and "metal men" worsened the situation. Not content with the pickings they removed from abandoned houses and sold, they turned on the entire building stock of neighborhoods, removing aluminum, copper, and other valuable metals from churches, homes, and commercial buildings. One local magazine likened these scavengers to ants, literally eating neighborhoods from the inside out, causing millions of dollars of damage and accelerating the process of urban decline. At times, metal men destroyed property as fast as it could be renovated. The St. Ambrose Housing Aid Center, for example, spent $200,000 to remodel four townhouses during the early 1990s; now all four houses are shells, stripped of every bit of metal.[2]

In January 1993, after a prolonged period of increasing violence and record-setting levels of murder, Mayor Kurt L. Schmoke appointed Thomas Frazier the new chief of police. Chief Frazier moved quickly to reorient the Baltimore Police Department—then reeling under charges of brutality, petty corruption, and internal racial strife—toward community policing. As a key element of this effort, he hand-picked district commanders and gave them broad new authority to respond to neighborhood problems. Yet even more significant for turning around individual Baltimore neighborhoods were the efforts of citizens themselves, mobilizing and then acting on their own and in concert with government agencies and the police.

Only a few years ago Boyd Booth, an old residential community on the southwest side of the city, for example, had become a battleground. As the *Baltimore Evening Sun* chronicled in May 1991: "Residents of Boyd Booth heard gunshots at night and found blood on their sidewalks in the morning. Many retreated into their homes, afraid to report the violence to the police, afraid that drug dealers would burn them out, or worse."[3] The story went on to document that everyone who was able to leave the neighborhood had done so, and with drug dealers attending their community meetings, residents and leaders were powerless. Over time, the Citizens Planning and Housing Association provided a part-time community organizer (funded by the Abell Foundation) to a reinvigorated and newly incorporated Boyd Booth association. To assist citizens to deal with problems, Mayor Schmoke set up a task force of city agencies and surrounding community associations that met regularly with citizens. One priority was community decay, especially abandoned housing. The state provided the neighborhood group with a small fund for boarding up vacant houses, erecting fences, improving lighting, and making other minor improvements to their neighborhood. Citizens themselves boarded up abandoned housing, fenced off or closed walkways between houses where drug dealers could flee or hide, cleaned up trash in the neighborhood, turned vacant lots into gardens, and, with the technical and legal assistance of Baltimore's Community Law Center, pursued nuisance abatement cases against six drug houses. The Law Center also helped residents identify irresponsible landlords and take legal action against them. To reclaim their streets, neighborhood residents conducted numerous vigils and street demonstrations (vigils took their spirit from the season—during Christmas holidays, for example, as caroling) and held ten neighborhood picnics. As a service to youth, the neighborhood association established a summer work program that concentrated on cleaning public spaces. A private drug-treatment program supported neighborhood efforts by providing access to a treatment program for local youths addicted to drugs; and residents provided a Christmas dinner for drug-treatment participants who had helped to clean the neighborhood. Bon Secours Hospital, the largest employer in the area, began to work closely with residents; and police reinvigorated their activities by providing special patrols.[4]

The results? Violent crime decreased 56 percent from 1993 to 1995; narcotics calls for service and arrests dropped by 80 percent.[5] Moreover, violent crime continues to drop even with a gradually declining police presence. Citizens with whom Kelling walked in Boyd Booth late in 1995 proudly testified to their reduced fear and their control over the streets. Quality of life in the area is dramatically improved: streets and alleys are clean; and even elderly people and children can move about in public areas without fear of being victimized. Several times in the last two years drug dealers have attempted to return to the area to resume their activities: none have been successful.

The restoration of order in Boyd Booth was the result of vigorous political leadership from Mayor Schmoke's office, aggressive policing that included foot patrol and the use of special antidrug units, coordinated city and private agency activities, but above all a citizenry mobilized to plan and implement a comprehensive strategy for reclaiming its community. The Mayor's Coordinating Council on Criminal Justice (MCCCJ) is now exporting this model to other troubled neighborhoods in Baltimore.

Notwithstanding the vitality of the downtown areas, during the mid and late 1980s "homelessness" became an increasing problem there. Estimates put the number of homeless persons at approximately 2,400, with two-thirds of the men and one-third of the women being chronic alcohol abusers. Moreover, nearly half of the homeless population were seriously mentally ill, with 10 to 20 percent meeting the criteria for chronic mental illness.[6] By the early 1990s, problems associated with "homelessness"—aggressive panhandling, litter, and crime—had become so serious in the downtown areas that the private business sector became involved in attempts to restore order and prevent crime. The vehicle for doing so was a business improvement district (BID), again with support from the mayor's office.

The Downtown Partnership of Baltimore originated in 1982 as the Charles Street Management Corporation, through the efforts of the business community and then Mayor William Donald Schaefer. Their goal was to revitalize Charles Street between Pratt Street and University Parkway. In 1990, with encouragement from Mayor Schmoke, the target area expanded to cover approximately 200 square blocks in the downtown area. Since its inception the partnership has provided business development, marketing, and management services to improve the downtown area. The explicit policy of the partnership is to create a "positive public environment for all citizens who live, work [in,] or visit the downtown area."[7]

In 1993, with the creation of the Downtown Management District by city ordinance, management services were expanded to cover safety and physical maintenance in the area.[8] Forty-two police-trained Public Safety Guides patrol the area, serving as "eyes and ears" looking out for the safety of members of the public. The guides, uniformed but unarmed, are in radio contact with the police, and are trained to report suspicious behavior, intervene in the behavior of persons obstructing pedestrian or vehicular traffic or intimidating other citizens, ask them to move along, and to call the police if necessary. They do not have the power to arrest. They also answer questions and give directions and information to anyone who approaches them on the streets, helping any citizens, especially the homeless, in need of assistance. In addition to the safety guides, uniformed "clean sweep" ambassadors sweep and clean sidewalks, weed tree wells, and clear graffiti. Some formerly homeless persons, after training, have received jobs as safety guides and in the maintenance program.[9] More importantly, however, the partnership has taken a leading role in helping homeless persons, working with service providers to develop better resources for the homeless, and referring and matching them to available services. The partnership has worked to increase training and employment opportunities, to actually place homeless individuals in jobs, and to encourage the business community to take responsibility for developing and expanding homeless services.

Working with the Baltimore City Police Department, the Downtown Partnership also initiated the Public Safety Coalition, a group of business and civic leaders, to develop programs for improving public safety in the downtown area. Among its many projects, the coalition has set up a computerized bulletin board and fax network to share information related to safety and security among seventy-five agencies and businesses (representing over 2,000 safety providers), and issued pagers to police officers working in the area and local security directors to facilitate rapid transmission of information. It provides training for private security forces operating downtown, and teaches building operators without private security forces how to operate safely. In addition, the Public Safety Coalition has sought to develop crime-prevention training programs in shoplifting, robbery and burglary prevention, and personal security awareness presentations for businesses and employees, and brochures with safety tips and information for distribution to travelers.[10]

What have been the results of these efforts? Police Department statistics showed drops of 10 to 25 percent in rates of various crimes in the downtown area by the end of 1994; and surveys of public perceptions indicated that 77 percent of respondents had positive impressions of the downtown area.[11] And in spite of the efforts of the Downtown Partnership to develop services for the homeless, as well as to address public safety concerns, in August 1993 the ACLU brought a legal challenge to both the partnership's program and police enforcement activities, describing them as an "effort to expel an entire class of citizen from the downtown area of Baltimore City based on their appearance and homeless status."[12] This legal action not only challenged efforts to restore order in downtown Baltimore, it exposed policy problems originating from decisions made during the 1980s.

The plaintiffs in *Patton v. Baltimore City* (1994), three formerly homeless individuals, were portrayed as society's victims, who "have been arrested or harassed in the past, and/or expect to be arrested or harassed in the future, for conduct which constitutes the ordinary and essential daily activities of their lives on the streets of Baltimore City."[13] They charged the mayor and city council of Baltimore, the commissioner of police, the Downtown Management Authority, and the Downtown Partnership with establishing policies that violated their rights under the United States Constitution to privacy and personal autonomy, to travel, to equal protection under the law, and to free speech and expression. Furthermore, the ACLU asserted that these policies constituted cruel and unusual punishment by punishing the plaintiffs solely because of their status as homeless persons.[14] In particular they objected to city police and safety guides employed by the Downtown Management Authority asking homeless persons and panhandlers to "move along," and "harassing" them when they panhandled or engaged in activities such as sleeping, eating, or "tending to personal needs."[15]

The ACLU also challenged the aggressive panhandling ordinance passed by the Baltimore City Council in December 1993, asserting that it infringed on the First Amendment right of the homeless to freedom of association. The ordinance specifically prohibited panhandling in combination with any of six types of conduct: (1) confronting a person in such manner as would cause a reasonable person to fear bodily harm or the commission of a criminal act upon a person or property in the person's immediate possession; (2) touching another person without his/her consent; (3) continuing to panhandle from or follow a person after he or she had refused to give money; (4) intentionally blocking or interfering with the safe passage of a person or vehicle; (5) using obscene or abusive language toward a person while attempting to panhandle from him or her; (6) acting with intent to intimidate another into giving money.[16] The ordinance also prohibited *all* panhandling, whether aggressive or passive, at locations where it could be "inherently intimidating": near ATM machines, in public transport vehicles or at stations or stops, on private residential property if an owner, tenant, or occupant requested or posted a sign indicating no panhandling, and from motor vehicle operators or occupants in traffic on a public street.[17]

The issues placed before the court in this case, then, were much the same as those we have considered in other legal challenges to order restoration efforts, such as the New York City and Transit Authority suits over panhandling legislation. In Baltimore, Federal District Court Judge Frederic N. Smalkin handed down his decisions in two separate opinions, in which he denied many of the ACLU's claims. Yet the outcome of the suit ultimately was more favorable to the Downtown Partnership than to the city and police department.[18]

Disposing of a number of constitutional claims, the court held that the fundamental right to privacy and personal autonomy did not extend to a "right to eat, sleep, or perform other essential activities in public,"[19] and therefore, the city's and partnership's policies did not infringe upon this right. Furthermore, the court found that the First Amendment right of association did not protect the "uncoordinated presence of certain similarly situated individuals in a relatively small geographic area" that the ACLU maintained as "homeless" individuals.[20] Finally, the court held that a police officer or public safety guide's direction to a panhandler to move on or cease panhandling did not constitute a "seizure" under the Fourth Amendment, and therefore was not unlawful.[21]

Turning to the issue of whether homelessness constituted a status and city policies impermissibly punished life-sustaining activities associated with it, the court declined to adopt the ACLU position. Specifically, Judge Smalkin contrasted the federal district court's holding in *Pottinger v. City of Miami*—that criminalizing the conduct of homeless persons who had no choice but to sleep and live in public constituted cruel and unusual punishment based upon their status[22]—with what he found to be more persuasive reasoning set forth by the court in *Joyce v. City and County of San Francisco* (discussed above in Chapter 2, and below in this chapter). He agreed with the *Joyce* court that "'homelessness,' as a matter of law, is not a 'status' as that term was utilized by the Supreme Court in *Robinson*.'"[23] Furthermore, he found that the defendants' customs and practices of moving persons along or discouraging panhandling were aimed at their acts, and not at their status as homeless persons or panhandlers.

The ACLU challenge to the aggressive panhandling ordinance was not as easily dismissed. Considering the ACLU's charge that the ordinance violated the First Amendment rights of the homeless, the court agreed that panhandling was fully protected speech, analogous to charitable solicitation since "the distinction between soliciting funds for oneself and for charities is not a distinction of constitutional dimension," and because it conveyed a message about how society treated the poor and homeless.[24] And because the ordinance regulated only aggressive *panhandling* as opposed to all types of solicitation, Judge Smalkin found that it imposed greater burdens on the speech of those soliciting for charity than for other purposes. This made it a content-based restriction.[25] Yet applying the strict scrutiny First Amendment analysis appropriate for a content-based restriction on speech in a public forum (recall that this constitutes the highest standard, and one especially difficult to meet), he found that compelling state interests made it necessary: protecting citizens and visitors from threatening, intimidating, or harassing behavior; promoting tourism and business in the downtown area; and preserving the quality of urban life. Clearly, the defendants, Downtown Partnership and the city, had provided a strong record in support of this conclusion. Furthermore, Judge Smalkin found the ordinance narrowly tailored, through its specific prohibition of certain acts such as assault, battery, extortion, following a person after he or she had refused to give money, directing obscene or abusive language, and interfering with safe passage, and to leave open alternative channels of communication. He contrasted Baltimore's ordinance with broader anti-begging statutes that had not survived constitutional challenges, such as the New York law considered in *Loper v. New York City Police Department* that banned all panhandling on city streets.[26]

Even though the ordinance emerged unscathed from a First Amendment analysis, it foundered when Judge Smalkin addressed the ACLU's claims that it violated the rights of the homeless to equal protection under the law. Here the standard required the city to demonstrate that the statute was finely tailored to further a compelling interest in *discriminating among speakers*. Judge Smalkin concluded that the city failed: "The City has made no showing that panhandling, or charitable solicitation, is inherently more intimidating than other types of solicitations for money."[27] He suggested, however, that this flaw could be remedied by amending the ordinance to include *all* aggressive solicitation for money, regardless of the purpose or intended use.[28] In light of the court's finding that Baltimore's aggressive panhandling ordinance violated the Equal Protection Clause, the city council drafted a new ordinance to prohibit *all* aggressive solicitation for funds in public places, whether for alms or organized charities.[29]

Yet this action was not sufficient to clear up the city's legal problems arising out of the suit—and here was the rub. Not only was the aggressive panhandling ordinance itself struck down by the court, but the ACLU brought to the court's attention that park rule 4, a prior ordinance banning the solicitation of money, alms, subscriptions, or contributions in parks without a permit, which had been declared unconstitutional by a federal district court in 1981, had nevertheless remained on the books and was being used by the police to arrest people.[30] Between January and November 1992, for example, thirty-three persons were arrested under it, even as prosecutors and judges were questioning police about its legality. Not until October 1993, after Chief Frazier was appointed and discovered through this litigation that rule 4 was still on the books and being enforced, were Baltimore police officers alerted to the illegality of park rule 4 and informed that they should not enforce it.[31] After the filing of the suit, the mayor and city council in March 1994 also repealed ordinances similar to the old vagrancy laws that many courts had long ago declared unconstitutional because they were based upon status and not acts.[32] Overall, the city's vulnerability in these areas made it liable for payment of substantial attorneys' fees and costs; therefore, the city and the Baltimore Police Department entered into a settlement agreement with the ACLU. Under the agreement, the city would repeal park rule 4 and the vagrancy ordinance, and amend the aggressive panhandling ordinance "to redress the constitutional issues" identified in Judge Smalkin's opinion.[33] Furthermore, the city and the police commissioner agreed that police officers would be instructed not to "'move along,' harass, arrest, or otherwise interfere with persons . . . not violating any law or applicable regulations." The city and the police commissioner also agreed to pay a confidential sum as full settlement in satisfaction of claims by the ACLU against them for attorneys' fees and costs.

The primary cost of this outcome was a weakened, if not untenable, position for police: that is, to permit them to intervene with needy and homeless persons only when they observed a clear violation of the law. Historically, police have always had the responsibility to help those who are vulnerable or who cannot help themselves. To be sure, they have engaged in abuses, and in the case of Baltimore it appears that during the 1980s, someone was at least asleep at the switch when it came to keeping police policy and practices in line with judicial decisions.

Either police were not made aware, or ignored, the court decisions striking down earlier vagrancy laws. Regardless, the consequences for the city are troublesome. Many interpret this decision in Baltimore to mean that police business is only to enforce the law; police efforts should be targeted only at serious crime; and all interaction with emotionally disturbed individuals, drunks, and youths should be left to social workers and advocates. The agreement is, therefore, a setback for Baltimore's Police Department, and a victory for an extreme libertarian ideology.

The Downtown Partnership emerged from the case in a much more favorable position. Clearly, it was not liable for legislation determined by the court to be unconstitutional, nor for the city's enforcement of legislation long ago declared invalid. In addition, the partnership prevailed with respect to nearly all of the ACLU's claims. Considering the safety guides' regularly asking individuals to "move along," Judge Smalkin found neither actual nor constructive knowledge by the partnership of any unconstitutional policy "put into practice on the street by the Public Safety Guides" nor deliberate indifference to the homeless expressed through a failure to train the guides.[34] Because the safety guides' actions were aimed at aggressive behavior by solicitors generally, and not simply by panhandlers, the court found no violation of the Equal Protection Clause. Similarly, Judge Smalkin found no infringement of the right to travel or to free speech, particularly since requests by the guides to move along often were coupled with attempts to assist a homeless or inebriated person find shelter or services, and the requests were not based upon any coercive, state police power.[35] In return for the Downtown Partnership not filing for reimbursement of attorneys' fees, the ACLU agreed not to appeal the decision.

The partnership was not a party to the city's agreement with the ACLU, and safety guides continue to carry out their activities in full in the downtown area. In the meantime, the police department has turned to a state statute that prohibits loitering within fifty feet of a liquor store as the basis for enforcement actions in the downtown.[36] Additionally, the city's amended aggressive panhandling ordinance now makes all aggressive soliciting, for any purpose, unlawful. And the partnership's safety guides and police continue to work cooperatively. Nevertheless, the *Patton* case concluded with the city and police department having learned a hard lesson. When police and city officials are ignorant of or disregard the law, they put themselves at the mercy of active and militant litigants and seriously jeopardize contemporary efforts at crime control.

## SAN FRANCISCO: THE POLITICS OF ORDER MAINTENANCE

San Francisco's ethnic and cultural diversity, coupled with its hills and valleys, has made it a city of legendary neighborhoods: Chinatown, Haight-Ashbury, the Castro District, Nob Hill, the Tenderloin, Japantown, Mission, and North Beach. It is also a city governed by a tradition of political activism on the part of residents, and an ethos of tolerance for differing life styles.[37] Haight-Ashbury is seen by many as the birthplace of the 1960s counter-culture revolution, and the city, especially the Castro District with its picturesque Victorian houses—"painted ladies" as they are known—has always accepted homosexuals. A climate that is hospitable for much of the year and a strikingly beautiful natural setting have also helped to promote both a vital street life and a profitable tourist industry.

These same qualities, however, also led to large numbers of aggressive beggars, "homeless," panhandlers, and prostitutes congregating on city streets during the 1980s—indeed, San Francisco may have the highest incidence of aggressive begging and panhandling of any American city. In spite of the city's generous social service and public welfare policies, by the 1980s and early 1990s conditions on public streets had deteriorated significantly. The downtown Civic Center became, in effect, a shantytown: local citizens dubbed it "Camp Agnos," after former San Francisco Mayor Art Agnos, who refused to break up encampments of the "homeless" in public spaces and parks until housing that he deemed adequate was created for them. At the same time, prostitutes, drug dealers and users, and persons "camping" were taking over city and neighborhood parks, prompting local residents to demand that the city remove children's play equipment and bulldoze play areas like Langton Mini Park. Park workers, accompanied by police to protect them from hostile street people, ventured daily into parks to clean up syringes, needles, feces, condoms, and every imaginable form of refuse. Commuter rail terminals and parking garages became surrogate flophouses, and many closed public restroom facilities. Concomitantly, downtown businesses and tourist industries suffered severe declines in commercial activity levels, and residents living near area parks and in old historic areas threatened to leave the city and move away rather than face daily battles with substance abusers, aggressive panhandlers, drug dealers, and prostitutes literally on their front stoops and sidewalks.[38] "Camp Agnos" became a dominant issue during the 1991 mayoral race between Frank Jordan and the incumbent. We have already recounted the attitudes of city and Bay area residents reflected in surveys conducted in 1991, expressing fear and concern for their physical safety arising out of encounters with aggressive panhandlers on city streets.[39] That same year, enough San Franciscans repudiated the Agnos policy to elect Frank Jordan mayor.

Even while citizens were voting to restore order with new leadership, however, they were losing in the courts. San Francisco lost its most effective piece of legislation for curbing and prosecuting aggressive begging and panhandling when a federal court declared California's anti-panhandling statute unconstitutional in *Blair v. Shanahan* (1991).[40] The statute, Section 647(c) of the California penal code, provided that anyone "who accosts other persons in any public place or in any place open to the public for the purpose of begging or soliciting alms" was guilty of a misdemeanor.[41] "Accost," according to a state court that had previously upheld the constitutionality of the statute, meant walking up to and approaching another, so as to distinguish soliciting in this manner from merely receiving a donation while standing in place.[42] In *Blair* a former panhandler, who no longer begged but had been arrested several times under the statute, sought to prevent the city from enforcing it, claiming it to be unconstitutional under both the First Amendment of the United States Constitution, and the California Constitution.[43]

The federal district court held that the restriction on begging and panhandling violated the First Amendment and the Equal Protection clause of the Fourteenth Amendment. Judge William Orrick reasoned that begging was protected under the First Amendment both because it could involve an exchange of protected speech and because it implicated the same interests present in charitable solicitation—communication of information, the spreading of views and ideas, and the advocacy of causes.[44] He rejected the city's argument that under the statute beggars could still communicate about homelessness and poverty through conversing with others, so long as they did not approach them to solicit money; rather, he believed beggars would be less likely to speak to passersby if they could not solicit funds, and therefore found that the statute impermissibly chilled protected speech. According to Judge Orrick, the act of begging was fundamentally intertwined with its message, and therefore deserved First Amendment protection.[45] He also emphasized that the statute was aimed at protected speech in a public forum, and therefore a standard of heightened scrutiny was warranted. Yet he found the statute not narrowly tailored so as to achieve even the potentially valid state interest of avoiding compelling, coercive, or intimidating behavior: *all* approaches to passersby were not inherently coercive, or intimidating, and the statute did not define the proscribed acts specifically to be avoided by those begging.[46]

Although Judge Orrick's opinion reflected a line of reasoning not unusual at the time, ultimately the decision would not stand, for *Blair* then became enmeshed in procedural disputes: first, it was appealed to the Ninth Circuit Court for review of the district court's finding that the California penal code section violated the First and Fourteenth amendments, as well as upon procedural grounds. The appeals court remanded the case back to the district court, which then vacated the original *Blair* holding—again on procedural grounds. Legally, the penal code section banning begging is still valid. Yet during the protracted legal battle it was useless as a tool for prosecutors and police attempting to restore order on the streets in San Francisco and elsewhere. Today, the city has chosen not to enforce the anti-begging statute.[47]

The city's liberal traditions notwithstanding, many San Franciscans during the late 1980s and early 1990s turned to police, prosecutors, and other government officials to demand that they take action. Prosecutors responded by working with police to target prostitution and aggressive panhandling on a neighborhood by neighborhood basis, especially in the Tenderloin area. The effort involved both the district attorney's office, which is responsible for the prosecution of criminal matters within the city and county of San Francisco, as well as the city attorney's office, which by charter deals with civil cases, but which also advises the police in legal matters such as those arising in the enforcement of city ordinances. Working with the police, neighbor-hood groups, and the ACLU, lawyers from both offices collaboratively developed specific enforcement and prosecution strategies and policies. When *Blair* was lost, the mayor called upon the city attorney's office to draft Proposition J, to prohibit harassing or hounding another person for money in any area to which the public had access, to replace it.[48] Voters supported this proposition, which passed in the November 1992 election.

In August 1993, Mayor Jordan, a former police officer, expanded the efforts of prosecutors and police by initiating a city-wide program, Operation Matrix, to deal with health and safety problems resulting from the massive levels of disorder that were affecting San Francisco's public spaces. Operation Matrix encompassed a wide range of social services. As the *New York Times* noted in 1993: "San Francisco alone spends $46 million a year on housing, food, and social services for its homeless, which works out to more than $7,600 for each of its esti-mated 6,000 street people."[49] Operation Matrix also emphasized order-maintenance activities by police to deal with public drinking and drunkenness, public urination and defecation, aggressive panhandling, camping and sleeping in public spaces, street prostitution, and other such offenses. Police enforced ordinances prohibiting many of these activities, while cooperating as well with health and social workers who offered services and referrals to those who needed and would accept them.[50] Throughout, the police were carefully advised by the city attor-ney's office legal staff.

Not surprisingly, the collision between San Francisco's historically liberal social attitudes and demands for order created another intense legal and political battle, testing the city's commitment and ability to restore order. Soon after the city initiated Operation Matrix, it was sued by the Lawyers Committee for Civil Rights of the San Francisco Bay Area and the ACLU on behalf of several "homeless" individuals. Recall, as we discussed in Chapter 2, that at least three of the four indi-viduals named as plaintiffs in *Joyce v. City and County of San Francisco* (1994) either had housing or were living on the streets at least in part because they had refused assistance from relatives or available city housing or shelter space.[51] Although the plaintiffs endorsed much of the Matrix program, they challenged the police order-maintenance efforts for penalizing the necessary "life sustaining activities" associated with their status as homeless individuals, in violation of the Eighth Amendment. They also alleged that the Matrix program violated the Equal Protection clause, asserting that through its implementation the city had discriminated against the homeless; it impermissibly burdened the constitutional right to travel; in "cleaning up the streets" the police had violated Fourth Amendment prohibitions against unlawful search and seizure by confiscating and destroying property belonging to the homeless; and code sections on which the Matrix program were based were both overbroad (that is, reaching a substantial amount of constitutionally protected activity) and vague.

Federal district court Judge D. Lowell Jensen first denied a request for a preliminary injunction against the city's continued enforcement of the Matrix program (March 1994), finding that the plaintiffs had not demonstrated a likelihood of success in their arguments that the program was unconstitutional. In a later decision, he upheld the constitutionality of the program itself (August 1995).[52] Addressing the issue of homelessness as a status, Judge Jensen followed the reasoning of the California Supreme Court in a recent case involving a camping ordinance in Santa Ana (1995),[53] as well as his reading of the U.S. Supreme Court's decisions in *Powell* and *Robinson*, to conclude that the plaintiffs had not shown homelessness to be a status, and that the Matrix program did not punish people for being homeless.[54] Examining the acts of persons who lodged in doorways and other prohibited sites, and who slept in parks and other public places during prohibited periods, Judge Jensen found these acts to be volitional, and therefore subject to legitimate regulation that was not barred by the Eighth Amendment.

Considering whether Matrix deprived the plaintiffs of equal protection under the law by imposing a special hardship on homeless people, he declined to find the homeless a suspect class that would warrant the application of strict scrutiny; instead, he subjected the program only to a rational basis equal protection review. Treated in this manner, Matrix easily passed the test: Judge Jensen found it rationally related to the city's interests in "protecting public safety and health, and preserving parks for their intended purposes. The city has submitted uncontradicted evidence that homeless encampments can lead to drug sales, vandalism, public elimination of body wastes, and other unhealthful conditions, as well as facilitation of a host of other crimes by and against homeless individuals."[55] This conclusion was in line with the recent findings of other courts.[56] And going on from this point, Judge Jensen found no pretext in Matrix for displacing or punishing the homeless:

> Plaintiffs . . . have not introduced any evidence showing that the City implemented Matrix in order to punish the homeless, or that Matrix fails to accomplish its purposes. They argue that the City could enact alternate legislation prohibiting the particular evils it fears. While such alternate legislation may be possible, given the virtually limitless societal problems related to criminal conduct, the Court finds unpersuasive the argument that regulating phenomena that contribute to them, such as lodging and encampments, is not a legitimate governmental approach.[57]

Judge Jensen disposed of the remaining claims in favor of the city as well. He held that the Matrix program did not burden the rights of indigent people to travel, since it did not treat residents and nonresidents differently.[58] He denied claims that the laws against lodging or camping were vague, giving police too much discretion in enforcement or citizens too little notice of prohibited acts. Overbreadth—reaching a substantial amount of constitutionally protected speech—was not an issue, since no speech was implicated. All in all, the city had compiled an excellent record of its efforts to care for the homeless and indigent, the police had worked carefully with the city attorney's office in implementing Matrix, and lawyers from the city attorney's office prepared and placed before the court both well-reasoned legal arguments and convincing factual accounts to support the city's efforts. Nevertheless, *Joyce* is now on appeal before the Ninth Circuit.[59]

Operation Matrix, having survived a legal challenge, nonetheless stirred up a political hornet's nest. In the Board of Supervisors, Supervisor Angela Alioto (who was to run for mayor in 1995) proposed an amnesty plan to dismiss charges against some five hundred people who had been arrested for sleeping or camping illegally. Fiercely opposed by the mayor and a majority of supervisors, amnesty lost by an eight to three vote. The *San Francisco Chronicle* noted the board's "clear law and order stand" and remarked that the vote "revealed unexpected maneuvering among members of the usual liberal-leaning panel, as several supervisors who had attacked Jordan's crackdown in the past did not flinch yesterday in voting down the amnesty plan."[60]

Similar maneuvering occurred during the 1995 mayoral race. In August, during the preliminary contest, candidate Willie Brown took a clear stance against Operation Matrix. In a five-way debate, Operation Matrix was the dominant issue, with all four of Jordan's opponents attacking it. Brown went so far as to describe the program as "'persons in uniforms operating as if they are occupational officers in a conquered land.'"[61] By October, although Brown was still opposing Matrix, the *Chronicle* noted: "One of the sharpest boundaries . . . is growing blurred: the line between Mayor Frank Jordan and his opponents on how to deal with street people. . . . Rival candidates Willie Brown and Roberta Achtenberg still condemn Jordan's Matrix program . . . though, they make it a point to declare that they, too, would send the police after people who camp in parks, drink alcohol in public and commit similar crimes."[62] The controversy over Matrix became an issue of such importance that the *San Francisco Chronicle* endorsed Jordan almost solely on the basis of the program, running an editorial entitled, "Jordan Deserves Re-election for Matrix."

> There was a time when Jordan's critics attacked him for what they called criminalizing homelessness. Homeless advocates still say this, but the politico pack seems to have clued into the fact that rap doesn't play well with voters. . . .
>
> Talk about not learning the lessons of history [referring to the need to provide the homeless with more and better services]. Remember Mayor Art Agnos? He didn't want to move the homeless without first providing enough services. The result: When the homeless broke the law, police were paralyzed. The Civic Center became the mecca of America's unwashed. The decision to not use the police turned San Francisco into a magnet for people who just want to hang out, not work, do drugs, and soil the city.[63]

Nevertheless, Mayor Jordan lost the December 1995 run-off election. Newly elected Mayor Willie Brown formally ended the Matrix program on January 12, 1996. His actions and words since then have created uncertainty as to whether the change is nominal or substantive. For example, he asserted that despite ending Matrix, "I've instructed (Police Chief Fred Lau) to enforce the law, but not to the extent that the homeless or the poor are singled out."[64] The ambiguity of this message has been widely remarked upon, even by homeless advocates. Paul Boden, of the Coalition for the Homeless, cautioned "that's exactly what Jordan said: that these laws apply to everybody. So, what does that mean? Does this mean that everybody will be allowed to take a nap in the park? Or does it mean that everybody who takes a nap in a park will be arrested?"[65]

The political and policy implications of Brown's election and subsequent moves are not fully apparent at present. Willie Brown, of course, is a California political happening: the impact of his charisma on the San Francisco mayoral race cannot be ignored. One question that can be raised, however, is the extent to which Jordan's opponents—both Brown and Achtenberg—were able to exploit the message that Matrix was targeted specifically at the "homeless." In the minds of the public, and even the police, Jordan evidently failed to link disorder and fear with crime itself, and to make clear the need for restoring order to stem the downward spiral into urban decline. The city attorney's office convinced the court of just these facts, prevailing on behalf of Matrix in *Joyce*; yet the public seemed not to have been persuaded.

## SEATTLE: WHOSE SIDEWALK IS THIS?
## A CITY ATTORNEY ANSWERS

As Baltimore and San Francisco faced growing problems of disorder in public spaces, so too did Seattle, Washington. In response to citizen and commercial requests, Seattle's city attorney Mark Sidran coordinated the implementation of what was, along with the New York City Transit Authority's effort, the most carefully designed program in the United States to restore order. Seattle, along with San Francisco, is proud of its liberal traditions, but is not as thoroughly sated with liberal ideology as San Francisco. Seattle's viewpoint is more "laid back": it has long tolerated a street population in its "skid row" area—including Pioneer Square—that until recently had mixed peacefully with the tourist, commercial, and resident population. Even the term "skid row" had its origins in Seattle where in early days it referred to the location where logs were "skidded" down the area's steep hills to Puget Sound. Later, when local logging practices changed, Seattle's skid row became the locale around which vagrants found cheap single occupancy rooms and "hung out." Seattle prided itself on its ability to "manage" its problems through civil and generous welfare programs and to share its famed quality of life with all of its citizens, the poor as well as the working and middle classes. Seattle, after all, was not New York, Los Angeles, or San Francisco.

But Seattlites were worried. As Mark Sidran noted in a speech to the Downtown Seattle Rotary Club in 1993: "[We] Seattlites have this anxiety, this nagging suspicion that despite the mountains and the Sound and smugness about all our advantages, maybe, just maybe we are pretty much like those other big American cities, 'back east' as we used to say when I was a kid and before California joined the list of 'formerly great places to live.'"[66] Of special concern during the late 1980s and early 1990s, the "homeless" were concentrating throughout Seattle's downtown and other commercial areas, and becoming increasingly aggressive in their actions toward passersby. The problem was especially serious in the area adjacent to the University of Washington. Business people as well as shoppers who attempted to use the area were frustrated: at times, congregations of persons lying prone on the street completely blocked sidewalks, virtually claiming the space as their special territory. Pedestrians, including parents with strollers, the visually impaired, and the elderly were regularly forced onto the roadway and into passing traffic as they attempted to navigate around the street people. Some of those stretched out on the sidewalk held cups, others asked for money—one person regularly asked for money for his dog—although few exceeded the limits of Seattle's ordinance prohibiting aggressive panhandling.[67]

Earlier, Seattle had attempted to address these problems by enforcing a portion of the same ordinance that prohibited the obstruction of pedestrian traffic. This pedestrian interference ordinance represented an attempt to write legislation aimed clearly at specific behaviors. It defined pedestrian interference (a crime punishable by a fine, imprisonment, or both) as begging with the intent of intimidating another person into giving money or goods, or intentionally blocking passage by another person so as to require that person to take evasive action to avoid physical contact.[68]

In *Seattle v. Webster* (1990), advocates for the homeless challenged the constitutionality of the pedestrian interference portion of the ordinance, a controversy that reached the Supreme Court of the State of Washington. The court upheld the ordinance on several grounds. First, it was not "facially overbroad," that is, the language of the ordinance did not reach constitutionally protected speech. It regulated behavior, not speech, and it appropriately limited the sweep of the legislation to the requirement of specific intent to block passage, since the innocent intentional acts that might provoke evasive action by others to avoid physical contact—collecting signatures for a petition, picketing, even mere sauntering—were not prohibited.[69] The ordinance was also not unconstitutionally vague, but provided adequate notice to citizens as well as sufficient guidelines to prevent arbitrary enforcement by the police.[70] Finally, the court rejected a Fourteenth Amendment equal protection challenge, finding that the pedestrian interference ordinance applied equally to all persons possessing the requisite criminal intent, and its language made no mention of economic circumstances or residential status. Further, the court found no precedent for declaring the homeless a protected class, even though the ordinance might disparately affect these individuals.

Even this legislation was not sufficient to stem the increase in disorderly behavior, however, nor the potentially ominous consequences for the university neighborhood, and many feared that it was only a matter of time until Seattle's vibrant downtown community would be destroyed by the increasingly brazen behavior of street people. Businesses reported falling revenues; citizens were unwilling to continue shopping in the area when it required wending their way through persons lying on the street who importuned them for money, insulted them, and urinated and defecated in public. The elderly living in the neighborhood were especially bothered, fearing not only for their own safety in the face of crime, but the dangers of being forced up and down curbs and into traffic. Although the pedestrian interference ordinance itself was constitutional, in application it was increasingly ineffective, since it required a showing of deliberate (criminal) intent to block

pedestrians in order to prosecute offenders, an intent not easily satisfied when many of those obstructing were mentally ill, drunk, or
drugged so as to be indifferent to the effects of their behavior. Clearly
something more was required.

Attempting to stay within the generous and civil traditions of Seattle, City Attorney Sidran responded by developing a narrow ordinance
aimed specifically at the behavior that was so troublesome on Seattle's
streets.[71] The "sidewalk" or "lounging" ordinance, as it was known,
prohibited a person from sitting or lying on a public sidewalk, or on any
object placed on a public sidewalk, from 7 A.M. to 9 P.M., in the downtown and neighborhood commercial areas. Unlike the pedestrian interference ordinance, violation of the sidewalk ordinance was a civil
infraction (punishable by a civil penalty of $50 or performance of com-
munity service) requiring no criminal intent but merely the commission of the prohibited act. Thus the ordinance was more easily
enforced.[72] Numerous exceptions to the prohibition included medical
emergencies, wheelchairs, sidewalk cafes, parades, rallies, demonstrations, performances or meetings for which street use permits had been
issued, and seats supplied by public agencies, private property owners,
or in bus zones while awaiting transport. Moreover, the law specified
that all citizens who violated the ordinance had to be given notice of
their violation before they could actually be cited. In other locations
such as parks, or during nonbusiness hours, people could lie down
when and as they pleased.

The outcry from advocates and libertarians was immediate and typically strident: the ordinance was called "anti-homeless," and Sidran
was labeled a fascist for introducing it. One local author wrote: "The
bottom line is that people are homeless not through fault of their own
but because of a failure of our political and economic systems."[73]
Sidran, however, had anticipated just such an attack. Understanding
from the beginning that Seattle would be taken to court, he considered
in advance all possible legal arguments that would be raised, canvassed
existing legislation nationwide, and crafted a narrow ordinance that he
believed would pass muster. He then developed a three-pronged plan
for establishing a strong record that would be placed before the court as
it judged the ordinance. First, local services had to be adequate for the
truly needy. Second, a clear and consistent record of legislative intent

by the city to restore order and not to target or scapegoat truly disadvantaged citizens had to be established. Finally, the city's enforcement practices had to be carefully implemented, so as not to violate the fundamental rights of any citizens.

Early on, Seattle Mayor Norman Rice assumed leadership by reviewing the city's efforts to care for the needy, and by communicating those efforts to the city council so it could incorporate into its records a history of generous provision for Seattle's poor and troubled citizens. Sidran investigated and gathered considerable information about the nature of the problem. He relied not only upon data from city agencies, but on testimony from those most seriously affected by street disorder: the elderly, infirm, vision-impaired, the poor, and street people who were themselves frequently victimized. He then responded to the clamor from homeless advocates about possible abuses with careful delineation of the real problem—lawlessness—by emphasizing the very limited nature of what he was proposing, and by fully supporting increased services to the poor. Finally, Sidran carefully set forth the basic rationale for restoring order through preventing crime and reversing urban decline. As part of this effort he invited Kelling to meet with city council members to carefully review and explain existing research about fear, disorder, crime, and urban decline, especially the dramatic crime reductions that had resulted from control of disorder in New York's subways.

Sidran knew that he had to be prepared to defend the ordinance not only in terms of legal jurisprudence, but on the legislative record and the facts of the case that would be brought before the judge. In his words,

When you get into trying to legislate in this area, you have to assume that there is at least as likely a chance as not that you are going to get in front of a judge whose political and policy instincts tell the judge that controlling disorder is not a good idea. With all due respect to the judiciary, when it gets down to it in these policy disputes in a constitutional context, it's a judgment call in which it's not just some kind of analytical argument that appeals to the intellect of the court, but a matter that has to be approached on a gut level. These judges are people and they have their views about the nature of the "homeless" issue and the kinds of policies that are "good" or "bad." Given the fact that the politics of these

issues are almost inevitably knee-jerk, on both ends of the spectrum . . .
one has to compel judges by the record to take a balanced view. . . .

How a case comes out depends on the city's ability to shape the record
to get past the ideological screens of the judge who will react to the
rhetoric of the advocates. . . . You have to balance the rhetoric of advocates with your own rhetoric, based on both the legislative record and the
facts of the case. You want a good case because bad facts make bad law.
. . . It was out of fear of drawing an unsympathetic judge [that] we spen[t]
a great deal of time assessing the nature of the problem, identifying the
most defensible constitutional position to be in, and how [to] . . . make
the best record.

Sidran understood that advocates would present to the court the most
heartrending examples of the nature of the problem from the perspec-
tive of their clients. He sought then to counter these examples with
equally heartrending stories about individuals who suffered the consequences of street people sprawling over the sidewalk—the blind, disabled, elderly, parents with children—and others who would suffer
greater victimization if good citizens withdrew from the streets. As
Sidran explains, "What you get into is some sort of balancing in the
hearts and minds of the court about whose sidewalk this is. The answer
to this question must be in your factual record." Thus Sidran made a
direct connection between the acts of street people and the consequences for safety and the vitality of commerce in the area. If street
people congregated on the curb side of the sidewalk, Sidran asked,
"What about people trying to cross the street? park their cars? deliver
products? Isn't it dangerous for people to block the curbside and force
people into the street to get by?" Sidran raised the consequences of
street people congregating alongside buildings: "That's where you can
expect to find the disabled, the elderly, the blind—the people who are
not likely to keep pace with the traffic and who want to be at the mar-
gins." Furthermore, if good citizens were so frightened that they withdrew from the streets, the homeless themselves would become victims
of predators in their midst. The question became "Whose rights prevail
here? People who must use the sidewalk because it is the only right-of-
way between points A and B, or those who want to sprawl over the

sidewalk in spite of having many options—parks, other streets, and so forth?"[74] And beyond the question of rights, the issue was the balance between the safety and security of all citizens, including street people, and the rights of a few.

When the ordinance was passed by the Seattle City Council in October 1993, along with an amendment to the aggressive panhandling ordinance, steps toward implementation were taken with great care: signs were posted; pamphlets were handed out to citizens; those violating the law were forewarned of upcoming enforcement; and the decision was made that early enforcement efforts would only be conducted by specially trained officers in consultation with the city attorney's office. Nevertheless, a number of homeless people, advocates for the homeless, as well as political, social, and community organizations, filed suit against the city in federal district court, charging that both the sidewalk ordinance and the aggressive begging ordinance were unconstitutional, violating the plaintiffs' rights to freedom of speech and association, to travel, to due process, and to equal protection under the law.[75] Again, the issue for plaintiffs was homelessness: "There can be little doubt that the sidewalk and begging ordinances, particularly when viewed in conjunction with ordinances enacted by the Seattle City Council on the same day, are aimed at the homeless population of the City of Seattle."[76]

The city's careful and thorough efforts to document its case and develop the law as narrowly as possible did not go unnoticed by the court. In *Roulette v. Seattle*, Judge Barbara Rothstein first addressed the sidewalk ordinance, and rejected immediately the plaintiffs' argument that the ordinance was unconstitutionally vague: instead, she found it to contain both a clear description of the proscribed behavior (thereby eliminating the danger of police exercising unfettered discretion), and adequate notice to citizens concerning both the acts restricted and zones in which the ordinance applied.[77] She also denied the claim that the ordinance violated the fundamental constitutional right to travel, because the right did not generally apply to street behavior. Distinguishing *Roulette* from two recent cases, *Pottinger v. City of Miami* and *Tobe v. City of Santa Ana*, Judge Rothstein noted that in these cases the ordinances had imposed criminal liability for sleeping, lying down, eating, and performing numerous life-sustaining activities in public places, and their enforcement "followed on the heels of concerted action by the police to target the homeless, including mass arrests together with confiscation and destruction of their property." In both these cases, the courts found evidence that the cities had attempted to force homeless people out of the area by seeking to remove them from places in which they gathered. In Seattle, Judge Rothstein found no basis on which to conclude that the city had sought to expel homeless individuals from its commercial areas. Clearly, Sidran's careful attention to creating a record of Seattle's treatment of the homeless through measures reflecting integrity, concern, and the provision of concrete services was effective.

Turning to the First Amendment claims, Judge Rothstein found that the sidewalk ordinance regulated only acts that did not "in and of themselves contain an expressive element," for the act of sitting or lying was not inextricably linked or necessary to speech or expressive conduct: the homeless could still perform other communicative acts without lying down. Furthermore, the mere presence of a homeless person lying or sitting on the sidewalk did not constitute protected expression: to the contrary, she maintained, "Plaintiffs' argument would require the conclusion that every public act by homeless people is expressive conduct protected under the First Amendment because they are by their very presence making a continuing social statement. The court rejects this argument as not supported by First Amendment precedent." Finally, in addressing plaintiffs' equal protection challenge the court found no violation of the plaintiffs' right to free speech, travel, or due process, no precedent recognizing the homeless as a suspect class, and no blatant discrimination in the ordinance or its enforcement. Therefore, Judge Rothstein applied a rational relationship test, which the city easily satisfied by showing that its legitimate interest in ensuring pedestrian safety and safeguarding the economic vitality of commercial areas was rationally related to and advanced by the prohibition against sitting or lying down on public sidewalks in commercial areas during certain hours.

The aggressive begging ordinance defined criminal begging as "to beg with the intent to intimidate another person into giving money or goods"[78] . . . "whether by words, bodily gestures, signs, or other means."[79] Amendments in 1993 added a definition of intimidate as "to engage in conduct which would make a reasonable person fearful or feel compelled"[80] and a list of circumstances to be considered in determining whether an actor intended to intimidate another into giving money, including touching or following a person, using profane or abusive language toward the person, or continuing to beg after the person solicited has given a negative response.[81]

Plaintiffs asserted that the ordinance unconstitutionally prohibited speech protected under the First Amendment because it was overbroad and vague. Both the court and the city accepted that at minimum peaceful begging and solicitation for charitable purposes were entitled to some First Amendment protection.[82] Judge Rothstein therefore found the ordinance not overbroad since it applied only to "threats to cause bodily injury or physical damage to the property of another which would make a reasonable person fearful of such harm." Such threats were not protected speech. However, she did find the section of the ordinance setting out circumstances to be considered in determining an actor's intention to intimidate another both lacking in specificity, and inclusive of some speech protected by the First Amendment. This section was therefore vague and overbroad, and the court could find the ordinance constitutional only by striking the circumstances section.[83]

In March 1996, the Ninth Circuit Court of Appeals upheld the city's position in *Roulette*. Writing for a two to one majority, Judge Alex Kozinski found that even though sitting itself might "possibly be expressive," this was not enough to sustain the claim that the ordinance was unconstitutional on its face: sitting or lying on the sidewalk were not forms of conduct "integral to, or commonly associated with, expression."[84] The case remains unresolved, however, with the plaintiffs' filing of a petition for *en banc* rehearing in the Ninth Circuit. In the meantime, the city is also contesting two challenges to the ordinance brought under the state constitution.[85]

## LESSONS WE HAVE LEARNED

From the New York City and Transit Authority, Baltimore, San Francisco, and Seattle experiences, we can draw a number of conclusions about what does and does not work in attempting to restore order. Four elements in particular contribute to successful efforts by city officials and police departments as they develop legislation and implement programs:

- Claim the high moral ground
- Learn to problem-solve
- Prepare to win in court
- Involve the community

*Claim the High Moral Ground*

Implementing a community-based crime-prevention model of crime control and order maintenance will inevitably require new legislation, programs, and policies. At first glance, much of the work involved in order maintenance can be viewed as distasteful or unpleasant and as ensuring order at the cost of freedom. As a matter of fact, restoring order can benefit the entire community, including those who are needy as well as those we might consider "troublemakers," and can be carried out in ways designed to ensure the fundamental liberty interests of all.

The purpose of order maintenance is to prevent fear, crime, and urban decay. Although order maintenance activities will put police into contact with homeless and poor people, those who are emotionally disturbed, youths, and substance abusers, order-maintenance efforts are not intended to solve society's problems regarding these populations. This message must be driven home to political leaders, media representatives, citizens, and police and criminal justice professionals alike. In the New York City subway, our purpose was to create a safe and unthreatening environment for all riders, including poor and troubled people. In Seattle, Sidran's purpose in restoring order was to maintain a safe and viable neighborhood shopping center for residents. Similar purposes characterized efforts in Baltimore and San Francisco. In each case, broader purposes were served and acknowledged: maintaining a community, supporting community institutions, and ensuring commerce—to name just three.

The first axiom of attempts to restore order then is: *claim the high moral ground by framing the issue in proper terms.* From the very beginning in the New York City subway, we understood that allowing others to frame the issue of disorder as "homelessness" would have been an organizational, legal, and political trap. Organizationally, it would have conceded to police that order maintenance was only a peripheral function—divorced from policing's core function of preventing crime. Legally, it would have permitted advocates to fix the terms of the litigation and ambush the MTA and police with legal arguments about "harassing the poor." Politically, it would have evoked knee-jerk responses to homelessness, a problem serious in its own right but fundamentally different from the one the MTA was dealing with—lawlessness. Sidran understood these pitfalls very well in Seattle. His question, "Whose sidewalk is this?" tinged with some indignation, and his powerful scenarios of the elderly and disabled struggling for safe places to walk illustrated vividly the competing values and entitlements that were at stake.

It may be that one pitfall of linking homelessness with order maintenance caused Mayor Jordan to lose in San Francisco. The significance of the election of Willie Brown in San Francisco and the role of Operation Matrix in the unseating of Frank Jordan is not clear at this time. Brown's extensive political history and his charisma are widely recognized and doubtlessly contributed to his victory. Yet the controversy regarding Operation Matrix might be instructive, especially in light of what is happening in New York City. While Mayor Jordan and other San Francisco officials might have sought or anticipated some fear-reduction and crime-control benefits from restoring order, this goal was not built into their efforts. This is not entirely surprising: Jordan's attempt to deal with disorder was one of the first city-wide efforts in the United States and he was no doubt improvising as he went along. In New York City, the impact of order maintenance in the subway was only starting to be recognized at this time, and the NYPD's efforts had not yet taken place.

It is clear, however, that the San Francisco Police Department was ambivalent about order maintenance and failed to integrate it into an overall crime control strategy. Despite a carefully crafted policy statement on disorder, the police department only begrudgingly authorized officers to deal with aggressive panhandlers. While enforcing the law against aggressive panhandling was designated as a responsibility of San Francisco police officers, their "primary enforcement objective is preventing and suppressing *serious* crime"[86] (emphasis added). In retrospect, by folding social welfare efforts for the homeless and order

maintenance into one highly visible and identifiable program, city officials might have made themselves vulnerable to charges that they were
harassing the poor and the unfortunates of society. Such charges put
Jordan on the defensive throughout the mayoral campaign. His opponents could have it both ways: they could support equitable law
enforcement; they could attack targeting the homeless. The fact that
social welfare programs targeted the homeless got lost in the political
rhetoric. Nonetheless, linking homelessness and disorder in one effort
made it easy to misrepresent the spirit of Operation Matrix.

With the advantage of hindsight, we can contrast Matrix with New
York's subway and street experiences. In the subway, Bratton portrayed
disorder, farebeating, and robbery as one seamless cloth—when police
dealt with one, they dealt with all. Today, for both Mayor Giuliani and
Bratton, NYPD order-maintenance activities are the cornerstone to
crime prevention and reduction. The message seems clear: decouple
homelessness and disorder. One is a condition, the other is behavior.
They are different sets of problems with surprisingly little overlap. Keep
the focus on the linkages among disorder, fear, crime, and urban decay.

Two final admonishments about coupling homelessness and disorder.
First, cities simply cannot ignore homelessness and still restore order.
Enough overlap exists between the two sets of problems that cities
ignore social problems at great peril to their order-maintenance efforts.
Second, despite the need to deal with social problems conceptually and
programmatically apart from disorder, police still have an important
responsibility to such problems. The homeless need police protection
and help, often help in finding social service agencies appropriate for
their problems. Caring for those who cannot care for themselves has
always been and will remain an essential function of police.

Claiming the high moral ground also includes a second axiom: *do
order maintenance right.* Not much more needs to be said about this.
Police officers must understand that they will never be asked to do
things for which there is not legal or moral justification. There is no
need for dirty work or "commando cleaning." Sweeps only get cities
and departments into trouble. From Newark during the 1970s, to New
York's subways, to Seattle, to cities throughout the United States, there
are plentiful examples about how to do order maintenance properly.
Under previous city and police administrations, Baltimore cut corners

with the law by either enforcing or continuing to apply laws that courts deemed unconstitutional. They got caught: now, the police department and city are paying high costs for what was either carelessness or irre- sponsibility. It is not just bad facts that make bad law, bad practices make bad law.

The basic message here is: *take time to prepare carefully, and do things right.* Do not act impulsively out of an unreasoned response to emo- tional charges made by your opponents. Take time to examine the actual issues at stake. Examine fundamental assumptions, and chal- lenge them if they are faulty, incomplete, or one sided. Go to the research. Be prepared to back up your own reasoning in every way— morally, practically, and legally. Review the law and change it if neces- sary. Engage the public fully in your deliberations; provide channels for and seek feedback; be prepared and willing to change directions. And if the policy and program lack a moral foundation and integrity, *don't back them even if they might pass a legality test.*

### Learn to Problem-Solve

To claim the high moral ground, officials and citizens must clearly understand the problems with which they are confronted, and then work to find appropriate solutions. To this end, police scholar Herman Goldstein conceived a powerful problem-solving method that is sophis- ticated, easy to understand, teachable, and practical.[87] Although devel- oped primarily as a police methodology, problem solving is applicable to other governmental and criminal justice agencies as well. It was this method that Kelling adopted for use and elaborated upon as he guided the New York City Transportation Authority through a number of steps to develop solutions for problems of disorder in the subway.

*Step 1:* The first step—problem identification—is probably most important in the problem-solving process. We may think we know what the problem is when one confronts us, but it is not that simple. Everyone "knew" that the subway's problem was homelessness—and attempts to deal with it as such led only to duplicity and trouble. Everyone "knew" that subway graffiti was a law-enforcement problem, so for years arrests were piled on arrests while the problem got worse. And so on.

*Step 2:* As crucial as problem-identification is, it is only the first step in a problem-solving methodology. In the subway, the next step was to identify programmatic options for all dimensions of the problem. Who needs help? What help would be most effective and appropriate? How can it best be provided?

*Step 3*: The task force then examined the morality, legality, and constitutionality of all programmatic options in light of the functions and basic values of the organization. What were the values of the New York City Transit Authority and its police? How were they best implemented? What tactics met those standards?

*Step 4*: All related and appropriate departments, governmental units, police departments, and service agencies were either involved in planning or notified to ensure that the program's goals were not undermined or blunted by conflicting operations carried out elsewhere. Service and enforcement gaps were identified, and community leaders and policy-makers were informed about the consequences of such gaps. What services were required above order maintenance? Who could best carry them out? What could be done about the hard-core, burned-out substances abusers who had literally gone into the subway to die?

*Step 5*: Subway rules and regulations were reviewed in light of constitutional law and changing legal, social, and moral traditions. What rules could pass constitutional muster? What was "obstructing" and how could a rule prohibiting it be enforced?

*Step 6*: Citizens and community leaders were informed about the nature of the problem and the proposed program, including constitutional and moral implications and the limitations on police, so they could adjust their expectations to legal and practical realities. What outcomes could we expect? How soon?

*Step 7*: Finally, the task force tried to identify effective and accurate feedback mechanisms to provide constant data about the program's effectiveness, its impact on various target groups, and unanticipated consequences. What were recognizable early wins? How could we get information back to interest groups? Valuable feedback confirmed fears that although a conceptually valid program had been initiated, lack of leadership was allowing it to wither. It also convinced Metropolitan Transportation Authority leaders that new transit police leadership was necessary if order was to be restored to the subway.

Such extensive problem identification and problem solving have characterized every police and criminal justice success story of which we know. "Conventional wisdom" and "common sense" are not the reliable guides that many claim them to be. This is the bad news. The good news, however, is that considerable wisdom, often unarticulated, is found in organizations once practitioners employ a problem-solving methodology. The Metropolitan Transportation Authority needed help and even new leadership to implement order maintenance in New York's subway, yet one captain had been successfully implementing an effort that contained virtually all the elements of good practice even before the problem-solving exercise was initiated or Bratton was recruited. A police lieutenant had the key to controlling squeegeemen in New York City, but his ideas needed to be brought forward and given credibility before they could be implemented. The lesson is not just that problem-solving methods should be employed by police and criminal justice agencies, but that the process involves line personnel—those who work with the problem on a daily basis and experience it.

The question then is how to implement a problem-solving orientation throughout criminal justice organizations so that they can respond quickly to problems, not after thousands of public transportation patrons have been lost, a city's housing stock has been seriously and irrevocably damaged, squeegeers have terrorized thousands of drivers, or drug dealers have taken over an entire neighborhood. We are not certain of the entire answer to this question; however, developing and maintaining a focus on the community—and the forces such a focus generates—is absolutely essential.

## Prepare to Win in Court

To have a chance at long-term survival and reaching its intended goals, any order-restoration policy must not only rest firmly upon moral and utilitarian bases, it must also be able to survive an intense legal battle. The wisest course is to assume from the beginning that you will be challenged in court, and plan legislation, programs, and policies accordingly. This effort will necessarily involve close coordination among city officials, police, other criminal justice agencies, and city and county legal counsel, and should include citizens as well. Carried out well, such coordination will provide a strong base on which legal counsel can mount a successful, two-pronged defense of the city's program: first, by developing a careful factual record of the city's efforts to place before the court; and second, by meeting legal arguments that will surely be raised by advocates for those opposed to order restoration.

CONVINCE THE COURT WITH THE FACTUAL RECORD. The factual record placed before the court of the city's efforts to develop legislation, programs, and policies to restore order will be as crucial to the outcome of the case as the legal arguments themselves. To begin, the city must be able to provide a clear account of the legislative intent to restore order as part of an overall effort to control crime and prevent further urban decline. If advocates for the homeless can make the case that city officials or the police were concerned primarily with displacing indigent street people, rather than turning neighborhoods around and preventing further decline, they will have a hand up. If the legislative record documents the fact that policy decisions were taken to develop an order-restoration program after city officials carefully considered recent empirical research linking disorder, fear, serious crime, and urban decline, a city will be better able to convince a court that its interest and intent are legitimate and constitutionally permissible.

Evidence of the city's intent will be provided as well in a consistent record of having met its responsibilities to the poor and indigent by attempting to offer social services, job training, counseling, housing, and other resources from within the community. These services need not all come from government—private sector resources may also be offered—but government must be actively engaged in marshaling them and monitoring citizen needs. The services also need not be linked directly to an order-maintenance program. Nevertheless, as an independent element in the city's record, their existence will serve to dispel the notion that the city intended in any fashion to discriminate against indigent, homeless, or otherwise disadvantaged persons through its order-maintenance efforts. In Seattle and San Francisco, records of the services provided to indigent and homeless individuals served just this effect.

The factual record amassed by a city must also show careful attention to the fundamental rights of all citizens in implementing legislation and the order-restoration program itself. Legal counsel should work closely with city and police officials to inform and educate the public and train police officers prior to implementation of new legislation or a new order-restoration program, just as they did in the New York City subway, and should be available for consultation as the program unfolds, as were lawyers from the city attorney's office in San Francisco. City and police officials should develop explicit guidelines for police to follow as part of their enforcement efforts.

Finally, the factual record should undertake to illustrate the effectiveness of the program in accord with stated goals—lessened fear, safer conditions on streets, neighborhood renovation, crime decreases—if such progress can be documented. Statements from citizens in Boyd Booth, reduced crime rates and restoration projects such as Bryant Park in New York City, greater citizen satisfaction with the downtown area in Baltimore, all attest to the achievements related to order restoration.

CONVINCE THE COURT THROUGH LEGAL ARGUMENTS. As a first step, the legislation undergirding any order-restoration and maintenance effort will need to be narrowly and precisely drafted so as to avoid vagueness and overbreadth challenges, and to address acts rather than status. Most courts today have found the act of begging to implicate First Amendment protections, a holding with which we do not agree: it is not congruent with the street experiences of citizens facing panhandlers, and ignores the contextual elements that give meaning to behavior. Ultimately this issue will be resolved by the Supreme Court. At present, legislation is most likely to succeed if it seeks to restrict aggressive begging or panhandling, or other narrowly defined behaviors, in particular places and at specific times. The examples provided by City Attorney Mark Sidran in Seattle, and the New York City Transit Authority, suggest the best mechanisms for drafting legislation.

Once engaged by a legal challenge to legislation, legal counsel should be prepared to offer convincing legal arguments to support the following assertions:

*Disorderly behavior is not protected by the First Amendment.* Advocates for the homeless and many courts continue to subscribe to the view that begging and other low-level offenses targeted frequently by order-maintenance programs constitute speech or at least expressive activity that is protected by the First Amendment. This conclusion is particularly troubling, given what we know about the nature of the "homeless" population and many of those who engage in disorderly behavior on our streets: while some may be passive or benign in their speech and acts, many more are scam artists, substance abusers feeding alcohol or drug habits, mentally ill, or have criminal records. Furthermore, we know that the speech and behavior of many in this population are intimidating and even threatening, and may become even more so depending upon the context in which they take place. What, indeed, is the "message" that such speech, or acts, is sending? Can it really be, as some courts have found, that "government benefits are inadequate" or "there are large numbers of poor and homeless today for whom our country is failing to provide"?

Cities and advocates of legislation restricting disorderly behavior must be fully prepared to assert that disorderly acts are not protected by the First Amendment and should not be accorded the highest degree of First Amendment protection.[88] They may find support in the opinion of the federal appeals court in *Young v. New York City Transit Authority*, that construing such messages out of the intimidating speech or acts of individuals influenced by mental illness, drugs, alcohol, or even criminal intent represents an "exacerbated deference to the alleged individual rights of beggars and panhandlers to the great detriment of the common good."[89] In a similar vein is Federal district court Judge Barbara Rothstein's refusal to find that every public act by homeless persons should be considered expressive conduct and accorded First Amendment protection.

*The government has a compelling interest in restricting disorder in public places.* Contesting the view that acts such as aggressive panhandling and squeegeeing are protected "speech" is made more difficult when they are carried out in public places, such as city parks or streets. The courts have designated these arenas, traditionally reserved for the free expression of ideas, as "public fora," and determined that the greatest possible degree of First Amendment protection applies. Yet as Harvard professor Mark Moore has recognized about traditional legal thinking in this area: "There is this interesting paradox that says that the places in which people can act out—streets and parks—are the places in which there are also the greatest dangers that result from their actions."[90] Stanley Fish recognizes this paradox when he discusses the balancing of individual rights and governmental interests that courts undertake in approaching restrictions on speech:

> It is only in the most peculiar and eccentric of social spaces, like a Hyde Park Corner, where the production of speech has no purpose other than itself that absolute toleration will make sense, and it is one of the oddities of "official" First Amendment rhetoric that such peculiar spaces are put forward as the norm. That is, First Amendment rhetoric presupposes the ordinary situation as one in which expression is wholly unconstrained and then imagines situations of constraint as special. But the truth is exactly the reverse: the special and almost-never-to-be-encountered situation is one in which you can say what you like with impunity. The ordinary situation is one in which what you can say is limited by the decorums you are required to internalize before entering. Regulation of free speech is a defining feature of everyday life, not because the landscape is polluted by censors, but because the very condition of purposeful activity (as opposed to activity that is random and inconsequential) is that some actions (both physical and verbal) be excluded so that some others can go forward.[91]

Conversely, recent Supreme Court opinions suggest that it may be moving toward defining even more arenas as public fora—airport terminals and other centers of mass transportation and communication, for example.[92] If this change is adopted, restrictions on "speech" or communicative acts (as are involved in begging and panhandling) in an increasing number of areas will have to pass the highest standard—strict scrutiny—by showing the existence of a compelling governmental interest.

Although the "compelling government interest" test is difficult to meet, it is not impossible to make the case that the government's interest in providing for the safety and welfare of its citizens requires order-restoration measures. Many courts have been unpersuaded by assertions of such an interest where it is based upon the discomfort or fear of citizens faced with beggars or persons camping in parks and on sidewalks. Many courts have also expressed the views of Judge Robert Sweet, in *Loper v. New York City Police Department*, who questioned what threat a single beggar could pose to the welfare of citizens or a community. Yet the work of Skogan and other social scientists, especially when coupled with the data linking order maintenance and reduction in serious crime, suggests a different conclusion: the governmental aim in restricting disorderly behavior such as begging goes far beyond obtaining relief from the uncomfortable or disturbing impact of beggars' speech or expressive acts upon listeners, which the courts have rejected as impermissible. As citizens faced with disorder abandon their use of streets, parks, and commercial areas, the secondary effects ultimately develop much more broadly into higher rates of index crimes, commercial decline, and widespread urban decay. It is not simply that an individual beggar poses a threat to society or will become involved in more serious criminal acts if permitted to continue begging (although this is not out of the realm of the possible, as shown by empirical research); rather, disorderly behavior draws and begets more serious criminal activities. In Baltimore, Judge Smalkin recognized this right where commercial viability was threatened in the downtown area;[93] and in San Francisco, Judge Jensen found the city to have a legitimate interest in protecting public safety and health and preserving parks for their intended purposes.[94] Both social scientists and legal counsel for cities must work much harder to develop this line of argument, and to convince the courts that an interest in restricting disorderly behavior merits according it full status as a compelling interest sufficient to justify restrictions on disorderly behavior.

*Disorderly behavior in public spaces is legitimately subject to time, place, and manner restrictions.* An important legal justification for regulation of disorderly behavior may be as time, place, and manner restrictions. Recall from our discussion of the New York City Transit Authority case that such regulations are judged according to a mere reasonableness standard so long as they are content-neutral, narrowly tailored to serve a significant government interest, and leave open alternative channels for communication. The Supreme Court has explained that the significance of the governmental interest must be viewed within the context of the particular forum involved (whether public or nonpublic). Furthermore, the validity of a narrowly fashioned regulation need not be judged solely on the basis of the specific incidents of speech or act at hand, but may be considered in light of the potential impact of other such acts as well.[95] In addition, the Court has held that to be judged "narrowly tailored" does not require the least restrictive means, only that a regulation further a substantial government interest "that would be achieved less effectively absent the regulation" and that any restriction not be substantially broader than is required to reach the government's interest.[96]

These standards offer perhaps the best opportunity for defending restrictions on disorderly acts: in particular, they permit the argument to be made that the aggregate effects of disorderly behavior could be sufficiently serious to warrant restrictions, even though individual acts, one by one, might appear insignificant.

*Head off a charge of municipal liability for failure to address disorderly behavior.* Recognizing a compelling governmental or public interest in restricting disorderly behavior must also remind us that the interest itself is a two-edged sword: if the interest in restricting disorder is so significant, then government also has a responsibility to address and deal with issues surrounding it—such as providing shelter and services for those legitimately homeless or mentally ill, treatment programs for substance abusers, and police training for dealing with those individuals. Failure to attend to such issues may subject a municipality to liability, including damages, where the constitutional rights of individual members of particular groups are frequently implicated in interactions with police or other officials. The Civil Rights Act as codified in 42 U.S.C. Sec. 1983 and interpreted by the Supreme Court assigns liability to municipalities where legislation, a policy, or even inactivity by municipal officials or police is found to infringe upon constitutional rights of those begging or panhandling, or engaging in other forms of disorderly behavior. Civil remedies are available to aggrieved parties who can show a policy not only through unconstitutional legislation, but through practices or failure to train employees.[97]

Therefore, to avoid liability a municipality can no more afford to *ignore* the disorderly behavior of its most troubled citizens than to attempt to restrict it. In fact, when statutory restrictions are challenged in court, municipalities able to document their efforts in addressing problems of the homeless, substance abusers, and the mentally ill, such as San Francisco in *Joyce v. City and County of San Francisco,*[98] and Seattle in *Roulette v. City of Seattle,*[99] are most likely to succeed in convincing the courts that they have not unfairly targeted these groups or discriminated against them in their efforts to control disorderly behavior.

Preparing to go to court has potential benefits that go well beyond

234 Fixing Broken Windows

mere legal preparation. Legislative debate and consideration should be invigorated; the resulting policies should be beneficial to a number of interests and constituencies, including those who are in genuine need of assistance. Finally, greater interaction among city officials, the police, the public, and city attorneys should provide a keener awareness of the potential resources that the entire community has at its command to address problems, particularly when citizens work together.

## Keep the Community Involved

Virtually all "experiments" in the control of disorder, fear, and crime now being conducted throughout the United States mix the "small change" of citizen control with that of governmental and criminal justice agencies, including the police. In fact, no efforts at restoring order in the community will be successful in the long run without the development of a full partnership between citizens in the community and the criminal justice institutions that affect conditions in their neighborhoods. This partnership must be fully inclusive of all racial, ethnic, religious, and economic groups; it must be subject to continuous renewal and reaffirmation; and it must provide the basis for the development of any efforts by the city to restore order, including the authority of police to implement an order-restoration program.

The goal of this partnership is for citizens themselves to "own" the problems facing their community, as well as the solutions that emerge. Along with police, prosecutors, the courts, and corrections, citizens must themselves become responsible for restoring order: they must participate fully in developing appropriate policies and programs, sharing in the public discourse and debate, and then support implementation efforts. Their involvement will not end when order returns to the community: instead, citizens must be prepared to play an active and ongoing role in maintaining order and preventing crime, just as have the residents of Boyd Booth and Manhattan, and private businesses working together as part of the Downtown Partnership in Baltimore and BIDs in New York City.

There is no single formula for the role that private initiatives need take. On the streets, residents and workers in neighborhoods must look out for each other's safety and well-being, help to enforce shared standards of civility and lawful behavior, and physically clean up streets and public places. Merchants can join together in BIDs to provide services and security in downtown areas, as they have in Baltimore, New York, and other cities. Private foundations can help support the creation of community courts and other locally based institutions to bring restorative justice to individual neighborhoods. All must work with schools, police, and other local institutions to make the community a safer place for children, the elderly, and those more vulnerable individuals.

One important role that local residents can play is to assist police entering very troubled areas. We should not underestimate the extent to which fear drives police officers' responses in situations, especially in inner-city and minority neighborhoods. At least two generations of police have been isolated from communities. The "old-timers" who knew neighborhoods and foot patrol practices are now retired, taking their knowledge and skill with them. Little in officer training today prepares police for the realities of street life. Yet community organizers, community lawyers, some criminal justice personnel, and leaders of neighborhood groups move through these communities regularly, if prudently: their safety arises primarily from familiarity with residents and other users of the community. Community residents in most of these neighborhoods will need to work with criminal justice officials and take to the streets with them—as they have already done in Baltimore and other cities. By taking such actions, citizens indicate publicly that they are conferring authority on officials to act on their behalf, and that they themselves have assumed responsibility for their neighborhood.

Perhaps more than anyone else, Sir Robert Peel has captured the essence of such a partnership between the public and criminal justice officials, drawing attention in his principles to a tradition in which "the police are the public and . . . the public are the police." The police are unique members of the public in that they "give full-time attention to duties which are incumbent on every citizen in the interest of the community welfare." Such a characterization places equal weight on the shoulders of citizens and police—and other officials—for maintaining order in the community. It also captures the essence of the new community-based paradigm of crime prevention and control that many communities are implementing today.

C H A P T E R     7

<hr/>

# FIXING BROKEN WINDOWS

WHILE WORKING WITH THE MASSACHUSETTS BAY TRANSIT AUTHOR-
ity (MBTA) Police Association (the police union) during the summer
of 1995, Kelling rode the Boston subways with off-duty officers and visited a number of transit stations. One was of particular interest: a tiny
neighborhood station on the Red Line, it had become the focus of an
increasing number of muggings, especially targeting Asian immigrants
moving into the nearby residential area. As the officers and Kelling
approached the station by car one afternoon, four youths sat tightly
pressed together on a small bench on a porch directly across the street
from the subway entrance. The street was narrow, and from their perch
the youths commanded a view of the comings and goings of the station,
as well as of the area just inside the station doors. Upon leaving the station, Kelling stopped and looked at the youths directly, at some
length—something he would not have done had the officers not
accompanied him. None of the boys could have been older than thir-
teen or fourteen, weighed more than 140 pounds, or been taller than
five foot three. All were African Americans, dressed identically in a
dark sweatshirt with hood up, dark baggy pants, and black sneakers.
The bench was at the front of the porch and each youth slouched forward—shoulders hunched over, vulture-like—with hands in sweatshirt
pockets. Despite the obvious fact that Kelling's companions were

police, the four did not shrink back when observed: they simply stared, eyeing Kelling impassively but menacingly.

After a few moments—haunted by the experience—Kelling got into the police car and left with the officers. Not more than a mile away, a dispatch over the police radio informed them that an Asian male had been mugged directly outside that very station. It took only a couple of minutes to get back to the scene. Two Boston Police Department officers were already there, but the four youths were gone, as was the victim. A neighborhood resident had observed the four rob the man and had called the police. She was talking to one of the officers. As best she could tell the man had lost his wallet, but was unwilling to stay and talk to the police. Kelling stood off to the side and looked back at the porch he had earlier observed. A middle-aged Asian woman and a young boy about eleven or so were sweeping off the porch and repositioning the bench back against the house. Even though they were off duty, the officers drove around the neighborhood for a short time, and then gave up—they did not even have a victim.

To be viable, crime-control policies must acknowledge and be prepared to deal with the tragic realities that are imbedded in this incident: the inability of family, neighborhood, and community institutions to control and protect children; the tragically damaged children themselves, and their incognizance of or resignation to their fate—for most if not all will go to prison and/or be killed, it is only a matter of time; their calculating viciousness and the terror and damage they cause to others in the community; and the loss that all of this represents for the community itself. Restoring order and reducing fear are not enough where such trauma is being inflicted daily upon a community: crime-control policy must assume responsibility for such youths and the terror they spread. Yet the broad debates about welfare, education, and family values, or more narrow arguments about gun control, capital punishment, or "three strikes you're out," seem to offer little hope of immediate relief or value.[1]

The feared future—of marauding bands of armed and vicious youths, and frightened children and adults alike carrying weapons to protect themselves—is already with us in many cities. Citizens and neighborhoods are in trouble *now*; they need help *today*. Short of imprisoning a whole generation of youth, can policies be developed and implemented that offer hope for the immediate present, while not ignoring long-range requirements? The answer is an unequivocal yes. And while imperfect and inchoate in its present form, the outline for such policies and practices exists in virtually every city in the United States, in the shape of a new paradigm of crime control already manifest in our communities.

In preceding chapters, we developed the story of how this new model of crime control emerged by looking backward, at the previous model that failed us. We began with the public "criminal justice system"—a radical mid-twentieth century invention that redefined how crime was to be controlled in a community. Police were the "front end" of this system, responsible for arresting serious offenders and presenting them to prosecutors for judicial processing and ultimately correction. Citizen concerns, whether for maintaining order or seeking justice, were largely discounted in favor of "objective" calculations by prosecutors, police, and other criminal justice professionals of what constituted the "true" crime problem and the appropriate means of handling miscreants, whether petty or felonious. The preoccupation of each part of this "system" was a process: arrest for police, plea bargaining and case processing for prosecutors, interviewing probationees and parolees for corrections, and holding prisoners for jails and prisons. The different agencies of the "criminal justice system" atomized problems into incidents or cases, treating each as best they could—a classic example of the law of the instrument. Ironically, however, as every part of this "system" was improved and made more efficient, neighborhood and community problems continued to worsen. If an arrest went nowhere, police blamed prosecutors or soft-hearted judges; prosecutors and judges blamed police for ineptness or lack of attention to required legal procedures. Everyone could blame the fictive "system" with impunity. Meanwhile, while each agency was doing its self-defined job, no one "owned" the neighborhood and community problems that were increasing daily.

Confronted with the failure of professional crime control and the excesses of disorderly and predatory behavior, citizens inexorably mobilized and struggled to regain control over their communities. In Boston alone, the one hundred or so named and active community crime-control groups that existed in 1982 expanded to more than six hundred. In Baltimore, historic neighborhoods like Boyd Booth, Harlem Park, and Sandtown organized around issues like drug dealing, abandoned and vacant houses, trash (often the result of abandoned houses), and having police patrol their neighborhoods on foot—all with considerable success. Similar examples could be given from virtually every city in the United States. Private or corporate security, which had its contemporary origins during the post–World War II era, also increased, with the current 1.5 million–agent private security industry in the United States now dwarfing public police forces, which number approximately half a million. As businesses turned to private security for protection, developing business improvement districts (BIDs) along the way, private security programs began operating in public areas— sidewalks, parks, and other public spaces—causing police to rethink their approach to private security. Pioneer Square, the heart of downtown Portland, Oregon, is policed jointly by private and public police, with private police having the primary responsibility for order maintenance and keeping the peace. In New York City, the NYPD, the Metro North Police (public police responsible for Grand Central Terminal and Metro North trains and facilities), the Grand Central BID, and First Security (a Boston-based security firm responsible for the Met-Life building) now form the Grand Central Alliance, apportioning policing responsibilities in the area and, like the Portland public and private police in Pioneer Square, share common radio bands. In Austin, Texas, District Attorney Ronnie Earle has created, in his office, one of the most thoroughly problem-oriented agencies in criminal justice today. Even courts are starting to concentrate on community problems. Drug courts spreading across the country show equal concern for the protection of communities and the rehabilitation of drug users. Likewise, the Midtown Community Court provides a model for managing neighborhood problems while simultaneously providing help for minor offenders.

Together these efforts reflect the evolution of a new community-based paradigm of crime prevention and control that is revolutionizing criminal justice. The foundation of this new movement is a partnership between private and public forces. Its most significant aspects are, first, the definition of crime prevention and control in new and broader terms, and second, the location of a significant source of authority for criminal justice processes in the community and delineation of a crucial role for citizens. The model representing this movement is summarized in Figure 7.1.

**FIGURE 7.1**

*The "Criminal Justice System" Versus Community-Based Prevention*

|  | Criminal Justice System | Community-Based Prevention |
|---|---|---|
| The Crime Problem | INDEX CRIME: the more serious the crime, as determined by traditional measures, the more energy criminal justice agencies should expend dealing with it. | DISORDER, FEAR, SERIOUS CRIME: seriousness determined by context, neighborhood priorities, and the extent to which problems destabilize neighborhoods and communities. |
| Priorities in Crime Control | APPREHEND AND PROCESS OFFENDERS. | PREVENT AND CONTROL CRIME, RESTORE AND MAINTAIN ORDER, REDUCE CITIZEN FEAR. |
| Role of Citizens | AID POLICE: Since crime control is best left to criminal justice professionals, citizens "aid" professionals in controlling serious crime by calling police, being good witnesses, and testifying against wrongdoers; all else is vigilantism. | CITIZENS ARE KEY: control of disorder, fear, and crime has its origins in the "small change" of neighborhood life; citizens set standards for the neighborhood and maintain order; police and other criminal justice agencies support and aid citizens, especially in emergencies. |
| Police, Prosecutors, Courts and Corrections: Structure | CENTRALIZED ORGANIZATION. | DECENTRALIZED AGENCIES: allow for flexible responses to local problems and needs. |
| Methods | PROCESS INDIVIDUAL CASES: when crimes occur. | PROBLEM-SOLVING APPROACH: identify and solve larger problems within which individual cases are embedded. |
| Use of Discretion | DISCOURAGED, UNRECOGNIZED: assumption that little guidance is needed for law enforcement processing; clear and precise rules and regulations developed as required; attempt to limit/eradicate discretion with mandatory arrest and prosecution policies, determinate sentences. | FUNDAMENTAL AND IMPORTANT TO CRIME CONTROL EFFORTS: controls developed through statements of legislative intent; carefully crafted laws that address the complexity of issues; formulation of guidelines, procedures, rules, and regulations with input from citizens and line police officers. |

**FIGURE 7.1** (*continued*)

|  | Criminal Justice System | Community-Based Prevention |
|---|---|---|
| Order v. Liberty Interests | INDIVIDUAL LIBERTY INTERESTS PREDOMINATE: most nonviolent deviance should be tolerated in the name of individual liberty interests. | BALANCED: liberty interests not absolute, but balanced against need to maintain basic levels of order for neighborhoods and communities to function. |
| Public-Private Relationship | POLICE NEUTRAL AND REMOVED: should intrude into community life as little as possible. | POLICE ACT ON BEHALF OF COMMUNITY: are intimately involved in local life, but also act justly, equitably, in accord with established legal principles. |

Citizen or neighborhood-based groups are a key element in this paradigm. They are bound by a common purpose—the restoration of order—and a commitment to prod criminal justice agencies into helping them solve neighborhood problems. Moreover, neighborhood organizations, with support from local and national foundations, community action groups, and even government, have developed a coherent set of tactics for restoring order and controlling crime that are clearly identifiable and can be taught to other neighborhood groups, as well as to criminal justice organizations. Individuals and organizations like Felice Kirby of the Citizens Committee for New York City, Roger Conner of the American Alliance for Rights and Responsibilities, and Michael Sarbanes of Baltimore's Mayor's Coordinating Council on Criminal Justice, have developed step-by-step guides for dealing with specific neighborhood problems and gaining the attention of criminal justice agencies. Opportunity reduction,[2] problem solving,[3] and crime prevention through environmental design (CPTED),[4] as well as political and legal action, have all become part of the vernacular of community groups and are included in their banks of skills. Neighborhood residents can now say, as one did recently to Kelling in Baltimore's Boyd Booth neighborhood, "We let the neighborhood get out of control. It was our fault. We took it back. We know how to keep it."

Today we are beginning to see the impact of this new paradigm in our communities, particularly in its emphasis on restoring order. Wherever one goes in cities, when neighborhood residents have organized, established priorities, and brought pressure to bear on governmental agencies to provide them with assistance, citizens report improvement in the quality of their lives. They also believe that along with restoring order, serious crime has also been reduced. Limited empirical evidence notwithstanding, we find these accounts of crime reduction persuasive. But a caveat is in order. Let us suppose that police order-maintenance activities have not reduced crime and have little potential for doing so, in spite of the fact that we do not believe this to be true. Such an outcome would dampen only slightly our enthusiasm for restoring order. Both disorder and the fear it generates are serious problems that warrant attention in and of themselves. Disorder demoralizes communities, undermines commerce, leads to the abandonment of public spaces, and undermines public confidence in the ability of government to solve problems; fear drives citizens further from each other and paralyzes their normal, order-sustaining responses, compounding the impact of disorder. Restoring order is key to revitalizing our cities, and to preventing the downward spiral into urban decay that threatens neighborhoods teetering on the brink of decline, regardless of whether a reduction in crime results. Even those neighborhoods struggling with significant levels of predatory criminal behavior—as the area around the Boston subway station victimized by young males that we described above—can benefit from taking the first steps toward attempting to restore order. Citizens organizing cooperatively, taking responsibility for their streets and parks, developing working relationships with police, prosecutors, and other criminal justice officials, learning about resources available to them—all will reduce fear and strengthen the community in the long run.

More than this, however, there is growing reason to believe that order-maintenance activities will have a major impact on index crime, as well as low-level disorder. This is a finding of crucial significance for neighborhoods already facing high levels of crime, and living with the day to day trauma that such crime brings.

## THE EFFECTS OF RESTORING ORDER: CONTROLLING CRIME THROUGH ORDER MAINTENANCE

Four elements of the Broken Windows strategy explain its impact on crime reduction. First, dealing with disorder and low-level offenders both informs police about, and puts them into contact with, those who have also committed index crimes, including the hard-core "6 percent" of youthful offenders. Second, the high visibility of police actions and the concentration of police in areas characterized by high levels of disorder protect "good kids," while sending a message to "wannabes" and those guilty of committing marginal crimes that their actions will no longer be tolerated. Both of these elements ultimately bring greater control to bear to prevent crime. Third, citizens themselves begin to assert control over public spaces by upholding neighborhood standards for behavior, and ultimately move onto center stage in the ongoing processes of maintaining order and preventing crime. Finally, as problems of disorder and crime become the responsibility not merely of the police but of the entire community, including agencies and institutions outside but linked to it, all mobilize to address them in an integrated fashion. Through this broadly based effort, a vast array of resources can be marshaled, and through problem solving, targeted at specific crime problems.

*Establishing Control: Police Contact with Criminals
and the "6 Percent"*

By their nature, police order maintenance and minor crime enforcement activities increase police-citizen interactions. Usually, such contacts are not remarkable: police remind citizens of their responsibilities, educate them about rules, regulations, and laws, warn them about their infractions, and occasionally ask or order citizens to "move on"—all legitimate interventions when people are violating subway rules or city laws and ordinances. But these activities also put police into contact with troublemakers and serious offenders. The experience in the New York City subway is an example: a significant number of those arrested for farebeating either were carrying weapons or had warrants outstanding on felony cases. Similarly, many police contacts with "homeless" panhandlers revealed petty criminals, as well as those who had records for serious felonies.

The potential deterrent effect of such routine police activities on serious crime was first raised by James Q. Wilson and Barbara Boland in 1978.[5] In a controversial statistical study, Wilson and Boland suggested that aggressive police tactics in activities such as citing for moving traffic violations lowered the crime rate by increasing both the possibility of arrest for offenders and criminals' perceptions of social control. Robert Sampson and Jacqueline Cohen retested these ideas in 171 cities in 1980, and concluded: "Proactive policing has been shown to have significant and relatively strong inverse effects on robbery, especially adult robbery by both blacks and whites. . . . Hence, on strict empirical grounds the results suggest that cities . . . with higher levels of proactive police strategies directed at public disorders also generate significantly lower robbery rates."[6]

America's crime problem is a male youth problem, fourteen to seventeen year olds being the single largest offender group. Moreover, in terms of violence, the behavior of male youths is worsening. As Princeton policy analyst John DiIulio, Jr., has pointed out, the murder rate has increased 50 percent by white males and 300 percent by black males during the period from 1985 to 1992.[7] Not all male youths, even those who commit crimes, present equal risk to society, however. Since the 1970s, we have known that some 6 percent of youths who commit crimes in the United States account for more than 50 percent of all such crimes committed.[8] These figures have held over time, as the same findings were obtained in 1985 studies conducted in the United States,[9] as well as in London, England.[10] There is, however, a significant difference between the two cohorts reported on in the United States (the first group born in 1945; the second in 1958): while the *number* of criminal events committed by the 6 percent did not increase appreciably, the *severity of their crimes* did.

Considerable study has followed these findings, especially with an eye to identifying social and psychological characteristics of repeat juvenile offenders so that we can predict who they will be and determine how to prevent the mayhem they wreak on society. James Q. Wilson describes and compares the experiences of serious, hard-core offenders and the rest of us, in the face of conditions increasingly conducive to crime in society:

> The traits of the 6 percent put them at high risk for whatever criminogenic forces operate in society. As the cost of crime declines, or the benefits increase; as drugs and guns become more available; as the glorification of violence becomes more commonplace; as families and neighborhoods lose

some of the restraining power—as all these things happen, almost all of us will change our ways to some degree. For the most law-abiding among us, the change will be quite modest: a few more tools stolen from our employer, a few more traffic lights run when no police officer is watching, a few more experiments with fashionable drugs, and a few more business deals on which we cheat. But for the least law-abiding among us, the change will be dramatic: they will get drunk daily instead of just on Saturday night, try PCP or crack instead of marijuana, join gangs instead of marauding in pairs, and buy automatic weapons instead of making zip guns.[11]

Wilson likens the situation for the 6 percent, and the conditions that stimulate them into more serious crime, to the game of "crack the whip":

> When children play the school-yard game of crack-the-whip, the child at the head of the line scarcely moves but the child at the far end, racing to keep his footing, often stumbles and falls, hurled to the ground by the cumulative force of many smaller movements back along the line. When a changing culture escalates criminality, the at-risk boys are at the end of the line, and the conditions of American urban life—guns, drugs, automobiles, disorganized neighborhoods—make the line very long and the ground underfoot rough and treacherous.[12]

Police, prosecutors, and probation and parole agents know who these "6 percenters" are. In smaller cities like New Haven, chiefs like Nick Pastore can rattle off their names. In larger cities, precinct commanders, even in cities like New York, can be apprised of who in their neighborhood is a violent repeat offender or on probation or parole for serious violent crimes. Moreover, as we have seen in New York City, minor offenders and "wannabes" have important information about who is dealing drugs from where; about who carries weapons, and when; about who is planning to commit crimes or who has; about who has been "dissed"—humiliated—and intends to strike back. Some minor offenders and "wannabes" will provide such information because they want to strike a deal with police or prosecutors; others because they are fearful—"so-and-so is carrying a gun and wants me to roll some drunks"—both of the offender and/or of getting caught. Good citizens, especially in tough neighborhoods, also have pools of information about serious offenders that go untapped, either because no one asks them for it, because they have no opportunity to share it with police or correctional agents, or because they fear that the indiscretion of officials could result in reprisals.

Once they have identified serious offenders, police, prosecutors, and probation and parole agents must send very strong messages to these youths that their predatory behavior will result in immediate incarceration. A core part of this message must be that weapon carrying is absolutely unacceptable, and will result in re-incarceration for any known violent offender. Such messages must and can have teeth: great potential exists to exert control and influence over repeat and violent offenders. Many are under court orders that restrict their behavior, including where they can be and with whom; others have warrants outstanding for their arrest. Many commit minor offenses giving police legitimate opportunities to question them, search them for weapons, and if appropriate, arrest them.

All of this, of course, speaks to control. We believe gaining control in troubled neighborhoods to be a necessary first step to both restoring order and reducing crime. To strengthen communities and reinvigorate their institutions, order must first be restored and predators controlled. Granted, the issue of control in minority communities, especially by police, has been a sensitive one. To speak to the problem in black communities, Glenn C. Loury and Shelby Steele, prominent African Americans, while calling for black leadership in restoration of their communities, nonetheless specifically obligate larger society to restore order and control crime:

> We do not want our advocacy of black responsibility to represent a general absolution from responsibility for the larger society. Why doesn't America keep the peace in inner cities? . . . Suppose there were several hundred gang-related murders every year in suburban Chicago or Washington or Los Angeles. Would there be a different public response?[13]

If we are not going to flush an entire generation of youth, 6 percenters must learn for their own sakes, as well that of the community, that there are limits. As in Wilson's "crack the whip" metaphor, these youths are plummeting towards personal disaster: imprisonment, addiction, and death. Certainly, they need help: education, training, jobs. To use help, however, they need control first. Prison alone is not adequate—it is an all or nothing response. For those who commit serious crimes, control must pervade the communities in which they live or to which they return, serving as a clear disincentive to further criminal activity. It must take the form of closely coordinated citizen, police, prosecutorial, and correctional vigilance.

*Order Maintenance Protects "Good Kids" and Controls "Wannabes"*

Hard-core predators and gang members wreak havoc with other youths, especially in poor and ghetto neighborhoods. Education suffers and jobs flee the neighborhood, both making a tough situation worse for inner city youth. More directly, good youths fear the depredations of the 6 percent and many elect for their own protection to join gangs and/or carry weapons, in effect being pressured or forced into criminal activity. Unlike many adults who can retreat into their cars and homes, youths must expose themselves to urban life *on the streets*. It is not surprising that they should take protective action. Unfortunately, the situation is only exacerbated by a libertarian philosophy that offers levels of freedom to young people that they simply do not have the internal controls and experience to manage. It is further worsened by a police and criminal justice strategy that abdicates control over the streets to those most prepared to intimidate and bully. Politically and morally these are unacceptable consequences.

Order restoration and maintenance efforts offer help in two senses. By developing a community consensus about a moral order applicable within the neighborhood, and enforcing it, well-intentioned and behaved youths, adults, and police can regain control over streets, thereby reducing the level of fear of youths and their need to protect themselves. Additionally, controlling predators will send strong messages to children and youths coming up behind the 6 percent: there is a moral order in the community; offenders may get a second chance, but it will not be a joke, for the state has teeth; adults will control neighborhoods and set standards for children; vicious youths will not be permitted to interfere with the functioning of schools, churches, neighborhoods, and commerce.

The emphasis of order-maintenance programs upon low-level offenses is particularly important as a means of restraining "wannabes," the less-dedicated-to-crime friends and associates of repeat offenders. Many in this group, if pressured, or if schools and police pressure their parents, ultimately will change their behavior to conform to more appropriate and decent standards. They don't understand the impression they make or the terror they can instill by "horsing around" in public spaces, for other citizens who do not know them, especially the elderly, cannot always discern the potential for violence in their actions from that in the behavior of the hard-core 6 percent. The depredations of the 6 percent have become so vicious, and the braggadocio and boisterousness of the rest of the youths so indistinguishable from the menacing swagger of the 6 percent, that virtually all have become a source of fear, especially for the elderly or feeble. Many of these wannabes need instruction, some of it by police but by other institutions as well, about civil behavior. Restraining this group by enforcing rules, in the subway or on the street, reduces the criminogenic conditions—the disorder and chaos—that both stimulate and provide cover for those dedicated to serious crime.

## Increasing Citizen Control Over Public Spaces

When the Transit Authority initiated its program in New York, the vast majority of subway riders had lost patience with routine incivilities in the subway system. Asked what they thought about the content and style of signs delineating subway rules, one group of riders, mostly minority women, indicated that if they were to see such signs and police enforcing the rules they, too, would reprimand rule violators, especially smokers and "boom box" players. This attitude indicates what is perhaps the most significant effect of reducing disorder and offers the greatest potential for crime reduction in long-range terms: the development of a renewed commitment within the community for citizens themselves to take responsibility for maintaining civil and safe social conditions. This acceptance of responsibility by citizens is not trivial: experience after experience has demonstrated that while police might be able to *retake* a neighborhood from aggressive drug dealers, police could not *hold* a neighborhood without significant commitment and actual assistance from private citizens.[14]

Understanding the role of citizens in maintaining order and crime control has come full circle since 1961, when Jane Jacobs described, in *The Death and Life of Great American Cities*, a precinct captain's advice to fearful residents of a middle-income housing development never to hang around outdoors after dark or answer their doors without knowing the caller.[15] Faithful to reform-model policing, the officer believed the proper role of citizens to be observers of events, reporting them promptly to police, acting as good informants and witnesses, and generally supporting the local police. Only now do we comprehend fully the disastrous consequences of such advice. Atomistic, self-protective moves by citizens help to erode the quality of urban life, for when locked behind closed doors, individuals abandon their basic civic obligations. Not only does such withdrawal from urban life represent bad citizenship, it also contributes to relinquishing public spaces and streets to disorderly and criminal persons, whom Jacobs labeled "barbarians." When residents in Baltimore's Boyd Booth neighborhood admitted responsibility for conditions there getting out of hand, they exemplified this point: it might appear prudent to surrender to barbarians in the short haul, but the ultimate consequence of such surrender is the loss of one's freedom to live in a decent and civil urban environment.

How does citizen control over public spaces develop, especially when threatened or once lost? Although we have discussed numerous factors, such as crime control through environmental design and problem solving, the very first step in troubled, changing, or pluralistic communities must be police collaboration and negotiation with citizens to identify neighborhood standards of behavior that will then be enforced. A real police presence in neighborhoods, one that persists over time and is intimately familiar with the community and its strengths and problems, will be crucial to this consensus-building process, for good policing will help shape, identify, and give legitimacy to neighborhood standards. Newark police officers negotiated informally with local residents during the 1970s over neighborhood standards; the same informal process took place in Somerville, Massachusetts, when officers negotiated with youths and neighborhood residents over how parks could be used on warm summer nights. Negotiation of standards can also be highly structured and formal, as they were in Dayton during the late 1970s and in New York's subways during the early 1990s.

Regardless of whether such negotiation is formal or informal, all citizens who are affected by the establishment of the standards—street people and youths as well as residents and merchants—must participate. The outcome will be a consensus in the form of an agreement that contains, for all parties, an explicit recognition of mutual obligations as well as rights. If youths are granted the right to stay in a park, they must behave. The rights of homeless to use the subway are assured but they, like everyone else, must follow its rules. Students may be students and party, but they must do so at times and in a manner that does not interrupt the routines of working persons and children.

Once established, the terms of such agreements may need reinforcing in practice. Some youths may have to be reminded of their responsibilities; some adults may be unsympathetic to youths and need to be encouraged to be more tolerant. Even though a consensus has been developed, an active police presence will be required to deal with those who are not prepared to accept their obligations to others: those who absolutely refuse to cooperate and violate both the informal standards and the law may be arrested. For the most part, however, the standards will become self-enforcing after a period of time. Youths come to understand that they will suffer the 10 P.M. curfew if they do not help to control their more obstreperous peers. Neighbors understand that a complaining neighborhood crank can undermine a neighborhood's peace as surely as a few irksome youths.

Because such neighborhood standards are negotiated (and renegotiated under changing conditions as the need arises), widely understood, and accepted as legitimate by virtually all elements of the community, eventually all those who live there will have a stake in helping to uphold and enforce them. Residents, for example, will legitimately caution youths when their youthful exuberance leads to minor infractions—a little bit too much horseplay, music a little too loud—that erode community life. Police and other officials will assist citizens, restraining them if overzealousness edges toward vigilantism, acting as peacemakers where the consensus is under strain in a neighborhood, making certain that citizen enforcement does not violate the fundamental rights of individuals. In the final analysis, however, citizens must accept their responsibility to control their neighborhoods—and once invested in restoring order, they generally take on this role. Restoring order and controlling crime in neighborhoods are only in part the responsibility of police and criminal justice agencies.

*Order Maintenance and Crime Prevention Through*
*Integrated Problem Solving*

From the earliest efforts to eliminate graffiti in the New York City subway, every department was involved and committed. Station managers monitored conditions in their stations continuously to ensure that minimum standards were maintained. Maintenance and repair staff cleaned new graffiti promptly, secured token receptacles, and repaired and cleaned facilities. The police "homeless unit" referred vulnerable persons in the subway for services. And all transit staff had to help maintain order by reminding those who broke the rules of their responsibilities. Restoring order was not merely the responsibility of police, then, but an *integrated effort* involving a number of different agencies and social service providers, all of which engaged in a *problem-solving* process to target a specific set of problems. The end result was not only order restored, but crime reduced, and most probably, prevented.

The fact is that in other settings, when they work in isolation from each other neither police, citizens, nor today's criminal justice agencies have been able to reduce serious crime. Taking our cue from the New York experience, we believe that order-restoration and maintenance attempts are most effective and most likely to lead to crime prevention and reduction when a community mounts an integrated and comprehensive effort involving citizens, police, various criminal justice agencies, social service agencies, business, schools, and city officials. At first, this cooperation will serve an educational function, as each discrete actor learns about the capabilities and resources of others and information is shared. But even more importantly, when the effort is channeled through a problem-solving process, in which each actor or agency directs its attention and assets toward a single target, the splintered, atomizing tendencies of the criminal justice "system" can be overcome. Where each agency strives not merely to do its job, but to coordinate its actions as part of achieving a common goal, the potential for success increases significantly.

Coordinating efforts through problem solving is catching on across the country: in Salt Lake City, Community Action Teams, which include both prosecutors and correctional agents, set out to understand neighborhood and community problems and devise overall coordinated tactics for dealing with them. In Indianapolis, four street-level prosecutors operate out of offices in police district stations, working closely with citizen groups and as liaisons between the Marion County Prosecutor's Office and the police district. Each street-level prosecutor screens and files cases arising in the district to which he or she is assigned, selecting a limited number that he or she will prosecute personally, and otherwise assists detectives with investigative matters, advises police about enforcement issues, responds to local community concerns, and interacts with businesses, schools, churches, and governmental agencies to improve the quality of life in the district. At the same time, prosecutors and Corporation Counsel staff, cooperating with the Indianapolis police and fire departments, are shutting down drug houses for health and safety code violations. In Boston, Operation Nightlight is a coordinated on-street response to serious offenders by police and the Massachusetts Department of Probation. Boston's (Suffolk County) District Attorney Ralph Martin has overseen the development of a number of "Safe Neighborhood Initiatives," in which prosecutors based in local district courthouses work with the police and citizen advisory councils to identify citizen concerns and develop strategies for addressing them that include law enforcement as well as other components.[16] These endeavors are all fledgling examples of the shift to integrated, community-based problem-solving efforts, akin to those undertaken in the early days of community policing when police were trying to respond to neighborhood problems in new and creative ways. The difference now is that not only police, but prosecutors, correctional agents, and courts must learn to speak with one voice—and that voice should reflect neighborhood interests and controls.

As the problem-solving process works itself out, officials around the country representing different criminal justice agencies are beginning to question and redefine their "mission," their jobs, and the nature of their role in the community. For prosecutors, the shift is from case processing alone to working more closely with citizens in neighborhoods and communities, and responding to their concerns. Austin, Texas, District Attorney Ronnie Earle's efforts are a case in point. Earle views his job as more than running an office efficient in trying and winning cases: instead, he has attempted to build institutions and processes to implement his concept of community justice. He has led in the development of a community justice program, seeking to have low-level offenders incarcerated in local county jails, apart from more violent offenders, so that they can receive appropriate punishment, treatment, and counseling, remain close to the community, and be reintegrated into it upon release. The goal is to restore and maintain the health of the community by changing the behavior of offenders so that they become contributing members—a much harder task than simply locking them away, and one that, if successfully achieved, will prevent recidivism. In addition to his community justice program, Earle has also sought to make justice for victims, particularly victims of violent crimes, a central focus of the Travis County District Attorney's Office. Justice is achieved in part with the successful prosecution of a case, resulting in a finding of guilt and appropriate punishment for the offender, but also by using the prosecution process itself to help the victim heal. Assistant district attorneys, aided by victim advocates, can contribute to this healing—by educating, showing strong support for, and advocating on behalf of the victim and his or her family—even when a case is lost in court. To reduce the trauma for child victims or witnesses of violent crime or abuse, District Attorney Earle also initiated the creation of a Children's Advocacy Center, bringing together in a home-like setting all law enforcement, prosecution, and social and medical services needed to examine, counsel, interview, and prepare a child victim or witness for trial.[17] Today the center operates as a public/private nonprofit organization, supported by a number of public agencies (including prosecution, law enforcement, social services), but under the control of private citizens in the community. Just as some prosecutors are doing, so too correctional officials and even the courts must eventually redefine their roles, making commitments to citizens and their concerns, to neighborhoods, and to making their presence felt in them. Most thus far have been slow to do so.

Each of these elements of an order-maintenance program—addressing disorder through a comprehensive community-wide problem-solving effort, forcing a change in the behavior of wannabes away from disorderly acts, increased police contact with and control over perpetrators of index crimes, and causing citizens to accept a greater role in order maintenance in public spaces in their community—also holds the potential for preventing and reducing crime. While the linkages between these elements and crime reduction are most apparent at this time in the New York City subway experience, they are being replicated in order-maintenance efforts around the country.

## PROSPECTS FOR RESTORING ORDER

Those who alert us to the "echo baby boom"—the cohort of youths that will pass through the population in the last years of the twentieth century—do us a service. They remind us of the consequences of failed social policies in dealing with youth, as well as with the emotionally disturbed and alcohol/drug abusers, during the last thirty years. For us, however, neither the programs of the right nor left offer much promise. While we object little to imprisoning many repeat violent offenders (regardless of their age) forever, more prisons and harsher mandatory sentencing laws will have limited impact overall on fear, public safety, and quality of urban life. Similarly, while we support efforts at social and economic justice, no consensus exists about how these goals can be achieved, in what time frame (probably decades, at minimum), and what impact they would have on crime. In the meantime, children are in peril, citizens cannot protect themselves or their property, a generation of African-American male youths is near to being lost to death and imprisonment, and the quality of life of all citizens has been diminished.

Nevertheless, we are optimistic about the ability of American society to restore order and control crime. Our optimism has three sources. First, the public has lost confidence in the idea of a public criminal justice system that controls crime through case processing. Recognition of the failure of this "system" is explicit and growing. Its demise is long overdue. Second an alternative paradigm to crime control and prevention is in place, albeit in incipient form, and is producing remarkable outcomes in the early stages of implementation. Finally, there is little evidence that vengeance and/or vigilantism will result from following more democratic values in crime-control processes, suggesting that fears of this danger have been exaggerated and misguided.

Private citizens and researchers alike recognize the failures of the criminal justice system paradigm. From the epochal findings of the

American Bar Foundation during the 1950s, to the discovery of the linkage between disorder and citizen fear during the 1960s, through studies of foot patrol in the 1970s and Skogan's work linking disorder, fear, crime, and urban decay, research has been essential to overthrowing the dominant criminal justice ideology. For most of this century, police professionals were assumed to know best: about crime, society's best response to it, and the role of citizens in crime control. Yet, research turned the argument, at first giving tentative voice to citizen concerns, and later, fueling attempts by a new generation of reformers to bring police and criminal justice policies in line with citizen concerns. Now research is crucial to overturning social policies and legal dogma that give undue weight to liberty interests and ignore personal responsibility and community interests.

The salient point here is that, aside from cynical or naïve politicians, no one really believes that "professional" reform model policing and improved case processing will obtain the quality of life for which citizens yearn. Moreover, American society is confronted with the dilemma that the more efficient its criminal processing becomes, the more likely it is that African Americans will be its "products"—a moral and socially unacceptable solution to the crime problem. Citizens have found their own answer to the dilemma—the new paradigm that we have described as community based, rooted in citizen ideals of an ordered, civil society, blending informal social control with recognition of fundamental, constitutionally protected rights and liberties, and integrating order maintenance with crime prevention and control.

There is no lack of support for this new model. In Kansas City, Missouri, voters in Jackson County in 1989 willingly imposed a quarter cent sales tax, now called COMBAT (Community Backed Anti-Drug Tax), to support a massive anti-drug effort in their community. COMBAT is a true representative of the new paradigm in action: drawing upon wide citizen support and input, marshaling resources for an assault on the community's drug-related problems, marrying enforcement and prosecution with prevention and treatment. Originally spearheaded by County Prosecutor Albert Riederer, the program has been expanded and revitalized by current Prosecutor Claire McCaskill since she took office in 1993. Its goals are to jail dangerous criminals and drug dealers; treat nonviolent offenders who sincerely want to get off drugs; and prevent children from experimenting with drugs. Funds now totaling close to $15 million a year are allocated to a comprehensive effort that addresses all aspects of the drug problem including: law enforcement and community crime prevention; investigation, prosecution, and judicial processing; incarceration; and treatment and rehabilitation.[18] The results? To recognize only a few—as of August 1995, violent crime was down 32 percent over the previous thirty months; with fifty-one new police officers drug arrests are up over 300 percent; more than 1,300 drug houses have been closed through the efforts of code and fire inspectors, police officers, and county prosecutors working together; nearly 100,000 students in twelve school districts have participated in drug abuse prevention programs; neighborhood-based crime and drug prevention programs are increasing; twenty-six agencies are providing inpatient and outpatient substance abuse treatment; and first-time nonviolent offenders are receiving court-ordered drug treatment, education, and employment training. COMBAT is working, and citizens know it: 71 percent of voters supported it in the last referendum, held in November 1995.

Finally, we are optimistic about prospects for restoring order and bringing crime under control because today we see citizens taking firm steps to reclaim their rightful role in a democratic society—defining the terms of civility in their neighborhoods and communities and insisting that these terms be respected. To be sure, they do this within the context of a legal system that is properly vigilant about protecting individual rights. Yet the idea that left to their own devices citizens necessarily will be overly restrictive, vengeful, and punitive—a point of view that has dominated criminal justice thinking—is belied on the streets of Somerville, Massachusetts, in Manhattan's Midtown Community Court, in Baltimore's Boyd Booth neighborhood, and in other neighborhoods throughout the United States. Despite outrageous levels of crime in some communities, vigilantism remains extremely rare in the United States.

Can citizens go too far? Will there be injustices? Yes, at times. Part of the responsibility of police, prosecutors, courts, and correctional officials will be to restrain citizens and encourage tolerance. But it is a form of narrow elitism to believe that only government has a corner on justice and tolerance. Government officials must let democracy work, even in matters of crime control. Preemptively usurping citizen obligations, whether in the name of preventing abuse, efficiency, or narrow profes-sional interests, does for citizens what they should do for themselves and encourages bad citizenship. Not only that, it does not work.

The good news, however, is that windows can be fixed, and order restored. In some of the most difficult circumstances imaginable—New York City, New Haven—the quality of urban life is improving and crime is decreasing. The results are better than we could have imag-ined, and perhaps we have not seen them all yet.

# POSTSCRIPT

ON APRIL 15, 1996, WILLIAM BRATTON RESIGNED AS NEW YORK City's police commissioner. This was not surprising: Bratton had long expressed a desire to enter the private sector and it was no secret that his relationship with Mayor Giuliani was deteriorating. Besides, commissioners do not last long in New York: the average tenure during this century has been about two and a half years. Bratton's incumbency was about two and a quarter. The media "spin" focused on who would get credit for the decline in crime—Bratton or Giuliani? If crime did worsen again, how would this reflect on Giuliani and his new commissioner, Howard Safir? And if it continued to drop after Bratton's departure, certainly Giuliani would be given the credit![1]

The media focus on personalities and their interactions—the "great men" view of politics and history—might make for salacious and gossipy news; however, it wholly ignores the true meaning of what occurred in New York City, and its significance in national terms. Neither Bratton's nor Giuliani's contributions to New York City and policing are demeaned by recalling that Benjamin Ward initiated the basic shift in New York's policing strategy during the mid-1980s; that former Mayor David Dinkins and Police Commissioner Lee Brown accelerated this strategic change and developed state and local political support for adding thousands of new officers; and that Commissioner Raymond Kelly opened the door to aggressive order maintenance in the NYPD. Nor does it diminish the contributions of either to acknowledge the roles played by David Gunn in eliminating graffiti in the subway, Robert Kiley in restoring order in the subway, Herb Sturz in pushing for neighborhood responses to disorder, and by a legion of others in restoring order to Grand Central Terminal, Penn Station, the Port Authority Bus Terminal, Bryant Park, and the Times Square and Grand Central neighborhoods.

Mayor Giuliani and Commissioner Bratton will be remembered properly as a forceful team that clearly articulated and rapidly accelerated movements inchoate in New York City from the late 1970s onward. They were innovative, creative leaders who greatly contributed to the city's capacity to maintain order and reduce crime. Yet, New York City's story is bigger than the Bratton–Giuliani saga. It is the tale of an entire community reclaiming its public spaces.

# NOTES

## Introduction

1. Helen Hershkoff, "Aggressive Panhandling Laws: Do These Laws Violate the Constitution? Yes: Silencing the Homeless." *ABA Journal*, vol. 79 (June 1993): 40.

2. Kent S. Scheidegger, *A Guide to Regulating Panhandling* (Sacramento, Calif.: Criminal Justice Legal Foundation, 1993), 4.

## Chapter 1

1. A. D. Biderman, L. A. Johnson, J. McIntyre, and A. W. Weir, *Report on a Pilot Study in the District of Columbia on Victimization and Attitudes Towards Law Enforcement*, Department of Justice (Washington, D. C.: U.S. Government Printing Office, 1967).

2. The study was commissioned by the City of San Francisco in preparation for a legal suit against its enforcement of a statute banning accosting for the purpose of begging, and was conducted by the Stanford Research Institute. See Declaration of Susan Russell in Support of Defendants' Motion for Summary Judgment at 4–6, Blair v. Shanahan, 775 F. Supp. 1315 (N.D. Cal. 1991), *appeal dismissed and remanded*, 38 F.3d 1514 (9th Cir. 1994), *cert. denied* by California v. Blair, 115 S.Ct. 1698 (1995), district court decisions vacated by No. C-89-4176 WHO (N.D. Cal. January 31, 1996).

3. "The New York Newsday Interview with Jeremy Travis," *Newsday*, August 11, 1994.

4. See Amici Curiae Brief of Senior Achievement Non-Profit Housing Association and Seattle Indian Center on Behalf of Appellees, Roulette v. City of Seattle, No. 94–35354 (9th Cir., September 1, 1994 [appealing Federal District Court Judge Barbara Rothstein's Order Granting Defendants' Motion for Summary Judgment and Denying Plaintiffs' Cross-Motion for Summary Judgment, Roulette v. City of Seattle, 850 F.Supp. 1442, W.D. Wash., 1994]).

5. Jane Jacobs, *The Death and Life of Great American Cities* (New York: Vintage Books, 1961), 72.

6. For a discussion of the program and description of the research see *The Newark Foot Patrol Experiment* (Washington, D.C.: Police Foundation, 1981).

7. International Association of Chiefs of Police, Field Service Division, A Survey of the Police Department (mimeo, 1962).

8. Fowler and his colleagues, while evaluating an early experiment in community policing in Hartford, Connecticut, found similar connections. Floyd J. Fowler, Jr., and Thomas Mangione, *Neighborhood Crime, Fear, and Social Control: A Second Look at the Hartford Program*, National Institute of Justice, U.S. Department of Justice (Washington, D.C.: U.S. Government Printing Office, April 1982). Other surveys of specific populations, especially the elderly and residents of public housing, found the same results.

9. Robert Trojanowicz, *An Evaluation of the Neighborhood Foot Patrol Program in Flint, Michigan* (East Lansing: Michigan State University, 1982).

10. James Q. Wilson and George L. Kelling, "The Police and Neighborhood Safety," *The Atlantic* (March 1982), 29–38. Wilson was also on the Board of Directors of the Police Foundation, which had funded the Newark Foot Patrol Study. He has written extensively on policing. *Varieties of Police Behavior* (Cambridge, Mass.: Harvard University Press, 1968) is considered a classic in police literature and includes discussions of policing disorder.

11. Wilson and Kelling, "The Police and Neighborhood Safety," 31.

12. Ibid., 32.

13. Ibid., 34.

14. See Arthur L. Stinchcombe et al., *Crime and Punishment in Public Opinion* (San Francisco, Calif.: Jossey-Bass, 1980); and Wesley G. Skogan and Michael Maxfield, *Coping with Crime: Individual and Neighborhood Reactions* (Newbury Park, Calif.: Sage Publications, 1981).

15. Among those who responded strongly and immediately to the implications of "Broken Windows" was James K. (Chips) Stewart who, while not yet director of NIJ when the solicitation was published, would become the director soon after and be responsible for administering the grant. At the time the solicitation was published Stewart was a White House Fellow. Formerly, he had been an Oakland police officer who rose to head its detective unit. As Stewart has since put it:

> "Broken Windows" was a breakthrough in thinking about the practical things that police could do to reduce fear and crime. It may not have made sense to the criminological establishment, focused as it was on correlational studies and serious crime, but to a former police officer it made a lot of sense. I believed, and only a few of the staff were with me on this, that NIJ both had to do more experimentation with ideas like "Broken Windows" and more work—I call it anthropological—on the streets and with officers and offenders to try to discover what works. (Personal conversation with George Kelling, 20 July 1994.)

Stewart's goal was to turn NIJ into a criminal justice policy "think tank" and to focus its research on policy in all areas of criminal justice. Given his interest in "Broken Windows," and his commitment to large-scale policy-relevant experimentation, Stewart moved to expand the original order-maintenance research effort that he inherited into a major experiment in Newark and Houston that would cost well over a million dollars.

16. The Police Foundation research team included Mary Ann Wycoff, Tony Pate, Lawrence Sherman, and Wesley Skogan.

17. Robert C. Black, "Police Control of Disorder: Legal Bases and Constitutional

Constraints," Report Submitted to the Fear Reduction Project, Police Foundation, Washington, D.C., January 18, 1983.

18. Lawrence Sherman, personal conversation with George L. Kelling, July 21, 1994.

19. For a summary of this research see Tony Pate et al., *Reducing Fear of Crime in Houston and Newark: A Summary Report* (Washington, D.C.: The Police Foundation, 1986).

20. Wesley G. Skogan, *Disorder and Decline: Crime and the Spiral of Urban Decay in American Neighborhoods* (New York: Free Press, 1990). For a discussion of these data bases, see "Methodological Appendix," 187–194.

21. Ibid., 54–57.

22. Ibid., 74–75.

23. Ibid., chap. 4 generally.

24. Ibid., 75.

25. Research in England based on the British Crime Survey (a victimization survey similar to those conducted in the United States) adds further credence to the "Broken Windows" hypothesis. While more cautious than Skogan because of the limits of the data they used, the authors conclude:

> This chapter has sought to shed some light from the British Crime Survey on two themes. . . .
> (i) the relationship between incivility and crime in neighborhoods; and (ii) the distribution . . .
> of crime across different kinds of residential neighborhoods. Some support is given to the general relationship between incivility, crime, and neighborhood deterioration described in a number of theoretical models, . . . of which Wilson and Kelling's (1982) "broken windows" hypothesis is one version.

See Tim Hope and Mike Hough, "Area, Crime, and Incivilities: A Profile from the British Crime Survey," in *Communities and Crime Reduction*, ed. Tim Hope and Margaret Shaw (London: Her Majesty's Stationery Office, 1988), 43.

26. David Firestone, "Stopping Blight at the Border; Two Paths for Ridgewood, Queens, and Bushwick, Brooklyn," *The New York Times* (August 25, 1994), B1.

27. *Crime in the United States*, Federal Bureau of Investigation, Department of Justice (Washington, D.C.: U.S. Government Printing Office, Published annually).

28. Thomas Repetto, "Bruce Smith: Police Reform in the United States," in *Pioneers in Policing*, ed. Philip John Stead (Montclair, N.J.: Patterson Smith, 1977), 171–206.

29. For a discussion of the development of most of the measures used to evaluate police during the reform era—crime rates, clearances, clearance ratios, cost per citizen, and number of police per 100,000 population—see Bennet Mead, "Police Statistics," *The Annals*, vol. CXLVI (November 1929), 74–96.

30. In Chicago during the early 1980s, for example, reported rapes of black women were regularly *unfounded* by the Chicago Police Department. That is, although black victims reported that they had been raped, and good reason existed to believe them, police refused to record their rapes as such. Aside from involving serious injustice to the women victims, and sending a message to rapists that black women could be raped with impunity, these acts by police resulted in the incidence of reported rapes being kept at a spuriously low level. Personal knowledge based upon observations made by George Kelling in Chicago, 1982.

31. To deal with this problem, national victimization surveys were developed during the 1960s and are now published annually under the title *Criminal Victimization in the United States* by the Department of Justice. They are reported only on national and regional bases. Unless specially funded and adapted for evaluation purposes, they are not useful in attempting to measure local crime trends.

32. *Criminal Victimization in the United States, 1993*, NCJ-151657 (Washington, D.C.: U.S. Department of Justice, 1995), Table 27.

33. This final shortcoming will be alleviated somewhat when the National Incident-Based Reporting System (NIBRS), the planned replacement of the UCR, is fully implemented. NIBRS is being pretested in locations throughout the country at the present time. NIBRS will collect much more detailed information about the criminal event, including information about the victim and perpetrator (such as any relationship between them). See Brian A. Reaves, "Using NIBRS Data to Analyze Violent Crime," Bureau of Justice Technical Report, U.S. Dept. of Justice, Office of Justice Programs, Bureau of Justice Statistics, Washington, D.C., October 1993.

34. Thorsten Sellin and Marvin E. Wolfgang, *The Measurement of Delinquency* (New York: Wiley, 1964).

35. Marvin Wolfgang, Robert M. Figlio, Paul E. Tracy, and Simon I. Singer, *The National Survey of Crime Severity*, Bureau of Justice Statistics, NCJ-96017 (Washington, D.C.: U.S. Government Printing Office, June 1985).

36. Ibid., vi; the following statistics are on pp. vi–x.

37. Peter Tira, "No Place for Kids; City Will Bulldoze Blighted Mini-Park," *San Francisco Independent*, vol. 39, no. 12 (January 28, 1994), 1.

38. Jane Jacobs, *The Death and Life of Great American Cities*, 72.

## Chapter 2

1. Candace McCoy, "Policing the Homeless, " *Criminal Law Bulletin*, vol. 22, no. 3 (1986): 266.

2. James S. Kunen, "Quality and Equality: The Mayor tries something that works, at a cost," *The New Yorker* (November 28, 1994), 9–10.

3. Loper v. New York City Police Dept., 802 F.Supp. 1029, 1032 (S.D.N.Y. 1992), *aff'd*, 999 F.2d 699 (2d Cir. 1993).

4. See, for example, David H. Bayley, "Ironies of American law enforcement," *The Public Interest* 59 (Spring 1980): 45–56; Myron Magnet, *The Dream and the Nightmare: The Sixties' Legacy to the Underclass* (New York: William Morrow and Company, 1993); Fred Siegel, "Reclaiming Our Public Spaces," *The City Journal*, vol. 2 (Spring 1992): 35–45.

5. Lawrence M. Friedman, *The Republic of Choice* (Cambridge, Mass.: Harvard University Press, 1990), 9.

6. See, e.g., Mary Ann Glendon, *Rights Talk: The Impoverishment of Political Discourse* (New York: The Free Press, 1991).

7. Mapp v. Ohio, 367 U.S. 643 (1961); Escobedo v. Illinois, 378 U.S. 478 (1964); Miranda v. Arizona, 384 U.S. 436 (1966).

8. Quinn Tamm, executive director of the International Association of Chiefs of Police (IACP), asked and answered the question "Whose Rights Are Being Defended?"

as follows: "This is a logical question to ask in view of the 5–4 decision by the Supreme Court of the United States on June 13 which virtually eliminated police-station inter-rogation of suspects and further hamstrung the police in their fight against crime. Whose rights—those of the lawbreaker or those of society?" Quinn Tamm, "Whose Rights Are Being Defended?" *Police Chief*, vol. 33 (July 1966): 6. Even earlier, North-western University law professor Fred Inbau railed against the exclusionary rule in a speech to the 1961 National District Attorneys' Associations: "We are not only neglecting to take adequate measures against the criminal element; we are actually facilitating their activities in the form of what I wish to refer to as "turn 'em loose" court decisions and legislation. . . . What particularly disturbs me . . . is the dangerous attitude that has been assumed by the United States Supreme Court. The Court has taken upon itself, without constitutional authorization, to police the police." Fred E. Inbau, "Public Safety v. Individual Liberties," *Police Chief*, vol. 29 (January 1962): 29.

9. V. A. Leonard, *Survey of the Seattle Police Department*, Seattle, Washington (June 1, 1945).

10. Citzens' Bureau of Milwaukee, *Survey of the Milwaukee Police Department* (September 1938).

11. City and County of San Francisco, California, Police Department, Annual Report (1947), 68; City and County of San Francisco, California, Annual Report (1954), 58.

12. Sociologist Egon Bittner, who has studied police handling of the mentally ill, notes the "unofficial" character of police handling of disturbed persons at this time: "By far the larger number of police encounters with mentally ill persons results neither in dejure nor in defacto emergency apprehensions. Rather, the involvements begin and end in the field. No other social agency, either legal or medical, participates in these cases and the policeman acts as the terminal, all-purpose remedial agent." Egon Bittner, "Police Discretion in Apprehension of Mentally Ill," in *Aspects of Police Work* (Boston: Northeastern University Press, 1990), 75.

13. Philip B. Taft, Jr., "Dealing with Mental Patients," *Police Magazine* (January 1980), 20–27.

14. Thomas Szasz, *The Myth of Mental Illness: Foundations of a Theory of Personal Conduct* (New York: Hoeber-Harper, 1961); Erving Goffman, *Asylums; Essays on the Social Situation of Mental Patients and Other Inmates* (Garden City, N.Y.: Doubleday, 1961); R. D. Laing, *Divided Self: An Existential Study in Sanity and Madness* (Baltimore: Penguin Books, 1965).

15. O'Connor v. Donaldson, 422 U.S. 563, 575–576 (1975).

16. President's Commission on Law Enforcement and Administration of Justice, *The Challenge of Crime in a Free Society* (Washington, D.C.: U.S. Government Printing Office, 1967), 234.

17. Robin Room, "Comment on 'The Uniform Alcoholism and Intoxication Treat-ment Act,'" *Journal of Studies on Alcohol*, vol. 37, no. 1 (1976): 123.

18. President's Commission on Law Enforcement, *The Challenge of Crime in a Free Society*, 236.

19. Christopher Jencks, *The Homeless* (Cambridge, Mass.: Harvard University Press, 1994), 40.

20. Rael Jean Isaac and Virginia C. Armat, *Madness in the Streets: How Psychiatry and the Law Abandoned the Mentally Ill* (New York: The Free Press, 1990), 7.

21. Christopher Jencks, *The Homeless*, 39, and n. 22.

22. For a detailed history of Larry Hogue and a summary of the deinstitutionalization issue, see Heather Mac Donald, "Have We Crossed the Line: The Human Costs of Deinstitutionalization," *The City Journal* (Winter 1993): 35; Janet Allon, "For Hogue, A Step Toward Freedom," *The New York Times*, Sunday Edition (October 22, 1995), Sec. 13, p. 6.

23. City and County of San Francisco, California, Police Department, *Annual Report* (1967), 140.

24. President's Commission on Law Enforcement, *The Challenge of Crime in a Free Society*, 233.

25. *Bureau of Justice Statistics Sourcebook of Criminal Justice Statistics—1992*, U.S. Department of Justice, Office of Justice Programs (Washington, D.C.: U.S. Government Printing Office, 1993), 422.

26. *Sourcebook of Criminal Justice Statistics—1992*, 603.

27. Mark A. Kleiman, *Against Excess: Drug Policy for Results* (New York: Basic Books, 1992), 221.

28. See, e.g., Garcia v. San Antonio Metropolitan Transit Auth., 469 U.S. 528 (1985); National League of Cities v. Usery, 426 U.S. 833 (1976); L. Tribe, *American Constitutional Law*, 2d ed. (Mineola, N.Y.: The Foundation Press, 1988), Sec. 6–3 at 405–06; 7–3 at 554–55.

29. Kent S. Scheidegger, *A Guide to Regulating Panhandling* (Sacramento, Calif.: Criminal Justice Legal Foundation, 1993), 4.

30. See, e.g., Amitai Etzioni, *The Spirit of Community: Rights, Responsibilities and the Communitarian Agenda* (New York: Crown Publishers, 1993).

31. Harry Simon, "Towns Without Pity: A Constitutional and Historical Analysis of Official Efforts to Drive Homeless Persons from American Cities," 66 *Tulane Law Review* 638, 639 (March 1992). See also Arthur H. Sherry, "Vagrants, Rogues and Vagabonds—Old Concepts in Need of Revision," 48 *California Law Review* 557, 558 (October 1960).

32. The first were Connecticut, Georgia, Massachusetts, New Hampshire, New York, Pennsylvania, South Carolina, and Virginia. Maryland, New Jersey, Rhode Island, and Vermont passed such regulatory statutes between 1796 and 1805. See Brief of Defendants-Appellants at 19–20, Young v. New York City Transit Authority, 729 F. Supp. 341 (S.D.N.Y.); Cohens v. Virginia, 19 U.S. 264, 276–89, 284 (1821).

33. J. Crouse, *The Homeless Transient in the Great Depression: New York State, 1929–1941* (Albany: State University of New York Press, 1986), 15–19.

34. In the United States, many (although certainly not all) current statutes aimed at restricting disorderly behavior have their roots in early British vagrancy laws that were directed at vagrancy as a way of life, at those idle and disorderly people considered to make up the "dangerous classes." In 1859, the *Oxford English Dictionary* included a reference to the "dangerous classes," according formal recognition to the notion of the poor as a criminal class. See Robert Teir, "Maintaining Safety and Civility in Public Spaces: A Constitutional Approach to Aggressive Begging," 54 *Louisiana Law Review* 285 (1993), for a discussion of the history of vagrancy laws in Europe as ancestors to the U.S. experience.

From the mid-fourteenth century, vagrancy was thought to threaten the economic stability of the country in its potential for depleting the work force. When high death rates from the Black Plague resulted in labor shortages in 1348, the English government recognized wandering and vagrancy as a crime through the Statutes of Labourers. 22 Edw. 3, c.12; 23 (1348) (Eng.); 23 Edw. 3, chap. 1 (1349) (Eng.); 25 Edw. 3, chap. 1 (1350) (Eng.). See also C. J. Ribton-Turner, *A History of Vagrants and Vagrancy and Beggars and Begging* (London, Chapman and Hall, 1887), 42–43; James F. Stephen, *A History of the Criminal Law of England* (London: MacMillan, 1883), 3: 267. Similarly in 1530 Parliament made "being a vagrant" a crime if the individual was able to work. 22 Hen. 8, c.5.

During the sixteenth and seventeenth centuries the government enacted punitive vagrancy laws, and while compulsory taxation of the landed aristocracy provided support for the poor, able-bodied indigents were set to work. Following the Napoleonic Wars, Parliament, perceiving a threat from large numbers of returning soldiers, again attacked vagrancy by passing the Vagrancy Act 1824, "for the punishment of idle and disorderly persons, rogues and vagabonds." Section 3 of the Act reads: "Every person wandering abroad, or placing himself or herself in any public place, street, highway, court or passage, to beg or gather alms . . . shall be deemed an idle and disorderly person within the true intent and meaning of this Act." Vagrancy Act, 1824, 5 Geo. 4, c.83. This act remains the basis of English law, although section 70 of the Criminal Justice Act 1982 abolished imprisonment for the offense of begging. Criminal Justice Act 1982. Neil Corre, "A Proposal for Reform of the Law of Begging," 1984 *Criminal Law Review* 750, 750.

35. Mayor of New York v. Miln, 36 U.S. (11 Pet.) 102, 142 (1837). A historical account of the development of laws against begging in New York State is provided in Appendix A, Defendants' Memorandum of Law in Support of their Renewed Motion for Summary Judgment at 5–14, Loper v. New York City Police Department, 802 F. Supp. 1029 (S.D.N.Y. 1992).

36. In West Virginia vagrancy was a common law offense. See Sherry, "Vagrants, Rogues and Vagabonds," 557, n. 1.

37. See Simon, "Towns without Pity," 642, for sources documenting the criticism of vagrancy and loitering laws that originated in legal scholarship as early as the 1950s.

38. The Court conceded that the reasoning expressed in the earlier *Miln* decision was outmoded, since "Poverty and immorality are not synonymous." Edwards v. California, 314 U.S. 162 (1941); Miln, 36 U.S. (11 Pet.) 102.

39. Shapiro v. Thompson, 394 U.S. 618, 629–31, 642 (1969).

40. Robinson v. California, 370 U.S. 660, 666 (1962).

41. Powell v. Texas, 392 U.S. 514, 517 (1968). Powell was tried first in the Corporation Court of Austin, Texas, and found not guilty; he appealed to the County Court of Travis County, and after a trial *de novo* was again found guilty. He then appealed to the U.S. Supreme Court since there was no further right to appeal within the Texas judicial system.

42. Powell, 392 U.S. at 532, 533–34.

43. Id. at 553–54 (White, J., concurring opinion).

44. See, e.g., Tobe v. City of Santa Ana, 27 Cal. Rptr. 2d 386, 393–94 (Cal.App. 4 Dist. 1994), *rev'd*, 892 P.2d 1145 (Cal. 1995).

45. For example, in 1992, the Third Circuit Court of Appeals upheld rules prohibit-

ing certain conduct in a public library against an equal protection challenge brought by a homeless man, using the lowest standard of review since "the homeless do not constitute a suspect class." Kreimer v. Bureau of Police for Town of Morristown, 958 F.2d 1242, 1269 (3rd Cir. 1992). See also Johnson v. City of Dallas, 860 F.Supp. 344, 355 (N.D. Tex. 1994), *rev'd, vacated, and remanded* on other grounds, 61 F.3d 442 (5th Cir. 1995).

46. Tobe v. City of Santa Ana, 892 P.2d at 1167 (Cal. 1995), overturning 27 Cal. Rptr. 2d 386 (Cal.App. 4 Dist. 1994). See also Kent S. Scheidegger, Brief Amicus Curiae of the Criminal Justice Legal Foundation in Support of Respondents, Tobe v. City of Santa Ana, 892 P.2d 1145; Patton v. Baltimore City, Civil No. S-93–2389, slip op. at 50–53 (D.Md., filed Aug. 19, 1994) (unpub. memorandum opinion and order).

47. Joyce v. City and County of San Francisco, 846 F. Supp. 843, 857 (N.D. Cal. 1994) (citations omitted).

48. Federal district courts in Pottinger v. Miami (Florida) and Church v. City of Huntsville (Alabama) have recognized homelessness as a status, and regulation of acts of the homeless as unconstitutional status restrictions. In *Pottinger*, the court ordered that "safe zones" be set up in which homeless persons could remain and carry out harmless, life-sustaining activities without being arrested. On appeal, however, the Eleventh Circuit Court of Appeals sent the case back to the district court for a clarification of whether recent events, including the city's construction of shelters for the homeless, justified modification of the lower court's holding. Pottinger v. City of Miami, 810 F. Supp. 1551, 1561–65 (S.D. Fla. 1992) (Eighth Amendment limits criminal prohibition of innocent conduct deriving from status of homelessness), *remanded*, 40 F.3d 1155, 1157 (11th Cir. 1994) (for determination of factual issues and clarification of the court's holding). And in *Church*, the district court's grant of a preliminary injunction against the City of Huntsville was overturned by the Eleventh Circuit Court of Appeals, which held that homeless plaintiffs had failed to establish a likelihood of prevailing on the merits of their claim that a city policy existed to arrest, harass, and remove them. Church v. City of Huntsville, No. 93–C–1239–S, slip op. at 2 (N.D.Ala. Sept. 23, 1994) (city enjoined from harassing, intimidating, detaining, or arresting homeless solely because of their status, for walking, talking, sleeping, gathering in parks or public places), *vacated*, 30 F.3d 1332, 1343–47 (11th Cir. 1994).

49. See, e.g., Goldman v. Knecht, 295 F. Supp. 897 (D. Colo. 1969); Wheeler v. Goodman, 306 F. Supp. 58 (W.D.N.C. 1969), *vacated*, 401 U.S. 987 (1971); Fenster v. Leary, 229 N.E. 2d 426 (N.Y.1967); Parker v. Municipal Judge, 427 P.2d 642 (Nev. 1967).

50. Papachristou v. City of Jacksonville, 405 U.S. 156, 158–59, 162–63, 164–65, 169 (1972) (citing United States v. Harriss, 347 U.S. 612, 617 (1954); Thornhill v. Alabama, 310 U.S. 88 (1940); Herndon v. Lowry, 301 U.S. 242 (1937); *Jacksonville Ordinance Code* Sec. 26–57.

51. Kolender v. Lawson, 461 U.S. 352, 354 (1983); *Cal. Penal Code Ann.* Sec. 647(e) (West 1970). In an earlier decision the California Court of Appeals had construed the statute to require a person to provide "credible and reliable" identification when requested by a police officer to do so: credible and reliable meant "carrying reasonable assurance that the identification is authentic and providing means for later getting in touch with the person who has identified himself." People v. Solomon, 33 Cal. App. 3d

429, 108 Cal. Rptr. 867, *cert. denied*, 415 U.S. 951 (1974). The Court relied on a line of cases to support its conclusion in applying the void for vagueness test: Hoffman Estates v. Flipside, Hoffman Estates, Inc., 455 U.S. 489 (1982); Smith v. Goguen, 415 U.S. 566 (1974); Grayned v. City of Rockford, 408 U.S. 104 (1972); Papachristou v. City of Jacksonville, 405 U.S. 156; Connally v. General Construction Co., 269 U.S. 385 (1926). Kolender, 461 U.S. at 359–61.

52. Shuttlesworth v. City of Birmingham, 382 U.S. 87, 91 (1965) (italics added).

53. See Annotation, "Validity of Loitering Statutes and Ordinances," 25 *American Law Reports* 3d 836, 842, Sec. 3[c].

54. Hoffman Estates v. Flipside, Hoffman Estates, 455 U.S. at 499; People v. Superior Court (Caswell), 758 P. 2d 1046, 1052–54, 1056 (Sup. Ct. Cal. 1988).

55. For example, a municipal loitering ordinance in Akron, Ohio, that prohibited loitering or remaining in a public place for the purpose of engaging or soliciting sexual activities for hire, or loitering or remaining in the area of any school, college, or university absent any legitimate reason or relationship of custody or responsibility for a student, survived a vagueness challenge because it specified what activities were prohibited, and connected loitering to a criminal activity. Akron v. Massey, 381 N.E. 2d 1362 (Ohio 1978).

56. City of Milwaukee v. Nelson, 439 N.W. 2d 562, 563, 567 (Wisc. 1989) (quoting Smith v. Goguen, 415 U.S. 566, 581 (1974).

57. Charles Theis, Chief Prosecutor, Office of City Attorney (Milwaukee, Wis.), personal conversation with Catherine Coles, July 10, 1995.

58. Wyche v. State, 619 So.2d 231, 233–34 (Fla. 1993); *City of Tampa Code*, sec. 24–61 A.10 (1987).

59. Loper v. New York City Police Dept., 999 F.2d 699 (1993), affirming 802 F.Supp. 1029 (S.D.N.Y. 1992).

60. See, e.g., Loper v. New York City Police Dept., 802 F. Supp. 1029, in which plaintiffs attacked the statute under the First, Eighth, and Fourteenth Amendments; however, the court addressed only First Amendment claims, found the Eighth Amendment claim contending that the statute created a status offense without merit, and declined to address Fourteenth Amendment claims entirely.

61. City of Cleburne v. Cleburne Living Center, 473 U.S. 432, 439 (1985).

62. The court applies an intermediate, heightened level of scrutiny where action or legislation classifies by gender or illegitimacy: here, the government must show that the classification is substantially related to an important state interest.

63. Maher v. Roe, 432 U.S. 464, 470–71 (1977).

64. Harris v. McRae, 448 U.S. 297, 322–23 (1980).

65. San Antonio Independent School Dist. v. Rodriguez, 411 U.S. 1, 29 (1973). The Court followed the same reasoning in Kadrmas v. Dickinson Public Schools, 487 U.S. 450, 458–59 (1988), holding that those who could not afford to pay a user fee for a public school bus service did not constitute a suspect class for equal protection purposes, and in addressing the housing issue, in Lindsey v. Normet, 405 U.S. 56 (1972).

66. First Amendment (speech) restrictions are subject to a number of tests developed by the Court. These are considered in greater detail in Chapter 6.

67. Roulette v. City of Seattle, 850 F. Supp. 1442, 1449 (W.D. Wash. 1994) (Judge Barbara Rothstein's Order Granting Defendants' Motion for Summary Judgment and

Denying Plaintiffs' Cross-Motion for Summary Judgment), *aff'd*, no. 94–35354 (9th Cir., March 18, 1996).

68. Berkeley Community Health Project v. City of Berkeley, 902 F. supp. 1084, 1092 (N.D. Cal. 1995), *appeal docketed*, No. 95-16060 (9th Cir. 1995). At issue were two sections of the Berkeley Municipal Code, sec. 13.37 (a solicitation ordinance), and sec. 13.36.015 (a sitting ordinance).

69. Alice S. Baum and Donald W. Burnes, "Analyses of Issues in *Joyce et al. v. City and County of San Francisco*" 14, prepared for Joyce v. City and County of San Francisco, No. C-93–4149 (N.D. Cal.), Oct. 27, 1994. This argument is provided in greater detail in Alice S. Baum and Donald W. Burnes, *A Nation in Denial: The Truth about Homelessness* (Boulder, Colo.: Westview Press, 1993).

70. Tobe, 892 P. 2d at 1145.

71. Joyce v. City and County of San Francisco, 846 F.Supp. 843, 850 (N.D. Cal. 1994).

72. Memorandum of Points and Authorities in Support of City and County of San Francisco's Motion for Summary Judgment, or Alternatively, Partial Summary Judgment at 3–5, Joyce v. City and County of San Francisco, No. C-93–4149 (N.D. Cal., filed Apr. 5, 1995).

73. Observations were conducted at this time by George Kelling. See also Rita Schwartz, *The Homeless: The Impact on the Transportation Industry*, Port Authority of New York and New Jersey, 1987.

74. Celia W. Dugger, "New York Report Finds Drug Abuse Rife in Shelters," *The New York Times* (February 16, 1992), 1.

75. Alice S. Baum and Donald W. Burnes, *A Nation in Denial*, 2.

76. Christopher Jencks, *The Homeless*, 46–48.

77. Memorandum of Points and Authorities in Support of City and County of San Francisco's Motion for Summary Judgment, or Alternatively, Partial Summary Judgment at 11–12, Joyce v. City and County of San Francisco, No. C-93–4149 (N.D. Cal., filed April 5, 1995).

78. Brad Lichtenstein, "Yet Another Reason to Arrest the Homeless," *The New York Times*, letter to the editor (October 24, 1994), A1.

79. Kent S. Scheidegger, Brief Amicus Curiae of the Criminal Justice Legal Foundation in Support of Respondents (filed October 25, 1994), Tobe v. City of Santa Ana, 892 P. 2d 1145 (Cal. 1995).

## Chapter 3

1. Quoted in Arthur Woods, *Policemen and Public* (New Haven, Conn.: Yale University Press, 1919), 13–15.

2. Eric H. Monkkonen, *Police in Urban America: 1860–1920* (New York, N.Y.: Cambridge University Press, 1981), 96. Monkkonen estimates that between 10 and 20 percent of the U.S. population in the late nineteenth century had at least one family member who had used police lodging facilities.

3. See Robert Fogelson, *Big City Police* (Cambridge, Mass.: Harvard University Press, 1977), 37.

4. Egon Bittner, "The Rise and Fall of the Thin Blue Line," *Aspects of Police Work* (Boston, Mass.: Northeastern University Press, 1990), 356.

5. For a fascinating account of American police history, especially the attempts to reform police, see Thomas Repetto, *The Blue Parade* (New York: The Free Press, 1978).

6. Sidney L. Harring, *Policing a Class Society: The Experience of American Cities, 1865–1915* (New Brunswick, N.J.: Rutgers University Press, 1983), 87.

7. Gene E. Carte and Elaine H. Carte, *Police Reform in the United States: The Era of August Vollmer, 1905–1932* (Berkeley, Calif.: University of California Press, 1975), 42.

8. Ibid., 45.

9. See George L. Kelling and William J. Bratton, "Implementing Community Policing: The Administrative Problem," *Perspectives in Policing* 17 (Washington, D.C.: National Institute of Justice, and Program in Criminal Justice Policy and Management, John F. Kennedy School of Government, Harvard University, July 1993).

10. International City Management Association, *Local Government Police Management* (Washington, D.C., 1991), 4, quoting August Vollmer, "Police Progress in the Last Twenty-Five Years," *Journal of Criminal Law and Criminology* 24, no. 1 (May-June 1933).

11. The 1953 *Manual of the New Haven Police Department* was typical: "Patrolmen, when they meet on the confines of their post, must not walk together or talk to each other, unless to communicate information pertaining to their police duties, and in such cases, the communication should be as brief as possible; they must not engage in conversations with any person on any part of their beat, except in regards to matters concerning the immediate discharge of their duties, but shall furnish such information and render such aid as is consistent with their duty" (rule 4, p. 43).

12. Jonathan Rubinstein, *City Police* (New York: Farrar, Straus and Giroux, 1973), 20.

13. Roscoe Kent, "Catching the Criminal by Police Radio," *The American City*, vol. 45 (November 1931): 106.

14. Orlando W. Wilson, *Police Administration*, 2d ed. (New York: McGraw-Hill, 1963), 240.

15. Samuel Walker, a historian who has published widely about the police reform movement, understands the disdain reformers had for line personnel: "The rank-and-file police officer was the 'forgotten person' of reform. Most reformers had contempt for ordinary officers." Samuel Walker, *The Police in America: An Introduction*, 2d ed. (New York: McGraw-Hill, 1992), 14.

16. Egon Bittner, *Aspects of Police Work* (Boston, Mass.: Northeastern University Press, 1990), 6–7.

17. Francis "Mickey" Roache, Boston Police Department Commissioner, personal conversation with George Kelling, 1985.

18. Two notable exceptions were Patrick V. Murphy and Clarence Kelley. Murphy ultimately became commissioner of the New York City Police Department and president of the Police Foundation. Kelley was chief of the Kansas City, Missouri, Police Department and director of the FBI. Murphy was so disliked by some of his colleagues for his outspoken opposition to much of what passed as police professionalism during the 1960s and 1970s that they tried to drum him out of the New York State Police Chiefs Association. Murphy, of course, practically made a career out of running against police chiefs.

19. President's Commission on Law Enforcement and Administration of Justice,

*Task Force Report: The Police* (Washington, D.C.: U.S. Government Printing Office, 1967).

20. Herman Goldstein and Charles Rogovin, personal communication with George Kelling, 1992.

21. Interview conducted by George Kelling with Herman Goldstein, Frank Remington, and Lloyd Ohlin, Madison, Wis., 1993.

22. For a detailed discussion of these issues, see George L. Kelling, "Toward New Images of Policing: Herman Goldstein's Problem-oriented Policing," *Law and Social Inquiry*, vol. 17, no. 3 (Summer 1992): 539–59.

23. Antony Pate, Amy Ferrara, and George L. Kelling, "Foot Patrol: A Discussion of the Issues," *The Newark Foot Patrol Experiment* (Washington, D.C.: The Police Foundation, 1981), 12.

24. Albert J. Reiss, Jr., *The Police and the Public* (New Haven, Conn.: Yale University Press, 1971), 95–97.

25. George L. Kelling et al., *The Kansas City Preventive Patrol Experiment* (Washington, D.C.: The Police Foundation, 1974).

26. Ibid., xvi, and chap. 6, 239–391.

27. Mary Ann Wycoff, *The Role of Municipal Police Research as a Prelude to Changing It* (Washington, D.C.: The Police Foundation, 1982).

28. Bittner, *Aspects of Police Work*, 7–8.

29. See George L. Kelling,, "How to Run a Police Department," *City Journal*, vol. 5, no. 4 (Autumn 1995): 34–45; George L. Kelling and Robert B. Kliesmet, "Police Unions, Police Culture, the Friday Crab Club, and Police Abuse of Force," in *And Justice For All*, ed. William A. Geller and Hans Toch (Washington, D.C.: Police Executive Research Forum, 1995).

30. Bittner, *Aspects of Police Work*, 43–44.

31. W. Blackstone, *Commentaries on the Law of England*, vol. 1, 1st ed. (1769), 290–91.

32. Tony Pate et al., *Police Response Time: Its Determinants and Effects* (Washington, D.C.: The Police Foundation, 1976), 49.

33. Kansas City Police Department, *Response Time Analysis: Volume II—Part I Crime Analysis*, Kansas City, Mo. (1977).

34. William Spelman and Dale K. Brown, *Calling the Police: Citizen Reporting of Serious Crime* (Washington, D.C.: Police Executive Research Forum, 1981).

35. Ibid., xxix.

36. Ibid., xi.

37. J. Thomas McEwen et al., *Evaluation of the Differential Police Response Field Test*, National Institute of Justice, United States Department of Justice, Washington, D.C. (1986).

38. The other side of this story is told by Sheriff Charles Berry of Grafton County, New Hampshire. Police received a call from a young child calling for her "mommy." Because enhanced 911 was in operation, police had access to the address, so dispatchers quickly sent a patrol car. "Mommy" was washing clothes in the basement, and refused to oblige her child's desire to come immediately. Having learned about 911 from her parents and television, the child called police to demand that her mommy come upstairs.

39. Spelman, *Calling the Police*, xxxiv.

40. David Bayley, "The Best Defense," *Fresh Perspectives* (Washington, D.C.: Police Executive Research Forum, n.d.): 3–4.

41. Ibid., 11.

42. This dynamic was evidenced recently in Indira A. R. Lakshmanan, "Police Wary of Bystanders Obstructing Arrests," *The Boston Globe* (March 18, 1994), 23, recounting a struggle that occurred when police tried to arrest a youth who had been speeding in a stolen car. A deputy superintendent of police commented: "If you really want to be safe as a police officer, you have to come in with a show of force that would convince the would-be attacker not to attack."

43. David Bayley, "The Best Defense," 2.

44. Readers familiar with private security will recognize that we are drawing upon a well-known set of goals, "prevent, limit damage, and restore functioning," made explicit to us by Robert Johnson, president of First Security.

45. Clifford Krauss, "Shootings Fall as More Guns Stay at Home," *The New York Times* (July 30, 1995), 29.

46. David M. Kennedy, "The Strategic Management of Police Resources," *Perspectives in Policing* 14 (Washington, D.C.: National Institute of Justice, and Program in Criminal Justice Policy and Management, John F. Kennedy School of Government, Harvard University, January 1993): 2.

47. To achieve rapid response for calls for service, police departments traditionally have tried to keep the uncommitted time of patrol cars somewhere between 40 to 60 percent of total time spent patrolling, whether one- or two-person cars. This amount of free, in-service time is generally thought to be desirable, although as calls have increased over time it has been difficult for police in many cities to maintain such a figure. Regardless, if one were to calculate the costs of uncommitted time (which serves very little purpose other than call availability since we know that both preventive and interception patrol contribute little to crime control or quality of neighborhood life), it would be a substantial portion of any police budget. If one were to allocate the costs of keeping police in-service to ensure rapid response to calls, even for serious crimes or emergencies, the cost for each successful response—recall that research indicated rapid response made a difference in less than 3 percent of cases—would likely be so high as to be politically and socially unacceptable.

48. "Serial Rapist Stalks E. Side Girls; Ages of 11 Victims Attacked by Stranger Range from 9 to 16," *Buffalo News* (April 27, 1991), A1.

49. Jane Jacobs, *The Death and Life of Great American Cities*, 31–32.

50. Peel's Principles cited in Louis A. Radelet and David L. Carter, *The Police and the Community*, 5th ed. (Englewood Cliffs, N.J.: Prentice-Hall, Inc., 1994), 9, quoting W. L. Melville Lee, *A History of Police in England* (London: Methuen, 1901), chap. 12.

## Chapter 4

1. The effort originated under Herbert Sturz, Deputy Mayor for Criminal Justice under Mayor Koch and former director of the Vera Institute. Sturz's influence was widely felt, both in New York City and nationally. Three of Sturz's protégés—Jeremy Travis, Carl Weisbrod, and John Feinbladt—would play pivotal roles not only in New

York City, but in criminal justice nationally, working to restore order to public spaces. Carl Weisbrod pioneered in the use of civil, as against criminal, laws to regulate disorderly behavior and conditions; he is now director of the Downtown (Wall Street) Business Improvement District (BID). Jeremy Travis became Deputy Commissioner for Legal Affairs in the New York City Police Department, where he installed a nationally recognized program to regulate disorderly behavior through the use of civil remedies; he is now director of the National Institute of Justice, the U.S. Department of Justice's research unit. Finally, John Feinbladt now directs the Midtown (Manhattan) Community Court, which blends private and public funding in a community-based effort to restore order and justice within urban neighborhoods.

2. Jonathan P. Hicks, "Court Cleanup Foils Giuliani Campaign for Quality of Life," *The New York Times* (September 20, 1995), A1.

3. George Kelling, "Measuring What Matters. A New Way of Thinking About Crime and Public Order." *The City Journal* 21 (Spring 1992): 28–30.

4. Dan Biederman, interview with George Kelling and Catherine Coles, February 9, 1995.

5. A study of criminal incidents in the district involving sixteen categories of crime was conducted by the Grand Central Partnership in cooperation with the NYPD.

6. See James Traub, "Street Fight," *The New Yorker* (September 4, 1995), 36.

7. Ibid., 40.

8. Nathan Glazer, "On Subway Graffiti in New York," *Public Interest* (Winter 1979): 4.

9. George L. Kelling, "Reclaiming the Subway," *The City Journal*, vol. 1, no. 2 (Winter 1991): 17–28. See also Maryalice Sloan-Howitt and George L. Kelling, "Subway Graffiti in New York City: 'Gettin' Up' vs. 'Meanin' It and Cleanin' It'," *Security Journal*, vol. 1, no. 3 (1990): 131-36, for a more detailed discussion of eradicating graffiti from subway cars.

10. Some officials in city government proposed bringing in portable showers, toilets, and kitchens—a move that would have turned the entire system into a gigantic flophouse.

11. See Wolfgang Saxon, "4 Deaths on the Subway Attributed to Cold Wave," *The New York Times* (December 19, 1989), B3; Robert R. Kiley, "The Homeless Are Dying in the Subway," *The New York Times* (February 17, 1990), A27.

12. For a detailed account of these data and the MTA's efforts to deal with the problem, see George L. Kelling, "Reclaiming the Subway," *The City Journal*, vol. 1, no. 2 (Winter 1991): 17–28.

13. The process used by the study group was an adaptation of Herman Goldstein's problem-oriented approach. Although his book, *Problem-Oriented Policing*, had not yet been published, Goldstein allowed me to use material from the book in the study group's activities. Herman Goldstein, *Problem-Oriented Policing* (Philadelphia, Pa.: Temple University Press, 1990).

14. The memo stated in part:

> With the return of cold weather, the incidents of homeless persons entering the subway system seeking shelter will increase greatly.
>
> This presents a number of problems. . . . The homeless who congregate on the system litter the area with cardboard boxes, discarded furniture, and other refuse. . . . (M)any also urinate

and defecate on the system. . . . Some . . . are alcoholics, drug addicts, emotionally disturbed persons and criminals who have perpetrated serious crimes against passengers as well as homeless individuals. Homeless individuals continue to be victims of serious crimes which range from homicide to sexual assaults and robberies.

. . . We as police officers cannot ignore these problems. This condition is contributing to the public's negative perception of the subway as a whole and the police in particular, because we are no doubt perceived as condoning the violation of many laws and regulations.

In an effort to deal with this problem the following guidelines will be used when addressing the homeless problem:

a) in instances when the homeless person is not violating any laws, they will not be the subject of any police action other than inquiry as to whether medical attention is indicated or to ascertain if the person wishes to avail himself of shelter or other assistance which may be needed.

b) When an individual is observed violating any laws or regulations . . . including but not limited to . . . obstructing . . . littering . . . urinating . . . defecating . . . occupying more than one seat . . . drinking of alcoholic beverages . . . these violations must be corrected and appropriate actions taken such as ejection, summons, or arrest.

Excerpts from Gollinge's "Homeless Persons," memo to District 1 police officers, November 11, 1988.

15. The most recent statement of Transit Authority Rules is contained in New York City Transit Police, "Legal Bulletin 1, 1995 Amendments to the TA Rules," March 24, 1995. The Transit Authority Rules, "Rules Governing the Conduct and Safety of the Public in the Use of the Facilities of New York City Transit Authority and Manhattan and Bronx Surface Operating Authority," constitute Sec. 1050 of "New York Codes, Rules and Regulations." N.Y. Comp. Codes R. & Regs. tit. 21, Sec. 1050.

16. Young v. New York City Transit Auth., 729 F.Supp. 341 (S.D.N.Y.), *rev'd and vacated*, 903 F.2d 146 (2d Cir. 1990). Also at issue was the constitutionality of N.Y. Penal Law Sec. 240.35(1), which provided in part that "A person is guilty of loitering when he . . . loiters, remains, or wanders about in a public place for the purpose of begging." A similar case was brought in the New York state courts challenging the regulations as violating the New York State Constitution. See Walley v. New York City Transit Authority, Index. No. 177/91 (Supreme Court of N.Y., County of Kings, June 3, 1991).

17. R.A.V. v. City of St. Paul, Minnesota, 505 U. S. 377 (1992).

18. Spence v. Washington, 418 U.S. 405, 410–11 (1974); Texas v. Johnson, 491 U.S. 397, 404 (1989).

19. See Tinker v. Des Moines School Dist., 393 U.S. 503 (1969) (students wearing armbands); Texas v. Johnson, 491 U.S. 397 (flag burning); and Grayned v. City of Rockford, 408 U.S. 104 (1972), Shuttlesworth v. City of Birmingham, 394 U.S. 147 (1968), Cox v. Louisiana, 379 U.S. 536 (1965) (picketing and parading).

20. United States v. O'Brien, 391 U.S. 367 (1968).

21. Perry Education Association v. Perry Local Educators' Association, 460 U.S. 37 (1983).

22. See United States v. Albertini, 472 U.S. 675 (1985); United States v. Kokinda, 497 U.S. 720 (1990); International Society for Krishna Consciousness, Inc. v. Lee, 505 U.S. 672 (1992).

23. Cox v. New Hampshire, 312 U.S. 569 (1941); Cox v. Louisiana, 379 U.S. 536, 558 (1965); International Society for Krishna Consciousness, 505 U.S. at 703-04; Ward v. Rock Against Racism, 491 U.S. 781, 798-800 (1989); Clark v. Community for Creative Non-Violence, 468 U.S. 288 (1984).

24. Schaumburg v. Citizens for a Better Environment, 444 U.S. 620, 632 (1980); see also Riley v. National Federation of the Blind of North Carolina, 487 U.S. 781, 796–98 (1988).

25. Young, 729 F.Supp. 341.

26. Young v. New York City Transit Authority, 903 F.2d 146, 155 (1990). Judge Altimari reasoned: "Neither *Schaumburg* nor its progeny stand for the proposition that begging and panhandling are protected speech under the First Amendment. Rather, these cases hold that there is a sufficient nexus between solicitation by organized charities and a 'variety of speech interests' to invoke protection." Id. at 161–62; 156.

27. Id. at 153–54.

28. Id. at 160; 149–50.

29. Id. at 158; see also 158–61.

30. Bratton and his Boston accent became well known as a result of his radio announcements and interviewing. When shopping one time in a department store, he was asked to repeat his request for service. After he repeated his request, the clerk responded: "The voice. The voice" and introduced herself to Bratton.

31. George L. Kelling and Maryalice Sloan-Howitt, "Station Managers and Police," a report submitted to the New York City Transit Authority by the St. Germain Group, n.d., 2.

32. Jane Jacobs, *The Death and Life of Great American Cities*, 37.

33. On a small scale, such activities reflect the thinking of Newman, who argued that the design of much public space, especially public housing, is such that it discourages the territorial "instincts" of residents and other persons with legitimate vested interests in public spaces, thereby giving rise to the depredation of those spaces by criminals. Oscar Newman, *Defensible Space: Crime Prevention Through Urban Design* (New York: MacMillan, 1972).

Most recently, Newman's work in the Five Oaks neighborhood in Dayton is an example of his use of urban design to prevent crime in a large public space. The situation in Five Oaks was grim prior to Newman's involvement:

> In the summer of 1991, this integrated, middle-class area just north of downtown seemed on the brink of collapse.
>
> Suburban commuters dodging a nearby interstate clogged the residential streets at rush hour. Chipped paint and rotting porches testified to sinking home values and absentee landlords. Open-air drug deals, random gunfire and prostitution were snaking from the neighborhood's scruffy periphery into its heart.
>
> After conventional police crackdowns failed, the city and neighborhood association, almost in desperation, brought in architect Oscar Newman.

Ronald Brownstein, "Taming the Mean Streets," *Los Angeles Times* (May 4, 1994), A1. Newman's focus was on restoring control of streets to residents by limiting traffic to pedestrians and residents. To this end, he closed off thirty-five streets and twenty-six alleys. As Brownstein reported, at the end of a year, "Traffic has plummeted, neighborhood watch activities have increased, housing prices are up 15%, violent crime has dropped in half and arrests for burglary, auto theft, and vandalism have fallen sharply." Id.

34. Dean Ronald V. Clarke of the School of Criminal Justice at Rutgers University pioneered this approach. See Ronald V. Clarke, ed., *Situational Crime Prevention: Successful Case Studies* (New York: Harrow and Heston, 1992), 3. Clarke initially developed this approach in England, where he directed crime prevention research in the Home Office.

35. N.Y. Penal Law Sec. 240.35(1).

36. Loper v. New York City Police Dept., 802 F.Supp. 1029 (S.D.N.Y. 1992), *aff'd* 999 F. 2d 699 (2d Cir. 1993).

37. Loper, 802 F.Supp. at 1037–40.

38. Id. at 1042–46.

39. New York City Police Dept. v. Loper, 999 F.2d 699 (1993).

40. Young v. New York City Transit Auth., 903 F.2d 146.

41. Seattle v. Webster, 802 P.2d 1333 (Wash. 1990) (en banc), *cert. denied*, 111 S. Ct. 1690 (1991).

42. Colum Lynch, "War on Windshield Washers," *The Boston Globe* (December 18, 1993), 3.

43. Jonathan P. Hicks, "Court Cleanup Foils Giuliani Campaign for Quality of Life," *The New York Times* (September 20, 1995), A1.

44. New York, N.Y., Ordinance Int. No. 456 (introduced October 12, 1994).

45. Panhandling Control Emergency Act of 1993, District of Columbia Code Sec. 22–3302 (1995 Supp.) (D.C. Acts 10–34; 10–54; 10–98; 10–131, 1993).

46. As of early 1996, this bill was still moving through the city council.

47. *The Midtown Community Court Experiment: A Progress Report*, unpub. doc., Midtown Community Court, 314 West Fifty-fourth Street, New York, NY 10019, p. 4. The court has received government, foundation, and corporate support.

48. Chief administrator for the court, John Feinblatt, oversees community service programs as well as numerous social services available in-house, which are aimed at providing immediate crisis intervention for offenders: drug and prostitution counseling, job counseling and referrals, long-term drug treatment placement, AIDS and TB testing, referrals for housing, and classes in English as a second language.

49. Many of these data are compiled through assessment interviews conducted at the court with each offender.

50. Meryl Gordon, "Street Justice," *New York Magazine* (December 5, 1994), 55.

51. New York City Crime Control Indicators & Strategy Assessment, New York City Police Department, November 1995. Rape has not declined appreciably and those data are hard to interpret. It could reflect that rapes really did not decline or it could reflect an increase in women willing to report being raped. Short of much more intensive study, no means of determining which is true is possible.

52. Quinnipiac College Poll, Surveys of New York, New Jersey, and Connecticut, Press Release (Hamden, Conn.: Quinnipiac College Polling Institute, November 6, 1995): 2.

53. Harvard Professor Mark H. Moore of the John F. Kennedy School of Govern-

ment has reflected on this issue in considerable depth and this enumeration of issues reflects his thinking.

54. See, for example, Richard Moran, "More Police, Less Crime, Right? Wrong." *The New York Times* (February 27, 1995), A15.

## Chapter 5

1. James Q. Wilson and George L. Kelling, "The Police and Neighborhood Safety," *The Atlantic* (March 1982), 35.

2. Pratt v. Chicago Housing Authority, 848 F.Supp. 792 (N.D. Ill., 1994); see also Summeries et al. v. Chicago Housing Authority, 88 C 10566.

3. "AARR Defends Chicago Public Housing Residents," *Re: Rights & Responsibilities*, Newsletter, American Alliance of Rights & Responsibilities, Washington D.C. (March-April 1994).

4. "Judge Blocks Weapons Sweeps," in *Re: Rights & Responsibilities*, Newsletter of American Alliance of Rights & Responsibilities, Washington, D.C. (October 1995): 2.

5. This propensity toward secrecy by police departments, fortunately has diminished considerably. It is within recent memory, however, that Harold Breier, Milwaukee's chief of police from 1961 to 1983, fought for years to keep the department's rules and regulations, not only from the press, but from the city council that demanded it.

6. Lloyd Ohlin, "Surveying Discretion by Criminal Justice Decision Makers," in Lloyd Ohlin and Frank J. Remington, eds., *Discretion in Criminal Justice: The Tension Between Individualization and Uniformity* (Albany: State University of New York Press, 1993), 6.

7. Herman Goldstein, "Confronting the Complexity of the Policing Function," in Lloyd Ohlin and Frank J. Remington, eds., *Discretion in Criminal Justice: The Tension Between Individualization and Uniformity*, 35.

8. Kenneth Culp Davis, *Discretionary Justice: A Preliminary Inquiry* (Baton Rouge: Louisiana University Press, 1969), 166.

9. Ibid., 222.

10. See also George L. Kelling, "Toward New Images of Policing: Herman Goldstein's Problem Oriented Policing," *Law and Social Inquiry*, vol. 17, no. 3 (Summer 1992): 545.

11. The final reports were published in five books, all edited by Frank Remington and published by Little and Brown: Wayne LaFave, *Arrest: The Decision to Take a Suspect into Custody* (1965); Donald J. Newman, *Conviction: The Determination of Guilt or Innocence without Trial* (1966); Lawrence P. Tiffany, Donald M. McIntyre, Jr., and Daniel Rotenberg, *Detection of Crime: Stopping and Questioning, Search and Seizure, Encouragement and Entrapment* (1967); Robert O. Dawson, *Sentencing: The Decision as to the Type, Length and Conditions of Sentence* (1969); and Frank W. Miller, *Prosecution: The Decision to Charge a Suspect with a Crime* (1970).

12. Mary Ann Wycoff, *The Role of Muncipal Police Research as a Prelude to Changing It* (Washington, D.C.: Police Foundation, 1982).

13. Joseph Goldstein, "Police Discretion Not to Invoke the Criminal Process: Low-Visibility Decisions in the Administration of Justice," 69 *The Yale Law Journal* 587 (1960).

14. Prosecutorial discretion in handling of domestic violence was also highlighted by early ABF reports. Frank Miller, *Prosecution: The Decision to Charge a Suspect with a Crime,* ed. Frank J. Remington (Boston: Little, Brown, 1969). See Raymond J. Parnas, "Criminal Justice Responses to Domestic Violence," in Lloyd Ohlin and Frank J. Remington, eds., *Discretion in Criminal Justice: The Tension Between Individualization and Uniformity,* 175–210.

15. Lawrence W. Sherman and Richard A. Berke, "The Specific Deterrent Effects of Arrest for Domestic Assaults," *American Sociological Review,* vol. 49, no. 2 (April 1984): 270.

16. See Raymond J. Parnas, "Criminal Justice Responses to Domestic Violence," 175–210.

17. Herman Goldstein, "Confronting the Complexity of Police Functioning," 53.

18. In respects, the history of criminal processing itself can be viewed as a struggle among the judicial, legislative, and executive branches of government as well as outside interest groups for control of decision-making within criminal justice agencies. See Lawrence Friedman, *Crime and Punishment in American History* (New York: Basic Books, 1993).

19. See Anthony Amsterdam, "The Supreme Court and the Rights of Suspects in Criminal Cases," 45 *New York University Law Review* 786–93 (1970).

20. This discussion relies heavily on Gregory Howard Williams, "Police Discretion: The Institutional Dilemma—Who Is in Charge?" *Iowa Law Review,* vol. 68, no. 3 (March 1983): 431–93.

21. George L. Kelling and Catherine M. Coles, "Disorder and the Court," *The Public Interest,* 116 (Summer 1994): 69.

22. See Roulette v. Seattle, 850 F. Supp. 1442, 1451 (W.D. Wash. 1994) (quoting SMC Sec. 12A.12.015(A) (2); see also Patton v. Baltimore City, No. S-93-2389, slip op. at 6 (D.Md., August 19, 1994), citing Baltimore, Md., Code art. 19, Sec. 249 (1994), later revised by the city.

23. Roulette v. Seattle, 850 F. Supp. at 1453.

24. See, e.g., Wych v. State, 619 S.2d 231, 234 (Fla. 1993) (loitering for the purpose of prostitution ordinance).

25. Wayne R. LaFave, "Police Rule Making and the Fourth Amendment: The Role of the Courts," in Lloyd E. Ohlin and Frank J. Remington, eds., *Discretion in Criminal Justice: The Tension Between Individualization and Uniformity,* 211–77, 213.

26. Frank J. Remington, "Police in a Democratic Society," *The Journal of Criminal Law, Criminology and Police Science,* vol. 56 (Chicago: Northwestern University School of Law, 1965): 361–65.

27. *The Challenge of Crime in a Free Society: A Report by the President's Commission on Law Enforcement and Administration of Justice* (Washington, D.C.: U.S. Government Printing Office, 1967): 104. Guidelines were also strongly endorsed by the report of the American Bar Association's Committee on the Urban Police Function (1973), and the report of the Kerner Commission, the National Advisory Commission on Civil Disorder, created to study the problem of urban rioting (1968). Scholars, reformers, and lawyers added their voices to the call for police themselves to develop their own professional guidelines as a means of shaping discretion.

28. LaFave, "Police Rule Making and the Fourth Amendment," in Lloyd Ohlin and Frank J. Remington, eds., *Discretion in Criminal Justice*, 215.

29. Gerald M. Caplan, "The Case for Rule-making by Law Enforcement Agencies," *Law and Contemporary Problems*, vol. 36, no. 4 (1971): 500–14, 501.

30. *The Challenge of Crime in a Free Society*, 103.

31. LaFave, "Police Rule Making and the Fourth Amendment," 249–53.

32. Ibid., 252.

33. Herman Goldstein points out the value of such rigor in the development of guidelines:

> A judge fully informed on all of the circumstances related to a given police practice is obviously in a better position to pass judgment upon its legality and propriety than one whose knowledge of the procedure is limited to what is revealed in the typical hearing on a motion to suppress evidence.

Herman Goldstein, "Trial Judges and the Police," *Crime and Delinquency*, vol. 14, no. 1 (January 1968): 14–25.

34. James J. Fyfe, "Administrative Interventions on Police Shooting Discretion: An Empirical Evaluation," *Journal of Criminal Justice* 7 (Winter 1979): 309–24.

35. Confidential field notes of Ms. Jinney Smith, in the possession of George Kelling.

36. San Francisco Police Department, Department General Order, No. J-6: Aggressive Soliciting (January 6, 1993), p. 2; field notes of Jinney Smith.

37. New Haven, Connecticut, Police Department Memorandum (n.d.).

38. Frank J. Vandall, *Police Training for Tough Calls: Discretionary Situations Limited Edition* (Atlanta, Ga.: Center for Research in Social Change, Emory University, 1976), 3.

39. Patton v. Baltimore City, Civil No. S-93-2389 at 47 (N.D. Md., August 19, 1994) (Smalkin, J., unpub'd Memorandum Opinion and Order). See Chapter 6 for a more detailed discussion of this case.

40. Patton v. Baltimore City, Settlement Agreement, No. S-93-2389 (D. Md., September 13, 1994) (Smalkin, J.).

41. Herman Goldstein, "Police Policy Formulation: A Proposal for Improving Police Performance," 65 *Michigan Law Review* 1123, 1127 (1967); Sheldon Krantz, Bernard Gilman, Charles G. Benda, Carol Rogoff Halistrom, and Eric J. Nadworny, *Police Policymaking* (Lexington, Mass.: Lexington Books, 1979), 3–4.

42. Igleburger and Schubert's police/public model of policy formulation was also funded by the Police Foundation in 1972.

43. It is instructive to reproduce parts of the general order:

> The Department of Police has as one of its primary responsibilities the development and maintenance of peaceable relations between citizens. Police officers are expected to act in an appropriate and effective manner so as to maintain a standard of public order which is generally acceptable to the life styles of both the student and nonstudent residents of the area in the vicinity of the University.
>
> It should be recognized that divergent life styles frequently generate conflict which is not conducive to the well being of either students or nonstudents and that compromises must be made by all concerned. Other communities have attempted to deal with this campus-community situation by general suppression through use of police power. The record seems to indicate

that this response has not resolved the problem but, rather, increased the polarization of the parties.

I believe that we should seek to develop a police response to the problems which will permit an evolutionary and improving relationship based on respect and a concern by all for the mutual welfare of the community. Such a police posture can only be justified, however, if the situation shows improvement.

The following problems were identified by student and nonstudent residents meeting with police personnel as being of legitimate police concern:

Fires—The residents have indicated that they believe fires should not be permitted in the streets as they constitute a serious threat to life and property. Residents expect police crews to act appropriately to prevent the lighting of fires and to put out existing fires.

Loud Noise After 12:00 Midnight—The residents have indicated that it is reasonable to expect that loud noises should cease after midnight. Both students and nonstudents believe this compromise to be fair and acceptable. I expect police crews to act so as to protect the rights of persons to peace and quiet in their residences after midnight.

Traffic Blockages—The residents recognize that large numbers of students in attendence at parties may require the temporary use of the streets. It is important, however, vehicles be permitted to pass through these crowds so that residents can gain access to their property and so emergency vehicles can pass. Police crews are expected to insure vehicles are not being blocked unless barricades have been erected in accordance with our block party procedures.

It should be emphasized that the burden for complying with the standards discussed in this memo should be on the residents, both student and nonstudent. The problem is unlikely to be resolved by police force; however, in the event we need to respond to situations such as those discussed above, we will act to implement the identified standard as the situation requires.

We are committed to persuasion as the primary method of dealing with these problems because it is constructive, and not destructive as is the confrontational approach. Conflict management personnel are to be called up to assist whenever it is felt they can be of aid to the crew.

The second District Sergeants and beat crews are encouraged to confer with residents, Project South (telephone #), and the University Student Government so as to make use of their services in dealing with problems in a "non-police" fashion to the greatest extent possible.

The officers are to feel free to consult with the Conflict Management Director, their superiors, or myself if they have any questions about this policy. It is the responsibility of the Supervisors to assure all officers have read and understand this order and respond accordingly.

*Director of Police*

44. Frank A. Schubert, interview with George Kelling, January 24, 1994.

45. Robert M. Igleburger and Frank A. Schubert, "Policy Making for the Police," 58 *American Bar Association Journal* 307 (March 1972).

46. Mary Ann Wycoff, conversation with George Kelling, December 8, 1994.

## Chapter 6

1. The importance of neighborhoods in the governance of Baltimore has been described in a wonderful book by Matthew A. Crenson, *Neighborhood Politics* (Cambridge, Mass.: Harvard University Press, 1983).

2. David Simon, "The Metal Men," *Baltimore Sun Magazine* (September 3, 1995), 8–13.

3. "Boyd-Booth Battleground," *Baltimore Evening Sun* (May 13, 1991), A4.

4. George L. Kelling, interview with residents of Boyd Booth, December 1, 1995.

5. *Baltimore Comprehensive Communities Program Summary*, Mayor's Coordinating Council on Criminal Justice, 10 South Street, Baltimore, Maryland 21202, Attachment A.

6. Patton v. Baltimore City, No. S-93–2389, slip op. at 3 (D. Md. August 19, 1994) (Smalkin, J., Unpub. Memorandum and Order on motions).

7. "Policies of the Downtown Partnership and the Authority Relative to Homelessness and Panhandling," Downtown Partnership of Baltimore, unpub. document, n.d.

8. The activities of Baltimore's BID, the Downtown Partnership of Baltimore, are patterned after Portland, Oregon's EID. In Portland, private guides provide information to tourists and help deal with problems of disorder, especially aggressive panhandling. They do so in a variety of ways, including referring street people for services, "shadowing" panhandlers (staying close to them in order to reassure citizens and tourists and attempting to dissuade the street people from panhandling), and calling police if someone becomes too obstreperous. For a description of Portland's program, see Philip Langdon, "How Portland Does It: A City that Protects Its Thriving, Civil Core," *The Atlantic* (November 1992), 134–41.

9. A minimum of one-third of the clean sweep ambassador slots are set aside for homeless individuals. See "Policies of the Downtown Partnership and the Authority Relative to Homelessness and Panhandling."

10. "Downtown Public Safety Coalition 1994 Committee Accomplishments, 1995 Committee Goals" Downtown Partnership of Baltimore, unpub. doc.

11. Reported in "FY '94 Annual Report," *Clean and Safe Update* (Downtown Partnership, December, 1994), 1.

12. Complaint for Declaratory and Injunctive Relief Class Action at 2, Patton v. Baltimore City, No. S93–2389 (D. Md., filed August 18, 1993).

13. Id. at 4.

14. Patton v. Baltimore City, Civil No. S-93–2389, slip op. at 4 (D. Md., filed August 19, 1994) (Smalkin, J., unpub. Memorandum Opinion and Order on motions); Patton v. Baltimore City, Civil No. S-93–2389 (D. Md., September 14, 1994) (Smalkin, J., Oral Opinion). In August 1993, the ACLU filed suit against the mayor and city council, Downtown Management Authority, and Downtown Partnership for their "move along" policy; the complaint was amended early in 1994, challenging the city's newly enacted aggressive panhandling ordinance and adding the commissioner of police as a defendant. The plaintiffs sought injunctive and declaratory relief under 42 U.S.C. Sec. 1983.

15. Patton, Civil No. S-93–2389, slip op. at 11–12.

16. Baltimore, Md., Code art. 19, Sec. 249 (B) (1994).

17. Plaintiffs also alleged that the city's policies violated their Fourth Amendment protections against unreasonable intrusion and seizure, and challenged several different ordinances and rules as violative of due process. They brought analogous state law constitutional claims. Patton v. Baltimore City, Civil No. S-93–2389, slip op. at 11–12, 29–30 n. 6 (August 19, 1994).

18. Patton v. Baltimore City, Civil No. S-93–2389, slip op. (D. Md., filed August 19,

1994) (Smalkin, J., Memorandum Opinion and Order on motions); Patton v. Baltimore City, Civil No. S-93-2389, Reporter's Official Transcript of Proceedings (D.Md. September 14, 1994) (Smalkin, J., Oral Opinion).

19. Patton v. Baltimore City, No. S-93-2389, slip op. at 49 (August 19, 1994), citing Zablocki v. Redhail, 434 U.S. 374, 384 (1978) (recognizing fundamental right to privacy includes right to marry); Roe v. Wade, 410 U.S. 113, 152–55 (1973) (fundamental right to privacy and personal autonomy includes right to terminate pregnancy); Griswold v. Connecticut, 381 U.S. 479, 481–86 (1965) (recognizing right to privacy in choices concerning contraception).

20. Instead, Judge Smalkin noted that the United States Supreme Court had found such a right to exist in two circumstances: in certain intimate relationships, and in organized associations for the purpose of engaging in activities protected by the First Amendment such as speech, assembly, expressing political grievances, and the exercise of religion. Patton, slip op. at 69–72 (citing Dallas v. Stanglin, 490 U.S. 19, 23–24 (1989), Roberts v. United States Jaycees, 468 U.S. 609, 617–18 (1984), and Bd. of Directors of Rotary Int'l v. Rotary Club, 481 U.S. 537 (1987).

21. The court also granted summary judgment in favor of the defendants on charges of violation of due process for the enforcement of various other Baltimore city ordinances and park rules, finding no problematic enforcement by the city and no injury to plaintiffs.

22. Pottinger v. City of Miami, 810 F. Supp. 1551, 1561–65 (S.D. Fla. 1992), *remanded*, 40 F.2d 1155 (11th Cir. 1994).

23. Joyce v. City and County of San Francisco, 846 F. Supp. 843, 853–58 (N.D. Cal. 1994); Patton, No. S-93-2389, slip op. at 52–53 (August 19, 1994).

24. Patton, No. S-93-2389, slip op. at 55–56.

25. Judge Smalkin declined to adopt defendants' reasoning that the ordinance was content-neutral because it was enacted not with the purpose of discouraging panhandling for the message it conveyed, but in order to prevent negative "secondary effects" on the surrounding community. Distinguishing *Renton* and following the Supreme Court's holding in *Boos v. Barry*, Judge Smalkin noted that "the effect that protected speech has on its listener . . . cannot be considered to be the type of secondary effect that was contemplated by the Renton decision." Id. at 59; see also Renton v. Playtime Theatres, Inc., 475 U.S. at 48; Boos v. Barry, 485 U.S. 312, 321 (1988).

26. Patton v. Baltimore City, No. S-93-2389, slip op. at 62–63.

27. Id. at 67.

28. In offering this suggestion, the court explicitly departed from the federal district court's holding in *Blair v. Shanahan*:

> This Court disagrees with the conclusion in *Blair* that *no* prohibition on solicitation can withstand Equal Protection scrutiny because any such prohibition necessarily draws an impermissible distinction between those who ask strangers for money and those who ask strangers for directions, the time of day, or to sign a petition, for example. Yet common sense and everyday experience tell us that requests for money are inherently more threatening than requests for directions.

Id. at 68 (citations omitted). See below.

29. Baltimore, Md., Code art. 19, Sec. 249 (revised, September 1994).

30. International Society for Krishna Consciousness vs. Schmidt, 523 F. Supp. 1303 (D.Md. 1981) (striking down Baltimore Park Rule 4); Patton at 7–8.

31. See Pls' Opp'n to Def. Police Comm'r's Mot. for Summ. J. Exs. J., K., Patton v. Baltimore City, S-93–2389 (D. Md., submitted June 13, 1994).

32. Code of Public Local Laws of Md. art. 4, Sec. 24–2 (1980). The ordinance provided that those without visible means of support or who begged or solicited alms were deemed beggars or vagrants.

33. Patton v. Baltimore City, S-93–2389, Settlement Agreement at 3–4 (D. Md., September 13, 1994).

34. Patton, S93–2389, transcript at 16 (D. Md. September 14, 1994) (Smalkin, J., Oral Opinion).

35. Id. at 27.

36. Frank Derr, Baltimore City Law Department, Jan. 18, 1996, personal conversation with Catherine Coles.

37. Political activism by citizens started early in San Francisco. The discovery of gold in 1848 and the influx of prospectors in subsequent years resulted in the breakdown of social order. Consequently citizens formed the Vigilance Committee that served as police, judge, and jury. The committee not only executed several criminals, it drove others from the area.

Currently, activism has its costs for the city: prosecutors report that numerous public demonstrations consume substantial local resources through policing requirements and prosecution of offenders. Many demonstrations have become so routine, however, that they are not policed at all: personal observations during a site visit of a demonstration on the steps of city hall by members of Coyote, a group advocating prostitutes' rights, found no police present.

38. See, for a detailed discussion of conditions in San Francisco and Operation Matrix, Heather MacDonald, "San Francisco Gets Tough with the Homeless," *The City Journal* (Autumn 1994), 30–40.

39. See Chapter 1, n. 2.

40. Blair v. Shanahan, 775 F. Supp. 1315 (N.D. Cal. 1991), *aff'd* in part, *dismissed* in part, *remanded*, 38 F.3d 1514 (9th Cir. 1994), *cert. denied* by California v. Blair, 115 S.Ct. 1698. In 1983, the U.S. Supreme Court, in Kolender v. Lawson, had declared the state's loitering statute, Sec. 647(e) of the California Penal Code, unconstitutional. Kolender v. Lawson, 461 U.S. 352 (1983).

41. California Penal Code, Sec. 647(c).

42. In *Ulmer* the state appeals court upheld the statute, finding that it was based upon a legitimate government interest of protecting members of the public from the annoyance of being approached by beggars in public locations. Further the court held that begging and soliciting involved no communication of an opinion or information, and thus were not within the First Amendment's protection. Ulmer v. Municipal Court for Oakland-Piedmont Judicial District, 55 Cal. App.3d 263, 127 Cal. Rptr. 445 (1976). Ulmer, 55 Cal. App.3d at 266–67, 127 Cal. Rptr. at 447–48.

43. The plaintiff also sought damages, under 42 U.S.C. Sec. 1983, against the city and the arresting officers. Blair vs. Shanahan, 775 F. Supp. 1315, 1322.

44. Relying on First National Bank of Boston v. Bellotti, 435 U.S. 765, 777 (1978), Judge Orrick found that the beggar's representation of himself rather than an organized

charity should not cause his speech to fall outside of First Amendment protection. Blair, 775 F. Supp. at 1323.

45. Id. at 1322, n.6, 1323.

46. Relying upon this same reasoning, Judge Orrick held that the statute violated the Fourteenth Amendment right to equal protection in that it discriminated "between lawful and unlawful conduct based upon the content of . . . communication," that is, asking for funds. Id. at 1324–25 [quoting Carey v. Brown, 447 U.S. 455, 460 (1980)].

With respect to the liability of the city and arresting officers under 42 U.S.C. 1983 and the First and Fourteenth Amendments, the court considered whether San Francisco's policy or custom resulted in the deprivation of his constitutional rights either in the execution of the policy, or through a failure to train police officers that constituted a de facto policy of deliberate indifference to the rights of those begging. Although a section of the San Francisco Police Code banning begging on any public street or in any public place demonstrated the existence of a policy that may have led to the plaintiff's arrests, the court remained unconvinced that this policy had caused the violation of his First and Fourteenth Amendment rights, and accordingly denied summary judgment to the plaintiff. However, the court also held that the city's reliance on the *Ulmer* decision as to the "accosting" statute's constitutionality, and its failure to inform police officers otherwise, did not constitute deliberate indifference to the rights of beggars: therefore, summary judgment was granted to the city. Id. at 1326.

47. In the intervening period, Blair and the city agreed upon damages, and a consent judgment was entered pursuant to Federal Rule of Civil Procedure 68, settling Blair's claim for damages against the city for $4,000. The appeal dealt primarily with various procedural matters arising out of the effect of the consent judgment. See Blair v. Shanahan, No. C-89-4176 WHO (N.D. Cal. January 31, 1996) (Orrick, J., Unpub. Memorandom, Decision and Order), vacating 775 F. supp. 1315.

48. Proposition J was proposed as an addition to the Municipal Police Code, to replace, at least temporarily, California Penal Code Sec. 647(c). San Francisco Municipal Code, Part II, Chap. 8 (Police Code), Sec. 120–1 (November 3, 1992). The ordinance states in part:

(a) *Findings*: The people of the City and County of San Francisco find that aggressive solicitation for money directed at residents, visitors, and tourists in areas of the City open to the public imperils their safety and welfare. This conduct in turn jeopardizes the City's economy by discouraging visitors and prospective customers from coming to San Francisco for business, recreation, and shopping. This conduct also threatens to drive City residents out of the City for their recreational and shopping activities. Further, the people find that aggressive solicitation undermines the public's basic right to be in and enjoy public places without fear that they will be pursued by others seeking handouts. The people further find that no state laws address or protect the public from these problems.

(b) *Prohibition*: In the City and County of San Francisco, it shall be unlawful for any person on the streets, sidewalks, or other places open to the public, whether publicly or privately owned, including parks, to harass or hound another person for the purpose of inducing that person to give money or other thing of value.

(c) *Definitions*: For the purpose of this ordinance, an individual (solicitor) harasses or hounds another (solicitee) when the solicitor closely follows the solicitee and requests money or other thing of value, after the solicitee has expressly or impliedly made it known to the solicitor that the solicitee does not want to give money or other thing of value.

49. Timothy Egan, "In Three Progressive Cities, It's Law vs. Street People, *The New York Times* (December 12, 1993), 26.

50. Joyce v. City and County of San Francisco, 846 F. Supp. 843, 846–49 (N.D.Cal. 1994), No. C-93–4149 DLJ (N.D. Cal. August 18, 1995), *appeal docketed*, No. 95–16940 (9th Cir. 1996).

51. See Chapter 2 discussion of the dangers of confusing homelessness and disorderly acts.

52. Joyce v. City and County of San Francisco, 846 F. Supp. 843 (N.D.Cal. 1994) (Jensen, J., denying plaintiffs' motion for preliminary injunction); No. C-93–4149, slip op. (N.D.Cal., August 18, 1995) (Jensen, J., granting defendant's motion for summary judgment).

53. Tobe v. City of Santa Ana, 892 P. 2d 1145 (Cal. 1995).

54. He did not hold, on the factual record presented, that as a matter of law homelessness was or was not a status. Joyce, No. C-93–4149, slip op. at 8 (N.D.Cal., August 18, 1995).

55. Id. at 13.

56. He cited Pottinger, 810 F. Supp. at 1582 (Miami case, court found cities have a compelling interest in ensuring parks are free of crime), and Johnson v. City of Dallas, 860 F. Supp. 344, 351–58 (N.D. Tex. 1994) (Dallas case, court applied rational basis review and found rational basis), rev'd, 61 F.3d 442 (5th Cir. 1995).

57. Joyce, No. C-93–4149, slip op. at 14 (N.D.Cal., August 18, 1995).

58. "Courts have traditionally required such differentiation before applying strict scrutiny and striking programs and laws unsupported by compelling interests." Id. at 15.

59. Joyce, *appeal docketed*, No. 95–16940 (9th Cir. 1996).

60. Dan Levy, "S.F. Board Votes Down Matrix Amnesty Plan," *San Francisco Chronicle* (October 26, 1993), A1.

61. John King, "Matrix Dominates S.F. Debate; Mayoral Hopefuls Blast Crackdown Against Homeless," *San Francisco Chronicle* (August 17, 1995), A21.

62. John King, "Mayoral Hopefuls Talk Tougher on Homeless Issue; Jordan Rivals Shift Stance," *San Francisco Chronicle* (October 11, 1995), A13.

63. Debra J. Saunders, "Jordan Deserves Re-election for Matrix," *San Francisco Chronicle* (September 1, 1995), A23.

64. Erin McCormick, "Matrix Gone, at Least in Name," *San Francisco Examiner* (January 12, 1996), A4.

65. Ibid.

66. Mark Sidran, speech given to Downtown Seattle Rotary Club on August 4, 1993, p. 1.

67. SMC 12A.12.015, the pedestrian interference ordinance, was enacted in 1987.

68. Seattle v. Webster, 802 P.2d 1333 (1990), *cert. denied*, 111 S.Ct. 1690 (1991). The aggressive begging portion of the ordinance was challenged later in Roulette v. City of Seattle, 850 F. Supp. 1442 (W.D. Wash. 1994), *aff'd*, No. 94–35354 (9th Cir. March 18, 1996).

69. Seattle v. Webster, 802 P.2d at 1337–38.

70. Id. at 1338–39.

71. Sidran proposed the anti–lying down ordinance as part of package of ordinances that addressed alcohol-related offenses, public urination, and aggressive panhandling, and permitted the closing of certain alleys. These parts of the package, however, were refinements or elaborations of existing ordinances. The new ingredient, and the one that caused most consternation in elements of the community, was the anti–lying down ordinance.

72. Refusal or failure to sign a notice of civil infraction, or to respond to a notice, constituted a misdemeanor, however, which was a criminal offense. See Roulette v. Seattle, 850 F. Supp. at 1444, and n. 2.

73. George Howland, Jr., "Sidran-ization and Its Discontents: Attacking the Homeless," *The Stranger* (September 6-12, 1993).

74. Interview with Seattle City Attorney Mark Sidran by George L. Kelling, June 27, 1995.

75. Memorandum in Support of Plaintiffs' Motion for Summary Judgment at 1, Roulette v. City of Seattle, 850 F.Supp. 1442 (W.D. Wash., 1994).

76. Id. at 3.

77. Roulette v. City of Seattle, 850 F.Supp. at 1446–47. The court also rejected a substantive due process claim which plaintiffs had brought by arguing that merely sitting on a sidewalk was an innocent activity that could not be prohibited because targeting such behavior bore no rational relationship to any legitimate government interest. Plaintiffs' claim rested on the Due Process clause of the Fourteenth Amendment which has been interpreted by the courts as protecting against infringement of substantive liberty interests as well as procedural due process. The court found that ensuring pedestrian safety and safeguarding commercial activities within the neighborhoods were legitimate government interests rationally related to the ordinance's prohibitions. Id. at 1447.

78. SMC Sec. 12A.12.015 (A) (1).

79. SMC Sec. 12A. 12.015 (A) (3).

80. SMC Sec. 12A.12.015 (A) (2).

81. SMC Sec. 12A.12.015 (C).

82. Citing among other cases, and in particular, Loper v. New York City Police Dept., 999 F.2d 699, and Blair v. Shanahan, 775 F.Supp. at 1322, 1324.

83. The Seattle ·Municipal Code contained a severability clause, SMC Sec. 1.04.010; striking the circumstances section did not impugn the validity of the remaining sections of the ordinance.

84. Roulette v. City of Seattle, No. 94–35354 at 3545, 3549 (9th Cir. March 18, 1996) (Kozinski, J.).

85. City of Seattle v. Hoff, No. 94-2-29610-8, and City of Seattle v. McConahy, No. 95-2-13008-9 (King County Superior Ct.), consolidated on appeal, *cert. accepted*, No. 36995-4-I (Wash. Ct. App. September 19, 1995).

86. See Chapter 5, note 36.

87. Herman Goldstein, *Problem-Oriented Policing* (Philadelphia, Pa.: Temple University Press, 1990). See above, Chapter. 4, n. 13. The steps that follow were developed by George Kelling in reliance upon Goldstein's suggested method.

88. Robert C. Ellickson, "Controlling Chronic Misconduct in City Spaces: of Pan-

handlers, Skid Rows, and Public-Space Zoning," 105 *The Yale Law Journal* 1165, 1230 (March 1996). Ellickson's comprehensive and thoughtful treatment of legal issues pertaining to panhandlers in public spaces appeared just as this manuscript was going into production. It is a valuable resource for any cities attempting to anticipate and understand the various arguments that are likely to be raised by advocates for panhandlers and others engaging in troublesome and disruptive behavior on streets.

89. Young v. New York City Transit Authority, 903 F.2d 146, 158 (2d Cir.), *cert. denied*, 398 U.S. 984 (1990). See also Judge Rothstein's opinion in Seattle.

90. Personal communication from Professor Mark Moore, John F. Kennedy School of Government, Harvard University, to George Kelling.

91. Stanley Fish, "Jerry Falwell's Mother, or, What's the Harm?" *There's No Such Thing as Free Speech: And It's a Good Thing Too* (New York: Oxford University Press, 1994), 129.

92. International Society for Krishna Consciousness v. Lee, 505 U.S. at 700.

93. Patton, slip op. at 62 (Memorandum Opinion, and Order, August 19, 1994).

94. Joyce v. City and County of San Francisco, 846 F.Supp. 843, 860 (1994).

95. Heffron v. International Society for Krishna Consciousness, Inc., 452 U.S. 640, 653-54 (1981).

96. See Ward v. Rock Against Racism, 491 U.S. at 798-99 (1989); Clark v. Committee for Community Non-Violence, 468 U.S. 288, 299 (1984); United States v. Albertini, 472 U.S. 675, 689 (1985).

97. See Ellickson, "Controlling Chronic Misconduct in City Spaces: of Panhandlers, Skid Rows, and Public-Space Zoning," 1212–13.

98. Joyce v. City and County of San Francisco, 846 F. Supp. 843 (N.D. Cal. 1994).

99. Roulette v. City of Seattle, 850 F. Supp. 1442 (W.D. Wash. 1994), *aff'd*, No. 94-35354 (9th Cir. March 18, 1996).

## Chapter 7

1. We wish, however, that the disputants would be forthright about it when they are raising utilitarian values (reduced crime), justice (punishing someone who deserves to be punished), or equity (punishing different people similarly for similar crimes).

2. Ronald V. Clarke, ed., *Situational Crime Prevention: Successful Case Studies* (New York: Harrow and Hetson, 1992), 3.

3. Herman Goldstein, *Problem-Oriented Policing* (Philadelphia, Pa.: Temple University Press, 1990).

4. Oscar Newman, *Defensible Space: Crime Prevention Through Urban Design* (New York: MacMillan, 1972).

5. James Q. Wilson and Barbara Boland, "The Effect of Police on Crime," *Law and Society Review*, vol. 12, no. 3 (1978): 367.

6. Robert J. Sampson and Jacqueline Cohen, "Deterrent Effects of the Police on Crime: A Replication and Theoretical Extension," *Law and Society Review*, vol. 22, no. 1 (1988): 163–89, 184–85.

7. John J. DiIulio, Jr., "The Coming of the Super-Predators," *The Weekly Standard* (November 27, 1995).

8. Marvin Wolfgang, Robert Figlio, and Thorsten Sellin, *Delinquency in a Birth Cohort* (Chicago: University of Chicago Press, 1972).

9. Paul Tracy, Marvin Wolfgang, and Robert Figlio, *Delinquency in Two Birth Cohorts* (Washington, D.C.: Office of Juvenile Justice and Delinquency Prevention, 1985).

10. Alfred Blumstein, Donald Farrington, and W. Moitra, "Delinquency Careers: Innocents, Desisters, and Persisters," in Michael Tonry and Norval Morris, eds., *Crime and Justice* (Chicago: University of Chicago Press, 1985), 187–219. For a highly readable account of the literature on career criminals and the precursors of criminal offending, see John H. Laub and Janet L. Lauritsen, "The Precursors of Criminal Offending Across the Life Course," *Federal Probation* (September 1994): 51–57.

11. James Q. Wilson, "What to Do About Crime," *Commentary*, vol. 98, no. 3 (September 1994): 27.

12. Ibid.

13. Glenn C. Loury and Shelby Steele, "A New Black Vanguard," *Wall Street Journal* (February 29, 1996), A18.

14. Accounts of citizens taking back neighborhoods have been documented most systematically in Saul N. Weingardt, Francis X. Hartmann, and David Osborne, *Case Studies of Community Anti-Drug Efforts* (Washington, D.C.: National Institute of Justice, October 1994), and Roger Conner and Patrick Burns, *The Winnable War: A Community Guide to Eradicating Street Drug Markets* (Washington, D.C.: American Alliance for Rights and Responsibilities, 1991). Both clarify the pivotal role of citizen initiative in controlling public spaces, even in face of the most dedicated and vicious opposition. Moreover, wherever one looks for crime-prevention success stories, "community," "partnership," and "collaboration" are almost certain to be a central part of the story.

15. Jane Jacobs, *The Death and Life of Great American Cities* (New York: Vintage Books, 1961), 31.

16. Boston, Indianapolis, Austin, and Kansas City, Missouri, are all sites included in a National Institute of Justice study, "Prosecution in the Community: A Study of Emergent Strategies," conducted by Catherine Coles (on prosecution) and George Kelling (on police) through the Program in Criminal Justice, John F. Kennedy School of Government, Harvard University (October 1995–December 1996).

17. Rosemary Lehmberg, assistant district attorney and director of the family justice division of the Travis County District Attorney's Office, also played a pivotal role in developing the Children's Advocacy Center.

18. Funds are allocated as follows: local police 19 percent; prosecution 9.5 percent; deferred prosecution (drug court) 6 percent; grant match fund 10 percent; corrections 15 percent; court 12 percent; treatment 15 percent; prevention 7.5 percent; DARE 6 percent. See "COMBAT: Community-Backed Anti-Drug Sales Tax" Mimeo, Jackson County Prosecutor's Office, Kansas City, Missouri, n.d.

## Postscript

1. See, for example, "The Mayor's New Police Commissioner," *The New York Times*, March 29, 1996 (editorial), A20.

# BIBLIOGRAPHY

"AARR Defends Chicago Public Housing Residents." *Re: Rights & Responsibilities*, Newsletter. Washington, D.C.: American Alliance of Rights & Responsibilities (March-April 1994).

Allon, Janet. "For Hogue, a Step Toward Freedom." *The New York Times*, October 22, 1995, sec. 13, p. 6.

Amsterdam, Anthony. "The Supreme Court and the Rights of Suspects In Criminal Cases." 45 *New York University Law Review* 785 (October 1970).

Annotation, "Validity of Loitering Statutes and Ordinances." 25 *American Law Reports* 3d 836.

*Baltimore Comprehensive Communities Program Summary*. Baltimore, Md.: Mayor's Coordinating Council on Criminal Justice, n.d.

Baum, Alice S., and Donald W. Burnes. *A Nation in Denial: The Truth about Homelessness*. Boulder, Co.: Westview Press, 1993.

Bayley, David. "The Best Defense." *Fresh Perspectives*. Washington, D.C.: Police Executive Research Forum, n.d.

——. "Ironies of American Law Enforcement." *The Public Interest*, vol. 59 (Spring 1980): 45–56.

Biderman, A. D., L. A. Johnson, J. McIntyre, and A. W. Weir. *Report on a Pilot Study in the District of Columbia on Victimization and Attitudes Towards Law Enforcement*. Department of Justice. Washington, D.C.: U.S. Government Printing Office, 1967.

Bittner, Egon. *Aspects of Police Work*. Boston: Northeastern University Press, 1990.

Black, Robert C. *Police Control of Disorder: Legal Bases and Constitutional Constraints*. A report submitted to the Fear Reduction Project of the Police Foundation, January 18, 1983.

Blackstone, William. *Commentaries on the Law of England*. 1st ed.. Vol. 1 (1769).

Blumstein, Alfred, Donald Farrington, and W. Moitra. "Delinquency Careers: Innocents, Desisters, and Persisters." In *Crime and Justice*, edited by Michael Tonry and Norval Morris, pp. 187–219. Chicago: University of Chicago Press, 1985.

"Boyd-Booth Battleground." *Baltimore Evening Sun*, May 13, 1991, A4.

Brownstein, Ronald. "Taming the Mean Streets." *Los Angeles Times*, May 4, 1994, A1.

Caplan, Gerald M. "The Case for Rulemaking by Law Enforcement Agencies." *Law and Contemporary Problems*, vol. 36, no. 4 (1971):500–514.

Carte, Gene E., and Elaine H. Carte. *Police Reform in the United States: The Era of August Vollmer, 1905–1932*. Berkeley: University of California Press, 1975.

Citizens' Bureau of Milwaukee. *Survey of the Milwaukee Police Department*. September 1938.

Clarke, Ronald V., ed. *Situational Crime Prevention: Successful Case Studies*. New York: Harrow and Heston, 1992.

Conner, Roger, and Patrick Burns. *The Winnable War: A Community Guide to Eradicating Street Drug Markets*. Washington, D.C.: American Alliance for Rights and Responsibilities, 1991.

Corre, Neil. "A Proposal for Reform of the Law of Begging." 1984 *Criminal Law Review* 750.

Crenson, Matthew A. *Neighborhood Politics*. Cambridge, Mass.: Harvard University Press, 1983.

*Crime in the United States*. Federal Bureau of Investigation, Department of Justice. Washington, D.C.: U.S. Government Printing Office. Annual publication.

*Criminal Victimization in the United States*. Office of Justice Programs, Bureau of Justice Statistics. Washington, D.C.: U.S. Government Printing Office, 1994.

Crouse, Joan M. *The Homeless Transient in the Great Depression: New York State, 1929–1941*. Albany, N.Y.: State University of New York Press, 1986.

Davis, Kenneth Culp. *Discretionary Justice: A Preliminary Inquiry*. Baton Rouge: Louisiana State University Press, 1969.

Dawson, Robert O. *Sentencing: The Decision as to the Type, Length and Conditions of Sentence*. Boston: Little, Brown, 1969.

DiIulio, John J., Jr. "The Coming of the Super-Predators." *The Weekly Standard*, November 27, 1995, pp. 23–28.

Dugger, Celia W. "New York Report Finds Drug Abuse Rife in Shelters." *The New York Times*, February 16, 1992, p.18.

Egan, Timothy. "In Three Progressive Cities, It's Law vs. Street People." *The New York Times*, December 12, 1993, p. 26.

Ellickson, Robert C. "Controlling Chronic Misconduct in City Spaces: Of Panhandlers, Skid Rows, and Public-Space Zoning." 105 *The Yale Law Journal* 1165 (March 1996, no. 5).

Etzioni, Amitai. *The Spirit of Community: Rights, Responsibilities and the Communitarian Agenda*. New York: Crown Publishers, 1993.

Firestone, David. "Stopping Blight at the Border: Two Paths for Ridgewood, Queens and Bushwick, Brooklyn." *The New York Times*, August 25, 1994, B1.

Fish, Stanley. *There's No Such Thing as Free Speech: And It's a Good Thing Too*. New York: Oxford University Press, 1994.

Fogelson, Robert M. *Big City Police*. Cambridge, Mass.: Harvard University Press, 1977.

Forero, Juan. "Serial Rapist Stalks E. Side Girls; Ages of 11 Victims Attacked by Stranger Range from 9 to 16, Investigators Say." *Buffalo News*, April 27, 1991, A1.

Fowler, Floyd J., Jr., and Thomas Mangione. *Neighborhood Crime, Fear, and Social Control: A Second Look at the Hartford Program*. National Institute of Justice, U.S. Department of Justice. Washington, D.C.: U.S. Government Printing Office, April 1982.

Friedman, Lawrence M. *Crime and Punishment in American History.* New York: Basic Books, 1993.

―――. *The Republic of Choice: Law, Authority, and Culture.* Cambridge, Mass.: Harvard University Press, 1990.

Fyfe, James J. "Administrative Interventions on Police Shooting Discretion: An Empirical Evaluation." *7 Journal of Criminal Justice* 309 (Winter 1979).

Glazer, Nathan. "On Subway Graffiti in New York." *Public Interest* (Winter 1979).

Glendon, Mary Ann. *Rights Talk: The Impoverishment of Political Discourse.* New York: The Free Press, 1991.

Goffman, Erving. *Asylums: Essays on the Social Situation of Mental Patients and Other Inmates.* Garden City, N.Y.: Doubleday, 1961.

Goldstein, Herman. "Confronting the Complexity of the Police Function." In *Discretion in Criminal Justice: The Tension Between Individualization and Uniformity*, edited by Lloyd Ohlin and Frank J. Remington, pp. 23–71. Albany: State University of New York Press, 1993.

―――. "Police Policy Formulation: A Proposal for Improving Police Performance." 65 *Michigan Law Review* 1123 (1967).

―――. *Problem-Oriented Policing.* Philadelphia, Pa.: Temple University Press, 1990.

―――. "Trial Judges and the Police," *Crime and Delinquency* 14, 1 (January 1968):14–25.

Goldstein, Joseph. "Police Discretion Not to Invoke the Criminal Process: Low-Visibility Decisions in the Administration of Justice." 69 *Yale Law Journal* 587 (1960).

Gordon, Meryl. "Street Justice." *New York Magazine*, December 5, 1994, pp. 46–55.

Harring, Sidney L. *Policing a Class Society: The Experience of American Cities, 1865-1915.* New Brunswick, N.J.: Rutgers University Press, 1983.

Hershkoff, Helen. "Aggressive Panhandling Laws: Do These Statutes Violate the Constitution? Yes: Silencing the Homeless." *American Bar Association Journal*, vol. 79 (June 1993):40.

Hicks, Jonathan P. "Court Cleanup Foils Giuliani Campaign for Quality of Life." *The New York Times*, September 20, 1995, A1.

Hope, Tim, and Mike Hough. "Area, Crime, and Incivilities: A Profile from the British Crime Survey." In *Communities and Crime Reduction*, edited by Tim Hope and Margaret Shaw. London: Her Majesty's Stationary Office, 1988.

Howland, George, Jr. "Sidran-ization and Its Discontents: Attacking the Homeless." *The Stranger*, September 6–12, 1993.

Igleburger, Robert M., and Frank A Schubert. "Policy Making for the Police." *American Bar Association Journal*, vol. 58 (March 1972): 307–310.

Inbau, Fred E. "Public Safety v. Individual Liberties." *Police Chief*, vol. 29 (January 1962): 29–32.

International Association of Chiefs of Police, Field Service Division. *A Survey of the Police Department.* Mimeograph, 1962.

Isaac, Rael Jean, and Virginia C. Armat. *Madness in the Streets: How Psychiatry and the Law Abandoned the Mentally Ill.* New York: The Free Press, 1990.

Jacobs, Jane. *The Death and Life of Great American Cities.* New York: Vintage Books, 1961.

Jencks, Christopher. *The Homeless.* Cambridge, Mass.: Harvard University Press, 1994.

"Judge Blocks Weapons Sweeps." *Re: Rights & Responsibilities*, Newsletter. Washington, D.C.: American Alliance of Rights & Responsibilities, October 1995.

Kansas City Police Department. *Response Time Analysis: Volume II—Part I Crime Analysis*. Kansas City, Mo., 1977.

Kelling, George L. "How to Run a Police Department." *The City Journal*, vol. 5, no. 4 (Autumn 1995): 34–45.

———. "Measuring What Matters: A New Way of Thinking About Crime and Public Order." *The City Journal*, vol. 2 (Spring 1992): 21–33.

———. "Reclaiming the Subway." *The City Journal*, vol. 1, no. 2 (Winter 1991): 17–28.

———. "Toward New Images of Policing: Herman Goldstein's Problem-Oriented Policing." *Law and Social Inquiry*, vol. 17, no. 3 (Summer 1992): 539–559.

———, and William J. Bratton. "Implementing Community Policing: The Administrative Problem." *Perspectives in Policing*, no. 17. Washington, D.C.: National Institute of Justice, U.S Department of Justice, and the Program in Criminal Justice Policy and Management, John F. Kennedy School of Government, Harvard University, July 1993.

———, and Catherine M. Coles. "Disorder and the Court." *Public Interest*, no. 116 (Summer 1994): 57–74.

———, and Robert B. Kliesmet. "Police Unions, Police Culture, the Friday Crab Club, and Police Abuse of Force." In *And Justice for All*, edited by William A. Geller and Hans Toch, pp. 187–205. Washington, D.C.: Police Executive Research Forum, 1995.

———, and Maryalice Sloan-Howitt. "Station Managers and Police." A report submitted to the New York City Transit Authority by the St. Germain Group, n.d.

———, and James K. Stewart. "The Evolution of Contemporary Policing." In *Municipal Police Management*, edited by William Geller. Washington, D.C.: International City Management Association, 1991.

———, et al. *The Kansas City Preventive Patrol Experiment*. Washington: D.C.: Police Foundation, 1974.

Kennedy, David M. "The Strategic Management of Police Resources." *Perspectives in Policing*, no. 14. Washington, D.C.: National Institute of Justice, U.S. Department of Justice, and the Program in Criminal Justice Policy and Management, John F. Kennedy School of Government, Harvard University, January 1993.

Kent, Roscoe. "Catching the Criminal by Police Radio." *The American City*, vol. 45 (November 1931).

Kiley, Robert R. "The Homeless Are Dying in the Subway." *The New York Times*, February 17, 1990, A27.

King, John. "Matrix Dominates S.F. Debate; Mayoral Hopefuls Blast Crackdown Against Homeless." *San Francisco Chronicle*, August 17, 1995, A21.

King, John. "Mayoral Hopefuls Talk Tougher on Homeless Issue; Jordan Rivals Shift Stance." *San Francisco Chronicle*, October 11, 1995, A13.

Kleiman, Mark A. R. *Against Excess: Drug Policy for Results*. New York: Basic Books, 1992.

Krantz, Sheldon, Bernard Gilman, Charles G. Benda, Carol Rogoff Halistrom, and Eric J. Nadworny. *Police Policymaking*. Lexington, Mass.: Lexington Books, 1973.

Krauss, Clifford. "Shootings Fall as More Guns Stay at Home." *The New York Times*, July 20, 1995, p. 29.

Kunen, James S. "Quality and Equality: The Mayor Tries Something that Works, at a Cost." *The New Yorker*, November 28, 1994, pp. 9–10.

LaFave, Wayne R. *Arrest: The Decision to Take a Suspect into Custody*. Boston: Little, Brown, 1965.

———. "Police Rule Making and the Fourth Amendment." In *Discretion in Criminal Justice: The Tension Between Individualization and Uniformity*, edited by Lloyd Ohlin and Frank J. Remington, pp. 211–277. Albany: State University of New York Press, 1993.

Laing, R. D. *Divided Self: An Existential Study in Sanity and Madness*. Baltimore: Penguin Books, 1965.

Lakshmanan, Indira A. R. "Police Wary of Bystanders Obstructing Arrests." *Boston Globe*, March 18, 1994, p. 23.

Langdon, Philip. "How Portland Does It: A City that Protects Its Thriving, Civil Core." *The Atlantic* (November 1992):134–141.

Laub, John H., and Janet L. Lauritsen. "The Precursors of Criminal Offending Across the Life Course." *Federal Probation* (September 1994):51–57.

Leonard, V. A. *Survey of the Seattle Police Department* (June 1, 1945). Seattle, Wash.

Levy, Dan. "S.F. Board Votes Down Matrix Amnesty Plan." *San Francisco Chronicle*, October 26, 1993, A1.

Lichtenstein, Brad. "Yet Another Reason to Arrest the Homeless." *The New York Times*. Letter to the editor, October 24, 1994, A16.

Loury, Glenn C., and Shelby Steele. "A New Black Vanguard." *The Wall Street Journal*, February 29, 1996, A18.

Lynch, Colum. "War on Windshield Washers." *Boston Globe*, December 18, 1993, p. 3.

MacDonald, Heather. "Have We Crossed the Line? The Human Costs of Deinstitutionalization." *The City Journal*, vol. 3 (Winter 1993): 35.

MacDonald, Heather. "San Francisco Gets Tough with the Homeless." *The City Journal*, vol. 4 (Autumn 1994): 30–40.

Magnet, Myron. *The Dream and the Nightmare. The Sixties' Legacy to the Underclass*. New York: William Morrow, 1993.

McCormick, Erin. "Matrix Gone, at Least in Name." *San Francisco Examiner*, January 12, 1996, A4.

McCoy, Candace. "Policing the Homeless." *Criminal Law Bulletin*, vol. 22, no. 3 (May-June 1986): 263–274.

McEwen, J. Thomas, et al. *Evaluation of the Differential Response Field Test*. Washington, D.C.: National Institute of Justice, U.S. Department of Justice, 1986.

Mead, Bennet. "Police Statistics." *The Annals*, vol. CXLVI (November 1929): 74–96.

*The Midtown Community Court Experiment: A Progress Report*. Midtown Community Court, New York, N.Y., n.d.

Miller, Frank. *Prosecution: The Decision to Charge a Suspect with a Crime*, edited by Frank J. Remington. Boston: Little, Brown, 1969.

Monkkonen, Eric H. *Police in Urban America: 1860–1920*. New York: Cambridge University Press, 1981.

Moran, Richard. "More Police, Less Crime, Right? Wrong." *The New York Times*, February 27, 1995, A15.

*The Newark Foot Patrol Experiment*. Washington, D.C.: Police Foundation, 1981.

Newman, Donald J. *Conviction: The Determination of Guilt or Innocence without Trial.* Boston: Little, Brown, 1966.

Newman, Oscar. *Defensible Space. Crime Prevention Through Urban Design.* New York: MacMillan, 1972.

New York City Police Department. New York City Crime Control Indicators and Strategy Assessment. November 1995.

"The New York Newsday Interview with Jeremy Travis." *Newsday*, August 11, 1994.

Ohlin, Lloyd. "Surveying Discretion by Criminal Justice Decision Makers." In *Discretion in Criminal Justice: The Tension Between Individualization and Uniformity*, edited by Lloyd Ohlin and Frank J. Remington, pp. 1–22. Albany: State University of New York Press, 1993.

Parnas, Raymond I. "Criminal Justice Responses to Domestic Violence Issues." In *Discretion in Criminal Justice: The Tension Between Individualization and Uniformity*, edited by Lloyd Ohlin and Frank J. Remington, pp. 175–210. Albany: State University of New York Press, 1993.

Pate, Tony, Amy Ferrara, Robert A. Bowers, and Jon Lorence. *Police Response Time: Its Determinants and Effects.* Washington, D.C.: Police Foundation, 1976.

———, Amy Ferrara, and George L. Kelling. "Foot Patrol: A Discussion of the Issues." In *The Newark Foot Patrol Experiment.* Washington, D.C.: Police Foundation, 1981.

———, Mary Ann Wycoff, Wesley Skogan, and Lawrence Sherman. *Reducing Fear of Crime in Houston and Newark: A Summary Report.* Washington, D.C.: Police Foundation, 1986.

President's Commission on Law Enforcement and Administration of Justice. *The Challenge of Crime in a Free Society.* Washington, D.C.: U.S. Government Printing Office, February 1967.

President's Commission on Law Enforcement and Administration of Justice. *Task Force Report: The Police.* Washington, D.C.: U.S. Government Printing Office, 1967.

Quinnipiac College Polling Institute, Quinnipiac College Poll Surveys of New York, New Jersey and Connecticut, Press Release, November 6, 1995.

Radelet, Louis A., and David Carter. *The Police and the Community.* 5th ed. Englewood Cliffs, N.J.: Prentice-Hall, 1994.

Reaves, Brian A. "Using NIBRS Data to Analyze Violent Crime." *Bureau of Justice Technical Report.* Washington, D.C.: U.S. Department of Justice, Office of Justice Programs, Bureau of Justice Statistics, October 1993.

Reiss, Albert J., Jr. *The Police and the Public.* New Haven: Yale University Press, 1971.

Remington, Frank J. "Police in a Democratic Society." 56 *Journal of Criminal Law, Criminology and Police Science* 361 (1965).

Repetto, Thomas. *The Blue Parade.* New York: The Free Press, 1978.

———. "Bruce Smith: Police Reform in the United States." In *Pioneers in Policing*, edited by Philip John Stead, pp. 171–206. Montclair, N.J.: Patterson Smith, 1977.

Ribton-Turner, C. J. *A History of Vagrants and Vagrancy and Beggars and Begging.* London: Chapman and Hall, 1887.

Room, Robin. "Comment on 'The Uniform Alcoholism and Intoxication Treatment Act.'" *Journal of Studies on Alcohol*, vol. 37, no. 1 (1976): 113–144.

Rubinstein, Jonathan. *City Police.* New York: Farrar, Straus and Giroux, 1973.

Sampson, Robert J., and Jacqueline Cohen. "Deterrent Effects of the Police on Crime:

A Replication and Theoretical Extension." *Law and Society Review*, vol. 22, no. 1 (February 1988): 163–189.

Saunders, Debra J. "Jordan Deserves Re-election for Matrix." *San Francisco Chronicle*, September 1, 1995, A23.

Saxon, Wolfgang. "Four Deaths on the Subway Attributed to Cold Wave." *The New York Times*, December 19, 1989, B3.

Scheidegger, Kent S. *A Guide to Regulating Panhandling*. Sacramento, Calif.: Criminal Justice Legal Foundation, 1993.

Schwartz, Rita. *The Homeless: The Impact on the Transportation Industry*. Port Authority of New York and New Jersey, 1987.

Sellin, Thorsten, and Marvin E. Wolfgang. *The Measurement of Delinquency*. New York: Wiley, 1964.

Sherman, Lawrence W., and Richard A. Berke. "The Specific Deterrent Effects of Arrest for Domestic Assaults." *American Sociological Review*, vol. 49, no. 2 (April 1984): 261–272.

Sherry, Arthur H. "Vagrants, Rogues and Vagabonds—Old Concepts in Need of Revision." 48 *California Law Review* 557 (October 1960).

Siegel, Fred. "Reclaiming Our Public Spaces." *The City Journal*, vol. 2 (Spring 1992): 35–45.

Simon, David. "The Metal Men." *Baltimore Sun Magazine*, September 3, 1995, pp. 8–13.

Simon, Harry. "Towns Without Pity: A Constitutional and Historical Analysis of Official Efforts to Drive Homeless Persons from American Cities." 66 *Tulane Law Review* 638 (March 1992).

Skogan, Wesley G. *Disorder and Decline. Crime and the Spiral of Urban Decay in American Neighborhoods*. New York: Free Press, 1990.

————, and Michael Maxfield. *Coping with Crime: Individual and Neighborhood Reactions*. Newbury Park, Calif.: Sage Publications, 1981.

Sloan-Howitt, Maryalice, and George L. Kelling. "Subway Graffiti in New York City: 'Gettin' Up' vs. 'Meanin' It and Cleanin' It.'" *Security Journal*, vol. 1, no. 3 (1990): 131.

*Sourcebook of Criminal Justice Statistics*. Bureau of Justice Statistics, U.S. Department of Justice. Washington, D.C.: U.S. Goverment Printing Office, 1992.

Spelman, William, and Dale K. Brown. *Calling the Police: Citizen Reporting of Serious Crime*. Washington: D.C.: Police Executive Research Forum, 1981.

Stephen, James F. *A History of the Criminal Law of England*. London: Macmillan, 1883.

Stinchcombe, Arthur L., R. Adams, C. Heimer, K. Scheppele, T. Smith, and D. G. Taylor. *Crime and Punishment in Public Opinion*. San Francisco, Calif.: Jossey-Bass, 1980.

Szasz, Thomas. *The Myth of Mental Illness: Foundations of a Theory of Personal Conduct*. New York: Hoeber-Harper, 1961.

Taft, Philip B., Jr. "Dealing with Mental Patients." *Police Magazine* (January 1980): 20–27.

Tamm, Quinn. "Whose Rights Are Being Defended?" *Police Chief*, vol. 33 (July 1966): 6.

Teir, Robert. "Maintaining Safety and Civility in Public Spaces: A Constitutional Approach to Aggressive Begging." 54 *Louisiana Law Review* 285 (1993).

Tiffany, Lawrence P., Donald M. McIntyre, Jr., and Daniel Rotenberg. *Detection of Crime: Stopping and Questioning, Search and Seizure, Encouragement and Entrapment*. Boston: Little, Brown, 1967.

Tira, Peter. "No Place for Kids: City Will Bulldoze Blighted Mini-Park." *San Francisco Independent*, vol. 39, no. 12 (January 28, 1994):1.

Tracy, Paul, Marvin Wolfgang, and Robert Figlio. *Delinquency in Two Birth Cohorts.* Washington, D.C.: Office of Juvenile Justice and Delinquency Prevention, 1985.

Traub, James. "Street Fight." *The New Yorker*, September 4, 1995, p. 36.

Tribe, Laurence H. *American Constitutional Law*, 2d ed. Mineola, N.Y.: The Foundation Press, 1988.

Trojanowicz, Robert. *An Evaluation of the Neighborhood Foot Patrol Program in Flint, Michigan.* East Lansing: Michigan State University, 1982.

Vandall, Frank J. *Police Training for Tough Calls: Discretionary Situations.* Limited edition. Center for Research in Social Change. Atlanta, Ga.: Emory University, 1976.

Walker, Samuel. *The Police in America: An Introduction.* 2d ed. New York: McGraw-Hill, 1992.

Weingardt, Saul N., Francis X. Hartmann, and David Osborne. *Case Studies of Community Anti-Drug Efforts.* Washington, D.C.: National Institute of Justice, October 1994.

Williams, Gregory Howard. "Police Discretion: The Institutional Dilemma—Who Is in Charge?" 68 *Iowa Law Review* 431 (March 1983).

Wilson, James Q. *Varieties of Police Behavior.* Cambridge, Mass.: Harvard University Press, 1968.

———. "What to Do About Crime." *Commentary*, vol. 98, no. 3 (September1994): 25–34.

———, and Barbara Boland. "The Effect of Police on Crime." *Law and Society Review*, vol. 12, no.3 (1978): 367–90.

———, and George L. Kelling. "The Police and Neighborhood Safety." *The Atlantic* (March 1982): 29–38.

Wilson, Orlando W. *Police Administration.* 2d ed. New York: McGraw-Hill, 1963.

Wolfgang, Marvin, Robert Figlio, and Thorsten Sellin. *Delinquency in a Birth Cohort.* Chicago: University of Chicago Press, 1972.

———, Robert Figlio, Paul E. Tracy, and Simon I. Singer. *The National Survey of Crime Severity.* Bureau of Justice Statistics. Washington, D.C.: U.S. Government Printing Office (NCJ-96017), June 1985.

Woods, Arthur. *Policeman and Public.* New Haven: Yale University Press, 1919.

Wycoff, Mary Ann. The Role of Municipal Police Research as a Prelude to Changing It. Mimeograph. Washington, D.C.: Police Foundation, 1982.

## CASES CITED

Akron v. Massey, 381 N.E.2d 1362 (Ohio 1978).

Berkeley Community Health Project v. City of Berkeley, 902 F. Supp. 1084 (N.D. Cal. May 5, 1995), *appeal docketed*, No. 95-16060 (9th. Cir. 1995).

Blair v. Shanahan, 775 F. Supp. 1315 (N.D. Cal. 1991), *aff'd in part, dismissed in part, and remanded*, 38 F.3d 1514 (9th Cir. 1994), *cert. denied*, 115 S.Ct. 1698 (1995), No. C-89-4176 WHO (N.D. Cal. January 31, 1996), *vacating* 775 F. Supp. 1315.

Board of Directors of Rotary Int'l v. Rotary Club, 481 U.S. 537 (1987).

Boos v. Barry, 485 U.S. 312 (1988).

Carey v. Brown, 447 U.S. 455 (1980).

Church v. City of Huntsville, No. 93-C-1239-S (N.D. Ala. Sept 23, 1994), *vacated*, 30 F.3d 1332 (11th Cir. 1994).

City of Cleburne v. Cleburne Living Center, 473 U.S 432 (1985).

City of Milwaukee v. Nelson, 439 N.W.2d 562 (Wisc. 1989).

City of Renton v. Playtime Theatres, Inc., 475 U.S. 41 (1986).

City of Seattle v. Hoff, No. 94-2-29610-8 (King County Superior Court), *cert. accepted*, No. 36995-4-I (Wash. Ct. App., Sept. 19, 1995).

City of Seattle v. McConahy, No. 95-2-13008-9 (King County Superior Court), *cert. accepted*, No. 36995-4-I (Wash. Ct. App. Sept. 19, 1995).

City of Seattle v. Webster, 802 P.2d 1333 (Wash. 1990) (en banc), *cert. denied*, 500 U.S. 908 (1991).

Clark v. Community for Creative Non-Violence, 468 U.S. 288 (1984).

Cohens v. Virginia, 19 U.S. 264 (1821).

Connally v. General Construction Co., 269 U.S. 385 (1926).

Cox v. New Hampshire, 312 U.S. 569 (1941).

Cox v. Louisiana, 379 U.S. 536 (1965).

Dallas v. Stanglin, 490 U.S. 19 (1989).

Edwards v. California, 314 U.S. 162 (1941).

Escobedo v. Illinois, 378 U.S. 478 (1964).

Fenster v. Leary, 229 N.E.2d 426 (N.Y. 1967).

First National Bank of Boston v. Bellotti, 435 U.S. 765 (1978).

Garcia v. San Antonio Metropolitan Transit Authority, 469 U.S. 528 (1985).

Goldman v. Knecht, 295 F. Supp. 897 (D. Colo. 1969).

Grayned v. City of Rockford, 408 U.S. 104 (1972).

Griswold v. Connecticut, 381 U.S. 479 (1965).

Harris v. McRae, 448 U.S. 297 (1980).

Heffron v. International Society for Krishna Consciousness, 452 U.S. 640 (1981).

Herndon v. Lowry, 301 U.S. 242 (1937).

Hoffman Estates v. Flipside, Hoffman Estates, Inc., 455 U.S. 489 (1982).

International Society for Krishna Consciousness, Inc. v. Lee, 505 U.S. 672 (1992).

International Society for Krishna Consciousness, Inc. v. Schmidt, 523 F. Supp. 1303 (D. Md. 1981).

Johnson v. City of Dallas, 860 F. Supp. 344 (N.D. Tex. 1994), *rev'd*, 61 F.3d 442 (5th Cir. 1995).

Joyce v. City and County of San Francisco, 846 F. Supp. 843 (N.D. Cal. 1994), No. C-93-4149 DLJ (N.D. Cal. August 18, 1995), *appeal docketed*, No. 95-16940 (9th Cir. 1996).

Kadrmas v. Dickinson Public Schools, 487 U.S. 450 (1988).

Kolender v. Lawson, 461 U.S. 352 (1983).

Kreimer v. Bureau of Police for Town of Morristown, 958 F.2d 1242 (3rd Cir. 1992).

Lindsey v. Normet, 405 U.S. 56 (1972).

Loper v. New York City Police Dept., 802 F. Supp. 1029 (S.D. N.Y. 1992), *aff'd*, 999 F.2d 699 (2d Cir. 1993).

Maher v. Roe, 432 U.S. 464 (1977).

Mapp v. Ohio, 367 U.S. 643 (1961).

Mayor of New York v. Miln, 36 U.S. (11 Pet.) 102 (1837).

Miranda v. Arizona, 384 U.S. 436 (1966).

National League of Cities v. Usery, 426 U.S. 833 (1976).

O'Connor v. Donaldson, 422 U.S. 563 (1975).

Papachristou v. City of Jacksonville, 405 U.S. 156 (1972).

Parker v. Municipal Judge, 427 P.2d 642 (Nev. 1967).

Patton v. Baltimore City, Civil No. S93-2389 (D. Md. August 19, 1994) (Memorandum Opinion and Order), September 14, 1994 (Oral Opinion).

People v. Solomon, 33 Cal. App.3d 429, 108 Cal Rptr. 867, *cert. denied*, 415 U.S. 951 (1974).

People v. Superior Court (Caswell), 758 P.2d 1046 (Sup. Ct. Cal. 1988).

Perry Education Ass'n v. Perry Local Educators' Ass'n, 460 U.S. 37 (1983).

Pottinger v. City of Miami, 810 F. Supp. 1551 (S.D. Fla. 1992), *remanded*, 40 F.3d 1155 (11th Cir. 1994).

Powell v. Texas, 392 U.S. 514 (1968).

Pratt v. Chicago Housing Authority, 848 F. Supp. 792 (N.D. Ill. 1994).

R.A.V. v. City of St. Paul, Minnesota, 505 U.S. 377 (1992).

Renton v. Playtime Theatres, Inc., 475 U.S. 41 (1986).

Riley v. National Federation of the Blind of North Carolina, 487 U.S. 781 (1988).

Ringsby Truck Lines v. Western Conference Teamsters, 686 F.2d 720 (9th Cir. 1982).

Roberts v. United States Jaycees, 468 U.S. 609 (1984).

Robinson v. California, 370 U.S. 660 (1962).

Roe v. Wade, 410 U.S. 113 (1973).

Roulette v. City of Seattle, 850 F. Supp. 1442 (W.D. Wash. 1994), *aff'd*, No. 94-35354 (9th Cir. March 18, 1996).

San Antonio Independent School Dist. v. Rodriguez, 411 U.S. 1 (1973).

Schaumburg v. Citizens for a Better Environment, 444 U.S. 620 (1980).

Shapiro v. Thompson, 394 U.S. 618 (1969).

Shuttlesworth v. City of Birmingham, 382 U.S. 87 (1965).

Shuttlesworth v. City of Birmingham, 394 U.S. 147 (1968).

Smith v. Goguen, 415 U.S. 566 (1974).

Spence v. Washington, 418 U.S. 405 (1974).

Texas v. Johnson, 491 U.S. 397 (1989).

Thornhill v. Alabama, 310 U.S. 88 (1940).

Tinker v. Des Moines School District, 393 U.S. 503 (1969).

Tobe v. City of Santa Ana, 27 Cal. Rptr. 2d 386 (Cal.App. 4 Dist. 1994), *rev'd*, 892 P.2d 1145 (Cal. 1995).

Ulmer v. Municipal Court for Oakland-Piedmont Judicial District, 55 Cal. App. 3d 263, 127 Cal. Rptr. 445 (1976).

United States v. Albertini, 472 U.S. 675 (1985).

United States v. Kokinda, 497 U.S. 720 (1990).

United States v. O'Brien, 391 U.S. 367 (1968).

Walley v. New York City Transit Authority, Index No. 177/91 (Supreme Court of N.Y., County of Kings, June 3, 1991).

Ward v. Rock Against Racism, 491 U.S. 781 (1989).

Wheeler v. Goodman, 306 F. Supp. 58 (W.D. N.C. 1969), *vacated*, 401 U.S. 987 (1971).

Wyche v. State, 619 So.2d 231 (Fla. 1993).

Young v. New York City Transit Authority, 729 F. Supp. 341 (S.D. N.Y.), *rev'd and vacated*, 903 F.2d 146 (2d Cir.), *cert. denied*, 398 U.S. 984 (1990).

Zablocki v. Redhail, 434 U.S. 374 (1978).

# INDEX

# ACKNOWLEDGMENTS

THE EXPERIENCE, DATA, AND RESEARCH IN THIS VOLUME HAVE
been gathered since the mid-1970s when Kelling began research on
foot patrols in New Jersey: both individuals and institutions have supported our research and writing.

Financial support for the research and production of this volume has
come from the Smith-Richardson Foundation, the Lynde and Harry
Bradley Foundation, the National Institute of Justice, the Randolph
Foundation, the New York City Police Foundation, and the Manhattan
Institute. The faculty and administration of Northeastern University
also granted Kelling a sabbatical leave during two quarters of the
1993–1994 academic year for work on the book.

Research assistants have been crucial to the book's development.
They include Jinney Smith, now a doctoral student at Northwestern
University; Steven Catalano, now on the staff of the United States
Department of Justice Community Oriented Policing Services; Gillian
Thomson, a graduate student at the Kennedy School of Government at
Harvard University; and Stephen Brimley, a research assistant at the
Kennedy School of Government at Harvard University.

We also thank our colleagues at Harvard University, especially Francis X. Hartmann, David Kennedy, Susan Michaelson, and Mark M.
Moore. They, and others, made specific contributions to our thinking
and created an intellectual atmosphere in which scholarship was
encouraged and valued. Kelling also thanks his colleagues at Northeastern University, especially James Fox, Lorraine Greene (now of the

University of Cincinnati), Michael Kass (now with the Commonwealth of Massachusetts Department of Public Safety), John Laub, and Frank Schubert for their individual contributions to the book. At Northeastern also, Robert Croatti offered both friendship and support. Roger Conner and Robb Tier of the American Alliance for Rights & Responsibilities and Michael Rushford and Kent Scheidegger of the Criminal Justice Legal Foundation deserve our thanks as well for keeping us up to date on what was going on in the field.

Mary Ann Wycoff has been our colleague for years. She was not only a constant source of support, but also searched her files for archival materials that were of great value. Patricia "Trish" Moore, Robert Kiley's former chief of staff at New York's Metropolitan Transportation Authority (MTA), made certain that although Kiley inserted Kelling as an unwanted consultant in the MTA and its police departments, he was there to stay as long as required. Robert Kiley not only placed Kelling in the MTA, he graciously read and commented on early drafts of chapters. Maryalice Sloan-Howitt was Kelling's colleague in the MTA and read and commented on early drafts of chapters. Kay Codish, who directs education in the New Haven Department of Police Service, was a valued reader of early drafts. Dean Esserman, chief of the Metro North Police Department, was an ongoing source of support and information. Seattle City Attorney Mark Sidran, San Francisco Assistant City Attorney Michael Olsen, and Michael Sarbanes of the Baltimore Mayor's Office on Criminal Justice all helped us gather information in their cities. Laurie Schwartz of Baltimore's Downtown Neighborhood Association also went out of her way to be helpful. Jeremy Travis, director of the National Institute of Justice, and Susan Herman of the Enterprise Foundation were especially helpful in understanding the history of events in New York City. William Bratton, former police commissioner of New York City, provided a laboratory for a "Broken Windows" approach in both the New York City Transit Police Department and the New York City Police Department; he also returned our calls throughout his busy stewardship of the New York City Police Department and helped us in every way he could. Finally, Robert Johnson, president of First Security, both taught us about private security and was a constant source of support throughout our writing.

We also thank our publishing colleagues. John Harney encouraged

us to seek the widest possible audience when he reviewed our first draft. Abigail Strubel, of the Free Press, helped us find our voice. And of course, along with his publishing colleagues, we mourn the late Martin Kessler, our first editor at the Free Press. We were inspired by the contact we had with him even though it was limited.

Three final expressions of appreciation. First, Larry Mone, president of the Manhattan Institute, supported us through every phase of the evolution of this manuscript. We thank him, sincerely, for all his support.

Second, from his support of Kelling's early research proposals as a Police Foundation board member during the early 1970s, through his support for this book, James Q. Wilson has been an unusually generous colleague. After Kelling's publication of the *Newark Foot Patrol Experiment* in 1981, Wilson offered to coauthor with Kelling an article in the *Atlantic*. In making the offer, Wilson particularly noted Kelling's emphasis on the neighborhood activities of foot patrol officers in Newark. Yet, Wilson could have met all of his responsibilities to Kelling by citing the Newark experiment in the article and writing it alone—a fact acknowledged by Kelling when Wilson first made his offer of coauthorship. While Kelling contributed substantially to the article, Wilson coined the "Broken Windows" metaphor—in retrospect, a powerful simile that captured the unarticulated and unrecognized concerns of citizens, the failed responses of police and criminal justice agencies, as well as the enormous capacity for good of well-meaning police officers once they are placed in neighborhoods. Jim's extraordinary generosity, intellectual and otherwise, has persisted throughout the conceptualization, production, and publication of this book.

Finally, we appreciate the help of hundreds of police, criminal justice officials, and citizens who opened their occupations, organizations, homes, and neighborhoods to us. We hope that we have reflected them respectfully and accurately. Nevertheless, the points of view or opinions expressed here, of course, represent those of the authors, not necessarily those of our friends, colleagues, or supporting institutions.

—*George L. Kelling and Catherine M. Coles*